Essen[illegible]osia

A Guide to Buddhist Contemplations

by

Taranatha

Translated by

Willa Baker

LIBRARY OF TIBETAN WORKS AND ARCHIVES

First print: 2005

ISBN: 81-86470-37-9

Published by Library of Tibetan Works and Archives, Dharamsala and printed at Indraprastha Press (CBT), 4 Bahadur Shah Zafar Marg, New Delhi-110002

Table of Contents

This book is dedicated to the Lama Norlha Rinpoche, whose compassionate activity constantly unfolds to benefit others, and to the sangha of Kagyu Thupten Choling monastery, whose prayers and practices bless the region of upstate New York.

FOREWORD

(Translation)

The Twelfth Tai Situpa

Ms. Palmo (Willa Baker), a disciple of His Eminence the Kalu Rinpoche, has studied and practiced Buddhism for many years. She has also formally completed a three-year meditation retreat.

I pray to the Three Jewels and call upon the unfailing Dharma Protectors that her translation of Tarantha's *Lamrim* (Stages of Path) guides and benefits all Dharma students and practitioners. May the merits gained through this noble deed ensure the acquirement of a conducive basis for happiness and well being to all sentient beings.

Tai Situ
Sherabling

10 January 2005

The Twelfth Tai Situpa

༄༅། །སྐྱབས་རྗེ་ཀ་ལུ་རིན་པོ་ཆེ་མཆོག་གི་ཞལ་སློབ་དད་ལྡན་མ་དཔལ་མོ་ནས་ལོ་མང་ནང་ཆོས་དང་སྒྲུབ་བརྒྱུད་ཀྱི་མཐོང་རྒྱུན་ཕྱག་བཞེས་སོགས་ལ་སྦྱངས་བརྩོན་དང་སྒྲུབ་པ་ཉམས་ལེན་ལོ་གསུམ་ཕྱོགས་གསུམ་སོགས་གནང་སྒྲིན་བྱུས་ཡོད་པར་བརྟེན་ད་ལམ་ཏཱ་ར་ན་ཐའི་ལམ་རིམ་ཞེས་པ་དབྱིན་སྐད་ཐོག་ཕབ་བསྒྱུར་བྱས་པའི་དེབ་འདིས་གནས་སྐབས་ནང་ཆོས་ལ་དོ་སྣང་ཅན་ཡོངས་ལ་ལམ་སྟོན་ཡོང་བ་དང་མཐར་ཐུག་དགེ་ཚོགས་ཅི་མཆིས་ཐ་དག་མཁའ་ཁྱབ་ཀྱི་སེམས་ཅན་ཀུན་ལ་འདི་དང་གཏན་གྱི་ཕན་བདེའི་གཞི་མར་གྱུར་པའི་མཐུན་སྦྱོར་མཆོག་གསུམ་གསོལ་སྨོན་དང་དམ་ཅན་རྒྱ་མཚོར་བདེན་བསྐུལ་བཅས་འཕགས་ཡུལ་བྱང་ཕྱོགས་གདན་ས་དཔལ་སྤུངས་ཤེས་རབ་རྣམ་པར་རྒྱལ་བའི་གླིང་ནས་ཀུན་ཏིང་ཏཱའི་སི་ཏུ་པས་ཕྱི་ལོ་༢༠༠༥ ཟླ ༡ ཚེས་༡༠ ཉིན་སྤེལ་བ་དགེ་ལེགས་འཕེལ།།

"SHERAB LING"
INSTITUTE OF BUDDHIST STUDIES
P.O. Upper Bhattu Via Baijnath -176125, District Kangra, Himachal Pradesh, India
Tel. No. (01894) 63758, 63013, 63757 Fax 62234

Publisher's Note

Library of Tibetan Works & Archives (LTWA) is happy to publish the 17th Century Lam-rim: Taranatha's *Essence of Ambrosia*, a stages of the path text designed as a series of meditations upon the key points of the path to state of Buddhahood, at a time when many people are interested in both meditation and in Tibetan Buddhism.

We are indebted to Willa Baker (Lama Palmo) for her fine translation and thank her for providing the funds to include the Tibetan text in this publication. We would also like to thank Mr. Sangye Tandar Naga for rechecking the translation and final proof reading of the Tibetan text and Ani Tenzin Choying for her valuable editorial assistance.

It is hoped that this publication will prove a useful guide and will benefit its readers and practioners.

Publication Department
LTWA

April, 2005

Acknowledgements

A number of people, perhaps more than I can name here, contributed to the translation of the *Essence of Ambrosia*. The translation would not have been possible at all without the inspiration, kindness and guidance of my root teacher Lama Norlha Rinpoche, who first bestowed teachings of this text to me and to a number of other fortunate individuals. If any value is derived from the words of this translation for the reader, it is certainly due to Lama Norlha's skillful presentation of the material and his ability to enliven Taranatha's texts with anecdotes stemming from his wealth of experience and wisdom. Likewise, I cannot repay the kindness of Kalu Rinpoche and Bokar Rinpoche who bestowed on me the reading transmission for this text and all the other Shangpa texts and practices. I am grateful to all the residents of Kagyu Thupten Choling monastery in New York for their kindness and support throughout the vicissitudes of time and change occurring while this translation was in progress. I am especially indebted to Ani Jamdron whose friendship, deep understanding of the Dharma and thorough knowledge of Tibetan was invaluable at various stages of the translation. I am deeply grateful to Derek Maher and Jeffrey Hopkins who provided the Sanskrit font, gave vital moral support and practical help with refining the translation, and whose erudition and attention to detail inspired me to be more meticulous. I am profoundly obliged to Ngawang Zangpo, who contributed valuable material on the Shangpa lineage and Taranatha while I was writing the introduction. I am also thankful to a number of individuals who contributed to this book directly and indirectly by offering their support while I was working on it: Khenpo Tsultrim Gyatso Rinpoche, Ari Goldfield, E. Gene Smith, Lama Chopal, Lama Surya Das, Lama Palden, Robert Kelly of Bard College, John Makransky of Boston College, Karen Lang and David

Germano of the University of Virginia, Janet Gyatso of Harvard University and Marilyn Goldberg of the University of Maryland. Sincerest thanks also goes to Tsering Namgyal and Sangye Tandar Naga and the staff at The Library of Tibetan Works and Archives for making this book possible. I am especially grateful to Mike Miller, my father Will Baker and my uncle Charley, who day in and day out offered their encouragement, love, constructive comments and uncompromising support.

Translator's Introduction

Words composed by a master with Taranatha's breadth of wisdom have their own unfathomable power. But many years of familiarity with the text have yielded some inkling of the magic that makes Taranatha's book so stirring and has made the text popular over the centuries. First, and perhaps foremost, is the text's sheer practicality. Taranatha composed *Essence of Ambrosia* as a simple, user-friendly, 'how to' guide for meditators. Unlike many other texts of this genre, Tsongkhapa's famed *Lamrim Chenmo* for example, Taranatha's text is pared down to its most basic structure. Like its title, *Essence* is the distillation of the most essential points of meditation practice for beginners on the Mahayana path.

Taranatha does not, however, expound these points in the form of a treatise on Buddhist thought but presents them in the most practical conceivable form for students and instructors: as a series of meditation exercises. Taranatha makes it abundantly clear, through his frequent directives, that he expects the students reading his text to formally meditate on the concepts he presents and to do so in sequence until the student gains some depth of understanding of each contemplation topic. Furthermore, many of the comments he makes between contemplation sessions are directed toward teachers, indicating that *Essence of Ambrosia* was designed as a teaching manual for lamas and instructors in the monastic context who would have benefited greatly from Taranatha's systematization of the Buddhist path when training young monks and nuns.

The text's appeal is amplified by the fact that Taranatha's literary voice is not couched in the formal language of many of his contemporaries but is conversational, colloquial and accessible. Taranatha liberally uses vernacular terms to enhance description and drifts off easily into the occasional pertinent digression. His writing manages to be both informal and organized, so that the reader feels as if

Taranatha is *speaking* rather than writing to the teachers and students for whom the text is composed. Taranatha offers the reader frequent and candid glimpses into his process of thought and composition.

Perhaps because *Essence of Ambrosia* is so accessible, simple and relatively short, it became the principal "stages of the path" (Tib. *lam rim*) text for the Jonang, Shangpa and Kagyu lineages and a favorite of a number of eminent lamas. Jamgon Kongtrul (1813-1899), the brilliant scholar of the 19th Century non-sectarian movement specified *Essence of Ambrosia* as one of three texts his students were required to read at the outset of participating in his Three Year Retreat Program (the other two being *The Jewel Ornament of Liberation* and *The Ocean of Certainty*).[1] In this century, Kalu Rinpoche (1904-1989), the principal heir of the Shangpa-Kagyu lineage, recommended this text to his beginning students, both at his home monastery in Sonada, Darjeeling and at his many centers in the West. The text is also taught in centers and monasteries of the Jonang lineage by Khenpo Tsultrim Dargye, Khenpo Ngawang Dorje and others in Tibet, India and the West.

For the most part, *Essence of Ambrosia* was not a difficult text to translate because Taranatha wrote in a simple, conversational tone. Three versions of the text were consulted for this translation: the *Sonada* version from Kalu Rinpoche's collection of Shangpa books that was copied from Jamgon Kongtrul's *Treasury of Oral Instructions,* the *Dzamtang* (Tib. *'dzam thang*) version and the *Phuntsok Ling* (Tib. *phun tshogs gling*) version. For use of the latter two, I am indebted to E. Gene Smith. While refining the translation, I consulted Lama Norlha Rinpoche, Khenpo Nyima Gyaltsen, Khenpo Ngawang Dorje, Dr. Derek Maher, Ani Jamdron and Dr. Jeffery Hopkins. Tibetan technical terms have been rendered in English when possible to make the book accessible to a broad audience. Taranatha's original structural outline is included in the translation where it appears in the text in bold. For the purposes of organization, numbering has been added by the translator to parts and chapters. In addition, titles have been added to some sections and contemplations where Taranatha did not provide explicit titles in order to make the content of those sections more accessible to the reader. Taranatha quotes from a number of sources throughout *Essence.* Wherever possible, the original sources of these quotes are provided. The first time a source is quoted, it appears in the footnotes in Sanskrit and Tibetan. Subsequent quotes are identified only by the English title and author. A Glossary of Technical Terms and Proper Names in the back defines technical terms with their Tibetan and Sanskrit equivalents. Throughout the text, Taranatha makes reference to standard classifications such as the five aggregates, the ten non-virtuous actions and so forth. In order to assist students of Buddhism and Tibetan who wish to familiarize themselves with these very common categories, they are included with Tibetan script in a separate Glossary of Classifications.

Taranatha (1575-1634)

Taranatha was born in 1575 in Drong County in the Tsang (Tib. *gtsang*) province of Western Tibet. Accounts of his life, corroborated by his autobiography, assert he was recognized by Kenchen Lungrik Gyamtso at an early age as an incarnation of the Jonang master Kunga Drolchok and was taken to a local monastery for training. Eventually, he settled at Jomonang, the monastic center of the Jonang order in Tsang. While Taranatha remained affiliated with Jomonang and other monastic institutions and hermitages, he was anything but a recluse. He spent much of his life traveling throughout Central Tibet (a penchant reflected in the nickname he gave himself, *Gyalkampa*, "the wanderer"); studying under a number of eminent lamas; teaching extensively; rebuilding temples and monasteries and composing an astounding number of texts on various aspects of Buddhist doctrine, practice and history. During his travels, Taranatha's activity was both intense and concentrated, the work of a man committed to devoting every waking moment of his life to the propagation and improvement of Buddhism. Taranatha studied under the great Indian scholar Buddhaguptanatha and several Tibetan teachers, including Je Draktopa, Yeshe Wangpo, Kunga Trashi and Jampa Lhundrup. Taranatha was an eager student, educing every possible detail on Buddhist history, language, biography, liturgical practice and method he could glean from his teachers. The eloquence and care that mark Taranatha's scholarship must have expressed itself as solidity and quality in architecture since many of the buildings designed and constructed under Taranatha's auspices, including the monastery at Takten Damcho Ling and the stupa at Jomonang, are still standing. While engaged in these various creative projects, he managed to find ample time to impart frequent teachings at retreat centers, monastic colleges, public gatherings and private meetings. In the later period of his life, he traveled to Mongolia where he passed away in 1634.[2]

The foci and content of Taranatha's scholarship define him as a master of all schools of tantric Buddhism and as one who believed in religious tolerance and a non-partisan approach to Buddhist doctrine. The breadth of knowledge and critical synthesis displayed in the seventeen large volumes containing his Buddhist histories, biographies, original compositions and commentaries on Buddhist practice mark him as an exceptionally brilliant and independent thinker. His historical works found their way into the libraries of all schools of Tibetan Buddhism, and his commentaries on tantric practices, especially Kalachakra tantra, were closely read and used by practitioners in a number of lineages. His most well-known historical work is *A History of Buddhism in India*, a text valued for its appealing mixture of anecdotes of the lives of Indian masters and historical information. It continues to be a valuable resource for historians of Indian Buddhism. His other historical works include his own autobiography, a history of the Kalachakra system, a history of the Yamantaka Tantra and a history of the Tara Tantra. He also contributed significantly to strengthening the Jonang transmission by composing commentaries to many Jonang practices and biographical accounts of the lives of Jonang masters. However, the vast majority of his compositions were pertinent to all Buddhist traditions in Tibet. Perhaps because political turmoil and religious sectarianism threatened the peace of Central Tibet in the 17th century (more on that below), Taranatha turned his attention to material that would be appreciated by and unite all Buddhists. His work would, in fact, later inspire a number of notable scholars in all schools of Buddhism, including the non-sectarian master Jamgon Kongtrul (1813-1899) and His Holiness, the Fourteenth Dalai Lama (b. 1935). Taranatha's life example so inspired Jamgon Kongtrul that he devoted three days a year in his retreat center to the celebration of Taranatha's memory, an honor he extended to no other single lineage holder. In his own words, "During this age of conflict, Taranatha was a great Buddha Vajra Bearer whose renunciation and realization were indistinguishable from those of the Land of the Exalted's accomplished masters."[3]

The Jonang Lineage

As a recognized incarnation of Kunga Drolchok, Taranatha was heir to the Jonang transmission, a lineage that included a few distinct traditions. The founder of the Jonang, Yumo Mikyo Dorje[4] (12th Century), specialized in Kalachakra tantra and the teachings extending from the Indian pandit Nalendrapa. In the 13th Century, the Jonang appropriated the Shangpa transmission, a collection of practices and teachings extending back to the great female adept Niguma (11th Century) and her disciple Khyungpo Naljor (978-1079)[5]. Also in the 13th Century, Kunpang Tukje Tsondru (1243-1313)[6] founded the first monastic seat of the Jonang lineage, Jomonang in Western Tibet. His student, Dolpo Sherab Gyaltsen (1292-1361)[7], also known as Dolpopa, wrote philosophical treatises on the "empty-of-other" view that helped further define the Jonang as a distinct transmission. By the time Taranatha lived at Jomonang, in the 16th and early 17th century, the Jonang was flourishing as an independent lineage, sandwiched between the powerful Sakya monastery to the West and the politically influential Gelugpa monasteries in Lhasa just to the East. Jomonang's proximity to these great monasteries must have been fodder for stimulating religious exchanges between lineages and teachers.

However, the early 17th century was a time of civil strife in Central Tibet, and Jomonang, like the other religious institutions in the region, was caught in political machinations that eventually erupted into civil war in the 1630's. Perhaps these pressures provided some of the impetus behind Taranatha's vision of a non-sectarian and apolitical Buddhism and fueled his aspiration to rebuild and extend Jonang's monasteries as well as to fill every gap in their library. In any case, his efforts were to encounter a serious setback as soon as he passed away. The king of Tsang (Karma Tseten Dorje's successor Karma Tenkyong) was assassinated by Gushri Khan in 1642 and Jomonang, left without the protection of its patron, was taken by the 5th Dalai Lama. The woodblocks of Taranatha's texts were sealed in the Puntsok Ling printing house at Jomonang, and their dissemination was prohibited.

Despite these events, the Jonang lineage would manage to survive and eventually prosper by going underground for a time and evading an affiliation with a single monastic institution. While many of its practices were absorbed into the Gelug, Sakya and Kagyu traditions, the integrity of the transmission was preserved by devoted individuals who adopted Jonang practices as their own. One institution that did manage to sustain its identity with the Jonang lineage was Sher Dzamthang, a monastery in Golok built by Dolpopa's disciple Kazhipa Rinchenpal. This institution became and remains the primary seat of the Jonang tradition.[8] In 19th century, the Zhalu master Losel Denkyong succeeded in having prints made from books sealed inside Putsok Ling, and Taranatha's complete works became widely available.

Essence of Ambrosia

Essence of Ambrosia: The Stages of the Path for Training the Three Types of Person Through Contemplations, as its title indicates, belongs to a genre of commentarial literature called "stages of the path" (Tib. *lam rim*). This genre was introduced to Tibet by the great Bengali master Atisha (982-1054) whose *Lamp on the Path to Enlightenment* became the prototypical "stages of the path" text for the Kadampa tradition and soon enjoyed popularity with other lineages. One major appeal of Atisha's *Lamp* was that it summarized and organized the voluminous sutras and Mahayana commentarial literature into a systematic, practical step-by-step path that most anyone could follow. Inspired by Atisha, Tsongkhapa, the founder of the Gelugpa order, composed *Lamrim Chenmo* in 1402, a text that remains a classic to this day. Taranatha's *Essence of Ambrosia* was intended as the definitive "stages of the path" text for the Jonang tradition although it was soon adopted as one of the principal manuals for beginning practice for the Kagyu Lineage as well.[9]

Like other texts in this genre, *Essence of Ambrosia* is neither a polemical work nor a strictly commentarial work. Rather, it is a synthesis, based loosely on an outline traced in Atisha's *Lamp on the Path to Enlightenment*, of exoteric Buddhist thought and practice that harkens back frequently to the teachings of the sutras and other basic Mahayana texts. Like other "stages of the path" literature, it rests on the proposition that certain developmental conceptual states are necessary to reach the pinnacle of Buddhist practice, enlightenment characterized by the non-conceptual realization of emptiness suffused with universal compassion. These conceptual states can be developed and refined gradually by a methodical process of self-reflection, analysis and meditation. As each developmental stage is reached, the mind becomes less self-centered, more concentrated, more motivated and more flexible than before. In other words, enlightenment is not out of anyone's reach: the mental qualities necessary for successful practice of meditation and for the attainment of buddhahood itself can be systematically cultivated by anyone determined enough to take the necessary steps.

Taranatha constructed *Essence* as a user-friendly guide for meditators by arranging the entire text around "Contemplation Sessions." In these sessions, Taranatha's voice alternates between directives and first-person contemplation material (i.e. what to think). In order to distinguish between the two, I have put directives in italics and contemplation material in ordinary type. Between sessions, Taranatha cites his sources, gives liturgical recommendations and offers suggestions for teachers. These comments are in non-justified type within braces {}. The simplicity and directness of the contemplation material is reflected in the title *Essence of Ambrosiar.* Taranatha has distilled from a wealth of Mahayana material what he considers to be the pith of the Buddha's instructions and has arranged them for easy practice.

As indicated in the subtitle, Taranatha organizes his text, following Atisha's lead, into contemplations for "three types of person": the person of lesser capacity, the person of average capacity and the person of greater capacity. These types of person represent three distinct motivations and capacities for understanding. Taranatha's commentary at various points in the text indicates that this model is developmental rather than indicative of absolute potential. In other words, this classification does not imply that the contemplations contained in each section are intended exclusively for different people. Rather, the text follows an instructional progression aimed at the expanding capacity of beginning students. All students begin as a "person of lesser capacity" and are eventually expected to become, by virtue of their practice of these contemplations, a "person of greater capacity."

The Person of Lesser Capacity (Part I)

Atisha, in *The Lamp for the Path to Enlightenment,* defines the person of lesser capacity:

> Know to be "least" those persons
> Who diligently strive to attain

Solely the joys of cyclic existence
By any means for their welfare alone.[10]

As Atisha's words imply, the person of lesser capacity is one whose orientation is generally self-centered and gives greater priority to protecting him or herself than to reaching out to help others. He or she, like many of us, is more attracted to rest and relaxation than to hard work and is easily motivated by fear. Therefore, the contemplations for the person of lesser capacity are aimed at cultivating renunciation of a lower rebirth[11] and strengthening the student's motivation to embark on the spiritual path with diligence and vigor. Four key conceptual topics, aptly called "the four thoughts that turn the mind," are employed in this section to gradually introduce the student to basic Buddhist concepts of humanity, impermanence, the suffering of cyclic existence and karma. These contemplations, employed pervasively in Tibetan Buddhist traditions as part of the preliminary practices (Tib. *sngon 'gro*), are designed to "turn the mind" away from worldly preoccupations and towards an interest in spiritual pursuits. In *Essence of Ambrosia,* the contemplations in Part I are divided into four chapters, each covering one of the four thoughts: "The Freedoms and Endowments of a Precious Human Life", "Impermanence and Death", "The Misery of the Lower Realms" and "The Instructions on the Causes and Effects of Actions." While the titles of these chapters are somewhat descriptive, the author—who was likely writing predominantly for Tibetan monks—assumes some previous exposure to basic Buddhist terminology. Therefore, some explanation of these topics may be useful for a Western audience.

The contemplations in Chapter 1, "The Freedoms and Endowments of a Precious Human Life", are intended to awaken a sense of deep appreciation for what it means to be born human. The Buddhist doctrine of reincarnation holds that each of us has been reborn again and again in every conceivable form, reaching back not centuries or millennia but for an eternity. To be born in a human form is, therefore, an unusual circumstance. What makes the human form even more difficult to attain, according to the sutras, is that the cause of being reborn human is preserving faultless moral discipline, specifically the discipline of the *vinaya*[12]. The contemplations on the precious human life encourage an awareness of the rarity of finding oneself in a human form. Furthermore, enlightenment, the goal of all Buddhist practice, can be attained only in a human body. Due to their inability to understand language, animals cannot attain it. Because they are intoxicated with their own bliss, Gods cannot attain it. Beings in the other realms described in Buddhist cosmology are prevented from attaining it by their various obscurations. The eight unfavorable states described in the second contemplation delineate these and other conditions that prevent beings from attaining Buddhahood.

Next, in Chapter 2 "Impermanence and Death", the student contemplates that although this body is precious and rare, it is impermanent. Conditions can change at any moment, sweeping this life, and all its promise of attaining buddhahood, away. These contemplations are designed to precipitate a recognition that death could be imminent and to instill in the student a profound sense of urgency to pursue the spiritual path. In the Buddhist view, death is not a blissful release from the pains of illness or a glorious entrance into heaven. Tibetan teachings on the after-death state (Tib. *bardo*) describe the mind of the deceased as a "mental body" that is not bound by the limitations of space and physicality. After a period of unconsciousness (that may last as little as a moment or as long as several days), the deceased awakes, realizes he or she is dead and is plunged into a state of overwhelming terror and confusion. Due to the degree of virtuous actions and meditation the deceased engaged in while alive, he or she is subjected to more or less frightening visions and has more or less control over the emotions that grip his or her consciousness. A person who has brought his or her practice of meditation to fruition before death, on the other hand, is not subjected to these terrors and may even have a chance to become fully enlightened at the moment of death. Therefore, a person's best bet is to follow a spiritual path, engage in virtuous actions, meditate, relinquish attachment and develop perfect control of mind before death.

The contemplations in Chapter 3, "The Misery of the Lower Realms", stimulate renunciation of secular pursuits by focusing on the suffering inherent in cyclic existence. The Buddha taught that six types of beings, living in six realms, experience cyclic existence. These six types of beings are hell beings, hungry ghosts, animals, humans, demi-gods and gods. These beings belong to their respective "realms" based on their common sufferings and mental obscurations. These realms are created by the karmic projections of the beings that inhabit each realm. Chapter 3 focuses only on the "three lower realms": the hell realm, the hungry ghost realm and the animal realm. The beings who suffer most intensely are those in the 18 hells. Taranatha paints a vivid picture of the agony beings in the 8 hot hells, 8 cold hells, the neighboring hells and the ephemeral hells endure as penance for their past actions. Taranatha then describes the sufferings of hunger and thirst that afflict hungry ghosts. Because they have subtle "mental bodies," beings in these two realms are invisible to humans. The suffering of animals, however, is familiar to humans. To some extent the detailed contemplations of the suffering of the three lower realms are intended to engender trepidation in the mind of the meditator, but that is not their primary purpose. Their purpose is to make the meditator aware that the causes of experiencing the suffering of the lower realms exist at this very moment in the mind of every sentient being in the form of latent emotions. These primary emotions of hatred, desire and ignorance, when acted on, become the seeds that ripen as rebirth in the lower realms. Contemplating the suffering of each of these realms, as unpleasant an endeavor as it may seem, awakens the motivation in the student to free him or herself from the cycle of rebirth. In addition, the student comes to identify with and feel for the beings in those realms, an important basis for the later contemplations on compassion.

The contemplations in Chapter 4, "The Instructions on the Causes and Effects of Actions", are designed to familiarize the student with the law of *karma.*[13] This law, in a nutshell, is that virtuous thoughts and actions lead to happiness and non-virtuous thoughts and actions lead to suffering. The Buddha Shakyamuni summarized the instructions on karma concisely in a famous phrase: "Do not do anything wrong. Engage in an abundance of virtue. Discipline your mind. This is the teaching of the Buddha." The Buddha's basic directive for action was to avoid ten non-virtuous actions and engage in ten virtuous actions in order to create the most conducive conditions for the attainment of buddhahood for oneself and others. Of all the actions, the most important are "mental actions" or motivations. The Buddha's premise was that if a person's motivation is in the right place, his or her words and actions will follow like a cart follows a horse. Therefore, cultivating the virtuous "actions" of mind, such as magnanimity, tolerance and wisdom, is of particular importance on the Buddhist path. The contemplations in Chapter 4 encourage the student to give up negative actions and adopt positive ones by cultivating mindfulness and vigilance with regard to every thought and deed.

The Person of Average Capacity (Part II)

Those people of average capacity, according to Atisha, "stop sinful actions, turn their backs on the joys of existence and diligently strive just for their own peace."[14] Having considered the human situation, the suffering of the lower realms and the infallibility of karma, the person of average capacity understands the reasons for shunning negative actions, abandons laziness and makes an effort at spiritual practice. However, he or she has not fully understood the causes of enlightenment and is, therefore, still interested primarily in personal salvation. Therefore, the contemplations in Part II synthesize the particulars of suffering into a perspective on the nature of existence in general, explore the causes of suffering and define liberation from suffering. The contemplations in Chapter 5, "The Misery of the Higher Realms," are aimed at dispelling illusions that there is any ultimate joy in the human, demi-god or god realms of cyclic existence. Even the 28 god realms are depicted as less-than-satisfactory. Although the gods enjoy the rewards of their past positive actions, when their karma is used up, they experience the agony of falling to a lower realm.

Chapter 6 synthesizes all the previous contemplations into the perspective that suffering pervades existence. From the 29th Contemplation:

> I am completely surrounded by suffering. Suffering burns like fire; it roils like water; it gusts like wind; it oppresses like a mountain. Wherever I am, it is a place of suffering. Whatever type of body I inhabit, it is a body of suffering. Whomever I befriend, it is a companion of suffering. Whatever I enjoy, it is an enjoyment of suffering.

After contemplating the sufferings shared by all living creatures in all realms, the student is lead to the conclusion that no hope for ultimate happiness exists as long as he or she remains in cyclic existence. The only possibility of relief lies in release from the cycle, a personal liberation from suffering. Chapter 7 explores the origin of cyclic existence: karma and the emotional and cognitive afflictions. In this chapter, the student considers the nature of the three primary afflictions: attachment, aversion and ignorance, and reflects on how they translate into action. Negative actions in turn strengthen the afflictions, and the cycle begins anew. Considering this situation, the student resolves to become free of the grip of the afflictions. Finally, Chapter 8 contains a brief contemplation on the causes and results of liberation. The contemplations in this section are primarily aimed at leading the student gradually to an understanding that personal liberation from suffering is not enough. To achieve enlightenment in the Mahayana, one must desire freedom from suffering and liberation for the sake of others.

The Person of Greater Capacity (Part III)

The contemplations in Part III include the meditations that are the apex of Mahayana practice, appropriate only for those who have the proper motivation. Atisha explains:

> Those persons are called "superior"
> Who sincerely want to extinguish
> All the sufferings of others
> By understanding their own suffering.[15]

The person with the greatest capacity, the "superior" person, is one who uses his or her own experience of suffering to identify with the suffering of others and who is motivated by the wish to relieve sentient beings from their suffering both in a temporary and ultimate sense. This kind of person is ripe for exposure to the key motivating factor of the Mahayana: the awakening mind.[16] From the relative point of view, the awakening mind is the wish to attain enlightenment for the sake of bringing all other sentient beings to that same state. From the ultimate point of view, the awakening mind is non-conceptual wisdom combined inseparably with spontaneous, non-referential compassion. Relative and ultimate awakening mind is developed both internally through meditation, the volitional method and externally through consciously directed action. The volitional method is to strengthen "the aspiration of awakening mind," the unselfish wish to attain enlightenment for the benefit of others. This is the subject of Chapters 9-11. Because the essence of the aspiration of awakening mind is impartial and unconditional love and compassion for sentient beings, the contemplations in these chapters are concerned with arousing feelings of love, compassion, kindness, and magnanimity towards all others. In order to move the student to unfeigned feelings of love for others, the contemplations begin with meditating on love for your own mother. From the 36th Contemplation:

> She cradled me with her ten fingers, warmed me with the heat of her flesh, nursed me from her breasts, tasted my food, and wiped the filth from my bottom with her own hands. At the time that I was unable to do anything for myself, was as helpless as a bug, she cared for me.

Through reflecting on the details of the care exhibited by his or her mother, the student develops an intense appreciation of her kindness and is moved to feelings of love and compassion for her. Once these feelings are stable, the student practices applying them to friends, enemies and eventually all sentient beings.

The active methods are subsumed under the topic "the application of awakening mind" and are the subject of Chapters 12 and 13. These chapters introduce the six perfections, six qualities that the aspirant must perfect in order to attain the goal of enlightenment in the Mahayana tradition. The perfections are generosity, patience, moral discipline, diligence, meditative absorption and wisdom. The perfections provide a guide to exemplary Mahayana behavior and supply a set of remedial resources to combat the afflictions of greed, anger, attachment, laziness and stupidity that stand in the aspirant's way of making progress on the path to enlightenment. Chapter 13, devoted to the perfection of wisdom, contains contemplation sessions on the selflessness of the individual and the selflessness of phenomena: the pinnacle of all Mahayana meditation practice and the basis for the realization of the empty nature of all phenomena.

As an appendix to his book, Taranatha includes the procedural instructions for the two most important ceremonies of the Mahayana tradition. The first is the formal engendering of the awakening mind in the presence of one's spiritual master and the second is the taking of the Bodhisattva Vow. The latter is the formal acceptance of the commitment to observe the precepts connected with the attitude of compassion and loving kindness.

Essence of Ambrosia is a valuable resource for reflection, study and inquiry both for beginning students of Buddhism and for those who have been practicing for a long time. Considering the almost inconceivable cultural and temporal gap between 16th century pre-modern Tibet and 21st century modern Europe and America, it is extraordinary how pertinent the material remains to the modern seeker, even those of us immersed in the preoccupations of jobs and families. Taranatha's fresh, informal use of language makes his book accessible across the bridge of centuries. It is the hope of this translator that other Westerners who read these words will be inspired and stirred by Taranatha's inconceivable wisdom. If I had a piece of advice for the readers of this book, whether they may be inclined to Buddhism or not, it would be to read the contemplations slowly, perhaps one per day, ruminating on the meaning. Make it a ritual; make it a session…

Prologue

Namo Buddha Bodhisattvaya[17]

Contained herein is *Essence of Ambrosia: The Instruction Manual for the Stages on the Path of the Three Types of Person to Enter into the Buddhist Teaching.*

> Homage to the Three Jewels.
> Having bowed to the Lama who holds the three lineages[18]
> That sparkle with the jewels of excellent qualities,
> I will now explain the supreme path of the great chariot,
> The meaning of the main treatise composed by the master Atisha.

{What is presented here is the very path meditated upon by all the noble beings of the three vehicles throughout the three times—the buddhas, bodhisattvas, solitary-realizers and hearers[19]—the very path they followed to reach the supreme level of liberation and omniscience. These spiritual methods are known collectively as "The Successive Stages Introducing the Aspirant to the Buddha's Teaching." They are also referred to as "The Graduated Path for the Three Types of Person," "The Graduated Path to Enlightenment," or "Introduction to the Great Chariot."}

This text has three main sections: (1) Relying on a spiritual master, the root of all paths; (2) the stages on the path for training the three types of person through contemplations; and (3) how to apply these teachings to the fruition of unsurpassable enlightenment.

Contemplation 1

Relying on a Spiritual Master, the Root of All Paths

In order to become acquainted with the characteristics of a spiritual master, and in order to develop the capacity to faithfully attend one, follow these steps during the meditation session: Observe the proper conduct preceding meditation by sitting cross-legged, straightening your posture, and so forth. Focus your attention on the buddhas and bodhisattvas who fill the expanse of space. Recite an expanded or abbreviated practice of homage and offering prayer as a preliminary; follow by reciting the seven-branch prayer[20] from the "Aspiration Prayer of Samantabhadra" three times while reflecting on the meaning. Then, very high in the sky in front of you, visualize an immeasurable number of buddhas and bodhisattvas. Directly in front of them in the sky, visualize your root lama, surrounded by a dense gathering of all the lineage lamas. Supplicate them fervently with the following prayer:

> Buddhas and bodhisattvas throughout the universe,
> And the perfect lama, my good and truly virtuous
> master—
> Please regard and bless me.
> Please pacify my faults completely.
> Please awaken genuine insights within me.
> Please dispel all obstacles to practicing the Mahayana way.

After praying thus, make visualized offerings [to the field of accumulation in front]. The root and lineage lamas then enter into the crown of your head and come to rest in a pavilion of light at your heart. Think that the buddhas and bodhisattvas disappear into suchness. Dedicate the merit using verses such as the following:

> May the roots of my virtuous practice become a cause
> for attaining the level of buddhahood for the sake of
> all sentient beings.

Or:

> By this virtuous activity,
> May all beings perfectly gather merit and wisdom,
> And obtain the two sacred states[21]
> Born from merit and wisdom.

Between meditation sessions, do not examine the lama for faults; reflect solely on his good qualities. Reflect as follows:

I have not had the opportunity to actually meet the Buddha [Shakyamuni]. But the compassion of all the buddhas who have existed throughout time has incarnated in the form of this spiritual master. Therefore, my lama is in truth a real Buddha. He has been kinder to me than all the Buddhas combined. Without concealing anything, he bestows the methods necessary to obtain whatever I wish—whether it be rebirth in the higher realms, freedom from suffering or buddhahood. If I develop a single good quality or suppress a single fault, it is due to my lama's kindness. How kind he is to impart these profound teachings that are so hard to come by!

I must use my body and all my possessions for the sake of the lama. With my body, I will carry out whatever acts of respect, offering and service are in harmony with the lama's wishes. With my speech, I will praise the qualities of the lama's body, speech and mind and will converse only as a means of spiritual service. I will behave in a way that pleases his mind and will do whatever he asks.

Think in this way again and again[22] *and strive to practice accordingly.*

To comment on the fourth line of the supplication at the beginning of the contemplation ["Please pacify my faults completely"], there are five faults: The fault being attached to this life, the fault of mistrusting the law of karma, the fault of clinging to cyclic existence as a source of happiness, the fault of thinking your own needs are most important and the fault of perceiving things and attributes as truly existent.

To comment on the fifth line ["Please awaken genuine insights within me"], there are five genuine insights: The insight that the next life is more important than this one, the insight of trusting the law of karma, the insight that cyclic existence is a state of suffering, the insight that the needs of others are more important than your own and the insight that the ultimate truth is emptiness, and that the relative truth is that things are like an illusion.

With regard to the sixth line ["Please dispel all obstacles to practicing the Mahayana way"], there are three kinds of obstacles. The outer obstacles are harm inflicted by human or non-human forces. The intermediate obstacles are illnesses that afflict the physical body. The inner obstacles are profane thoughts and negative emotions. Pray that these three obstacles may be dispelled. The instructions above comprise one visualization sequence.

The second section of this text, the stages on the path for training the three types of person through contemplations, has three sections: (1) Training in the common stages for the person of lesser capacity, (2) training in the common stages for the person of average capacity and (3) training in the extraordinary stages for the person of greater capacity.

Part I

Training in the Common Stages for the Person of Lesser Capacity

{There are many instructions on this topic stemming from the various traditions of practice. Even our tradition, which is based on the glorious oral instructions of Lord Atisha, has several versions. Some versions begin with the contemplation on the sufferings of cyclic existence. Some start with an explanation of karma. Some begin with an explanation of the difficulty of obtaining a human life with its freedoms and endowments. Most start off with the contemplation on impermanence and death.[23] Even though these variations exist, they all come down to the same point—there is no discrepancy in the meaning. Nevertheless, the most well-known presentations start with the contemplation on the difficulty of obtaining a human body with its freedoms and endowments because it is a good foundation for meditation on impermanence. Starting with the meditation on impermanence holds the risk that the practitioner will think, "I've never really existed in the ultimate sense, so only this moment is real. I may as well enjoy myself."[24] So we will use the following order.}

(1) The contemplation on the difficulty of obtaining a precious human life with its freedoms and endowments, (2) the contemplation on impermanence and death, (3) the contemplation on the suffering of the lower realms, and (4) the contemplation on the causes and effects of actions.[25]

Chapter One

The Freedoms and Endowments of a Precious Human Life

Contemplation 2

The Difficulty of Obtaining a Precious Human Life with its Freedoms and Endowments

Make prostrations and offerings and recite the seven-branch prayer[26] *as you did previously. Supplicate briefly as explained above [in Part I]. Then, carefully examine your situation—your body, home, possessions, environment and so forth—and reflect:*

A human life such as the one I have now obtained will be extremely hard to come by in the future, so I will not waste it in meaningless pursuits. I must use it in service to religion.

This basic reflection should precede all meditation sessions.

In brief:

> Hell beings, hungry ghosts, animals,
> Barbarians, long-lived gods,
> Those with distorted views, people unexposed to
> Buddha,
> And mutes—these are the eight unfavorable states.[27]

Beings born in the lower realms experience unavoidable misery. Because their bodies are extremely poor supports for pursuing religion, they have scant opportunity to practice. Even the gods of the desire realm are distracted due to their attachment to sense pleasures. The gods of the form and formless realms are for the most part intoxicated with the bliss of trance,[28] so they do not have the good fortune to listen to the teachings. The body of a demi-god[29]—even more than that of a desire-realm god—

is a poor support, comparable to the body of an animal. A being who is born in a world where a buddha has not come or one born as a barbarian in an outlying region where the inhabitants are ignorant of Buddhism has no chance to practice. The realms where a buddha has come and places where Buddhism has spread are very few. Even those born in a country where Buddhism has spread could develop perverted views and aversion to religion, or they could be born without the intellectual capacity to understand which actions should be abandoned and which adopted. These people also lack the good fortune to practice religion. At this time, I have obtained a body free from these eight unfavorable conditions, and therefore I have the ability to practice religion.

To sum up the ten endowments in a verse

> Born human, in the center, faculties complete,
> Karma uncorrupted and with faith.
> The Buddha came, taught the Way;
> The teaching survives, with many followers;
> There are those with loving hearts towards others.[30]

In general, I have been born human. In particular, I have been born in a central country where Buddhism has spread. More specifically, I have been born with my faculties complete so that I know what to adopt and what to abandon. And moreover, I have not been swayed by perverted views, I have not committed any extremely evil actions such as one of the five acts of immediate consequence[31] and have faith in an appropriate source—the sacred teachings and rules of discipline[32]. Therefore, the five inner endowments are complete. Furthermore, the Buddha has already come to this world. He has already taught the sacred teachings. His teachings have not declined but flourish. At this time, there are many new people starting to practice Buddhism. There are many sponsors who, moved by loving kindness towards religious practitioners, give them food, clothing and necessities. This is a time when the resources needed to support religious practice are available. Thus, the five outer endowments are fully complete. With things as they are, such a body that is free from the eight unfavorable states and replete with the ten endowments is extremely difficult to obtain. Therefore, I must exert myself in religious practice right now.

Contemplate this way again and again, recollecting the reasons the human body is so difficult to obtain. At the end of the meditation session, dedicate the merit to enlightenment as described earlier.

Contemplation 3

The Probability of Being Reborn Human

For this contemplation, the preliminaries and conclusion are the same as explained above

Among all sentient beings, those living in the lower realms are extremely numerous, and those born into higher existences are very few. It is like comparing the number of grains of dirt making up the earth with the number of dust motes that can rest on a fingernail. Or I could consider that if the number of beings in hell were equal to the atoms comprising the earth; then the number of hungry ghosts would be like snowflakes in a blizzard; the number of aquatic animals would be equal to the barley grains in a vat of malt; and terrestrial animals fill every mountain, valley and space on earth. If I look at these examples, it seems barely possible to be born as a god or human. A human rebirth is least likely of all. And humans born on earth are particularly rare. As for rebirth as a human who practices religion—it is almost impossible. Considering all of this, I must definitely resolve to exert myself in religious practice!

But why is a human rebirth so hard to obtain? From among all living creatures, most are inclined to act harmfully. In general, very few carry out virtuous activities. And even from among those who do, very few beings maintain the moral discipline necessary to make a human rebirth possible. Therefore, a human rebirth is difficult to come by. Moreover, I need to amass a great deal of merit in order to consolidate the ten endowments and encounter the teachings—a situation where I can do that is very hard to find. But now, because of my previous karma, I have—at this one time and in this one fortunate circumstance—accumulated enough merit to obtain a human body with all the freedoms and endowments. I must exert myself in the practice of religion right now!

Contemplation 4
Why This Human Life is Important

{At this point, several other texts include a section called 'understanding the difficulty of obtaining a human rebirth by way of example.' Since this section simply presents examples of how rare a human life is, it seems unnecessary in this case to consider it as a separate contemplation in itself.[33]}

The preliminaries and conclusion for this contemplation are the same as before. After the preliminaries, reflect on the reasons that a human rebirth is hard to obtain as explained above.

At this one exceptional time, I have obtained a human life that is so extremely difficult to come by—so I must achieve the great meaning of this life. If I want to live with an abundance of worldly comfort and happiness from one life to the next, I can accomplish that effortlessly by relying on this human body. If I want to achieve liberation from cyclic existence—the enlightenment of a hearer or solitary-realizer[34]—I can do that now without much hardship. Even if I want to achieve total and complete enlightenment, it would be easy to do so at this time. But if I had not obtained a human body such as this one, how could I even talk about liberation or buddhahood? I would not have any idea how to achieve even one aspect of worldly comfort. Therefore, at this time, I must assimilate the essential meaning of life. If, instead, I spend this human life that I have obtained just this one time in meaningless pursuits, it would be a tremendous waste. Shantideva's *Guide to the Bodhisattva's Way of Life*[35] says

> If, having obtained freedoms such as these,
> I do not practice virtuous actions,
> There could be no greater pretense.
> There could be no greater stupidity.

To waste this human life is to deceive myself! It is like traveling to an island of jewels and returning empty-handed. This body is an extraordinary support that can get me any extraordinary thing I desire, and I have found it just this once. If I do not do anything at all and, instead, let it slip through my fingers: that will be my own fault. Previously, I have let it go to waste. But now, from this day onwards, I will not waste a moment; I must assiduously practice religion.

Contemplate in this way again and again.

Furthermore, if I think the comforts and activities of this life are important considerations, I should remember that, even in a worldly context, the experience of long-term comfort requires the temporary sacrifice of leisure and contentment for a few days or months in order to work to earn that eventual security. In the same way, if I want to earn permanent happiness that lasts for all lifetimes, it is necessary to give up attachment to this life and work at religious practice. It is said

> This human life with its freedoms and endowments is
> very hard to obtain.
> If you find a meaningful life,
> But do not put it to good use,
> How will you ever receive this perfect gift again?[36]

Chapter Two

Impermanence and Death

Contemplation 5

You Will Certainly Die Soon

A sutra says

> Whoever has lived and will live,
> Must discard this body and depart.
> Frightened of that, the wise become realized.
> They come to abide in religion and definitely train
> in it.[37]

No matter where I live, I cannot avoid death. No matter whom I befriend, I cannot avoid death. All the transient beings that have lived on the face of the earth have died. All who will live in the future also will die. And among those who presently live, as well, there is no one who can escape death. From the time of my birth up until this day today, how many who were close to me have died? How many who were strangers or enemies have died? There is no reason to be confident that I shall remain when they have all died.

In general, no one is spared death. More especially, no one is capable of extending life. Starting from birth without pausing even for a moment, my life has been diminishing so that moment by moment death draws nigh. With each passing day, it comes closer. With each passing month, it comes much closer. With each passing year, it comes exceedingly close. I am swiftly approaching death.

Now while I am young, when I should be gaining experience in spiritual practice, I sometimes think, "I am still not old; if I do it gradually that will be okay." In this short life, to be leisurely like that will not work! For example, if I do not practice religion when young, then at the age of sixty, life will have passed. Even if in old age I decide to practice religion, because the power of the body and mind are depleted, the fruition will not arise[38]. Half the time remaining will be spent in sleep. Falling under the influence of such myriad meaningless things as preparing food, getting around, distractions and so forth, I waste this human life. Even taken from the perspective of one who has great motivation and perseverance, the full extent of time available for practicing religion and acquiring experience will not be very long.

I must quickly realize the truth, which has been realized by holy persons exerting themselves with every moment available. In this short life, I will never take the approach of postponing spiritual practice to the future from indolence or procrastination!

It is very important to meditate in this way again and again, thinking of the reasons to practice.

Contemplation 6

You Have No Idea When You Will Die.

In general, not only is life short but I have no indication when I will die. If I am fortunate, my life span—propelled by my past karma—might possibly extend as much as 60 or 70 years. But more likely, it won't be that much. Even allowing that I might live a long time, there is no calculating from today what my lifespan will be. It may be half over, or it may be mostly over. For some, because of their previous karma, it is possible that life will not extend beyond thirty or forty years.

In other words, the lord of death truly has arrived at my doorstep. The enemies, friends, wealth, material things, associates, servants and companions of this life, happiness, sadness and conversation—none will remain with me for long. What is the purpose of all this? As is said

> If the earth, mountains and oceans
> Will be incinerated by seven blazing suns,
> And none of these bodies will endure, even as ash,[39]
> It goes without saying that I should not rely on something so frail.[40]

This body, an aggregate of flesh, blood and fluid, is transient. The breath is unstable, like a mist in autumn: I have no idea when it may cease. Because I have not achieved freedom of mind[41], I am not sure of anything whatsoever and remain oblivious of when I will die. Maitreyanatha taught

> To say, "Today at least I will not die,"
> And to remain at ease is unwise.
> At the time when I become nothing,
> My fate will be beyond doubt.[42]

In the words of Nagarjuna

> The circumstances of death are many.
> Those that sustain life are few;
> Those very things, too, may cause death.
> Therefore, continually practice religion.[43]

The potential causes for death include sentient beings such as humans, animals and demons; the environment and elements such as precipices, fire and water; and inwardly the four hundred and four kinds of sickness of the body. In short, there is nothing about which it can be said, "This cannot be the cause of death." Those things asserted to be causes for not dying and remaining alive—food, clothing, my home, bed, medicine and so forth—at some point may become circumstances for death such as when food becomes rancid or when one takes the wrong medicine. I am living in the center of a swirling blizzard of circumstances adverse to my body and life and know nothing of when I will come to die!

Contemplation 7

At Death, Nothing Whatsoever Other Than Religion Will Help.

Shantideva says

> When I am seized by the messenger of the lord of death,
> What use are relatives? What use are friends?[44]

At the time of death, even if I have much wealth and many possessions, I will be powerless to bring along even one sesame seed's worth. Even if I am at the center of a vast number of family members, companions, workers, attendants, lords, chiefs and so forth, I will be powerless to bring with me even the lowliest servant or a single puppy, and they will be powerless to follow as well. All of this has the nature of parting and separation and will not provide any benefit whatsoever.

Meditate with utter disgust. Apply this in the same way to everything—friends, enemies, comfort, misery, good and bad circumstances.

If all that does not follow after me, what does follow? My accumulated karma, both positive and negative, will follow behind me. Once I have done something negative, it will continue to harm me. On the other hand, all the virtuous deeds that I have done will benefit me without a single exception. I should contemplate the words of Chöden Rabjor:

> All others will be left behind.
> Apart from virtuous and negative actions
> Nothing will follow behind you.
> Know this and analyze it well.[45]

Therefore, I should cultivate the thought that I am certain to die, will die soon, know not when I am to die and that nothing whatsoever will be of benefit when I die. From the moment of death onwards for boundless lifetimes, the only thing that can benefit me is sacred teaching: right now I must turn my efforts to practicing that teaching!

Contemplation 8

The Five Root Verses—The Instruction Used For Meditation Sessions on Impermanence and Death

The root verses

> First consider that nothing stays the same; everything changes.
> Think about the many others who have died.
> Think again and again about the many potential causes of death.

Meditate, 'What will it be like while I am dying?'
Contemplate what will happen after death.

1. "First consider that nothing stays the same; everything changes."

For each of us, from the time we are born until we die, this continuum of aggregates changes and develops. First, when I was a little baby, I was like that. When I was a child, I was thus. At the time of my youth, I was so. Now I am like this, coming closer and closer to death. Nothing has been of any benefit. In a subdued frame of mind, cultivate a sense of disenchantment.

2. "Think about the many others who have died."

Recall impermanence clearly. Then mentally enumerate individuals you have heard about or knew, who have died in your area of residence and reflect:

How many people older that me have died? How many people my age or younger have died? When I think about it, more people have died here than are alive now, and for the most part, people die in their prime. I am of the same nature as they are. I do not transcend this situation. Thinking I will not end up among them is idiocy. Before I die, I must practice religion purely.

With an acute awareness of impermanence, think about people and animals you have heard of or have known who have died. Think about those who are alive—acquaintances and those you have heard about—who went from being very powerful to very weak, or from weak to powerful, from rich to poor and so forth, then consider

I, my affairs, my enjoyments and so forth are of this nature. They too are transient.

3. "Think again and again about the many potential causes of death."

After contemplating as before on the many potential causes of death, reflect

I do not even know how all the things right around me might contribute to the circumstances of my death. I do not know how things may change spontaneously at any moment.

4. "Meditate: 'What will it be like while I am dying?' "

When I am dying, if my mind is in a non-virtuous state, I will experience terrifying suffering—the karma of my life force being severed and so forth. Death is not desired or joyfully welcomed. Undesired, it comes all of a sudden. People do not die happily and full of delight. They die accompanied by powerful, intense suffering. The next world is not one about which I know and am familiar. I am about to wander without directions in an unknown land.

5. "Contemplate what will happen after death."

When I die, my body and mind will separate. This body will be buried and become a mass of worms or be thrown in the water to be eaten by fish and otters, or be cremated and reduced to a handful of bones, or be carried to the mountains or plains to be strewn about and devoured by birds and jackals. In the end, after some days there will not even be a trace left. The demise of this body, nurtured so carefully now, will be like that. If the mind carrying the burden of karma must go to a birthplace unknown, is there any way I am not going to practice religion right now? Or, if I have been practicing, is there any way I am going to put it off to later?

After contemplating in this way, form a plan, thinking:

Now I am going to take up a pure spiritual practice. With the armor of this resolve, I will bring forth, reside in and guard spiritual practice. Then I will spend my life with great joy. After I die, others will say, "She was truly a religious person," and aspire to be like me. In living this life, I need to commit myself to a goal. For that, I should meditate on truth and attain a stable state. For that to happen, I need to become familiar with the practice of meditation and then become proficient.

If I do not achieve stability, then when I encounter negative circumstances, my mind will not be workable. There is the danger that I will not stick to my plans to practice religion. I may act contrary to religion and end up with regrets. Death will come amidst a din of disparagement from everyone else. There is no way I will let that happen; right now, in order to fulfill the aspirations of others and happiness for myself, I will engage in authentic spiritual practice and sustain it until I die.

Take this oath again and again. These days, for all religious people, this remedy is crucial.

Chapter Three

The Misery of the Lower Realms

{Include the preliminaries and the conclusion in each contemplation session as before. Then reflect as follows: "I do not have the freedom to remain in this human realm for a long time. Death will destroy me in the end. But death alone is not the only thing I have to fear. I am not just going to die—I will be compelled to take rebirth. This is what I should be worried about. If I do not engage in virtuous actions and instead engage in a lot of harmful actions, I will take rebirth in one of the three lower realms. How frightening!" All contemplations on the suffering of the lower realms should begin with this reflection.}

The Hell Realms

Contemplation 9

The Suffering of the Hot Hells

To summarize in verse

> Reviving, Black Lines, Crushing Together,
> Wailing, Great Wailing,
> Hot, Very Hot and Insufferable.[46]

All the hot hell realms have these characteristics in common: there are no mountains or valleys on the surface of the earth—the ground is made of burning iron; flames constantly blaze an arm's length in height; jagged ravines and precipices cut through the landscape; water here takes the form of scorching, molten copper, molten bronze, molten lead and boiling salt water— the rivers and lakes are composed of these substances; even the trees are made of scalding iron. These realms are full of harmful birds, carnivorous animals, karmic demons[47] and murderers. Beings in the intermediate state[48] who are destined to be reborn there first experience extreme cold—they may be blown by the wind, pelted by rain and so forth. By the force of their previous karma, they see one of the hot hell realms, crave to go there and run in that direction. They are then caught in that realm and take rebirth.

Fire made with sandalwood is seven times hotter than ordinary fire. The fire in the first hell realm, "Reviving," is seven times hotter than that. Likewise, the heat of each lower hell is seven times greater than the one above it. The mind of a being in the hell realms is extremely sensitive—it is stabbed and clouded by feeling. A hell-being's body is soft and his flesh tender, like that of a newborn baby. Both body and mind have little tolerance for pain, so his suffering is particularly intense.

The faculties and limbs of the beings in these realms are instantly restored[49] as if waking up from sleep. All beings that take 'miraculous birth' like the beings in hell[50] have similar experiences.

The particulars of each hot hell:

1. Reviving: The beings here see each other as enemies and assassins and, therefore, generate anger towards one another. Their raised arms turn into sharp weapons that they use to stab and cut one another to pieces. Eventually, they lose consciousness and fall over as if dead. Then a cold wind comes from the sky, and a voice calls out "Revive!" Their bodies are restored to their original state; they fight as before, die and are again revived in an endless cycle.
2. Black Lines: Wardens of hell[51] draw many black lines on the bodies of the sentient beings in this hell-realm then cut them with saws, chop them up with axes and pierce them with sharp weapons. While the upper part of their bodies is being cut up, the lower half heals. While the lower part of their bodies is being cut up, the upper half heals. This goes on constantly without interruption.
3. Crushing: The beings here experience the misery of being squeezed between or under the weight of huge, frightening animals such as rams. Or they may experience being crushed by huge boulders that take terrifying forms such as sheep, goat, water buffalo or lion heads. Or they might be crushed and smothered from the top by a great mountain. Sometimes a group of sentient beings in this realm will collect on top of an enormous iron bar, where they are ground and smashed by a club or hammer. When the mountain or club

lifts up, the bodies of the beings are restored to their original state. Their bodies are then again squeezed and crushed into dust.

4. Howling: Beings in this hell are pursued by many terrifying wild animals. From afar, they see a white house. Thinking they will be safe there, they flee to the house for shelter. But as soon as they are inside, it becomes an iron house with no doors. Fire scorches and burns them inside and out. With no hope of escape, they sob and howl.
5. Great Howling: this hell is similar to the one described above, but the iron house has two stories. The beings there are cooked inside of an iron pot filled with molten iron.
6. Hot: The beings in this realm are slowly impaled from the top of the head to the anus or from the anus to the top of the head with burning hot stakes or spears so that their entrails are cooked in the process. Fire and smoke come out of their nine orifices.
7. Very Hot: This hell is similar to "Hot," but the beings there are pierced with three-pointed spears and so forth.

   The suffering experienced in the higher hells is also experienced in the deeper ones, but the suffering in the deeper hells is much more intense.
8. Unceasing Torment: The misery here is immeasurable without even the slightest interim of comfort. The bodies of the beings in this realm are wrapped in a molten iron leaf, placed in an iron basket and shaken with hot sand. It is also taught that some of them experience the suffering of their tongues being plowed by 500 huge plows. Like butter lamp wicks, their bodies blaze with fire inside and out so that the fire and their bodies are indivisible. Except for their speech and cries, it would be hard even to identify them as sentient beings.

The beings in the hell realms experience intense suffering for a long time. The *Treasury of Phenomenology* says

> Fifty human years is equal to one day in the desire god realm. And they live for 500 god-years. The lifespan in the higher [realms] doubles as you go up... The lifespan and days in "Reviving" and the six others are equal to the desire god realm...

Fifty human years equals one day for the four great kings [of the desire god realm]. If you were able to live for five hundred hell-realm years, that would equal one day in "Reviving." The lifespan in "Reviving" is five hundred years. The lifespan of beings in the hells below that doubles as you go down. The length of each day in each lower hell is twice as long as the one above it. The hell directly above becomes the basis for calculating the length of the days and lifespan of the beings in the hell below.

At the conclusion of each session, think

The suffering in these hells is extreme. It lasts for a long time. Right now, if I merely burn the tip of my finger for a moment in a small flame, I can hardly stand it. If I end up in hell someday, I will not be able to bear the suffering at all. Once I have been born there, there will be no way for me to reverse the situation. But right now, I do have a way to reverse it; purifying the negative karma and evil actions that lead to rebirth there is the only way. In order that I do not take rebirth in a hell realm, I must exert myself in spiritual practice.

{In accord with your inclination, there is no problem with breaking these contemplations up into several sessions.}

Contemplation 10

The Suffering of the Cold Hells

To summarize in a verse

> Blisters, Bursting Blisters,
> Brrr, Alas, Chattering,
> Cracking like an Utpala, Lotus and Great Lotus.[52]

In all the cold hells, the ground, mountains and valleys are snow and ice slashed with crevices and ravines. Violent icy winds and snowstorms rage constantly over the landscape. The winds are so cold that they penetrate the skin and chill the flesh of the beings there to the very bone. Each of the eight hells is seven times colder than the one above it. The sentient beings destined to be born there first have the experience in the intermediate state of being burnt in a fire. They wish to cool off and, seeing the cold hell landscape from afar, run in that direction. Having entered that realm, they take rebirth there.

1. Blisters: The beings in this realm become so cold that blisters permeate their bodies inside and out.
2. Bursting Blisters: The beings in this realm are so cold that their blisters burst open. Pus covers their bodies and freezes, making them even colder. It says in *Letter to a Student*[53] that maggots infest the pus, bore into the beings' bodies and eat them.
3. Brrr!: The beings here are so cold that they are just able to make short monosyllabic sounds.
4. Alas!: The beings here are even colder than those and cannot utter even a syllable—they are just able to make slight, barely audible noises.
5. Chattering Teeth: The beings here are much colder still and cannot make any vocal sounds. Their bodies shiver uncontrollably; their chins shake, and their teeth chatter.
6. Cracking like an Utpala Flower: The bodies of the beings here freeze and crack into four or eight pieces.
7. Cracking like a Lotus: The bodies of these beings crack into a hundred or more pieces.
8. Cracking like a Great Lotus: This is the most extreme of the cold hells. Every section of the bodies of the beings here splits into hundreds and thousands of pieces.

How long is the life of the beings in Blisters? Suppose there was a silo that could hold eighty bushels of something, and it was completely filled with mustard seeds. If you were to take out one mustard seed every hundred years, the life of a being in Blisters would be over once the silo was empty. Thus it is explained. The lifespan of beings in each of the lower hells is twenty times longer than the one above.

The beginning and conclusion for the contemplation on the suffering of the cold hells is the same as for the hot hells.

Contemplation 11

The Suffering of the Neighboring Hells

The *Treasury of Phenomenology* says

> In addition to these eight, there are sixteen more.
> The four main ones are
> The Fire, Pit, Putrid Cadavers,
> Road of Razors, and the River.

Surrounding each of the eight hot hells, in the four cardinal directions, are four neighboring hells.

1. The Fire Pit: In this hell, there is an extremely wide pit full of hot embers. Some beings are born there from the start, and others wander there from the main hot hells. Because the misery of the sentient beings in the main hells is so intense, they become obsessed with the thought of escape. Eventually, some manage to run away and fall into the pit of embers. Depending upon the heaviness of their karma, they may sink up to their knees, up to their waist and so forth. When they wish to flee from the pit, they become confused and run back to the main hells. The terrifying wardens of the main hells surround and seize them, and they are not able to escape again for some time.
2. Swamp of Putrid Cadavers: But when they do again flee, they fall into a swamp called "Putrid Cadavers" that is filled with nine disgusting things.[54] The stench is so foul that it is enough to split open their heads and cause them to lose consciousness. The swamp is full of insects with iron and copper teeth that bore into and devour the beings' bodies as termites devour wood.
3. The Road of Razors and others: The beings first see a beautiful, verdant meadow from afar and run towards it. When they get there, the ground is covered with razors about four inches high, and they endure the misery of having their feet cut up.

   A related hell in this vicinity is "The Forest of Swords." The beings in the main hells, tortured by heat, are thrilled to see a cool, shady forest from afar. Running there, they find that all the leaves of the trees are swords and other weapons. The wind blows, causing the weapons to fall like rain and cut their bodies to pieces.

Yet another hell is "The Shamali Trees." The beings in this realm are first chased by vicious animals. The beings see a great shamali tree and scramble up its trunk. There are foot-long spines on the trunk, facing downwards, that gradually pierce their bodies all the way through. They experience other terrors as well, such as flocks of fierce birds pecking out their eyes and ripping their flesh. Then when they try to come down, the thorns turn upwards and pierce their bodies as they descend. Since the three neighboring hells described above are all associated with being hurt by weapons, they are classified under the same category.

4. The Impassable River of Hot Ash: The hell beings, tormented by heat, see a cool river flowing in the distance. Arriving there, they jump in without any hesitation only to find that the river is a mixture of fire and water. It is extremely hot, deep and wide. Their bodies sink into the water and are thoroughly cooked until their flesh separates from the bone. The flesh falls off, but the life force remains in the bones. The beings become skeletons and rise out of the water. As soon as that happens, their flesh is restored, and they again sink into the river. The length of time that they must endure this torture is indeterminate, but it is always a long time—a hundred, a thousand, or more years.

The beginning and the conclusion of the meditation session follow the pattern of the previous one.

Contemplation 12
The Ephemeral Hells

These hells exist below the earth and also in the mountains, plains and water upon the earth. The lifespan of beings in these hells varies. While some of them live longer than beings in the main hells, others live a very short time. The type of suffering they experience also varies. The sutras state that some beings in the ephemeral hells experience the happiness of the gods during the day and the suffering of hell at night. They may take the various forms in this hell, such as a seat, a wall, a pestle, a tree, a phantom, a broom and so forth.[55]

The beginning and conclusion of each session is the same as above.

{During the period when you are meditating on the suffering of the hells, generate confidence by listening, reflection and studying excerpts from the sutras such as the *Story of Sangharakshita.*[56]}

Contemplation 13
The Hungry Ghost Realm

The preliminaries and the basis of this contemplation are the same as above.

If I think, "What if I were not born in a hell realm and, instead, were born as a hungry ghost—would I be happy then?" When I consider the matter, I would not be happy. There are two types of hungry ghosts: those who live underground and those who live scattered about.

1. Hungry Ghosts Living in Serkya: The first type of hungry ghost lives 500 miles underground. They live in the hungry ghost city called Serkya, the empire of King Yamadharma, chief of the hungry ghosts. Countless hungry ghosts live around this city.
2. Hungry Ghosts Living Scattered About: There are countless hungry ghosts that move through space, on the earth and under the earth. If I had clairvoyance, I would be able to perceive that hungry ghosts are everywhere. They are unable to merely find a place to go and live. There are a few with great miraculous powers who are somewhat happy. But most of them experience a great deal of suffering. The great *Close Placement of Mindfulness Sutra*[57] mentions thirty-six kinds of hungry ghosts. If summarized, there are three main types: those with outer obscurations, those with inner obscurations and those with obscurations associated with food and drink.
3. Hungry Ghosts with Outer Obscurations: For many years, these hungry ghosts are unable to find food and drink. From time to time, they see heaps of food from a distance; but when they arrive, there is nothing left. Sometimes they see a great river; but when they arrive at the shore, it has dried up and there is nothing but sand and the stony river bottom. Sometimes a verdant tree laden with fruit appears in front of them, but it dries up when they

arrive at its base. At times, the food is guarded by many demons who keep them from getting at it.

4. Hungry Ghosts with Inner Obscurations: Their mouths are only as wide as the eye of a needle. At first, they are unable to get any food or drink into their mouths. When finally a bit of food gets in, it is lost in the enormous cavity of their mouths. If a little liquid gets in, it is dried up by the poison in their saliva. If they manage to swallow food or drink, it usually does not make it down their throats, which are as narrow as a bow-string. Even if some of it does make it down, since their stomachs are the size of mountains, they are never filled up.
5. Hungry Ghosts who have Obscurations Associated with Food and Drink: Whatever food and drink these hungry ghosts imbibe turns to fire that burns the inside of their bodies. In addition, all they can find to eat are disgusting things that cause them to suffer such as hot coals, feces, urine, pus and blood. They never find anything good to eat.

In general, all of these hungry ghosts suffer unbearably and constantly from hunger and thirst. They do not have clothing, so they are burned when it is hot and freeze when it is cold. In the winter, even the sunlight feels icy. In the summer, even the moonlight burns them. When it rains, they perceive the drops as hot coals scorching their skin. At all times, unable to find sustenance, they experience the misery of exhaustion and weariness, and their bodies become emaciated from lack of food and drink. Flames leap from the 360 dislocated joints in their bodies. Because they perceive one another as enemies, they catch, bind, beat and stab one another and experience the fear of being killed. Furthermore, because they are naturally timid and fearful, they feel extreme terror for no particular reason. Hungry ghosts experience this kind of intense suffering. Most hungry ghosts live to be about 15,000 human years old. The preliminaries and conclusion are the same as for the preceding contemplations.

{Although the above contemplations are comprehensive, there is a custom of setting aside a separate session to meditate on the hungry demons that move through space. Since these types of hungry ghosts harm others, they are born repeatedly in the lower realms. Some of these hungry ghosts harm others with poison[58] without intending to do so. Powerful ones harm others by striking and hitting them. When unexplained misfortune befalls people, they blame hungry ghosts saying "Even though I did nothing to deserve it, this demon harmed me!" Hearing this, the hungry ghosts feel mental anguish. It is also fine not to make this into a separate session; this contemplation can be included in one of the previous sessions.}

Contemplation 14

The Suffering of the Animal Realm

1. Animals Living Under Water: The animals living in the ocean have no source of protection and wander aimlessly, carried about by the waves. They eat one another. Constantly anticipating a predator's approach, they are afraid and miserable. They endure such unbearable miseries as being eaten alive and so forth.
2. Animals That are Scattered About: These are the animals living among humans and gods. Wild animals constantly live with an uneasy mind because they are innately anxious about approaching predators. Domestic animals endure the hardships of being shorn, having their noses pierced, of being beaten and being forced to carry heavy loads. They endure many sufferings associated with being enslaved or killed for their meat, blood, skin and bones. In addition, they endure hunger, thirst, heat and cold comparable to the suffering of the hell beings and the hungry ghosts. Their principal suffering is that of ignorance; not knowing better, they prey on one another and live in constant apprehension of being chased by a predator that is after their meat.

The preliminaries, basis and conclusion for this session are the same as above.

Contemplation 15

Summing Up the Points Above

Having contemplated the sufferings of the three lower realms, think as follows:

It seems that the situation in all of these realms is intolerable. I must find a source of refuge that is able to protect me from being reborn there. Who can protect me? If even Brahma, Indra or a universal monarch[59] cannot protect me, how could anyone else? Only the Three Jewels have that ability. I will, therefore, take the Buddha as my teacher. I will take his teaching as my practice, and I will take the spiritual community as my companions on the path.

As for refuge, although I take refuge in the Buddha, it is the teaching that protects me. Even the Buddha cannot pull me out of cyclic existence like pulling a hair out of a river current. In order to be protected, I must receive teachings on the Dharma and then put those teachings into practice.

Having meditated with faith on the Buddha, I will practice the teaching in just the way he explained it and will imitate the actions of the noble spiritual community.

At the beginning and end of this session, it is important to engage in the virtuous activity of reciting the refuge prayer. This completes the perfect method of taking refuge for the person of lesser capacity.

{At this point, it is important for the teacher to give the student a general explanation on taking refuge. It is also important for the student to thoroughly cultivate these contemplations in his or her mind.

In some of the ancient texts outlining the stages of the path, the stages for the person of lesser capacity are concluded at this point. There is also a custom of transmitting the teachings on actions and their effects throughout the presentation. In most texts presenting the stages on the path however, actions and their effects are taught separately, and so that is the way it will be imparted here.}

Chapter Four

The Instructions on the Causes and Effects of Action

{This chapter begins with the concept of action in general; the remaining contemplations concern specific types of action.}

Contemplation 16

The Concept of Karma in General

Happiness comes solely from positive or virtuous actions. Suffering comes only from negative or harmful actions. Since virtuous and harmful actions ripen inevitably in this way, I should adopt some actions and abandon others.

Whether my actions are virtuous or negative, at the time of the causal action, what I do may be minor. But at the time of the ripening of the action, the result increases considerably in magnitude. The smallest increases are a hundred or a thousand-fold. The largest increases are immeasurable. Therefore, giving up negative actions and adopting positive ones is very important.

If I do not take steps to repair the negative actions that I have committed, [the karmic imprints of] those actions will not diminish in the least until the action fully ripens as an effect. If I have not done something, it is impossible for the corresponding positive or negative karma to arise in my continuum. Therefore, it is very important for me to be careful about what I do and what I avoid.

CONTEMPLATION 17

The Causes of Negative Action

The preliminaries and conclusion for the meditation session are the same as before. Include the recitation of the Seven Branch Prayer, followed by the Refuge Prayer.

All of the suffering in the three lower realms and the higher realms does not arise without a cause or without supporting conditions. Its cause is non-virtuous actions. Think about this as the basis for the contemplation.

Although there are many enumerations of non-virtuous actions, the principal actions I should abandon can be roughly summarized as the ten non-virtuous actions.

The Three Non-Virtuous Actions of Body:

1. To take life means to kill another being, carrying that act to completion with the intention to take life. The act is complete if the intention to kill is not reversed before the victim dies.
2. To take what is not given means to take, either covertly or openly, something that belongs to another person with the intention of obtaining it for oneself.
3. To engage in sexual misconduct out of desire: Misconduct with respect to the object means to have sexual relations with an inappropriate partner, such as another person's spouse; a relative within seven generations; those who are under the guardianship of their parents, their employer or the government; an ordained person who holds the celibacy vow and so forth. Misconduct with respect to timing means to have sexual relations with someone who does not want to, who is ill or who is pregnant. Misconduct with respect to place means to have sexual relations near a shrineroom, stupa, lama's quarters or other sacred place. Misconduct with respect to the method means have sexual intercourse through an orifice other than the vagina because one's desire is not satisfied. There are four inappropriate methods. These are the guidelines for a layperson. For one who has taken vows of celibacy, every type of sexual intercourse is sexual misconduct.

The four non-virtuous actions of speech:

4. To tell lies means to alter what you perceive and intentionally say something untrue. The person to whom the lie is told must be a human being, and he or she must be able to hear it.
5. To slander means to speak words that cause further spite and malice between two people who are disharmonious. One or more people must hear the words.
6. To speak harsh words means to speak words that hurt another person, such as to speak of another's faults when he or she can hear.
7. To engage in meaningless conversation includes any speech, motivated by the negative emotions, that is not included in the previous three non-virtuous actions of speech. It includes insinuation, flattery and conversing about such mundane topics as war, prostitutes and business. It also includes frivolous singing, acting out and expressing distorted views.

The three non-virtuous actions of mind:

8. Having a covetous mind means being afflicted with the wish to possess someone else's wealth, spouse, family, retinue, land and so forth.
9. Having a harmful mind means being afflicted with the wish that harm may come to another person or that he or she may experience suffering.
10 Having a wrong view means distrusting the truth of actions and their effects, disbelieving in past and future lives and in the Three Jewels and holding this view as supreme.

If I look at these ten from the standpoint of perfecting the path of action, I should try to abandon all thoughts and actions that are even related to them: for example, unintentionally or accidentally killing another. These are the actions that I should definitely give up from the outset.

Contemplate in this way again and again.

Contemplation 18

The Effects of Negative Action

Each of these ten non virtuous actions can result in rebirth in any one of the six realms, depending on strength of the motivation behind the action. If the act is very powerful or if it is performed repeatedly, it may ripen as rebirth in one of the hell realms. If the action is of medium intensity, it may ripen as rebirth as a hungry ghost. If the action is weakly motivated or is only partial, it may ripen as rebirth as an animal. Rebirth as those kinds of beings who experience misery is called the "fully ripened result" of these actions.

Killing leads to a short life. Stealing leads to having a lack of possessions and enjoyments. Sexual misconduct leads to having many enemies. Lying leads to being maligned by others. Slandering causes friends to turn against you. Speaking harsh words ripens as hearing others say unpleasant things. Meaningless speech ripens as being ignored by others. Covetousness leads to disappointment. Having a harmful mind ripens as suffering and fear. Having a wrong view ripens as extreme stupidity and ignorance. These are called "resultant experiences that are in accord with the cause."

"Resultant actions in accord with the cause" are actions people like because of having done them in the past.

"Environmental results" are effects of actions reflected in the external environment.[60] The result of killing is having weak crops and medicine. The result of stealing is having a bad harvest. The result of sexual misconduct is living in a place where there are storms. Lying results in living where the mountains are steep and travel is difficult. Slander results in living in a place where the earth is alkaline. Harsh words results in hail and sleet. Meaningless speech ripens as seasonal imbalances; for example, the winter is too cold; the summer, too hot; the spring is dry, and the fall is too wet. The covetous mind ripens in the future as reaping a harvest with small grains. The harmful mind ripens as reaping a tasteless crop. Having wrong views results in crops that do not ripen properly.

Moreover, "results in accord with the cause" and "environmental results" may ripen in the same lifetime that the causal act was committed. Furthermore, the time of ripening is uncertain, so a being may have engaged in non-virtuous actions in this life and be born into the higher realms in the next life.[61]

Think again and again

Since these ten non-virtuous actions result in suffering and various unwanted occurrences, I will not engage in them even at the risk of my life. I will exert myself in methods for purifying the negative actions I have previously committed.

Contemplation 19
Positive Actions

Obtaining a physical body in the higher realms and all happy states in cyclic existence arise from virtuous actions. Even the super-mundane states, the three types of enlightenment, arise from virtuous actions. I should, therefore, give up all harmful actions and cultivate all virtuous actions as much as possible. Although there are many types of virtuous actions that can be practiced, the gateway to all virtue is the pure conduct of the ten virtuous actions.[62] Now that I have mentally given up the ten non-virtuous actions explained above, engendered the decision to modify my habits of body and speech and have put that intention into practice, I will make the commitment to continue in this fashion permanently.

In order to mentally give up the ten non-virtuous actions, I should understand that they are imperfections and that they cause problems. Knowing this will motivate me to get rid of them forever. On the basis of that, I will reverse habits of body and speech.

But if I engage in positive actions only sporadically or fail to engage in them during my leisure time, it is as if I am practicing them for profit. Then, even if the opportunity arises to practice them without effort, I will not.

By recalling my mental commitment to abandon harmful actions, I will prevent myself from starting down the wrong road in the first place. Therefore, mental abandonment alone is sufficient: The seven virtuous actions of body and speech are included in the three of mind.

Seeing non-virtuous actions as unethical is the basis of mental abandonment. Recognizing unethical actions for what they are is unconfused understanding on the relative level. This leads to the practice of the path of remedies and is the essence of moral conduct.

If the attitude of abandonment arises strongly several times, even if practice is interrupted by slumber, distraction and so forth, I will still recognize non-virtuous actions as mistakes and faults. Focusing on the conditions that awaken those tendencies, I will avoid and bind them. This process arises from the strength of the attitude [of abandonment], and that strength comes from the potency of the initial seed [seeing non-virtuous actions as unethical]. For that reason, the attitude of abandoning the ten non-virtuous actions together with its seed [awareness of the unethical nature of those actions] is the ten virtuous actions.

Contemplation 20

The Benefits of the Ten Virtuous Actions

The fully ripened result of practicing the ten virtuous actions extensively is rebirth as a god. Practicing them less extensively results in obtaining a human body. Practicing virtue with an impure attitude and so forth results in rebirth as a demi-god. Thus it is explained in the sutras.

"Results that are in accord with the cause" and "environmental results" are the opposite of the results explained above for the ten non-virtuous actions. So the virtuous results in accord with the cause are a long life, adequate wealth, freedom from enemies, praise, many friends, hearing pleasant things, noble speech, accomplishment of one's aims, a happy mind and expanding intelligence.[63] The environmental results of practicing virtue are having great power and excellent harvests and living in a pleasant place, where the terrain is even and the earth is workable, where grass and trees flourish, the climate is mild, the grains are large and delicious, and where fruit thrives.

In order to sustain the practice of the ten virtuous actions, reflect again and again

Since they are the cause for continual happiness in this and future lives, I will maintain my practice of the ten virtuous actions constantly.

{When engaging in these contemplations, it is important to examine the four divisions within the topic of actions and their effects meticulously. Therefore, the Lama should explain the topic repeatedly, and the student should cultivate it in his or her mind. Instead of being content with a mere intellectual understanding, the student should understand it on a personal level. This is an important point.}

CONTEMPLATION 21
The Essential Point of Practice

This session is the heart of these contemplations on actions and effects. First reflect on the positive and negative actions and effects explained above. Then consider that since you have already committed negative, non-virtuous actions, it is important to make a confession that is complete with the four powers. "The power of the support" is to take refuge and engender the awakening mind. "The power of fully engaging in remedial action" is to practice virtuous actions that purify negative karma as much as you are able. "The power of reparation" is to regret the harmful actions in which you have previously engaged. "The power of reversal" is to vow not to engage in them in the future.[64]

At the beginning of each session, practice this kind of confession several times. Between sessions, in the presence of your teacher, master, lama or the spiritual community, acknowledge and confess your wrongdoings again and again. If you cannot do that, visualize that the sky is filled with buddhas and bodhisattvas and offer confession to them. You can recite confession prayers from the texts such as The Sutra of the Three Heaps or The Confession of Sacred Golden Light. The essential point is to fully acknowledge and express, without hiding or concealing anything, that you have engaged in negative actions. Then reflect

Not only will I avoid the ten non-virtuous actions, I will also not commit any actions large or small that are associated with non-virtue. I will steer others away from negative actions, and I will not rejoice when I see others engaging in them. I will not praise or glorify these actions.

Not only will I practice the ten positive, virtuous actions, but I will also engage in everything that is related to virtue. I will save lives, give away sustenance and material things, maintain ethical conduct, make offerings to the Three Jewels, engender faith and so forth. I will encourage others to engage in virtue, will rejoice in the virtuous actions of myself and others and will praise virtue.

In addition, there are neutral actions that are neither virtuous nor evil, such as going, standing, sleeping, sitting and so forth. Although these do not have a fully ripened result, they are a meaningless waste of time. I will not let myself fall under the power of laziness and distraction! When I find myself in a state of indifference, I will turn my mind and behavior towards virtue.

In addition, between meditation sessions, you should reflect in this way. Spend your time engaging in the exceptional methods for accumulating merit from lifetime to lifetime, expressed as the eight qualities of a higher realm body:

1. Abandoning the intention to harm leads to a long life.
2. Offering butterlamps [to the buddhas], clothing [to the poor] and so forth leads to a healthy body.
3. Being humble and unselfish in the presence of your lama and your spiritual companions—whether they are above or below you—and respecting them leads to rebirth into a good family.
4. Giving necessities to those who have helped you, those who are suffering, those with good qualities and to other recipients leads to having strength, dignity and plentiful enjoyments.
5. Engaging only in virtuous speech leads to having noble speech.
6. Making offerings to your lama, the Three Jewels, your parents and so forth and making aspiration prayers to accomplish various positive qualities leads to having great power and influence.
7. Liking things associated with the human realm[65] and protecting animals from castration results in rebirth as a human.
8. Being helpful in religious activities without expecting rewards or praise from other people leads to the attainment of abundant powers.

Practice these as much as you are able.

{This concludes the section on the stages of practice for the person of lesser capacity.}

Part II

Training in the Common Stages for the Person of Average Capacity

This Part has two sections: the causes and results of cyclic existence [Contemplations 22-32] and the causes and results of liberation [Contemplation 33]. The first section is divided into two sub-sections: contemplations on the resultant suffering of cyclic existence [Contemplations 22-31] and types of origination [Contemplation 32]. The contemplations on the resultant suffering of cyclic existence is divided into contemplations on the misery of the higher realms [Chapter 5] and contemplations on the suffering of cyclic existence in general [Chapter 6].

Chapter Five

The Misery of the Higher Realms

Contemplation 22

The Suffering of Birth

Recite a slightly expanded version of the homage, offerings and confession. Then perform the seven branch offering and take refuge. For the contemplation, begin by reflecting

I have been considering the possibilities of being reborn as one of the six types of beings through the power of karma and am now familiar with the suffering accompanying rebirth in the lower realms. If I were to be reborn human, though, wouldn't I be happy? The answer is no; I would not.

For the most part, humans are born from the womb. During the nine months or so that the fetus remains in the womb, it constantly experiences the misery of fear, the misery of living in darkness and the misery of unpleasant odors.

When the mother is hungry, the fetus feels as though it is suspended in an abyss. When she is full, the fetus feels as if it is being crushed by a mountain. When the mother imbibes hot food or drink, the fetus feels as though it is being boiled in hot water. When she imbibes cold food or drink, it feels as if it is being frozen on an iceberg.

While the baby is being born, it is also miserable: while it is being expelled from the womb, it feels as if it is being squeezed between the pieces of wood on a sesame seed press. All of its joints feel as if they have been dislocated and crushed. Right after the birth, everything it touches feels harsh. Even if it is wrapped in the softest silk, it feels as though it has been thrown into a pit of thorns. When someone picks the baby up, it feels wretched, like a little bird being carried away by a hawk.

I do not remember what it was like to be born. If I did, I would not need convincing. Just by contemplating the suffering of birth alone, I would lose all interest in being born human.

I need a spiritual practice that will allow me to escape the power of karma and subsequent rebirth in cyclic existence. While the suffering of being born from a womb as a human is intense, there is suffering wherever one is born in the three realms[66]. As whatever type of being one is born, there is suffering. Into whatever situation one is born, there is suffering.

To elaborate, birth involves five types of suffering:

1. The birth process itself is miserable: It is accompanied by intensely uncomfortable feelings.
2. Birth involves accepting a negative situation: It plants the seeds for the arising and development of the afflictive emotions.
3. Birth becomes the basis for further suffering: From birth arise the further sufferings of old age, sickness and death.
4. Birth is the basis for the afflictive emotions: Once you have taken birth, when you encounter unpleasant conditions later, many afflictive emotions will arise. Based on those, you accumulate a lot of karma.
5. Birth involves the suffering of inevitable demise: The moment you are born, you begin to die—instant by instant.

Thus, birth is suffering.

Contemplation 23
The Suffering of Aging

Furthermore, humans experience the suffering of aging. When I grow old, I will experience five sufferings of deterioration:

1. Deterioration of complexion: My healthy color and radiance will decline. My complexion will become unattractive, with dark spots. My face will turn ashen in color, and my hair will become white as a trawa flower. All my senses will lose their acuity.

2. Deterioration of shape: My teeth will fall out. My posture will become stooped; my arms and legs will become arthritic; my muscles will shrink, and my skin will get loose. My face, full of wrinkles like an old cushion, will become unpleasant to look at.
3. Deterioration of strength: When I stand up, I will need to use all four limbs. When I walk, I will be unsteady. When I sit down, it will be like cutting the rope on a load of salt. When I speak, my voice will quaver.
4. Deterioration of the sense faculties: My eyes will not see clearly, and I will start to go deaf. Other people will no longer take me seriously.
5. Deterioration of enjoyment: I will no longer enjoy the sense pleasures—If I eat a little, I will be hungry. If I eat a lot, I will get indigestion and so forth.

I cannot escape the suffering of aging. Even if I have a long life, at the end of it I will grow old. My friends, relatives, and enemies are also like that.

Contemplation 24

The Suffering of Illness

Based on previous karma and unexpected circumstances, various illnesses arise. There are five types of the suffering of illness:

1. Illness involves physical misery and mental distress: When ill, I experience the suffering of manifest pain.
2. Illness involves spontaneous physical changes: My muscles wither away; my skin dries out and so forth.

3,4 I no longer enjoy pleasant things and must rely on unpleasant things: Delicious food and the other things I used to enjoy are no longer pleasurable. Instead, I must take medicine, receive injections, endure moxibustion and so forth.

5. I will be separated from my life force: Illness involves the suffering of dying and fear of death. Illness causes the anxiety of anticipating the imminent suffering of death itself. Until I am cured, this fear stays with me.

My relatives, friends, enemies—in fact, all beings—are just like me in this regard.

Contemplation 25

The Suffering of Death

There are even further sufferings shared by all beings in the human realm. The suffering of death has five aspects:

1. I will be separated from the wealth of possessions and enjoyments.
2. I will be separated from the wealth of power and the ability to defend myself.
3. I will be separated from a wealth of associates and friends.
4. I will be separated from my beloved and coveted body.
5. Death itself is accompanied by suffering and by an intense feeling of unhappiness.

I will be separated from all the things [and people] I love and cherish most: my family, wealth, master, servants and friends. I will die with the great suffering of having my life-force cut off.

If you wish to expand this contemplation, meditate in accord with the section on impermanence and death explained earlier.

Contemplation 26

Other Human Sufferings

The suffering of seeking what you want but not finding it: I struggle and risk my life just order to acquire a little wealth, fame or power. I embark on projects that take many months or years to complete. I labor continuously season after season but do not receive any reward for my efforts. Making the strength of my legs the burden, the strength of my arms the plow, my calves the horse and head the whip, I drive myself south and pull myself north, but none of my aims are reached. I willingly endure hunger and thirst, torment myself with heat and cold and have no respite day or night. While my flesh-and-blood body wastes away, I am not able to acquire even enough food or clothing. Because all my efforts are unsuccessful, my mind becomes weary.

The suffering of encountering what is unpleasant: This type of suffering includes being at the mercy of an enemy, being stricken by a virulent illness or intense suffering, encountering a murderer who intends to kill me, falling off a cliff, being carried away by water, hearing negative gossip, being thrown into prison, being banished and other experiences of loss.

The suffering of being separated from what you love: When I am separated from my parents, relatives, spouse, home and friends—the people that it seems impossible to do without—unbearable misery arises in my mind to the point where I may even walk bent over with sorrow. Similarly, I feel unhappy whenever I spend or loose my wealth, my influence deteriorates, my strength fails, I am deprived of freedom, I lose something to which my mind is attached or I miss something in which I have interest. Even if I have not yet experienced all these sufferings, I will not avoid their influence forever.

Add whatever might be suitable from the above contemplations here.

{Even though beings other than humans experience these seven sufferings, they are mainly experienced by humans and, therefore, have been mentioned in this section. There is a tradition of meditating on an eighth suffering[67] at this point, but I have chosen to include it in a subsequent contemplation as it works better that way.}

Contemplation 27

The Suffering of the Demi-god and God Realms

I might wonder if I were born in the demi-god realm, would I not be happy there? On consideration, I would not. Jealous of the splendor of the gods, my mind would constantly be ridden with anxiety. Occasionally, the demi-gods fight with the gods. Because their merit is weaker, they must endure the suffering of being killed or beaten, sometimes of maiming or losing their limbs. Because most of them are inclined toward vice, they dislike the Dharma. Although some of them are inclined to practice, their minds are obscured by fully ripened karma and, therefore, do not have the good fortune of achieving extraordinary realization.

"Well," I may then wonder, "if I were born in the desire-god realm, surely I would be happy there?" No, I would not be happy there either. Without my even being aware of it, my life would be exhausted as I carelessly indulged in the sense pleasures. Furthermore, the weaker gods are pushed out of their places by the stronger gods. Those with even less merit are so poor that they have no possessions except a single guitar. When they see the great wealth of the other gods, they experience mental anguish and despair over their lack of merit.

The gods living in the Heaven of the Four Great Kings and the Heaven of the Thirty-three[68] are particularly prone to fighting with the demigods, and this causes them intense suffering. All desire-realm gods experience the ordinary sufferings of death and transference, as well as the "suffering of decline." With regard to the latter, seven days before a desire-realm god dies, he sees five death omens: The color of his body becomes unattractive; he feels depressed and forlorn; the garlands of flowers that adorn him wither; his clothes take on a foul odor, and his body begins to sweat. When these signs appear, he is abandoned by his servants and friends of both sexes. Then, in the midst of the company of other gods, he becomes aware that despite his attachment to the desirable enjoyments of the god-realm, he will be torn from it without choice. Without any chance of averting his inevitable fate, he suffers as a mother camel who has lost her calf, a snake carried off by a hawk, a fish writhing on hot sand or a lone boat adrift on the great ocean. Although the length of this period of grief is seven god-days, this amounts to at least 10,400 human years, as in the case, for example, of the Land of the Four Great Kings. After a god endures this long period of grief and decline, he dies. After that, it is barely possible that he will be reborn again as a god. Those born as humans are also extremely rare. Most are reborn in the lower realms. As is said

> After a being leaves the world of gods,
> If he does not have some merit left unspent,
> He will be reborn without choice as an animal, hungry ghost
> Or hell being, whichever is suitable.[69]

Since a god has clairvoyance, he is able to see the beings in the realms below him and perceive where he will be reborn. If he will be reborn as a human, his pleasure-eyes are dismayed, and he sees many humans who are suffering.[70] If he is to be reborn in the three lower realms, he realizes he is destined to experience the sufferings there. The unbearable mental anguish he feels is even worse than the physical suffering experienced by beings of the three lower realms.

Contemplation 28

The Suffering of the Higher God Realms

Then I may think, "Well, if I were born in one of the higher god realms, wouldn't I be happy there?" Alas, there is no happiness there either. Ordinary beings are unable to perceive the manifest suffering in the higher god realms, but noble beings[71] can detect that the experience of gods does not transcend the suffering of composite existence.[72] Because gods are intoxicated with trance, their positive qualities do not increase. As long as they are savoring that experience of trance, they cannot bear to be separated from it. Moreover, when their trance deteriorates, they die. The previous meritorious karma they accumulated as ordinary beings is used up, and they are again reborn in the desire realm. It is true that the worldly trance meditation of humans and the trance of formless meditative absorption mentioned here are states endowed with an experience of intense bliss and extreme relaxation, but these states alone do not stabilize the mind, and those practicing them eventually deteriorate into an ordinary beings. Their emotional afflictions become even coarser and their suffering greater than before. What is the point of living in that state?

Chapter Six

The Suffering of Cyclic Existence in General

Contemplation 29

The Three Types of Suffering

Begin with the preliminaries as presented above. Contemplate briefly the suffering of the hell realms. Then go on to contemplate the sufferings of hungry ghosts, animals, humans, demi-gods, desire-gods and the gods of the form and formless realms. Considering all this, think

Cyclic existence with its three realms has the nature of the three or six or eight types of suffering. It is a storehouse of misery. I am completely surrounded by suffering. Suffering burns like fire; it roils like water; it gusts like wind; it oppresses like a mountain. Wherever I am, it is a place of suffering. Whatever type of body I inhabit, it is a body of suffering. Whomever I befriend, it is a companion of suffering. Whatever I enjoy, it is an enjoyment of suffering.

Three types of suffering pervade all existence. The "suffering of suffering" (manifest suffering) refers to all suffering that manifests as feelings of discomfort, such as feelings of heat, cold, illness and so on. The "suffering of change" refers to feelings of happiness from life and enjoyments to the bliss of meditative absorption. The "suffering of composite existence" is the basis for the other two types of suffering. It refers merely to the composite phenomena of these adopted aggregates[73] that are the origin and field of cultivation for all suffering. When the aggregates are experiencing a state of simple neutrality, the term "the mere suffering of composite existence" is used. If I do not become free of this suffering, I will not become free of the other two. I must, by all means, become free from the three types of suffering.

Contemplation 30

The Eight Sufferings

So far, seven sufferings of the human realm have been explained: the suffering of birth, the suffering of aging, the suffering of illness, the suffering of death, the suffering of encountering what is unpleasant, the suffering of being separated from what you love and the suffering of not finding what you seek. The eighth suffering is the suffering of the five closely adopted aggregates, the body-mind organism itself. This kind of suffering also has five aspects:

1. The organism is the vessel for manifest suffering: It is the place where the suffering of future lives is cultivated.
2. The organism is the vessel for suffering that supports pain: It is the origin of all other sufferings, such as the sufferings of birth, aging, sickness and death.
3. The organism is the vessel for the suffering of suffering.
4. The organism is the vessel for the suffering of change: The suffering of suffering and the suffering of change both arise on the basis of the aggregates.
5. The organism is the nature of the suffering of composite existence: The organism itself defines the suffering of conditioned existence.

The whole of cyclic existence with its three realms is the essence of the eight types of suffering.

Contemplation 31

The Six Sufferings

The suffering of cyclic existence has several additional facets. First, cyclic existence has the fault of suffering because it is undependable. My enemies, friends, parents, children, places, body and enjoyments are all undependable. As is said[74]

> Fathers becomes son, and mother, one's wife.......

Second, there is the fault of dissatisfaction. No matter in how much pleasure I indulge, I am never satisfied. No matter how much suffering I experience, I am never weary. As the verse continues

> ...each filling more than the four great oceans...

Third, there is the fault of having to give up my body again and again. The verse continues

> ...must again and again experience death. In each
> type of existence, I have left a mountain of bones.

Fourth, there is the fault of having to take rebirth again and again. Beings are compelled to take endless rebirths:

> Those who have been my mothers are infinite as
> juniper berries..[75]

Fifth, there is the fault of fluctuating again and again between high and low. Even if I become Indra, I will fall to earth. Even if I become a universal monarch, I will be born as the lowliest servant. Even in this single life, I can have no sense of mental certainty whatsoever about the state of our happiness and suffering, highs and lows, wealth and poverty. It is expressed in the line,

> Even if I become Indra, worthy of worldly offerings...

Sixth, there is the fault of suffering because I am ultimately alone, without a companion. When I was born, I was born alone. When I die, I will die alone. Aging and illness are also experienced alone. In the bardo, I must travel alone. My friends, relatives and spouse are of no use. This applies to the line

> I am sure to grieve in the end.

Therefore, all of cyclic existence is suffering, by having the nature of these six facets of suffering. Even if I were born at the very peak of existence, it is easy to tumble to the depths of hell. I simply move from one suffering to the next. It is as if I were in a house on fire, as if I were stranded on an island of flesh-eating demons and as if I were wandering through the wilderness without a guide. I must free myself from this situation immediately!

Contemplate in this way again and again.

Chapter Seven

Aspects of Origination

Contemplation 32

The Original Cause of Suffering

All of these great sufferings of cyclic existence do not arise without causes and conditions. Once the cause of suffering is given up, it is possible to avert cyclic existence. What is the cause?

All sufferings arise from the accumulation of karma. For karma to arise, the emotional afflictions must be manifestly present. If there were no emotional afflictions initially, karma would not ripen in the future. Therefore, the root of all suffering, the basic cause of myself and all sentient beings wandering in cyclic existence, is the emotional afflictions. They are described using various classifications. Sometimes they are presented as six: attachment, anger, pride, ignorance, having perverted views and harboring doubts. Sometimes they are presented as nine. No matter what the presentation, the root of all of them is the three poisons; attachment, aversion and ignorance.

There are also many classifications of karma, but all of them can be subsumed under the three types of actions that drive cyclic existence: non-meritorious action, meritorious action and unmoving action. Non-meritorious action includes harmful actions that drive us to the lower realms.

Meritorious action includes meditative absorption and virtuous actions of the desire realm, such as generosity that goes on the path to liberation, moral discipline that binds desire and so forth. These types of actions are cause for rebirth as a desire-realm god or human.

Unmoving action includes the four meditative stabilities, or the trances of the four formless realms, that are solely meritorious. This kind of action propels an individual to the form or formless god realms.

All types of karma are tainted by the ignorance of not realizing the natural state.[76] Ignorance leads to self-cherishing. Action that is motivated by self-cherishing becomes the cause of cyclic existence. If I wonder whether I have this affliction of ignorance, I need only examine my mind. I do not know the nature of cyclic existence, nor when or how it began. I do not know the nature of liberation or the methods of attaining it. I do not even know how to become certain about these things. It is possible I may have a rudimentary understanding through study and reflection, but when I examine the way things appear in my own mind, no matter how I look at it, finding truth is like trying to imagine a distant country I have never visited. I am left with just a vague, blurry, uncertain concept. Because I do not understand the condition of cyclic existence and liberation, doubts about ultimate truth arise. From that, all wrong views, such as clinging to a self where there is no self, arise; hence, all wrong views proceed from basic ignorance.

Furthermore, initially I am attached to my body and mind. Based on that, I become attached to other sentient beings—the opposite sex, my close friends, servants and so forth. I also become attached to things—food, clothing, possessions, my house, field, wealth, goods, country and so forth. The sense of painful mental longing and liking I feel towards my body and possessions is the emotional affliction of attachment. Based on this, pride, greed and jealousy arise.

Towards anything that harms me or my possessions, I feel aversion. With a feeling of discomfort, I fixate mentally on sentient beings who harm or threaten to harm me or anything I hold dear. This mental state is anger or aversion. Sometimes I even become angry at inanimate objects. For example, a place or dwelling may trigger mental discomfort. I may become irritated that my field is flooded by a river. All of these are examples indicating the presence of aversion. The coarse mental state arising from strong anger that wishes to harm others, wrath, irritation, malice and so forth are all forms of aversion.

Think to yourself, ingraining it in your stream of being:

Since these three poisons cause me and all sentient beings to wander in cyclic existence, I will abandon them as much as possible. I will recognize the emotional afflictions that arise in my continuum and identify the actions that proceed from those afflictions.

{At this time, it is of great benefit to supplement these contemplations with whatever presentation of karma and the emotional afflictions is appropriate for the student.}

Chapter 8

The Causes and Results of Liberation

Contemplation 33

Contemplation on the Causes and Results of Liberation

Having abandoned cyclic existence, I should attain liberation. Therefore I should consider what is the nature of liberation? What is called "liberation" is not a place, another country or direction to which I can travel. Rather, it is an uprooting of the latent potential of the emotional afflictions that exist in my mind, so that they never arise in the future and are purified within the expanse.[2] Once this potential is purified, it is no longer necessary to deliberately renounce actions because karmic results cannot arise. The entire cycle of karmic accumulation disappears into the expanse. In the religious terminology of the Buddhist canon: "Once the seeds are abandoned, the fruit cannot arise." Once karma and the emotional afflictions have been forsaken, cyclic existence will not arise anew. Whatever trace remainder of karma is left over will quickly disperse. The final result of the exhaustion of all the emotional afflictions of the three realms of cyclic existence is simply stainless awareness—that is liberation.

"Abandonment without regressing" means that after the moment liberation is attained, it is impossible for this level to deteriorate. The cause for attaining liberation is non-deteriorating wisdom that realizes the true nature of the selflessness of persons and the selflessness of phenomena and that relinquishes all obscurations. The cause of that realization is training the mind in one-pointed trance. If my mind is to attain one-pointedness, I need pure moral discipline. Moral discipline means holding to a pure attitude of renunciation and cultivating the view of selflessness. Hence, renunciation and the view of selflessness are the unfailing, incipient cause of liberation.

> In order to become liberated from cyclic existence, I will guard moral discipline starting now. I will cultivate trance. Having developed wisdom through meditation, I will realize the meaning of impermanence, suffering, emptiness and selflessness.

Contemplate in this way again and again.

{At this time, it is excellent to explain to the student the common presentation of the fruition, peace and nirvana and a rough presentation of the three trainings. However, although the instructions on tranquility meditation[3] and the meditation on the selflessness of the individual might be imparted at this point, an individual of average capacity cannot yet grasp the central point of this practice. Therefore, instructions on tranquility meditation and selflessness fall into the category of the contemplations for the person of greater capacity. In Chapter 8, the practice is to gradually develop the wish to train on the path to liberation. This completes the practices for the individual of average capacity.}

Part III

The Extraordinary Contemplations for the Person of Greater Capacity

Part III consists of a preparatory contemplation [Contemplation 34] and contemplations that expand the limits [of the awakening mind] [Contemplations 35-64].

Chapter 9

The Preparatory Contemplation and the Causal Links

Contemplation 34
Preparation

Once you have contemplated the faults of cyclic existence as presented in the previous sections, you are ready to relinquish cyclic existence and attain the state of nirvana. In order to reach nirvana, you need to study the three trainings. The nirvana to be obtained can be divided into three types of enlightenment: the enlightenment of a hearer, the enlightenment of a solitary-realizer and the enlightenment of a perfect Buddha.

The first two types of individuals—those who obtain the enlightenment of a hearer or solitary-realizer—have not perfected abandonments and realization for their own benefit. They lack interest in accomplishing the vast benefit for sentient beings. Furthermore, their abandonment is incomplete: They give up emotional obscurations but fail to relinquish cognitive obscurations. Their realization is also incomplete: They realize only the selflessness of the individual and relative interdependence but do not understand the selflessness of phenomena or ultimate interdependence. They develop a few distinct special qualities but not the kind that spread limitlessly. They do not lead kind sentient beings away from suffering but, instead, practice methods to liberate themselves alone. They have no integrity, a limited aspiration and no future: It is a liberation that has abandoned the benefit of others.

On the other hand, the good qualities of noble beings, who do not revert to samsara and rest in a state free from complication, cannot be encompassed by the mind of an ordinary person like me. However, if I compare the liberation of a buddha or a bodhisattva with the liberation of a hearer or solitary-realizer, it underscores the totality of the buddhas' and bodhisattvas' abandonment of the two obscurations, the expansiveness of their wisdom that knows the nature and multiplicity of everything[79], the limitlessness of their qualities, the strength and effectiveness of their unflagging compassion and the vigor of their activity for the benefit of sentient beings. It is like comparing a sesame seed to Mount Meru. Therefore, I will perfect all of the abandonments and realizations for my own benefit. I will then attain enlightenment by perfecting the factors of liberation that have the nature of inexhaustible activity for the benefit of others. One way or another, I will attain buddhahood!

Make this resolution again and again.

The contemplations that aim to expand the limits [of the aspiration of awakening mind] consist of the contemplation on the causal links [Contemplation 35] and contemplations on the meaning of those links [Contemplations 36-64].

Contemplation 35

The Causal Links that Lead to the Attainment of Buddhahood

Using the previous contemplations as a basis, reflect as follows:

I need to attain buddhahood. I therefore need to cultivate awakening mind since it is the cause of buddhahood. The cause of awakening mind is compassion. The cause of compassion is love. The cause of love is appreciation and gratefulness. The cause of appreciation is recognizing that all sentient beings have been my parents. I should meditate on developing these qualities in stages.

Meditate again and again

All sentient beings are my parents—they have been so kind to me. Wouldn't it be right if they were to be free from suffering? Wouldn't it be right for them to be comfortable and happy? I will, therefore, attain buddhahood in order to establish all of them in happiness. Once I have attained buddhahood, I will also place all sentient beings on the level of buddhahood.

{Pertaining to the above material, the special instructions passed down by the disciple of master Sharawa, Geshe Tumtonpa Lodro Drak[80], present five cause and effect connections just as explained above. However, within the lineage of Jayulwa's disciple Tsangpa Rinpoche,[81] as written down by Geshe Mumen[82] in the annals of the graduated teachings called *The Necessary Stages of Mind Training in the Mahayana*[83], this quote appears: "You should train your mind by stages in the seven causal links found in Atisha's extraordinary Mahayana teachings."

Atisha's presentation of the seven causal links states that buddhahood is not without causes and conditions. Buddhahood arises from the cause of awakening mind. Awakening mind is born from a pure and excellent motivation. A pure motivation arises from great compassion. Great compassion arises from great love. Love arises from seeing sentient beings with affection. Seeing sentient beings with affection arises from appreciation and gratefulness. Appreciation and gratefulness arise from developing the perception of sentient beings as your mothers.

These are the seven causal links [as expressed by Atisha]. However, the name "seven causal links" was not applied to these until later. I mention this here to establish that I did not invent the classification myself.}

The contemplations elaborating on meaning of the causal links may be divided into three sections: meditation on love [Contemplations 36-38], meditation on compassion [Contemplation 39] and meditation on awakening mind [Contemplations 40-64].

Chapter 10

Meditation on Love and Compassion

Contemplation 36

Love for Your Mother

The mother who gave birth to me in this life has been extremely kind to me. First she held me in her womb for nine or ten months. During her pregnancy, she protected me, cherishing me more than her own life. She gave me my human body, my life, my energy.

Then from the time I was born, she helped me with her own body. She cradled me with her ten fingers, warmed me with the heat of her flesh, nursed me from her breasts, tasted my food and wiped the filth from my bottom with her own hands. At the time that I was unable to do anything for myself and was as helpless as a bug, she cared for me.

She helped me with her speech. She called out to me in terms of endearment. She praised me without reason. She extolled my qualities when I had none. Even when my performance of tasks was mediocre, she was overjoyed.

She benefited me with her mind. She was constantly concerned about my welfare thinking, "I must ensure that this child of mine has a long life. I must make sure he does not get sick. I must make sure he is honored by others. Will people admire him? Will he be successful?"

When I first learned how to sit up, learned to walk and spoke my first words, she was overwhelmed with joy. As I grew older, not only was she free of anxiety about giving me whatever she possessed, she did so joyfully. She wouldn't have had the slightest hesitation about giving me all the wealth and clothing in the universe.

How exceedingly my mother helped me and cared for me! She loved me and was so kind to me! Would it not be right for her to be comfortable now and always? Would it not be right for her to be happy? I must establish my mother in unsurpassable comfort and happiness.

{This meditation on love for one's own mother is the root of all practices focusing on the development of love. Because it is easy to develop love this way, it is important to continue practicing this contemplation until the experience of love wells up in you.}

Contemplation 37

Recognition of the Extent of Your Mother's Love

I have just meditated on the ways my mother benefited me in this lifetime. But her generosity is not limited to just this one lifetime or two lifetimes. Rather, for an infinite number of lifetimes she has been my mother, benefiting me throughout countless incarnations just as she did in this lifetime. Sometimes, she has been born as my father, benefiting me countless times in that form. She has appeared infinite times as my family members, relatives, companions, spouses, teachers and so forth just to benefit me. For my sake alone, she has amassed a heap higher than Mount Meru of clothing to swathe me and of jewelry to adorn me. The amount of milk she has offered from her breast could not be contained by the volume of the four great oceans. My dear mother, incarnating as my fathers, mothers, children, and relatives with a mind so full of love that she vows she would die before letting anything happen to me, has cried more tears for my sake than could fill 100 million rivers. When my welfare was at stake, she placed herself in danger. She disregarded suffering. She ignored gossip. She thought of my benefit alone. How amazingly much she has benefited me and cared for me! She loved me and has been so kind to me! Would it not be right for her to be comfortable now and always? Would it not be right for her to be happy? I must establish my mother in unsurpassable comfort and happiness.

Contemplation 38

The Expansion of the Mind of Loving Kindness to All Sentient Beings

Repeat the previous contemplation but replace the focus with five or six people in your family or circle of friends such as your father, spouse and so forth. Then reflect

In this life, some of these people have benefited me a great deal. Some have helped me to an average degree. Some have helped me only a little. However, if I consider that cyclic existence is without beginning, there is no difference between how much each of these people has benefited me and how much my mother has. There is no difference in the degree of their kindness. All these people have benefited me so very much! Is it right that they should be comfortable? Is it not right that they should be happy? I must place them in a state of ultimate happiness and comfort.

> You can augment this contemplation with some of the ideas [contained in the 36th Contemplation].

In a similar way, gradually apply the meditation to others. The tradition of Master Jayulwa[84] *and Nartangpa*[85] *suggests widening the contemplation by stages to cover a larger and larger geographical area. This method, explained below, seems to be the most effective one for beginners in contemplative practice.*

After engaging in the contemplations described above, extend your focus to include the people who live in your region: your enemies, friends and acquaintances. Then include animals: those living below, on and above the earth. Next consider hungry ghosts: the demons as well as the indigent ones, the superior as well as the poor and ordinary ones. All of them have been your mothers and fathers for countless lifetimes. Consider how they have benefited you and how they have shown you kindness. Apply to them the meditation on love as in the previous contemplations.

Then extend the contemplation to include larger and larger areas of the country until—in the context of being a Tibetan—you include the three types[86] of beings inhabiting the whole of Tibet. Next include China to the east of Tibet, India to the south, Nepal to the west and Mongolia to the north, extending your visualization to include the tigers, leopards and all the other beings of the three types living in those great countries.

Then meditate on the three types of beings inhabiting the Land of Jambu[87]. Meditate as above on the hungry ghosts who live below the earth, the beings in the eight hot hells and the eight cold hells. Then extend your contemplation to include the three types of beings filling the rest of the four continents: eastern Majestic Body[88], western Bountiful Cow[89] and northern Unpleasant Sound[90]. Also include the various beings of the three lower realms. On the four steps of Mount Meru are the gods of the Heaven of the Four Great Kings. On the peak of Mount Meru are the gods of the Heaven of the Thirty-three. On the four substeps leading up to the shore of the water are the villages where the leaders of the demi-gods live. Meditate as previously on the beings living in these places.

Then contemplate the gods, demons[91] and animals living above the water on the seven golden mountains and the outer circle of iron mountains, and the various demi-gods, hungry ghosts and animals living below the surface of the water. Within and around the seven swirling lakes and outer ocean live ordinary amphibious nagas, demi-gods and animals. Meditate on each of these as objects of your loving kindness.

Three types of animals possess miraculous powers: garudas who fly through space, phantoms who live on the surface of the earth and the nagas who live underground or in the water. Specifically meditate on these beings as well.

This meditation covers the area as far down as the great, powerful golden ground, as far out as the iron mountains and as far up as the Heaven of the Thirty-three.[92] Above the Heaven of the Thirty-three are the heavens called Free from Strife, Delighting in Creation and Enjoyment of Pleasures in layers one above the other. Above those realms are the three heavens of the first stage of absorption[93] that are each the size of one four-continent universe: Brahma's Realm, Acolytes of Brahma and Brahma's Great Heaven. Original sources[94] explain that these levels are the habitats of the form realm, where only gods of the form realm can live—beings of the other five types are not found there. Even desire-realm gods cannot live there. From this level up, only gods belonging to each specific god realm can exist in that realm.

In general, below the Brahma realms[95] is a universe with the four continents, where the beings of the six types live. Meditate on all of them as before. There is a collection of a thousand of these world-systems, and at the edge of those is a ring of iron mountains. Above that whole system are the three heavens of the second stage of absorption: Small Light, Immeasurable Light and Clear Light. Clear Light covers one thousand universal systems. Meditate as before on the beings of the six realms within that area.

At the edge of an arrangement of one thousand of those universes is a ring of iron mountains. Above that are the three heavens of the third absorption: Small Virtue, Immeasurable Virtue and Infinite Virtue. Infinite Virtue covers the six types of beings living in the universal system comprised of a million world system.

At the edge of an arrangement of one thousand of those universes is yet another vast ring of iron mountains. Each universal system at this level has a golden foundation, below which is a water mandala. The billion water mandalas are supported by a single wind mandala. Therefore, below this entire system is a wind mandala, and above are the three ordinary places of the fourth absorption: Cloudless, Awakening Merit and Great Fruition. Above those are Incomparable, Peaceful, Glorious Appearance, Magnificent, and the Highest Heaven. The Highest Heaven alone covers the one billion world system.[96]

That which is called "a great one billion world system" is covered up above by the innumerable sentient beings in the formless god's realm. Meditate on the six types of beings in the three realms as before.

Then, to the east of this world-system are innumerable, uncountable world-systems. To give some idea of how many world-systems stretch to the east, if you were to fill one world-system with mustard seeds and then place one over each of the world-systems to the east, you would eventually run out of mustard seeds. But even then, the world-systems to the east would continue. If you started the process again in any direction, it would be the same as before. Even if you engaged in this exercise infinite times, the universes would not end. They are all full of the six types of beings. Recognizing each of them to be your mother, meditate as before on loving kindness for them.

Reflect:

There is no end to the space that stretches in all directions. Wherever space pervades, universes exist. All sentient beings have been my kind mothers and fathers. They have been my parents infinite times. Each time they have been my parents, they have benefited me in numerous ways. They have protected me from copious harms. May all sentient beings, my previous mothers, be content! May they be happy! I will establish them in unsurpassable contentment and happiness.

There are many aspects to this contemplation, so it is possible to divide it up in various ways. How to break it up is not specified because it depends on the disposition of the individual. But since the aspects of the contemplation all relate to the expansion of the mind of loving kindness, I have included everything in one long contemplation cycle.

{At this time, it is an important point for the student to become familiar with this presentation of the system of the universes [cosmology]. This completes the contemplations on loving kindness.}

Contemplation 39
The Meditation on Compassion

The preliminary and conclusion of each session are as usual. After briefly recollecting the previous contemplation, consider

I must establish all these sentient beings in contentment and happiness. But when I look at the realms of sentient beings, it is apparent they do not live with happiness or the causes of happiness. They live with suffering and the causes of suffering. When they wish, they wish for happiness. They do not want suffering, but they experience it anyway. Happiness does not occur for them—misery is their only lot. For the most part, the suffering they experience is apparent. In the hell realms, they endure heat and cold. In the hungry ghost realms, they endure hunger and thirst. In the animal realm, they eat each other. In the higher realms, there is not one of us who does not experience manifest suffering of some kind: we have short lives, many illnesses, little freedom, famine and destitution and are forced to work, are injured by weapons and so forth. All beings in general amass the immeasurable causes of suffering. Some individuals are not experiencing intense, undesired suffering right now but are accumulating serious negative karma. They will go straight to hell when their breath stops. This kind of individual is even more worthy of my compassion than those who are actually experiencing suffering now.

How confused we are by appearances! Alas, what is to be done? What if my own mother's eyes could not see and her legs were broken? What if she were without a guide, without a walking stick? What if she were about to fall from the edge of a precipitous cliff? What would I do? I wouldn't hesitate for an instant but would run to grab her to keep her from falling off the cliff.

All these beings who have been my mothers in previous lifetimes are in this very predicament—their eyes of wisdom are blind; their legs of method are broken. They are without a guide. They have lost their walking stick. They again and again engage in all kinds of negative actions, sometimes even when they know the action is wrong. They are slipping away from the path to the higher realms. It is as if they were on the verge of plunging into the abyss of the lower realms. How tragic that these beings are overpowered by the causes of suffering! How could I fail to protect them from suffering right now?

Furthermore, beings in the three lower realms experience primarily manifest suffering. The beings in the three pleasant realms, on the other hand, experience mainly the causes of suffering.

Recollect the kinds of suffering all these beings experience from the explanations given in the context of the contemplations for the persons of lesser and average capacity.

If those sufferings were to suddenly befall me, I would be unable to bear it even to a small degree. If I could not stand it, how do they manage to bear their misery? Those who actually undergo these sufferings, who experience the endless causes of suffering over the course of their lifetimes, who go from misery to misery without break, how I feel for them! May they be free from all suffering! May they be free from the causes of suffering—karma and the emotional afflictions. May I protect my previous mothers, the six types of sentient beings, from all negative actions and suffering. May I lead them out of cyclic existence, the place of suffering.

Reflect in this way again and again.

{Another custom divides the session above into three sessions. In that case, you should start with a contemplation session on the experience of manifest suffering of a person of your choosing. Then do one contemplation session on that person's experience of the causes of suffering. Then do a contemplation session combining the foci of the first two sessions. It is excellent if you continue to gradually expand the visualization to relate to all beings as in the contemplation on loving kindness explained above.

Another option is to teach the instructions on loving kindness and compassion at the same time and have the disciple practice them together by alternating between the first part of loving kindness, followed by a session on the first part of compassion and so forth alternating back and forth until both are completed. It is also fine not to break the session into parts at all.}

Chapter Eleven

Meditation on the Aspiration of Awakening Mind

This chapter has three parts: training in the aspiration of awakening mind [Contemplation 40], training in recollecting the benefits [Contemplation 41] and the commitments of training [Contemplations 42-44].

Contemplation 40

The Aspiration of Awakening Mind

Inspired by the meditation on loving kindness and compassion think

I must establish these mothers in happiness. I must establish them in comfort. They remain in a state of unhappiness, discomfort and suffering—Alas! There is no way that I will stand by indifferently without relieving their suffering! There is no way I will fail to establish them in happiness!

But I do not have that ability. Not only that, even Brahma, Indra and universal monarchs do not have it. Who does have it? Only the perfect buddha has it. Only if I attain buddhahood will that power be in my hands. Therefore, I must attain buddhahood. If I attain it, I can guide sentient beings out of cyclic existence. In order to benefit all sentient beings I must attain buddhahood.

Think this way again and again.

{When the student is training [in the context of the 34th Contemplation, the Preparatory Contemplation], he or she becomes familiar with the qualities of the Buddha and the difference between the great and small vehicles. Through this awareness, he or she comes to perceive perfect enlightenment as being the most valuable goal. However, awakening mind generated on the basis of mere knowledge of its qualities is not sufficient. Therefore, [the 40th contemplation] focuses on the value of perfect enlightenment based on its benefit for others—in this the qualities of awakening mind are complete. Although indeed [the 34th Contemplation] is about benefiting others, until love and compassion are mastered through the ensuing contemplations, benefit for others cannot really be the principal focus.}

Contemplation 41

Training in Contemplating the Benefits of Awakening Mind

Awakening mind has potential to accomplish all my own aims. A sutra says: "Awakening mind is like a seed because it gives rise to all the attributes of buddhahood." It has the benefit of accomplishing the aims of others as well: "It is like a field because it causes the virtuous tendencies of all beings to grow." It has the benefit of dispelling all faults: "It is like fertile bottom soil because it exhausts all faulty conduct." It has the benefit of attracting qualities: "Because it magnetizes all qualities, it is like a great ocean." Thus, it has four benefits. This very meditation on awakening mind that I am now engaged in plants the seed of liberation in my mind and awakens all virtuous habits. This excellent attitude actually benefits sentient beings and gives me the ability to help others. From just this meditation, I am purifying a great deal of negative karma. By surmounting such negative emotions as attachment, aversion, pride and jealousy and by softening the mind, awakening mind nurtures all qualities. Once I have made the commitment to accomplish buddhahood, all the other qualities I need to acquire will arise naturally. From now until the end of the path, realization for my own sake, activity for the benefit of others, purification of faults and the attainment of qualities are all generated by awakening mind. In brief, whatever qualities the omniscient one has, awakening mind has as well. Whatever value that a buddha has, awakening mind has as well.

Giving rise to it with enthusiasm and clarity, again meditate on awakening mind as above. Repeat these contemplations over many times. Between sessions, engender awakening mind by maintaining the focus of taking on the accumulated [negative karma, illness, suffering and so forth] of others again and again. When you are not able to engender awakening mind as extensively as described above, say to yourself continually, "For the benefit of beings, I will attain buddhahood" because this resolution is itself engendering awakening mind. Also recite the seven branch prayer again and again.

CONTEMPLATION 42

The Commitments of the Training

The first commitment in which I need to train is never abandoning sentient beings with my mind. There are two ways to mentally abandon sentient beings: abandoning them as a whole and abandoning them individually. Abandoning them as a whole occurs if I mentally renege on my initial commitment to practice religion. Reneging on my commitment means having thoughts such as "I will never accomplish my own benefit or the benefit of others, so I might as well just be an ordinary, non-religious person." It also includes mentally turning away from the Mahayana by thinking such things as "Since I will never be able to accomplish the benefit of sentient beings, I should cultivate the motivation of a hearer or solitary-realizer."

Abandoning sentient beings individually occurs when someone contradicts me or goes against me, and I think, "Even if I get a chance to help you out, whether it is in a temporary or ultimate way, I will not do it." This attitude is without loving kindness.

Whether I mentally abandon sentient beings as a whole or individually, if I maintain the attitude of abandonment for one session (about four hours) without applying a remedy, I have deserted the practice of engendering awakening mind. May I never give rise to the mind that abandons sentient beings! If it should arise beyond my control, may I apply a remedy immediately by confessing it right after it arises. May I eventually benefit all those whom I am unable to benefit right now.

Contemplation 43

Making an Effort to Accumulate Merit

As my qualities gradually develop, expanding the two accumulations is important. Therefore, from this very day forward, I need to train in the two accumulations. I will train in the accumulation of merit by making offerings to the Three Jewels whose great benevolence is described in the sutras and commentaries, serving the spiritual community, offering tormas[97] to spirits, prostrating, giving, circumambulating, reciting mantras, cultivating faith, meditating on love and compassion, meditating on patience and so forth.

I should train in the accumulation of wisdom through listening to the dharma, apprehending the words, thinking about the meaning, and challenging its ideas. In this way, my intelligence will cut through doubts. Through studying, I will come to apprehend and understand; through contemplation, I will come to trust; and through meditation, I will directly realize the seal of not conceiving the three spheres[98], that the entirety of cyclic existence and nirvana are untrue. This is the single thing I need to understand and realize. Through the view that perceives the activity of offering and so forth[99] as unreal and through training to sustain that view, merit becomes wisdom, and wisdom becomes merit. This is practicing the union of the two accumulations.

Contemplate in this way again and again. Between sessions, always implement these points in practice as much as possible.

Contemplation 44

Training in the Eight Deeds

The four black deeds in general are serious faults. Specifically, they are the cause for forgetting bodhicitta once I have passed on from this life. In general, the four white deeds are of great benefit. Specifically, they are the cause for remembering awakening mind in all lifetimes. Therefore, I should give up the eight black deeds and train in the four white deeds.

1. The First Pair—Lying Versus Being Honest: It is a black deed to mislead a lama who is the recipient of generosity or to mislead anyone worthy of offerings. Misleading means deceiving him or her with lies.

   The remedy for that is to completely give up intentionally telling any lies. Since I should not intentionally tell even the slightest lie to an ordinary person, how could I deceive someone worthy of offerings?
2. The Second Pair—Inducing Inappropriate Remorse Versus Teaching Virtue: It is a black deed to make someone feel remorse for something he or she should not regret. Although I should inspire remorse for negative actions that deserve to be regretted, I should not try to make someone feel bad for doing something virtuous. It does not matter if they actually feel bad or not—it is still a black deed. Some examples of ways that make others regret their positive actions include saying to someone, "If you give all that away, what are you going to eat?" or "If you take ordination, your social status will be lower than a woman's" or "If you do not take revenge on your enemy, your reputation will be impaired."

   To remedy this tendency, I will train in the white deeds that ripen sentient beings to the virtue of the three vehicles. I will introduce sentient beings to the attitudes associated with the three vehicles depending on their dispositions and establish as many beings as possible in the great vehicle. I will encourage others to practice virtuous actions as much as possible and to make aspiration prayers towards enlightenment. If it is my duty to encourage even the worldliest people to practice virtue, how could I possibly instill remorse in anyone for practicing it?
3. The Third Pair—Harsh Speech Versus Praise: It is a black deed to speak harsh words to a person who has taken the precepts of awakening mind. Speaking harshly is a fault whether the speech is uttered privately or publicly and whether the person has actually engendered awakening mind or not is irrelevant. Moreover, it does not matter whether the person thinks I have hurt them or not. If a person has so much as uttered the words "I take the vow of awakening mind," I should never slander them.

   All sentient beings have the buddha nature. Moreover, they facilitate gathering the accumulations and purifying obscurations and are, therefore, similar to buddhas. It is said, "Sentient beings and buddhas are the same with regard to accomplishing buddhahood and following the teaching." Therefore, thinking of sentient beings as buddhas, I will constantly admire and praise them. If I should not blame but instead praise even ordinary people, how could I possibly blame someone who has engendered awakening mind?

4. The Fourth Pair—Deception Versus the Altruistic, Beneficent and Heroic Attitude: It is a black deed to deceive sentient beings. Deceiving includes setting the law onto someone or going behind his or her back to accomplish my own aims. It even includes something as slight as cheating. If there is deception of any kind, it is a black deed. As a remedy, the white deed is to cultivate the altruistic, beneficent and heroic attitude directed toward sentient beings. Altruistic and beneficent means wanting to establish them in happiness in this life and the next. Heroic means taking up the burdens of others as my own. I should train in not vacillating due to insincerity but, instead, speak directly and honestly to others as a parent speaks to his or her child without hiding things inside. Since I should abide by the heroic mind that wants to benefit all sentient beings, how could there be chance for me to deceive them?

    I should assiduously cultivate these white deeds as the heart of practice. From today onwards, I will never again engage in the four black deeds. I will train in the four white deeds as much as I possibly can.

{There is an alternative precedent for making a contemplation out of each of the four pairs. This method helps a person of narrow intellectual capacity to gain certainty. Things will get better and better as he or she goes along.

Another option is to classify contemplations according to the eight trainings. These consist of (1) recollecting the benefits of engendering awakening mind, (2) training in engendering awakening mind during the six times of day and night, (3) not abandoning sentient beings, (4) training in the two accumulations and (5-8) training in each of the four pairs. Use whichever method of training seems appropriate.

The student can formally take the vow of awakening mind[100] after the instructions on compassion [the 39th Contemplation] have been imparted and before the instructions on the aspiration of awakening mind [the 40th Contemplation]. Inserting the vow here seems like the most orderly fashion.

Another possibility is to teach the contemplations up to this point and insert the Ceremony of the Vow of Awakening Mind here [after the 44th Contemplation]. It is important that at the time of the vow-taking ceremony the disciple has certainty about the meaning. Therefore, this is also an excellent place to insert it. Alternately, it is acceptable to have the student engender awakening mind [through the Ceremony of the Vow of Awakening Mind] after all the instructions in this book are completed in their entirety and before the Bodhisattva Vow Ceremony. Insert it whenever you find it most convenient.}

Chapter Twelve

Training in the Application of Awakening Mind

Contemplation 45

The General Reflection on the Application of Awakening Mind

If I want to attain buddhahood, I must train in the conduct of a bodhisattva[101]. Wanting to achieve buddhahood but not cultivating bodhisattva conduct is like wishing for an excellent harvest but being unwilling to till the soil. Although it is indeed true that there are many benefits of aspiring towards enlightenment, if I do not practice bodhisattva conduct, whatever good qualities I might have will not develop fully. Therefore, I must train in the conduct of a bodhisattva.

The essence of bodhisattva conduct is the six perfections and the four ways of gathering disciples. There is nothing else to practice other than the perfections and the four ways. I should therefore take up the practice of the six perfections, explain them to others and encourage others to practice them. Encouraging others to practice the six perfections is itself one of the perfections and the ways of gathering disciples. I will earnestly and thoroughly practice the ten perfections[102]. I will not procrastinate but will start at this very moment! At this time, while my promise and practice is not hazy, I should practice as much as I possibly can. I have to practice from this very day forward!

Cultivate this aspiration again and again.

Contemplation 46

The Perfection of Generosity

If I am to engage in bodhisattva conduct, I need to start by training in the perfection of generosity. Generosity can be classified as three types: material generosity, the generosity of offering protection from fear and the generosity of giving the Dharma.

1. Material generosity: I will give generously to all sentient beings until they are satisfied.

If you are not able to give that much, think

In the future, when I am a universal monarch, I will give everything I have away. Right now, I will give away whatever food, clothing and so forth I can afford without adversely affecting my spiritual practice. Except for keeping myself from falling into debt or going hungry, I must by all means give everything else away. I will not leave this as merely a contemplation—I must definitely put this generosity into practice!

2. Giving protection from fear: I will protect all sentient beings from such fears as those caused by illness, weapons, robbers, poison, by such predators as wild animals, poisonous snakes and so forth, by precipices, treacherous roads, fire, water, attackers, up to and including the fear of the lower realms. Right now, I will do everything I possibly can to protect others from the fears of illness, demons, enemies, the four elements and so forth. Visualizing this alone is not enough: I will practice it as much as I can without impairing my moral discipline and spiritual practice. At the very least, I will comfort others with helpful words.

This is training by application.

Giving protection from fear is synonymous with benefiting suffering sentient beings. So if the time is not right or if the attempt to help would involve negative actions, then the loss outweighs the profit and the action is potentially dangerous. In this case, although you should still train mentally, it is not appropriate to act.

3. Giving teaching: *Train by thinking:* I will satisfy all sentient beings by giving spiritual teachings. Through teaching the truth, I will

ripen sentient beings who have not been ripened. I will liberate those who have been ripened. I will cause those who do not understand to understand. I will cause those who have not yet realized to realize. I will cause those who have not yet attained freedom to attain it. Furthermore right now, if I have the ability to explain the truth, I should benefit others by explaining it to them without regard for wealth and fame. If I am not someone who can do that, I should aspire to teach the truth to humans and non-humans. While cultivating that intention, I should actually engage in the recitation of sutras and chanting of texts. I will not merely visualize this: I will definitely put this into practice. I will train by way of application.

Hence, the three types of generosity have both a contemplative and engaged aspect, so there is a total of six ways of training. If you put them all together, this is the training in the perfection of generosity.

Contemplation 47

The Perfection of Moral Discipline

Apply the concept of the contemplative and engaged methods of training to all the perfections that follow.

Next I should train in the perfection of moral discipline. There are three types of moral discipline: the moral discipline that binds faulty conduct, the moral discipline that gathers virtuous attributes and the moral discipline that accomplishes the benefit of beings.

1. The moral discipline that binds faulty conduct: In general, I should avoid all actions that are obviously wrong, such as the ten non-virtuous actions. In particular, I should not transgress whatever precepts I have taken such as the lay, novice or monastic vows; the training of the bodhisattva vow; or the commitments of secret mantra. In brief, I will turn away from everything that is taught to be wrong in the Buddhist canon. I must train in this immediately!
2. The moral discipline that gathers virtuous attributes: Without limiting myself to one type of virtuous action, I will constantly

train in everything that is included in the six perfections. From right now onwards, I will practice this as much as possible.

3. The moral discipline that accomplishes the benefit of beings: I will accomplish the benefit of beings by establishing them in various types of happiness and virtue. From right now onwards, I will as much as possible—as much as I am able—help sentient beings and bring them to happiness.

   Binding faulty conduct is not something I can put off until later. As soon as I learn an action is morally wrong, I should stop that action and turn away. Of two possible futures, there is only one that will come to pass. Therefore, I must use whatever force of mind I have to practice now as much as I possibly can. If I do not practice now, I am tacitly consenting to becoming a mere object of other people's prayers.[103] If a bodhisattva does not work for the benefit of others, that is a monumental fault! Therefore, I need to cultivate the moral discipline of accomplishing the benefit of others. Because I must ripen my own mind in order to help others, I need to practice virtuous deeds. It is not enough to be free of faults myself, but as an initial basis it is important to bind faulty conduct. Without this basis, even if I try to develop the other two aspects of morality, the result will be unsatisfactory.

Contemplation 48

The Perfection of Patience

There are three types of patience: The patience of not weighing harm, the patience of accepting suffering and the patience of certainty about truth.

1. The patience of not weighing harm: When someone harms me by beating me or stealing my wealth, I react with impatience and anger. But how can I be impatient with such trivial harms that are the cause for my accomplishment of buddhahood?[104] Even if the sentient beings in the three realms become my enemy and harm me in all sorts of ways, I will plant myself firmly in patience. If I cannot be patient with even this much harm, my hope for attaining

buddhahood and my hope of becoming a religious person is just self-deception.

2. The patience of accepting suffering: When practicing religion, I will sometimes encounter the suffering of heat, cold, hunger, thirst and so forth. At times, I will be required to travel on treacherous roads, will have trouble establishing favorable conditions for practice, and may become depressed, tired and discouraged. These are but trivial hardships! How can I not be patient? For the sake of wealth or a woman, I would without hesitation endure suffering a hundred or a thousand times greater than this. In order to attain buddhahood, I must first follow the examples of previous bodhisattvas. If I am impatient with just these slight hardships endured for the sake of religion, my commitment to the Mahayana is a joke.

Thinking thus, apply the remedy of patience firmly and immediately.

3. The patience of certainty about truth: Being certain about the truth means being unintimidated by profound methods, by various skillful means, vast activity, infinite qualities, the true nature beyond elaborations and so forth. It also entails being able to rest the mind in emptiness for an extended period of time. Likewise, I should consider all the harm and suffering I now experience to be like an illusion or a dream. Since it is ultimately empty, appearing yet not truly existent, what is the point of being impatient with it?

Contemplation 49

The Perfection of Diligence

Next I must train in the perfection of diligence. There are three types of diligence: armor-like diligence, the diligence of application and the diligence that does not turn back.

1. The armor-like diligence: I will not be contemptuous, thinking that among all virtuous activities I do not need to observe some, and therefore it is all right to kill for example. Likewise, I will not be timid, deeming some virtuous projects too big to undertake. Instead, I will accomplish every virtuous activity. I have the ability

to accomplish all of them. I will accomplish them now! I will accomplish them constantly!

Thinking in this way is having the attitude that is committed, enthusiastic about virtuous actions and undaunted. In order to make virtue a mental habit, meditate in this way again and again.

2. The diligence of application: When putting virtuous actions into practice, I will not give in to laziness and distractions but, instead, enthusiastically engage in virtue. While remaining enthusiastic, I will prolong any given virtuous activity as much as possible.
3. The diligence that does not revert: If the signs of heat[105] and benefits of practice do not quickly arise or if a project that I start cannot be completed easily, no matter how long it lingers or how much hardship I have to endure, I will not let my enthusiasm wane. One of the oral instructions of the instructional handbooks states

> The diligence of body is cultivated through prostrations and circumambulations and so forth. The diligence of speech is cultivated through recitation, chanting and so forth. The diligence of mind is cultivated generally through virtue and specifically through enthusiasm for spiritual practice.

Since these are the various forms of diligence, I will strive to be diligent in these ways. Not giving in to laziness and procrastination, I will practice virtue enthusiastically.

Contemplation 50

The Causes of Perfect Absorption[106]

I should abide in the causes of absorption from now on. For absorption to develop, I must reduce my aims and occupations. To reduce my aims, I must have few desires and be content. To have few desires, I must be satisfied with meager food, clothing, shelter and a poor bed. Whatever possessions I may have, I will not be attached to them but will meditate to develop trance.[107] If I do not have possessions, I will consider being destitute as good—not an obstacle to Dharma. Whatever happens, I will be content with that.

Contemplate in this way again and again.

Contemplation 51

The Perfection of Absorption—The Main Contemplation

Although there are many classifications of absorption, this contemplation will consider three: The absorption that abides at ease with visible phenomena is the attainment of the ease of mental and physical flexibility. The absorption that accomplishes the emergence of good qualities generally causes the attainment of clairvoyance, the ability to perform miracles, and so forth. The absorption that achieves the benefit of beings blesses the minds of others by relying on the power of trance or acts for the benefit of sentient beings by relying on various types of clairvoyance. To master these absorptions, I must cultivate a faultless state of tranquility and perfect the attributes [required for successful meditation]. I will start by resting the mind evenly in tranquility. Then, I will accomplish all of the other particular trances.

Meditate in this way again and again.

{At this time, it is good to confer a concise explanation of tranquility meditation until the student experiences certainty.[108] However, although it is indeed valuable to confer instructions on tranquility meditation at this point, the student's meditation need not become stable: it is sufficient for the student to attain some certainty and gain some experience. Moreover, it is the intention of all the great texts that the student should accomplish insight by first achieving an excellent, stable state of tranquility and then sustaining the view after that. This is indeed the path outlined in the great texts. However people these days have dull faculties and take a long time to achieve a faultless, stable state of tranquility, and I fear that they might be deprived of the opportunity to meditate on the perfection of wisdom. Moreover, if mental calm is achieved within the process of searching for an experience of the view, tranquility can be achieved simultaneously with insight. Therefore, for the convenience of students with regard to teaching and understanding, I have not explained the practice of tranquility meditation in detail here.}

Chapter Thirteen

Wisdom

Contemplation 52

The Perfection of Wisdom

The perfection of wisdom is the primary and most superlative among all forms of training and the ultimate of all practices. There are three kinds of wisdom: the wisdom that realizes the ultimate truth, the wisdom that realizes relative truth and the wisdom that knows how to benefit others. The first is the wisdom that realizes the true nature, emptiness. The second is the wisdom that realizes without error the essence of all objects of knowledge, their classifications and the interdependence of causes and conditions. The third is the wisdom that knows how to benefit others through the four ways of gathering disciples. These are

1. Giving: The first way to gather disciples is to give material possessions and to know how to inspire beings in many ways to practice religion.
2. Speaking pleasantly: The second way entails knowing how to speak pleasantly when imparting religious instructions appropriate to the dispositions of those beings.
3. Helping others: The third way is to be familiar with how to establish others in the meaningful activity of the six perfections.
4. Acting in accord with the meaning:[109] The fourth way entails helping others without transgressing the conduct of the six perfections oneself. From among these, establishing others in the six perfections involves knowing which methods are appropriate for which disciples.

Furthermore, I should develop the wisdoms of listening, reflecting and meditating. By way of listening, understanding develops. By way of reflecting, doubts are cut. Through meditation, true realization is attained. I will definitely engender these three wisdoms in my mind.

This is the general training in the contemplation of wisdom.

{Next you must train in the practice of the perfection of wisdom. The practice of wisdom has three steps: meditation on the selflessness of persons, meditation on the selflessness of phenomena and training in emptiness endowed with the heart of compassion.}

Contemplation 53

The Selflessness of Persons

The preliminaries for a session and the conclusion are the same as explained before. For the main practice, sit with your legs crossed[110] *and your hands in the position of meditative equipoise. Straighten your spine. Pull in your chin (lit. crook your neck). Square your shoulders. Let your jaw and lips rest naturally. Join your tongue with your upper palate. Look at the tip of your nose. Exhale slowly and deeply through your nostrils three times, then just breathe naturally. First, meditate on renunciation and weariness intensely. Then meditate on love and compassion until you feel deeply moved. Finally, mentally focus on your body, speech and mind—scrutinize them. Contemplate as follows:*

Throughout beginningless cyclic existence, having become accustomed to clinging to the concept of "I" as being the "self," I have become convinced that a continuous self exists. However, this "I" or "self" in truth has never existed.

This is the basis of the contemplation.

If that which is called an "I" or a "self" truly exists, there must be something designated as an independent personal entity, a self of person. But the material existence of such a thing has never been established. Therefore, since no material existence can be found, the essence of a self of person[111] cannot be proven either. Nevertheless, the ego has a way of clinging to this non-existent self as if it did exist. In accord with this deluded perception, I believe the self to be permanent, singular, and independent. From that, I have the thought "Last year I did that" and "This year I will do this" and "Last year's self was like that" and "My self in the present is like this." Thinking that I will continue to exist like this is what is called "clinging to the self as permanent."

When these present thoughts arise, I consider outer and inner occurrences to be other than I. It seems to me that there is an essence of a self that is established at the core of my being that is unmixed with this multitude of experiences and appearances. That is "clinging to a self as singular."

It seems to me as if the self is the owner of certain enjoyments, substances and possessions. That is "clinging to a self as independent."

Even though those various ways of clinging are my mode of perception, things cannot be proven to be like that in truth. If the self were permanent, then if I experienced happiness one time, I would always have to experience it. If I experienced suffering one time, I would always have to suffer. If I were initially trapped in cyclic existence, a time of future liberation would never occur. Similarly, using the same logic in reverse, if a time of future liberation did come about, it would mean that a previous cyclic existence was never experienced. However, happiness and suffering are both experienced and individual incidents of bondage and liberation do occur. Therefore, I should resolve that there is no permanent self.

The self as singular is also not an acceptable proposition. Although it seems as if the various parts that make up the body and mind exist, the eyes are not the self. The ears, nose, tongue and mind are also not the self. If each of them were the self, then there would be many selves. If each one of them is not the self, then a self cannot be found.

Moreover, if the self were an aggregate, it would have to be impermanent.[112] If it were something other than an aggregate, then, when something is seen by the eye consciousness, it would contact the entire body of the seer.[113] I would have the perception that I touched the object. Therefore, an "I" or "self" that has the nature of singularity is not established. Since its singularity is not established, neither is its independence. Moreover, since I can patently see that all occurrences depend on conditions, the existence of an independent self is impossible.

Hence, a self cannot be established outside of the aggregates. A self does not abide within the aggregates. Each of the aggregates individually is not the self. The self is not some kind of sheath encasing the aggregates.

The self is not the aggregates taken as a whole. It is not a whole that is other than each of the aggregates. Therefore, the so called "self" is a mere mental imputation, a mere mask of confusion, only a distortion. It does not ultimately exist at all.

{This meditation on the selflessness of persons can be divided into several contemplation sessions in accord with the intellectual capacity of the student.}

Contemplation 54

The Selflessness of Phenomena

Phenomena is defined as the aggregates, constituents and sources.[114] Beings do not perceive these as mental imputations: they seem to exist as material things with a solid identity. Although the term "self of phenomena" is used to identify the aggregates, constituents and sources, such a thing has never existed. All phenomena are without a self of phenomena. Even though that is the case, throughout infinite rebirths in cyclic existence, I have become habituated to the concept that perceives the aggregates, constituents and sources as possessed of a solid identity. Therefore, I need to meditate on the selflessness of phenomena.

First, I should meditate that the aggregates of my own continuum[115] are without a true nature. If I examine the phenomena of the form aggregate of my body, it is nothing but a conglomeration of various things that seems to be one thing. I give it the generic label "body" and think there is a thing that is equivalent to the name. Except for my mistaken cognitive perception, it does not exist.

This body can be separated into discrete parts such as the visual sense, the auditory sense, the olfactory sense, the gustatory sense and the tactile sense. There are also inner faculties that rely on each of the senses but are not the same as those senses. The body form aggregate is made up of various parts: the head, neck, chest, back, waist, stomach, gut, the two upper arms, two shoulders, two elbows, two lower arms, two hands, two thighs, two calves, two feet, the body's internal organs such as the five critical organs and the six secondary organs, the nine orifices and so forth. Except for the mental imputation "body," this collection is not ultimately real. If each of these parts were the body, then there would be many bodies. If the body were none of these parts, then the body cannot be found. If I think it is the entire conglomeration of parts, I should consider that the body cannot be something other than each of its parts. Therefore, I am compelled to conclude that it is merely a mental imputation.

Contemplation 55

The Selflessness of the Form Aggregate

To reinforce that the form aggregate is not established as a valid entity, reflect as follows:

Each of my four limbs is made up of many parts. It has an upper and lower part, a joint and its extension, an outside and an inside. If I wonder "Is each part established as a valid entity?"[116], it is not. Each part is connected by three joints and so forth. If I wonder "Is each joint ultimately real?", it is not. For example, the fingers have many joints. If I wonder "Is each part of the fingers established as a valid entity?", it is not. Each finger has seven parts. Each of these parts is also not real. After mentally dividing the fingers into seven parts, each part can be broken down further into coarse particles: "soma" particles, "sunlight" particles, "cow" particles, "sheep" particles, "rabbit" particles, "water" particles, and "iron" particles.[117] Each of these particles, when divided into seven parts, yields the next type of particle in the list [each is seven times smaller than the previous one]. If I wonder whether the "iron" particle [the smallest in this list] is truly existent, it is not. If I scrutinize the "iron" particle, it is made up of seven "subtle" particles. The "subtle" particle is also not established: it is made up of seven "minute" particles. In other words, when I scrutinize and try to measure the course sevenfold particles, each of the previous particles is split into the subsequent particles to yield a total of 343 particles [7x7x7]. Hence, there are a total of seven types of coarse particles and forty-nine possible divisions. Even the smallest of these particles can be broken into seven.

Contemplation 56

The Selflessness of Minute Particles

If I wonder whether a minute particle can be established as a valid entity, it cannot. Each one has sides, a top and a bottom. And each one must have a middle part. If this were not the case, then if I looked at the particle from the east or west, I would be unable to see it.[118] If I divide each of these seven-part particles in this way, they are found to be not established. This division can go on infinitely: The process is endless. Consequently, what I call the "body" is merely a mental imputation. In reality, its existence is completely unfounded. Therefore, these mere, unimpeded, illusion-like appearances are by nature primordially non-existent. On the basis of this logic, these seemingly material things are not established as singular. Since they are not established as singular, they cannot be established as multiple. The reasoning is that in order to prove that a collection of many things is established, one must first prove that one thing can be established.

Contemplation 57

The Selflessness of the Other Four Aggregates[119]

Well, what if I think that, although the form aggregate is not real, the mind is real? Mind, too, can be divided into parts. The seeing of forms, the hearing of sounds and so forth make up consciousness, the principal part of the mind. There are eight distinct consciousnesses.[120] Therefore, the existence of multiple aggregates of consciousness is confirmed. Feelings such as happiness, suffering and neutrality are also experienced as part of the mind. Hence, "feeling" cannot be established as a singular entity either. There are also perceptions designated by definitive terms such as high and low, good and bad and so forth. "Perception" cannot, therefore, be characterized as singular. Finally, there are multiple concepts such as attachment, aversion, faith and so forth. All of these concepts collectively are designated "mental formations." Therefore, "thinking" is also not a singular entity. Because these aspects of mind cannot be established as singular, they also cannot be established as multiple.

Contemplation 58
The Selflessness of Awareness

All the epithets for consciousness refer to nothing other than this vivid, dynamic awareness. Nothing else can be established as true. The phenomena that appear to the mind are like a mountain reflected on the surface of a lake.[121] If I examine this dynamic awareness, the mind of the past has ceased and, therefore, does not exist. The mind of the future has not yet arisen; therefore, it too does not exist. The present momentary awareness is all there is. Nevertheless, from its own side, it is not established as true because this single moment of awareness cannot be established. It can be divided into a beginning of the moment, a ceasing part of that moment and a part that abides in the center. If I examine that middle part, it too can be divided into three parts. In this way, I can analyze infinitely *ad absurdum.* Therefore, nothing can be established as having a singular essence. If one cannot be established, many cannot be established either.

Contemplation 59
Meditation on the Emptiness of All Sentient Beings Inhabiting the World

By that reasoning, I can resolve that the aggregates of my own body are not real. On the basis of resolving that the five aggregates comprising my body and mind are not real, I can conclude that the five aggregates comprising the minds and bodies of all sentient beings are just like that. In particular, when I focus on a particular object that generates strong emotions such as an enemy that I despise or a friend that I love, I can analyze his or her body in the same way that I analyzed my own. Just as I analyzed the aggregate that I label my mind, I should analyze his or her mind. By mentally imputing names to people such as "Lisa" and "George,"[122] I decide that this person or that person exists. Although I make this mistaken imputation with certainty, the basis for the imputation does not exist at all. It is like an illusion.

Training in this way, apply this reasoning to all circumstances.

Contemplation 60

Meditation on the Emptiness of the Outer Environment

Not only are sentient beings who inhabit the world not real, the outer world itself is not real either. If I scrutinize the billion-world system, it can be broken into parts such as a million-world system, a thousand-world system, the four continents, our world, one country, a square mile, an acre, a square yard, a square foot, six square inches, the size of a grain, all the way down to the space of a minute particle. The latter ones prove the previous ones are not established. Even a minute particle, when carefully scrutinized, cannot be established as real in the end. If it cannot be established as one, it cannot be established as many. The reasoning is the same as the previous contemplation.

In brief, everything is like this. I say, "This is a home. This is a field. This is grain. This is wealth. This is a harvest." Likewise, there seem to be entities such as mountains, plains, lakes, kingdoms and so forth. However, these are merely compounded appearances that are not established as real. By mentally assigning names and imputing terms to them, I perceive them as being real. However, in truth, they are not in the slightest bit established.

By meditating as above, cultivate this outlook on the world.

Contemplation 61

The Emptiness of the Outer Environment and Its Inhabitants

All material things—my self, others, the environment, its inhabitants and forms that I see and hear—are comprised of the five elements of earth, water, fire, wind and space. The mind, with all its energy and movement, is comprised of consciousness. The previous reasoning, that nothing can be established as having its own true existence on the subtlest level, can be applied to the four material elements [earth, water, fire and wind]. Just as an atom of earth is not established, this can be applied to the other elements.

The thing we call "space" is the void that lacks all those material forms. Except for being a mental imputation, space does not do anything and has no manifest existence. Consciousness also is merely an aspect of appearance arising due to adventitious conditions. Other than that, it cannot be identified. Therefore, my self, others, the environment and its inhabitants are all by nature not truly existent. Although the projections of the confused mind of each sentient being are unimpeded, they are without an inherent nature, like an illusion.

Contemplation 62

The Meditation on Ultimate Freedom from Elaborations

So called "non-things" are merely imputed by mind depending on a concept of "things." They are not established even as objects on the conventional, functional level let alone as an ultimate truth. In other words, since nothing inherently exists at all and all these phenomena that appear or are heard have never been established, it can also be surmised that what is called "the phenomena of emptiness that has been primordially rootless" does not exist. It is like the example of the son of a barren woman. It is not possible for a son of a barren woman to be born in the first place. Therefore, it is not valid to say that "The son of a barren woman does not exist."[123] This kind of emptiness depends on an idea of non-emptiness and is, therefore, mentally imputed. Existence and non-existence, being and not being and so forth are not at all established.

Therefore, do not mentally cling to anything and instead rest vividly in a state of clarity and non-conceptuality. When a thought arises again, look at its essence: it is free from identification. Meditate directly on that. It is important to meditate again and again for short periods lucidly on this and the previous contemplation.

Contemplation 63

How to Sustain Meditation on Selflessness and Emptiness

Next, mediate synthesizing all of those previous contemplations on selflessness and emptiness. In order to synthesize the previous understandings, reflect as follows:

My self and others, the world and its inhabitants are all lacking a truly existent self. No creator made all of this. It appears merely due to the assemblage of interdependent connections. Nothing can be at all established to exist as one thing or many. It all merely appears as the face of delusion; in reality, none of it truly exists. If I examine the matter carefully, "not established" and "non-existent" are also newly fabricated attributes created by the mind. In order to indicate something that seems to be the opposite [of existence], I merely impute the terms "non-existent" and "not established" to it.

By analyzing back and forth in this way, the object of focus dissipates. In the void that is left, rest evenly without thinking about anything at all. After the previous object of focus is cleared away, a state arises that is free from all identification. For as long as that lasts, rest in that non-conceptuality. If that state deteriorates, rest in the mere non-conceptuality of the disappearance of the aspect of emptiness. Because it is necessary to do the meditation just described repeatedly, it is important to recognize the point at which this disappearance starts [to come to distinguish between the state of non-conceptuality and its deterioration].

At first, you will not be able to stay in this state for very long. Eventually, when you get the point of the experience, you will be able to sustain it for longer and longer periods than before. Concentrating the mind on the object of focus[124] is known as "placement"[125], and extending that experience is called "continuous placement". When you become able to stop thoughts as soon as they arise, that is "repeated placement". Then, when the state of non-conceptuality extends for longer and longer periods, that is "close placement." Eventually, remembering the good qualities of trance, you will start to meditate more frequently and with joy, and enthusiasm will arise. This is the stage called "disciplined". Sometimes, by recollecting faults such as distraction, distraction will cease on its own. This stage is called "pacification". These two phases as also known as "engendering enthusiasm" and "engendering renunciation." Whatever thoughts of hope and fear, attachment and aversion arise, look directly at their essence and seal them with the meditation on their unreality that you cultivated previously. This natural pacification is the stage known as "close pacification." As long as your mind sometimes uses and sometimes loses [its mindfulness], you should cultivate these methods again and again. At some point, when you concentrate the mind, you will be without the faults of dullness and restlessness and will be able to rest the mind for a long time on the object of focus, which is emptiness. At this time, it is necessary to concentrate, engaging in one-pointed focus of the mental continuum. Eventually, just by remembering the experience of the view that you cultivated previously, you will be able to simply rest and abide for a long time in the aspect of emptiness. At that time, you should relax your effort and rest naturally settled. At this point, you have achieved the state called "resting evenly."

{The way of sustaining meditation presented above comes from the tradition of the Treasury of Phenomenology. It is the single way to meditate on tranquility that is preceded by insight. It can be construed as the same as the tradition presented in Stages of Meditation[126] by Kamalashila and so forth known as "the method of meditating with the precedent of non-conceptuality". It can also be construed as the tradition of glorious Atisha from the great Master Potowa's Annals[127] called "the only necessary preliminary". These instructions are in accordance with the sutra tradition such as the many instructions on mind training imparted by Atisha and with the many tantric instructions such as the teachings on mahamudra. Although there are a great many instructions that take this approach, in this case I have wished to present the instructions in a graduated way so have needed to rely on the teachings of Shenyen Potowa. [128]

In Potowa's tradition of sustaining the view, once the mind comes to rest, then insight meditation is again practiced. It is also asserted that from the beginning tranquility and insight may be cultivated in union.}

CONTEMPLATION 64

Emptiness with the Heart of Compassion

Realizing emptiness alone is not sufficient to achieve the perfection of wisdom. I need to practice emptiness and compassion in union. Because compounded phenomena appear and exist as ultimate truth, they cannot be established whatsoever as having inherent existence. They are like space. If I truly realize that only the non-establishment of phenomena is established, then sentient beings who experience suffering do not exist. The suffering they experience does not exist. The way that they experience suffering due to the cyclic interactions of karma, emotions and suffering has primordially never been established. Nevertheless, until that realization occurs, the appearance of sentient beings who experience suffering arises. The appearance of their suffering arises. The way they experience suffering and the way they are caught in the cycle arise. All these phenomena do not truly exist and yet appear. Even so, sentient beings are deceived by this illusion and, therefore, experience these various sufferings. Poor dear ones! Having dispelled their delusion, I must establish them in buddhahood, the realization of the true nature.

Ultimately, I too do not exist. Those sentient beings do not exist. Delusion does not exist. Even the path that dispels delusion does not exist. However, from the point of view of relative confused appearances, suffering and obscurations seem to exist. The path seems to exist. Through the path of meditation, delusion is dispelled, and a person becomes a buddha who abides in the essence of the natural state. Therefore, my illusion-like self will show illusion-like sentient beings the illusion-like path and teaching. In this way, the adversities of their illusion-like suffering will be liberated into the expanse.

Since all experiences of suffering and those who experience it are not established as truly existent, it is also impossible to establish any phenomena of perception such as appearance or sound as truly existent. However, one might assert the extreme of permanence, suggesting that a second nature is superimposed on the non-existent nature. In this case, one might consider it possible that there is truly existent suffering. But there is no way to augment the experience of unreal suffering with some other experience of truly existent suffering.[129] If this suffering were realized to be non-existent, it would be self-liberated. How I feel compassion for those who have not realized this!

Meditate, thinking in this way again and again.

Chapter Fourteen

Ways to Progress in the Practice

Session 1

Enhancement

In order to enhance the recognitions taught above, for one day meditate only on emptiness. For one day, meditate only on compassion. For one day, meditate on emptiness and compassion in union as described in the previous contemplation. Meditating repeatedly in this alternating fashion will enhance the practice. Sometimes, meditate for one session on emptiness only. Meditate for one session on compassion only. Meditate for one session on emptiness and compassion in union. Meditating at times in this way will bring about another kind of enhancement.

Session 2

Dispelling Hindrances

When practicing the main meditation that integrates emptiness and compassion, there is a risk of encountering the hindrance of attachment to the happiness of this life. Life is full of enjoyments, pleasant exchanges and interesting conversations. Some religious practitioners think they are superior to ordinary people but, meanwhile, cling to the hope of success. Failing to develop sincere renunciation, they blame others and protect themselves. They engage in ostensibly positive actions such as restoring temples, enduring austerities and begging for alms. They act virtuous out of a desire for food. They complete deity practices for fame. They are conceited and hypocritical. They secretly want people to have faith in them. Because they hope to win out over others, they slander and deceive them. In the name of religion, they engage in activities that strengthen worldly aims. This is the opposite of emptiness and compassion, like mixing food with poison. Attitudes and actions that are worldly from the start are always negative and, therefore, blameworthy. However, it is even worse to mix these concerns with religion and present them under the false pretense of being positive. As a remedy for those tendencies, recollect the contemplations for the person of lesser capacity again and again.

There is also the hindrance of being attached to the future happiness of gods and humans. If you do not reverse the craving for worldly happiness, you might seem to be generous, seem to guard moral discipline and may scrupulously and neatly engage in virtuous actions. But if you aspire for the joys of amassing food, clothing, possessions, a nice house, women, friends, servants and power, then emptiness and compassion have become an interference. As a remedy, meditate repeatedly on the contemplations for the individual of average capacity.

Even though your mind turns towards religion, you think only of your own benefit. This is the opposite of emptiness and compassion. As a remedy for that, meditate on the equality of yourself and others and exchange self for others. It is very important not to leave meditation as a mere intellectual exercise but to attain certainty by applying the focus directly to your own body and mind.

These instructions are elucidated in the mind-training texts [by Atisha] and are elaborated on in *The Bodhisattva's Way of Life* and *Compendium of Trainings*[130]. The Bodhisattva Maitreya says

> The quintessential mind is the same for you and others. When you discover that
> others are more dear and beloved than yourself, you will know that the aims of
> others are more important than your own. Whatever your own aims are—these are also the aims of others.

When you meditate again and again on emptiness, the object to be understood, you will have the thought "Nothing is real. It is all like an illusion." Since this concept is subject to dissipation, you have not reached the essential point. Coarse thoughts of enemies, friends, enjoyments, conversations and so forth are elements that interfere with emptiness and compassion. Therefore, you need to apply the concept of things being like an illusion directly to your own body, mind, possessions, enemies and friends. It is important to attain resolute certainty in this way and sustain it.

Session 3

Integrating the Practices

Next, spend one day each on each of the following: the difficulty of attaining a human life; death and impermanence; the sufferings of cyclic existence; action; cause and result; faith in religion; the awakening mind of love and compassion; and the two selflessnesses. Inside each session, sometimes meditate on the entire sequence. Sometimes meditate on them in reverse. Sometimes meditate mixing them up. Sometimes, meditate on your strongest faults, the ones that are harming your mind the most. Sometimes, meditate upon you feel most inclined to focus on.

Session 4

What to Do at All Times

As your main, continual practice of meditation, focus on four topics: (1) intense recollection of impermanence, (2) carefulness and avoidance born of contemplating the meaning of action and result, (3) compassion for all beings in the three realms of cyclic existence and (4) resting evenly in the true nature, free from elaborations.

Meditate on the other topics by rotation as described above. Spend time with holy lamas who practice this teaching and with wholesome friends. Between sessions, reading and listening to the sutras will enhance your practice of meditation. Find certainty in the teaching. Supplicate with faith. In particular, as expressed in the *Annals*[131] of the Kadampa stages on the path tradition, it is an important, essential point to apply the teachings directly to your perspectives, thoughts, resolve and aims.

The four topics mentioned at the beginning of this session should be your continual practice, augmented by training to dispel hindrances and induce enhancement. These topics need not be made into their own contemplation sessions [they can be practiced at all times], but there is no fault in doing so.

Afterword

The Way of Achieving the Fruition of Unsurpassable Enlightenment

{The way enlightenment is achieved can be best understood by studying the original treaties[132]. The explanation offered here cannot compare to what is presented in original sources. The essential meaning according to master Nagarjuna is as follows:

> Moral discipline and generosity benefit others. Diligence and patience benefit oneself. Meditation and wisdom are the cause of liberation. Compassion accomplishes all aims... Each one of these seven perfections without exception is the sphere of unsurpassable wisdom. A Protector of the World will attain them.

By training in the attitude of awakening mind and the conduct of the six perfections, the mind stays fixed on religion by its own power and does not become distracted. Faith in the Three Jewels, vigilance with regard to action and result, and renunciation for cyclic existence naturally arise. If tireless enthusiasm for meditating one-pointedly on the teachings develops, it does not matter whether you develop stable trance or not: You have grasped the point of the path, and the lesser path of accumulation[133] has been born in your continuum.

The path of accumulation itself is reached when you attain to some degree a clear apprehension of the meaning of impermanence, suffering, emptiness and selflessness. This is called "the absorption of incipient, approximating conduct." Then, through developing the power of meditation and the power of accumulating merit, you will have an experience of form as being hollow and so forth. You will realize that the five aggregates are like an illusion and will gradually achieve a clear apprehension of the selflessness of phenomena. This is called, "the absorption that thoroughly distinguishes the meaning."

Beginning with the path of seeing and up through the ten bodhisattva levels, the wisdom that directly realizes freedom from elaborations is born. This is called "the absorption that focuses on suchness." From the first to the seventh bodhisattva level, the bodhisattva has only a partial grasp of "the virtuous absorption of a Tathāgata[134]." On the eighth, ninth and tenth levels, there is the lesser, average and greater [version of this meditation]. At the level of perfect buddhahood, there is "the ultimate virtuous absorption of a Tatāgatha." The fourth absorption is the emerging wisdom that directly realizes the essence. For an extensive explanation, you should look elsewhere. These four absorptions are not found in the writings previously referred to in this text: the explanation here is based on material found in the sutras.

At first, until you grasp the essential point of the path, there will be some degree of challenge in your practice. Therefore, it is important that you give up all other activities and apply yourself assiduously and exclusively to the practice of meditation. After a time, although you need to work on increasing your effort, the practice will become easier. At that time, broaden your activities: accumulate merit in a variety of ways and make a variety of aspiration prayers. By training your mind in this way, the wisdom of the path of juncture will arise. By its own impetus, this wisdom will develop and become easy to engage with. At this stage, there is a great deal of subtle negative karma to abandon, of hindrances to be dispelled and of enhancement to be refined. Then, gradually, the wisdom that directly realizes the true nature of all phenomena will arise. You will then experience only happiness upon happiness.

The buddhahood of the fruition is described as follows. The essence body[135] is the uncomplicated wisdom of natural luminosity. The enjoyment body[136] is the one who turns the ultimate wheel of truth to the pure retinue in the Highest Heaven. The emanation body[137] is the one who accomplishes the benefit of beings in impure realms by disciplining them in appropriate ways. By way of wisdom, love and power, the enlightened activity [of these bodies] benefits all sentient beings according to their propensities and establishes them in unsurpassable bliss.

The information above does not necessarily constitute a session—explain it in whatever way seems appropriate for the student. This completes the commentary called "Entering into the Buddha's Teaching."[138]}

APPENDIX

This section will explain the rituals for engendering awakening mind as the fruition of practice and taking the bodhisattva vow. This section has two parts: The Ceremony of Engendering Awakening Mind and the Ceremony of Taking the Bodhisattva Vow.

1. The Ceremony of Engendering Awakening Mind

Arrange a support[139] *and offerings. Offer a mandala.*[140] *Then repeat after the lama three times:*

> Buddhas and bodhisattvas abiding in the ten directions, please regard me. Master, please regard me. Just as the previous tathagatas, the conquerors, the completely perfect buddhas and the bodhisattvas abiding on the ten levels began by engendering the unsurpassable, completely perfect awakening mind, likewise I (your name) also—by the power of my master—pray to engender the unsurpassable, completely perfect awakening mind.

After repeating this passage three times, repeat it again three times, replacing the last part with

> I (your name), from this time forward until I arrive at the heart of enlightenment, take refuge in the best of human beings, the transcendent buddhas. I take refuge in the best of teachings, the teaching of peace that is free from attachment. I take refuge in the best of assemblies, the spiritual community of the noble bodhisattvas who are beyond regression.

The extended version requires adding a verse "please regard me" before each sentence of taking refuge. If you are doing a condensed version, what is written above is sufficient. At this point, accumulate merit by repeating three times the seven-branch prayer that comes from the *Aspiration Prayer for Excellent Conduct*[141].

Next comes the main part of the ceremony. The request to be regarded is as above. Then recite

> I (your name), in this lifetime and all other lifetimes, will engage in roots of virtue: the spirit of generosity, the spirit of moral discipline and the spirit of meditation. I will encourage others to engage in them and will rejoice in their engagement. By these roots of virtue, just as the previous completely perfect buddhas, the victorious conquerors and the great bodhisattvas who abide on the ten levels engendered the awakening mind, I (your name), from this time forward until I arrive at the heart of enlightenment, engender the attitude of great, completely perfect, unsurpassable enlightenment. May I guide those sentient beings who have not crossed over. May I liberate those who have not been liberated. May I shelter those who are oppressed. May those who have not transcended suffering completely transcend suffering.

Repeat this three times.

Teach from the previous explanations of the training in the aspiration of awakening mind, either in an expanded or an abbreviated version. An expanded explanation of the training and of the many benefits of awakening mind is available in sutras such as *The Sutra of the Seven Dharmas* requested by the noble Avalokiteshvara and the *Array of Stalks Sutra*[142]. You can recite these.

Finally, make whatever aspiration prayers are appropriate. For an abbreviated conclusion, recite "By this merit, may all beings…." And so forth. Again make offerings to the Three Jewels and offer gifts to the master. This is known as "The Ceremony of Engendering Awakening

Mind and Taking Refuge" and is the ceremony of aspiration of awakening mind.

> {Before the ceremony, it is not necessary to subject the disciple to assessment, and it is not necessary for the disciple to have initially taken one of the eight types of lay and monastic ordination[143] as a prerequisite. You can bestow the vow on anyone who has the inclination to take it. This lineage of engendering awakening mind, originating with Maitreya, yielded an alternate ceremony for engendering awakening mind renowned in India composed by the master, noble Asanga. It is included in a treatise called the *Bodhisattva Canon*[144] that is not the one in *Heap of Jewels*[145]. The intention of Asanga's text is in harmony with what is presented here. This presentation was based on what is clearly found in the ceremony of engendering awakening mind composed by Atisha.}

2. The Ceremony of Taking the Bodhisattva Vow

> {The basic training of a genuine bodhisattva is taught extensively in the Mahayana sutras: therefore, you should study many sutras. Alternately, it is excellent to study quotes from *Bodhisattva-būmi*[146] and *Letter to a Student*[147] because these are the essence of the entire Mahayana. At least listen to a reading transmission of a sutra such as the *Cloud of Jewels Sutra*[148] or the *Essence of Space Sutra.*[149] Meticulously maintaining the stages of the path instructions presented in this volume is like studying the heart of the Mahayana. However, there is no underestimating the value of studying the original words of a Mahayana sutra.}

To prepare for actually taking the Bodhisattva Vow, arrange offerings in front of the three supports[150]. Making three prostrations to the Master, join your palms and supplicate him three times:

> Master, I request to take the pure vow of the discipline of a bodhisattva from you. If no harm will come, pray turn your compassionate attention to me for a short while and bestow it.

If you have these words memorized, you can recite them alone. If not, you should recite them after the master or a friend.

Then the Master says: Noble child, listen! Do you wish to guide those sentient beings who have not crossed over? Do you wish to liberate those who have not been liberated? Do you wish to shelter those who are oppressed? Do you wish to completely bring to nirvana those who have not yet attained nirvana? Do you want to join the unbroken lineage of the buddha?

Disciple replies: That is my wish.

Master: You should rely on engendering awakening mind and should rely on the meditation deity. Do you wish to take this vow to compete with others?

Disciple: No.

Master: Are you taking the vow due to coercion by others?

Disciple: No.

Then make offerings while reciting the verses "The offerings generally…." And so forth. Offer praise and homage by reciting whatever verses are appropriate such as "Protector, endowed with great compassion…." And so forth. Then, with reverence for the Master, recite this supplication of request three times:

Disciple: Master, please bestow upon me without delay the pure vow of the discipline of a bodhisattva.

The Master replies [Disciple's name], noble child, are you a bodhisattva?

Disciple: I am.

Master: Do you make aspiration prayers towards enlightenment?

Disciple: I do.

Master: Noble child, listen! Do you wish to accept the foundations of training of all the bodhisattvas and the disciplines of all the bodhisattvas?

Disciple: I wish to accept them.

Then, for the main part of the ceremony,

The Master says: Venerable one, noble child, [disciple's name], will you receive from me—the bodhisattva [Master's name]—whatever preparation for training the past bodhisattvas have engaged in and whatever preparation for moral discipline they kept, whatever preparation for training the future bodhisattvas will engage in and whatever preparation for moral discipline they will keep, whatever preparation for training the present bodhisattvas are now making in the ten directions and whatever preparation for training in moral discipline they keep? Will you engage in whatever training all the bodhisattvas of the past have engaged in, whatever training the bodhisattvas of the future will engage in and whatever training the bodhisattvas of the present abiding in the ten directions now engage in as bases for bodhisattva training? Will you accept all the moral disciplines of bodhisattvas—the moral discipline of vows, the moral discipline that gathers virtuous attributes and the moral discipline that performs the benefit of beings? Will you receive these from me?

Disciple: I will completely receive them.

By repeating this exchange three times, the bodhisattva vow is awakened.

The Master now supplicates the buddhas and bodhisattvas to pay attention by reciting three times.

Noble child, bodhisattva [disciple's name] from me bodhisattva [master's name] perfectly received the pure vow of the discipline of a bodhisattva three times. This bodhisattva [disciple's name] perfectly accepted the vow of the discipline of a bodhisattva. I [Master's name] acted as a witness. Although the noble, supreme ones are hidden, all the phenomena comprising the world are not. Therefore, please pay attention to these commitments that are part of the phenomenal world.

It appears that the Master should stand while chanting this and scatter flowers in all directions.

In response, the student makes three prostrations to the Three Jewels and the Master and again sits down.

The Master says: Now that you have taken the bodhisattva vow, all the buddhas and bodhisattvas think of you as their child and brother or sister. They will always protect and take care of you. They will cause your accumulations of merit and wisdom to increase. This act of taking of the bodhisattva vow should not be spoken of and should be kept secret from those who lack faith. From now on, always abandon the four or eight downfalls, the 46 faults and so forth. Become skilled in the methods of guarding the discipline of a bodhisattva, in knowing how to weigh the severity of transgressions and knowing how to maneuver within the disciplines.

{If you wish to do an expanded version of the Vow Ceremony, you can speak generally here about the training [of a bodhisattva]. Usually, in this tradition of taking the bodhisattva vow, a full explanation of the trainings is given first and is followed by taking the vow. Therefore, if you do not explain the trainings within the ceremony, you will not commit the fault of denigrating it.}

Finally, offer gifts and dedicate the virtue to enlightenment. This completes the Ceremony of the Bodhisattva Vow.

CONCLUSION

{This concludes "The Stages of the Path for Entering into the Buddha's Teaching", also known as "The Practices and Results that Comprise the Instructions for the Three Types of Person Together with the Practice of Engendering Awakening Mind." Any person who wants to practice Buddhism, even if he or she is only interested in the sutra tradition, will find all the practices of the sutras contained here. These days, practitioners of the sutra tradition rely on no other texts (are insistent on keeping their lineage unadulterated). This very Dharma has the blessing of the sutra transmission and contains the main practices they need to undertake. If those who are interested in tantra do not start with these practices, there is a danger that their practice of secret mantra will become distorted. Therefore, anyone who wishes to fulfill the intention of all the buddhas and their progeny should train in these contemplations.}

Kadampa Lineage Prayer

Lord of compassion, the Arhat Buddha,
Holy regents the bodhisattvas, intractable protectors,
Master of all Dharma, Venerable Asanga,
The second omniscient one, Bodhisattva Vasubandhu,
I prostrate to you and supplicate.
From mChog sde up until King Serlingpa[151]
The supreme Lamas of the vast lineage of conduct;
The bodhisattva Manjushri, Noble Nagarjuna and so forth—
The supreme lineages of the profound view;
The secret master yogini, glorious Tilli and so forth—
The supreme lineages of practice blessing;
To these I supplicate respectfully—please bless me.
The one with a mind that is like a wish-fulfilling jewel—
Atisha,

The origin of the victors, Dromton Rinpoche[152],
The complete expansion of the mandala of knowledge, Potowa,
The one who mastered an ocean of textual traditions, Sharawa,[153]
The one who behaved in accord with the Dharma renowned as Tumton Lodro,[154]
The life-tree of the Kadampa teachings, Dotonpa (also known as Sherab Drak),[155]
Palden Dro who blazes with the splendor of wisdom (also known as Dutsi Drak),[156]
Protector Kyoton Senge, whose three trainings were pure,[157]
Crown ornament of the nine great ones, renowned as Chimchen Namka,[158]
Master of power and efficacy, Venerable Monlam Tsultrim,[159]
One who accomplishes limitless benefit for beings, Zeu Drakpa, also called Tsondru,[160]
Master of an ocean of manifest dharmas, Losang Chim,[161]
Droton Kungyalwa,[162] possessed of a pure mind,
Master Sherab Pangton,[163] Lord of Dharma,
Holy, supreme intellect, Sonam Chokdrup,[164]
Holder of the tradition of the profound meaning, Venerable Palden Dondrup,[165]
Heart-son, the arhat Sonam Drak,[166]
One who possesses bodhicitta, Venerable Kunga Chokdrup,[167]
Hero who accomplished Maitreya, Lord Drolchok,[168]
Seer of the meaning of the unborn, Venerable Lungrik Gyatso,[169]
To all these root and lineage lamas,
I supplicate and request your blessing.
Moreover, to the ones who follow the source of the Buddhas,
The ones who possess the eyes that blaze with morality and wisdom,
Jayulwa,[170] the one blessed by the holy lamas,
Tsangba Rinpoche,[171] the one who actualizes the natural state,
Mumenpa[172] who mastered an ocean of instructions,
After them, from the five great disciples[173] to Khenchen Sonam Chok Drup,[174]
I supplicate and request your blessing.
The one who has supreme qualities, Khenchen Kungyalwa,[175]
One who has perfect knowledge, Yeshe Rinchen,[176]

The one who practiced one-pointedly through diligence,
Lhachungwa,[177]
To my root Lama named Jampa,[178]
I supplicate and request your blessing.

You can supplement these verses as appropriate since there are many lineages that carry these teachings. You can add verses for your specific textual and instructional transmission lineages, using the format laid out in the prayer above. Then, supplicate as follows:

Pure faith: the path of the lesser person,
Pure renunciation: the path of the average person,
Pure excellent attitude: the path of the greater person,
May I attain the three pure paths.
If awareness of impermanence and death are not born in my continuum,
However much I try, it will just augment my worldly tendencies.
Bless me that I may be freed from the bonds of the eight worldly preoccupations
That cause my mind to stray from religion once it has turned there.
If trust in the infallibility of action and result does not awaken,
All religious activities are lost in a state of the pretense of good.
Even if you try to make up for it with earnest practice, it will pass as something else.
Bless me so that trust in truth awakens.
If love and compassion do not awaken in my continuum,
Even if I exert myself in practice, it will be consigned to the lower vehicle.
Carrying the suffering of all beings as my burden,
Bless me so that I may train in supreme awakening mind.
If I do not realize emptiness where all complications are liberated,
I will not apprehend all phenomena as being like an illusion
And, lost to the power of clinging to attributes, my mind will not be liberated.
Bless me that I may realize the ultimate natural state.

{In writing this Dharma text, I consulted the explanations contained in *Lamp on the Path to Enlightenment*, *Commentary on the Two Truths*[179] and *Special Instructions on the Middle Way*[180]. I also studied Mumenpa's commentary, the graduated teachings of

Bumpawa and Potawa's religious root commentary with the supreme scholar Jampa Lhundrup. From the great scholar Lungrik Gyatso, I received the reading transmission, extensive explanation and experiential clarification of Potowa's root commentary *Annals*, Narthanpa's[181] root commentary *The Supreme Path*[182] and Chim's[183] commentary *Daily Teachings*[184]. Although I have studied a number of other texts, the ones mentioned above are the mains ones consulted in the composing of this book.}

Through whatever merit is generated by this mere summary of
The intention of all the Buddhas and their progeny,
May all sentient beings without exception
Swiftly attain the level of the Omniscient Buddha.

Essence of Ambrosia: The Commentary on the Instructions for the Three Types of Person was definitely composed by Taranatha, "the wanderer."[185] The format of this text, as a series of foci for meditations that explain the way that the meaning should be understood by the intellect of the practitioner, is based on the works of previous holy ones. Through this composition, may the precious teachings spread and remain for a long time.

༄༅། རྒྱལ་བའི་བསྟན་པ་ལ་འཇུག་པའི་རིམ་པ་སྐྱེས་བུ་གསུམ་གྱི་མན་ངག་གི་ཁྲིད་ཡིག་བདུད་རྩིའི་ཉིང་ཁུ་ཞེས་བྱ་བ་བཞུགས།

༄༅། །ན་མོ་བུདྡྷ་བོ་དྷི་ས་ཏྭ་བྷྱཿ། རྒྱལ་བའི་བསྟན་པ་ལ་འཇུག་པའི་རིམ་པ་སྐྱེས་བུ་གསུམ་གྱི་མན་ངག་གི་ཁྲིད་ཡིག་བདུད་རྩིའི་ཉིང་ཁུ་ཞེས་བྱ་བ། དཀོན་མཆོག་གསུམ་ལ་ཕྱག་འཚལ་ལོ། །ཡོན་ཏན་དུ་མའི་ནོར་གྱིས་བརྗིད་པ་ཡི། །བརྒྱུད་པ་གསུམ་གྱི་བླ་མ་ལ་བཏུད་ནས། །མར་མེ་མཛད་དཔལ་བཞེད་གཞུང་སྙིང་པོའི་དོན། །ཤིང་རྟ་ཆེན་པོའི་ལམ་མཆོག་འདིར་བཤད་བྱ། །དེ་ལ་འདིར་དུས་གསུམ་དུ་བྱུང་བའི་སངས་རྒྱས་དང་བྱང་ཆུབ་སེམས་དཔའ་དང་རང་རྒྱལ་དང་ཉན་ཐོས་སུ་བཅས་པ་ཐེག་པ་གསུམ་གྱི་འཕགས་པ་ཐམས་ཅད་ལམ་འདི་ཉིད་བསྒོམས་ཏེ། ཐར་པ་དང་ཐམས་ཅད་མཁྱེན་པའི་གོ་འཕང་མཆོག་བརྙེས་པ་ལགས་ཏེ། ཆོས་ཚུལ་འདི་ལ་བསྟན་པ་ལ་འཇུག་པའི་རིམ་པ་ཞེས་ཀྱང་བྱ། སྐྱེས་བུ་གསུམ་གྱི་ལམ་རིམ་ཞེས་ཀྱང་བྱ། བྱང་ཆུབ་ལམ་གྱི་རིམ་པ་ཞེས་ཀྱང་བྱ། ཤིང་རྟ་ཆེན་པོའི་འཇུག་ངོགས་ཅེས་ཀྱང་བྱ་སྟེ། ཆོས་འདི་སྟོན་པར་བྱེད་པ་ལ། ལམ་ཐམས་ཅད་ཀྱི་རྩ་བ་དགེ་བའི་བཤེས་གཉེན་བསྟེན་པ་དང་། ལམ་རིམ་དངོས་སྐྱེས་བུ་གསུམ་གྱི་བསམ་པ་ལ་བསླབ་པ་དང་། དེ་ལས་འབྲས་བུ་བླ་ན་མེད་པའི་བྱང་ཆུབ་ལ་སྦྱོར་ཚུལ་ཏེ་གསུམ་མོ། །དང་པོ་ནི། དགེ་བའི་བཤེས་གཉེན་གྱི་མཚན་ཉིད་དང་དེ་ལ་གུས་པ་བསྟེན་ཚུལ་ཁོང་དུ་ཆུད་པར་བྱས་ནས། མཉམ་གཞག་ཐུན་གྱི་སྐབས་སུ་འདི་ལྟར་བྱ་སྟེ། ཀྱང་པ་སྐྱིལ་ཀྲུང་བཅའ་ལུས་དྲང་པོ་བསྲང་བ་སོགས་སྤྱོད་ལམ་རགས་པ་གཙང་སང་ངེ་བ་བྱས་

ནས། སངས་རྒྱས་བྱང་ཆུབ་སེམས་དཔའ་མཁའ་དབྱིངས་གང་བ་ལ་དམིགས། ཕྱག་འཚལ་དང་མཆོད་པ་རྒྱས་བསྡུས་ཇི་ལྟར་རིགས་པ་ཅིག་ཡན་ལག་བདུན་པ་ལས་ཡོགས་སུ་བྱེད་དགོས་པས། ཐོག་མར་ཕྱག་མཆོད་སྔོན་དུ་བཏང་། དེ་རྗེས་བཟང་སྤྱོད་ནས་འབྱུང་བའི་ཡན་ལག་བདུན་པ་དེ་དོན་དྲན་བཞིན་པས་ཚར་གསུམ་བརྗོད། དེ་ནས་མདུན་གྱི་ནམ་མཁའ་ལ་ཆེས་མཐོ་བའི་སྟེང་གི་ཕྱོགས་སུ་སངས་རྒྱས་བྱང་ཆུབ་སེམས་དཔའ་དཔག་ཏུ་མེད་པ་བཞུགས། མདུན་དྲང་ཐད་ཀྱི་ནམ་མཁར་རྩ་བའི་བླ་མ་ལ་བརྒྱུད་པའི་བླ་མའི་ཚོགས་ཐམས་ཅད་ཀྱིས་བསྐོར་བ་ཐིབས་སེ་བཞུགས་པར་བསམས་ལ། ཕྱོགས་བཅུ་ན་བཞུགས་པའི་སངས་རྒྱས་དང་བྱང་ཆུབ་སེམས་དཔའ་ཐམས་ཅད་དང་། བླ་མ་ཡང་དག་པ་ཡོངས་ཀྱི་དགེ་བའི་བཤེས་གཉེན་ཆེན་པོ་བདག་ལ་དགོངས་སུ་གསོལ། བདག་ལ་བྱིན་གྱིས་བརླབ་ཏུ་གསོལ། བདག་ལ་ཕྱིན་ཅི་ལོག་གི་དྲི་མ་ཐམས་ཅད་ཉེ་བར་ཞི་བར་མཛད་དུ་གསོལ། ཕྱིན་ཅི་མ་ལོག་པའི་རྟོགས་པ་ཐམས་ཅད་སྐྱེད་པར་མཛད་དུ་གསོལ། ཐེག་པ་ཆེན་པོའི་ཆོས་བསྒྲུབ་པ་ལ་བར་ཆད་ཐམས་ཅད་སེལ་བར་མཛད་དུ་གསོལ། ཅེས་གསོལ་བ་དྲག་ཏུ་གདབ་པོ། །མཐར་ཡང་ཡིད་ཀྱིས་སྤྲུལ་པའི་མཆོད་པ་ཅིག་ཕུལ་ལ། །རྩ་བརྒྱུད་ཀྱི་བླ་མ་རྣམས་རང་གི་སྤྱི་བོ་ནས་ཞུགས་ཏེ་སྙིང་འོད་ཀྱི་གུར་ཁང་དུ་བཞུགས། སངས་རྒྱས་དང་བྱང་ཆུབ་སེམས་དཔའ་རྣམས་དེ་ཉིད་དུ་མི་སྣང་བར་མོས། བདག་གི་དགེ་བའི་རྩ་བ་འདིས་སེམས་ཅན་ཐམས་ཅད་ཀྱི་དོན་དུ་སངས་རྒྱས་ཀྱི་གོ་འཕང་ཐོབ་པར་གྱུར་ཅིག། ཅེས་པ་དང་། དགེ་བ་འདི་ཡིས་སྐྱེ་བོ་ཀུན། །བསོད་ནམས་ཡེ་ཤེས་ཚོགས་རྫོགས་ཤིང་། །བསོད་ནམས་ཡེ་ཤེས་ལས་བྱུང་བའི། །དམ་པ་གཉིས་པོ་ཐོབ་པར་ཤོག །ཅེས་པ་ལྟ་བུས་དགེ་བ་བསྔོ། ཐུན་མཚམས་སུ་ཡང་བླ་མའི་སྐྱོན་ལ་མི་བརྟག །ཡོན་ཏན་ཁོ་ན་དྲན་པར་བྱ། བདག་ལ་སངས་རྒྱས་དངོས་སུ་མཐོང་བའི་སྐལ་བ་ནི་མེད། དུས་གསུམ་དུ་བཞུགས་པའི་སངས་རྒྱས་རྣམས་ཀྱི་ཐུགས་རྗེའི་རྣམ་འཕྲུལ་དགེ་བའི་བཤེས་གཉེན་གྱི་ཚུལ་

དུ་བསྟན་པ་ཡིན་པས། བདག་གི་བླ་མ་འདི་དོན་ལ་ནི་སངས་རྒྱས་དངོས་ཡིན། བདག་ལ་བཀའ་དྲིན་གྱི་སྒོ་ནས་ནི་སངས་རྒྱས་ཀུན་པས་ཀྱང་ཆེས་ལྷག མཐོ་རིས་ཐར་པ་སངས་རྒྱས་གསུམ་གང་འདོད་ཀྱང་ཐབས་གང་དགོས་བདག་ལ་མ་སྨྲས་པར་གནང་བ་ཡིན། བདག་གི་རྒྱུད་ལ་ཡོན་ཏན་སྐད་ཅིག་སྐྱེས་པ་དང་། སྐྱོན་སྐད་ཅིག་བྲི་བ་ཡང་བླ་མའི་བཀའ་དྲིན་ཡིན། ཤིན་དུ་རྙེད་པར་དཀའ་བའི་ཆོས་ཟབ་མོ་འདི་ལྟ་བུ་ཐོབ། བཀའ་དྲིན་རེ་ཆེ་སྙམ་དུ་བསམ། གཞན་ཡང་བདག་གི་ལུས་དང་ལོངས་སྤྱོད་ཐམས་ཅད་ཀྱང་བླ་མའི་ཕྱིར་དུ་གཏོང་དགོས། ལུས་ཀྱི་སྒོ་ནས་བླ་མའི་བཞེད་པ་དང་མཐུན་པའི་བཀུར་བསྟི་རིམ་གྲོ་འཕྲལ་གཡོག་གི་བྱ་བ་ཐམས་ཅད་ཀྱང་བསྒྲུབ་དགོས། ངག་གི་སྒོ་ནས་བླ་མའི་སྐུ་གསུང་ཐུགས་ཀྱི་ཡོན་ཏན་བསྔགས་པ་དང་། ཞབས་ཏོག་ཏུ་འགྱུར་བའི་གཏམ་ཁོ་ན་སྨྲ་དགོས། སྤྱོད་ལམ་གྱི་སྒོ་ནས་ཐུགས་གང་ལ་དགྱེས་པ་དང་། གསུང་ཅི་འབྱོན་པ་དེ་བསྒྲུབ་དགོས་སྙམ་དུ་ཡང་ཡང་བསམ་ཞིང་ལག་ལེན་དུ་ཐེབས་པར་བྱའོ། དེ་ལ་སྐབས་འདིར་གསོལ་འདེབས་ཀྱི་དོན་ནི། ཕྱིན་ཅི་ལོག་གི་དྲི་མ་ལྔ་སྟེ། ཚེ་འདི་ལ་མངོན་པར་ཞེན་པའི་དྲི་མ། ལས་རྒྱུ་འབྲས་ལ་ཡིད་མི་ཆེས་པའི་དྲི་མ། འཁོར་བ་ལ་བདེ་བར་འཛིན་པའི་དྲི་མ། རང་དོན་ལ་གཅེས་པར་འཛིན་པའི་དྲི་མ། དངོས་པོ་དང་མཚན་མ་ལ་ཡང་དག་ཏུ་འཛིན་པའི་དྲི་མའོ། །ཕྱིན་ཅི་མ་ལོག་པའི་རྟོགས་པ་ཡང་ལྔ་སྟེ། ཚེ་འདི་ལས་ཕྱི་མ་གལ་ཆེ་བར་རྟོགས་པ། ལས་འབྲས་ལ་ཡིད་ཆེས་པར་རྟོགས་པ། འཁོར་བ་སྡུག་བསྔལ་དུ་རྟོགས་པ། རང་དོན་པས་གཞན་དོན་གཅེས་པར་རྟོགས་པ། དོན་དམ་སྟོང་ཉིད་དང་ཀུན་རྫོབ་སྒྱུ་མར་རྟོགས་པའོ། ཆོས་སྒྲུབ་པའི་བར་ཆད་ལ། ཕྱི་མི་དང་མི་མ་ཡིན་གྱིས་གནོད་པ། བར་འབྱུང་བ་ལུས་འཁྲུགས་ཀྱི་ན་ཚ། ནང་ཆོས་འགལ་གྱི་རྣམ་རྟོག་ཉོན་མོངས་རྣམས་ཡིན་པས། དེ་གསུམ་སེལ་བར་མཛད་དུ་གསོལ་ཞེས་པའོ། དམིགས་སྐོར་གཅིག་གོ།

གཉིས་པ་ལམ་རིམ་དངོས་སྐྱེས་བུ་གསུམ་གྱི་བསམ་པ་ལ་བསླབ་པ་ལ། སྐྱེས་

བུ་ཆུང་ངུ་དང་ཐུན་མོང་གི་རིམ་པ་ལ་བསླབ་པ། སྐྱེས་བུ་འབྲིང་དང་ཐུན་མོང་གི་རིམ་པ་ལ་བསླབ་པ། སྐྱེས་བུ་ཆེན་པོའི་ཐུན་མོང་མ་ཡིན་པའི་རིམ་པ་ལ་བསླབ་པ་སྟེ་གསུམ་ལས། དང་པོ་ལ་སྤྱིར་སློབ་ཀ་སོ་སོ་ལ་འཁྲིད་ལུགས་མི་འདྲ་བ་དུ་མ་འདུག རྗེ་བཙུན་མར་མི་མཛད་དཔལ་གྱི་བཀའ་སློལ་གདམས་ངག་འདི་པ་རང་གི་ལུགས་ཀྱིས་ཀྱང་། འགའ་ཞིག་འཁོར་བའི་སྡུག་བསྔལ་བསམ་པ་ལ་འགོ་འཛིན། འགའ་ཞིག་ལས་འབྲས་ནས་འགོ་འཛིན། འགའ་ཞིག་དལ་འབྱོར་རྙེད་དཀའ་ནས་འགོ་འཛིན། ཕལ་ཆེར་འཆི་བ་མི་རྟག་པ་ནས་འགོ་འཛིན་པར་མཛད་པ་སོགས་སྣ་ཚོགས་ཡོད་ཀྱང་ཐམས་ཅད་གནད་གཅིག་ལ་འབབ། དོན་གྱི་སྟེང་ནས་ཁྱད་པར་མེད། འོན་ཀྱང་སྤྱི་ཁྱབ་གྲགས་ཆེ་བར་མཐུན་པར་དལ་འབྱོར་རྙེད་དཀའ་ནས་འགོ་བཟུང་ན། དེ་ཀ་མི་རྟག་པ་སྒོམ་པའི་གཞི་རྟེན་ཡིན་པས། མི་རྟག་པ་བསྒོམ་པའི་འགོ་འཛིན་པ་དང་། དོན་ལ་ཁྱད་ནམ་ཡང་མེད་པ་ལས་འཕྲུལ་འདི་དངོས་རྣམ་པ་བདེ་བར་སྣང་བས་དེའི་དབང་དུ་བྱས་ཏེ་བཤད་ན། འདི་ལ་དལ་འབྱོར་རྙེད་དཀའ་བསམ་པ། འཆི་བ་མི་རྟག་པ་བསམ་པ། ངན་སོང་གི་སྡུག་བསྔལ་བསམ་པ། ལས་རྒྱུ་འབྲས་བསམ་པ་སྟེ་བཞིའོ། དང་པོ་ནི། ཕྱག་མཆོད་ཡན་ལག་བདུན་པ་སྔར་བཞིན་བྱས། གོང་དུ་བཤད་པའི་གསོལ་འདེབས་དེ་ཡང་ཅུང་ཟད་བྱ་སྟེ། དེ་རྗེས་རང་གི་ལུས་དང་གནས་དང་ལོངས་སྤྱོད་དང་ཡུལ་ཕྱོགས་སོགས་ཐམས་ཅད་ལ་གཞིག་འགྲེལ་ཞིག་བཏང་སྟེ། བདག་གིས་ད་རེས་ཐོབ་པའི་མི་ལུས་འདི་འདྲ་བ་ལར་ནས་ཤིན་ཏུ་རྙེད་པར་དཀའ། འདི་དོན་མེད་དུ་མི་གཏོང་། ཆོས་ལ་འཁོལ་བ་ཅིག་བྱེད་དགོས་སྙམ་པ་དམིགས་པའི་གཞི་འདི་སྤྱི་ལྡོག་ནས་ཐམས་ཅད་ཀྱི་མགོར་སྦྱར་ནས་བསྒོམ་སྟེ། དེ་ལ་སྡོམས་ནི། དམྱལ་བ་ཡི་དྭགས་དུད་འགྲོ་དང་། །ཀླ་ཀློ་ཚེ་རིང་ལྷ་དང་ནི། །ལོག་ལྟ་ཅན་དང་སངས་རྒྱས་སྟོངས། །ལྐུགས་པ་འདི་དག་མི་ཁོམ་བརྒྱད། །ཅེས་པ་ལྟར་ལས། ངན་སོང་གསུམ་དུ་སྐྱེས་ན་ནི་སྡུག་བསྔལ་དོས་དྲག་པ་དང་། ལུས་དེ་ཆོས་ཀྱི་རྟེན་དུ་ཤིན་དུ་ངན་པས་ཆོས་

བྱེད་མི་ཁོམ། འདོད་ཁམས་ཀྱི་ལྷ་རྣམས་ཀྱང་འདོད་ཡོན་ལ་ཆགས་པས་གཡེངས། གཟུགས་ཁམས་དང་གཟུགས་མེད་ཀྱི་ལྷ་ཕལ་ཆེར་ཏིང་ངེ་འཛིན་གྱིས་མྱོས་པས་ཆོས་ཉན་པའི་སྐལ་བ་མེད། ལྷ་མ་ཡིན་ཡང་འདོད་ལྷ་དང་འདྲ་བ་ལས་ལྷག་པོར་ངན་སོང་བཞིན་དུ་ལུས་རྟེན་ངན། སངས་རྒྱས་མ་བྱོན་པའི་འཇིག་རྟེན་ཁམས་སུ་སྐྱེས་པའམ་སངས་རྒྱས་བྱོན་པའི་ཞིང་ཁམས་སུ་ཡང་ཆོས་དར་བའི་ས་ཆ་ནི་རྒྱ་ཆུང་། ཆོས་མེད་ས་ཆ་ཡུལ་ཕྱོགས་མཐའ་འཁོབ་ཀླ་ཀློར་སྐྱེས་པའམ། ཆོས་དར་བའི་ཡུལ་ཕྱོགས་སུ་སྐྱེས་ཀྱང་ལོག་ལྟ་ཅན་ཆོས་ལ་སྡང་བའམ། གླེན་ལྐུགས་སུ་གྱུར་ནས་བླང་དོར་གྱི་གནས་གང་ཡང་མི་གོ་བར་སོང་ན་ཆོས་བྱེད་པའི་སྐལ་བ་མི་འདུག་པ་ལས། བདག་གིས་ད་རེས་མི་ཁོམ་པ་བརྒྱད་ལས་ལོག་ནས་ཆོས་བྱེད་ནུས་སུ་རུང་བའི་ལུས་ཞིག་ཐོབ་འདུག་སྙམ་པ་དང་། སྨོས་ནི། མི་ཉིད་དབུས་སྐྱེས་དབང་པོ་ཚང་། །ལས་མཐའ་མ་ལོག་གནས་ལ་དད། །སངས་རྒྱས་བྱོན་དང་དེས་ཆོས་གསུངས། །བསྟན་པ་གནས་དང་དེ་རྗེས་འཇུག །གཞན་ཕྱིར་སྙིང་ནི་བརྩེ་བའོ། །ཅེས་པ་ལྟར་ཏེ། བདག་སྐྱེར་མི་ལུས་ཐོབ། དགོས་སུ་ཡུལ་དབུས་ཆོས་དར་བར་སྐྱེས། ཡང་དགོས་སུ་དབང་པོ་སྒོ་ལྔ་ཚང་བས་སྤང་བླང་ཤེས་སུ་རུང་། ཞེ་དགོས་སུ་ལྟ་བ་ལོག་པ་དང་མ་ཕྲད་ཙམ། འཚམས་མེད་ལྔ་བུ་ལོག་པར་ལྟ་བའི་ལས་ཀྱང་མ་བྱས་ཙམ། གནས་དམ་པའི་ཆོས་འདུལ་བ་ལ་དད་པ་སྐྱེར་རུང་བ་ཙམ་དུ་འདུག་པས་རང་གི་འབྱོར་བ་ལྔ་ཚང་འདུག །འཇིག་རྟེན་དུ་སངས་རྒྱས་ཀྱང་བྱོན་ཟིན། དམ་པའི་ཆོས་ཀྱང་གསུངས་ཟིན། བསྟན་པ་ཡང་མ་ནུབ་པར་གནས། ཆོས་ལ་གསར་དུ་འཇུག་པ་ཡང་མང་བའི་སྐབས་སུ་ཡོད། ཆོས་བྱེད་རྣམས་ལ་གཞན་གྱིས་སྙིང་བརྩེ་བའི་སྒོ་ནས། ཟས་གོས་ཡོ་བྱད་སོགས་ཀྱང་སྦྱིར་བ་པོ་མང་པོ་སྣང་བས་ཆོས་མཐུན་གྱི་འཚོ་བ་འབྱོར་དུ་རུང་བའི་སྐབས་སུ་འདུག་པས་གཞན་འབྱོར་ལྔ་པོ་ཡང་བདག་ལ་ཚང་། དེ་ལྟར་ན་མི་ཁོམ་པ་བརྒྱད་ལས་ལོག །འབྱོར་པ་བཅུ་ཚང་བའི་ལུས་འདི་ལྟ་བུ་ཤིན་དུ་རྙེད་དཀའ། སྐབས་འདིར་

ཆོས་ལ་འབད་དགོས་པར་འདུག་སྙམ་པ་རྒྱུ་མཚན་དྲན་པའི་སྒོ་ནས་ཡང་ཡང་བསམ། རྗེས་ཐུན་མཚམས་ལ་འཇུག་ན་གོང་བཞིན་དགེ་བ་བྱང་ཆུབ་ཏུ་བསྔོ། དམིགས་སྐོར་གཉིས་པའོ།

ཡང་སྟོན་འགྲོ་དང་རྗེས་སྔ་མ་བཞིན་ལས་སེམས་ཅན་རྣམས་ཀྱི་ནང་ན་ངན་སོང་གི་འགྲོ་བ་ནི་ཤིན་དུ་མང་། དཔེར་ན། ས་ཆེན་པོའི་རྡུལ་ཙམ་ཡིན། མཐོ་རིས་ཀྱི་འགྲོ་བ་ནི་ཤིན་དུ་ཉུང་། དཔེར་ན་སེན་མོའི་སྟེང་གི་རྡུལ་ཙམ་ཡིན། ཡང་དམྱལ་བ་ནི། ས་གཞི་ཆེན་པོའི་རྡུལ་ཕྲན་ཙམ། ཡི་དྭགས་ནི་ཁ་བ་བུ་ཡུག་འཚུབས་པ་ཙམ། དུད་འགྲོ་བྱིངས་ནི་རྒྱ་མཚོ་ཆེན་པོ་ལ་ཆང་གར་མའི་སྦང་མ་ཙམ། དུད་འགྲོ་ཁ་འཐོར་བ་ནི། ས་གཞི་རི་གླུང་བར་སྣང་ཐམས་ཅད་ཁེངས་པ་ཙམ། ལྷ་དང་མིའི་འགྲོ་བ་ནི། དེ་རྣམས་ལ་ལྟོས་ན་སྲིད་མཐའ་ཙམ་ཡིན་པར་འདུག །དེ་ལས་ཀྱང་སྤྱིར་མིའི་འགྲོ་བ་ཉུང་། དགོས་སུ་འཛམ་བུ་གླིང་པའི་མི་ཉུང་། ཡང་དགོས་སུ་ཆོས་བྱེད་པའི་མི་ལུས་ནི་སྲིད་མཐའ་ཙམ་དུ་འདུག་སྟེ། ད་རེས་ཅིས་ཀྱང་ཆོས་ལ་འབད་དགོས་སྙམ་པ་དང་། དེ་ལྟར་འབྱུང་བའི་རྒྱུ་མཚན་ཡང་སེམས་ཅན་གྱི་ནང་ན་སྡིག་པའི་ལས་བྱེད་པ་ནི་ཆེས་མང་སྟེ་མཐའ་མེད། དགེ་བའི་ལས་བྱེད་པ་ནི་སྤྱི་ཙམ་ནས་ཀྱང་ཤིན་དུ་ཉུང་། དགེ་བའི་ནང་ནས་ཀྱང་མི་ལུས་འཕེན་ཐུབ་པའི་ཚུལ་ཁྲིམས་སྲུང་བ་ནི་ཆེས་ཤིན་དུ་དཀོན་པས། དེའི་ཕྱིར་མི་ལུས་རྙེད་དཀའ་བ་ཡིན། དེའི་སྟེང་དུ་ཡང་འབྱོར་པ་བཅུ་ཚང་ཞིང་ཆོས་དང་མཇལ་བ་ལ་བསོད་ནམས་མང་པོ་གསོག་དགོས་པས་འདི་འདྲ་ཤིན་དུ་རྙེད་དཀའ་བ་ཡིན་ཡང་སྟོན་སྐྱེས་དབང་གིས་དགེ་བ་ཆེ་རབ་ཅིག་ལན་གཅིག་བསགས་ཡོད་འདུག་པས་ད་རེས་དལ་འབྱོར་གྱི་ལུས་འདི་ཐོབ་འདུག། སྐབས་འདིར་ཆོས་ལ་འབད་པར་བྱ་སྙམ་དུ་བསྒོམ། དམིགས་སྐོར་གསུམ་པའོ།

འདིར་ཁ་ཅིག་དཔེའི་སྒོ་ནས་རྙེད་དཀའ་བ་ཞེས་ཟེར་ཞིང་དེ་ལྟར་གྲགས་པ་ནི། དཀོན་པའི་དཔེ་བསྟན་པ་ཙམ་ཡིན་པས་དམིགས་སྐོར་ལོགས་པ་མི་དགོས་སོ། ཡང་སྟོན་འགྲོ་དང་རྗེས་སྔར་ལྟར་ལས་གོང་དུ་བཤད་པའི་རྒྱུ་མཚན་རྣམས་དྲན་པར་བྱས་ནས། དེ་

ལྟར་ཤིན་ཏུ་རྙེད་དཀའ་བའི་མི་ལུས་འདི་ལན་ཅིག་ཐོབ་པའི་སྐབས་འདིར་དོན་ཆེན་པོ་ཞིག་སྒྲུབ་དགོས་པར་འདུག །སྐྱེ་བ་ནས་སྐྱེ་བར་འཁོར་བའི་བདེ་བ་ཕུན་སུམ་ཚོགས་པ་འདོད་ན་ཡང་མི་ལུས་འདི་ལ་བརྟེན་ནས་འབད་མེད་དུ་སྒྲུབ་ནུས། འཁོར་བ་ལས་ཐར་བའི་ཉན་རང་གི་བྱང་ཆུབ་སྒྲུབ་ན་ཡང་ད་རེས་དཀའ་ཚེགས་ཙམ་མེད། བླ་ན་མེད་པའི་བྱང་ཆུབ་སྒྲུབ་པར་འདོད་ཀྱང་ད་རེས་ཀྱི་སྐབས་འདིར་བྱེད་བླ་བ་སྒྲུབ་བླ་བ་ཡིན་ལ། མི་ལུས་འདི་འདྲ་བ་ཞིག་མ་ཐོབ་ན། ཐར་པ་དང་སངས་རྒྱས་ལྟ་ཅི་སྨོས། འཁོར་བའི་བདེ་སྐྱིད་ཕུན་སུམ་ཚོགས་པ་གཅིག་ཀྱང་སྒྲུབ་མི་ཤེས་པས་ད་རེས་རང་མི་ལུས་ལ་སྙིང་པོ་ལེན་དགོས་སྙམ་དུ་བསྒོམ། དེ་བཞིན་དུ་གལ་ཏེ་མི་ལུས་ལེན་ཅིག་ཐོབ་པ་འདི་དོན་མེད་དུ་སོང་ན་ཤིན་ཏུ་གོད་ཀ་ཆེ་སྟེ། ཇི་སྐད་དུ། སྤྱོད་འཇུག་ལས། འདི་འདྲའི་དལ་བ་རྙེད་ནས་ནི། །བདག་གིས་དགེ་གོམས་མ་བྱས་ན། །འདི་ལས་བསླུས་པ་གཞན་མེད་དེ། །འདི་ལས་རྨོངས་པའང་གཞན་མེད་དོ། །ཞེས་གསུངས་པ་ལྟར་རང་གིས་རང་ཉིད་ལ་བསླུས་ཚབས་ཆེ། རིན་པོ་ཆེའི་གླིང་དུ་ཕྱིན་ནས་སྟོང་ལོག་བྱས་པ་དང་འདྲ། འདོད་དོན་ཁྱད་པར་ཅན་གང་བསྒྲུབས་ཀྱང་འགྲུབ་ཏུ་རུང་བའི་རྟེན་ཁྱད་པར་ཅན་ལན་ཅིག་ཐོབ་པ་ལ་བྱ་བ་གང་ཡང་མ་བྱས་པར་དོན་མེད་དུ་ཐལ་འགྲོ་བ་འདི་རང་སྐྱོན་ཆེ་བར་འདུག །སྔར་དེ་ཙམ་ཞིག་དོན་མེད་དུ་སོང་། ད་ནི་ཉི་མ་དེ་རིང་ནས་བཙམས་ཏེ་དོན་མེད་དུ་མ་ལུས་པར་ཆོས་ལ་འབད་དགོས་སྙམ་དུ་ཡང་ཡང་བསམ་པའོ། ཡང་ཚེ་འདིའི་བདེ་སྐྱིད་དང་བྱ་བྱེད་རྣམས་བློས་མི་ཐོངས་སྙམ་ན། འཇིག་རྟེན་ན་ཡང་ཕྱུགས་སྐྱིད་ཡུན་རིང་བ་ཅིག་ཡོད་ན། འཕྲུལ་ཞག་འགའ་ཟླ་ཤས་སོས་དལ་བའི་བདེ་བ་ལ་མི་ལྟ་བར་ཕྱུགས་ཀྱི་བདེ་སྒྲུབ་པ་ལ་འབད་རྩོལ་བྱེད་དགོས་པ་ལྟར་སྐྱེ་བ་གཏན་གྱི་བདེ་སྐྱིད་སྒྲུབ་པའི་ཕྱིར་ཚེ་འདིའི་བྱ་བ་ལ་མ་ཆགས་པར་ཆོས་ཀྱི་བྱ་བ་ལ་འབད་དགོས་སྙམ་དུ་བསམ་པའོ། དེ་དག་གིས་ནི། དལ་འབྱོར་འདི་ནི་རྙེད་པ་ཤིན་ཏུ་དཀའ། །སྐྱེས་བུའི་དོན་སྒྲུབ་ཐོབ་པར་གྱུར་པ་ལ། །གལ་ཏེ་འདི་ལ་ཕན་པ་མ་བསྒྲུབས་ན། །ཕྱིས་འདི་ཡང་

དག་འགྱོར་པར་ག་ལ་འགྱུར། །ཅེས་པ་ལྟར་མི་ལུས་རྙེད་དཀའ་ཞིང་རྙེད་པ་དོན་དང་ལྡན་པར་བསམ་པ་ཡིན་ཏེ། དམིགས་སྐོར་བཞི་པའོ།།

གཉིས་པ་འཆི་བ་མི་རྟག་པ་བསམ་པ་ལ་གསུམ་གྱི་དང་པོ། ངེས་པར་མྱུར་དུ་འཆི་བ་བསམ་པ་ནི། མདོ་ལས། བྱུང་དང་འབྱུང་བར་གྱུར་པ་ཇི་སྙེད་པ། །ཀུན་ཀྱིས་ལུས་འདི་བཏང་ནས་འགྲོ་བ་དང་། །དེ་ཀུན་འཇིག་པར་མཁས་པས་རྟོགས་བགྱི་སྟེ། །ཆོས་ལ་གནས་བགྱི་ངེས་པར་སྤྱད་པ་སྤྱོད། །ཅེས་གསུངས་པ་ལྟར། གནས་གང་དུ་གནས་ཀྱང་འཆི་བ་ལས་མ་འདས། གྲོགས་སུ་དང་འགྲོགས་ཀྱང་འཆི་བ་ལས་མ་འདས། ས་སྟེང་གི་འགྲོ་བ་སྔར་བྱུང་བ་ཐམས་ཅད་ཀྱང་ཤི། ད་གཟོད་འབྱུང་འགྱུར་ཐམས་ཅད་ཀྱང་འཆི། ད་ལྟ་དངོས་སུ་ཡོད་པ་འདི་ཐམས་ཅད་ཀྱང་འཆི་བ་ལས་གྲོལ་བ་སུ་ཡང་མེད། རང་རེ་བཙས་ནས་ཉི་མ་དེ་རིང་ཡན་ཆད་དུ་རང་དང་ཉེ་བ་ཡང་ཇི་ཙམ་ཞིག་ཤི། བར་མ་དང་དགྲ་ཡང་ཇི་ཙམ་ཞིག་ཤི། དེ་རྣམས་ཤི་སྐྱ་བདག་ལ་སྡོད་པའི་གདེང་ཡོད་པའང་མིན། སྤྱིར་འཆི་བ་ལས་འོས་མི་འདུག དགོས་སུ་ཚེ་ལ་སྣོན་ཁ་རྒྱག་མཁན་ནི་མེད། དུས་སྐད་ཅིག་ཀྱང་སྡོད་པ་མེད་པར་ཚེའི་སྟེང་ནས་འབྲིད་པ་ཡིན་པས་སྐད་ཅིག་རེ་རེ་སོང་ནས་འཆི་བ་ལ་ཇེ་ཉེ། ཞག་རེ་ཞག་རེ་སོང་ནས་དེ་བས་ཉེ་རུ་སོང་། ཟླ་བ་རེ་རེ་སོང་གིན་ལྷག་པར་ཉེ་རུ་སོང་། ལོ་གཅིག་གཅིག་སོང་གིན་ལྷག་པར་ཉེ་རུ་སོང་། དེ་བས་ན་མྱུར་དུ་འཆི་བ་ཡིན། བདག་ཆོས་ཉམས་སུ་ལེན་དགོས་ན། ད་རུང་རྒས་པ་ལ་ནི་མ་ཐུག་རིམ་པས་བྱས་པས་ཆོག་སྙམ་ན། ཚེ་ཐུང་འདི་ལ་དེ་འདྲའི་ལོང་ཡོད་བྱེད་མི་ཉན་པར་འདུག། དཔེར་ན་ལོ་དྲུག་ཅུ་ལ་གཞོན་པའི་དུས་སུ་ནི་ཆོས་མ་བྱུང་བར་ཡར་འདས། རྒས་ནས་ནི་ཆོས་བྱེད་བློ་བྱས་ཀྱང་ལུས་སེམས་ཀྱི་སྟོབས་ཟད་པས་བོགས་སྐྱེད་མི་འབྱུང་། དེའི་ལྷག་མའི་ཕྱེད་ནི་གཉིད་ཀྱིས་འདས། གཞན་ཡང་ལྟོ་རྒྱབ་ཀྱི་ཕྱིར་དང་། འགྲོ་འདུག་དང་གཡེང་བ་སོགས་དོན་མེད་སྣ་ཚོགས་ཀྱི་དབང་དུ་འགྲོ་བས་འདུན་པ་དང་བརྩོན་འགྲུས་ཆེ་བ་ཅིག་

གི་དབང་དུ་བྱས་ཀྱང་ཆོས་རང་ཉམས་ལེན་བྱས་པའི་ཚོད་ལ་ཡུན་རིང་མི་ཡོང་བ་འདུག །དམ་པ་རྣམས་ཀྱིས་དུས་ཇི་སྲིད་ཅིག་འབད་པ་བྱས་ཏེ་རྟོགས་པའི་ཆོས་དེ་བདག་གིས་མྱུར་དུ་རྟོགས་དགོས་ན། ཚེ་ཐུང་འདི་ལ་ཆོས་ལ་ཕྱི་འགྱངས་དང་། ལེ་ལོ་དང་བར་སྐབས་སུ་བཤོལ་བའི་ཐབས་ཡེ་མི་འདུག་སྙམ་དུ་བསམ་དགོས། དེ་ལྟར་རྒྱུ་མཚན་བསམས་ནས་ཡང་ཡང་སྒོམ་པ་གལ་ཆེ། དམིགས་སྐོར་ལྔ་པའོ།།

དོན་ཚན་གཉིས་པ་ནམ་འཆི་ཆ་མེད་བསམ་པ་ནི། འོ་ཀོལ་རྣམས་སྤྱི་ཙམ་དུ་ཚེ་ཐུང་བར་མ་ཟད་ནམ་འཆི་ཆ་མེད་པ་ཡིན། གལ་ཏེ་སྐྱེས་དབང་ལེགས་ན་སྔོན་གྱི་ལས་ཀྱིས་འཕངས་པའི་ཚེ་ལོ་དྲུག་ཅུ་བདུན་ཅུ་ཙམ་འཕངས་པ་སྲིད་ཀྱང་། རང་རེ་ལ་ཕལ་དུ་དེ་ཙམ་མེད་ཏེ་འོང་། ཡོད་དུ་ཆུག་ཀྱང་ཉི་མ་དེ་རིང་ནས་ཅི་རྒྱུ་མིན། ཕྱེད་ཙམ་སོང་ཟིན་ནམ་ཕལ་ཆེར་སོང་ཟིན། ཡང་ཅིག་ཏུ་ན་སྔོན་གྱི་ལས་ཀྱིས་ཚེ་ལོ་སུམ་ཅུའམ་བཞི་བཅུ་ཙམ་ལས་མ་འཕངས་པ་ཡང་སྲིད། འཆི་བདག་སྒོ་དྲུང་ན་སླེབ་ཚར་བའི་ཚོད་དུ་གདའ། ཚེ་འདིའི་དགྲ་གཉེན་ནོར་རྫས་འཁོར་གཡོག་གྲོགས་པོ། བདེ་སྡུག་གཏམ་གསུམ་འདི་ཀུན་དང་ཡུན་རིང་འགྲོགས་སྐབས་མི་འདུག །ཅེས་ཀྱང་ཅི་བྱེད་སྙམ་པ་དང་། ཇི་སྐད་དུ། ས་དང་ལྷུན་པོ་རྒྱ་མཚོ་ཉི་མ་བདུན། །འབར་བས་བསྲེགས་པའི་ལུས་ཅན་འདི་དག་ཀུན། །ཐལ་བ་ཡང་ནི་ལུས་པར་མི་འགྱུར་ན། །ཤིན་ཏུ་ཉམ་ཆུང་མི་ལྟ་སྨོས་ཅི་འཚལ། །ཅེས་པ་ལྟར་ལུས་ཤ་ཁྲག་རྣག་གི་ཕུང་པོ་འདི་ནི་ཉམ་རེ་ཆུང་། དབུགས་མི་བརྟན་སྟོན་ཀའི་ན་བུན་བཞིན་དུ་ནམ་ཡལ་འགྲོ་ཆ་མེད། སེམས་ལ་རང་དབང་མ་ཐོབ་གང་ལ་ཡང་གདེང་མི་འདུག་པས་ནམ་འཆི་ཆ་མེད། ཇི་སྐད་དུ། དེ་རིང་ཁོ་ན་མི་འཆི་ཞེས། །བདེ་བར་འདུག་པ་རིགས་མ་ཡིན། །བདག་ནི་མེད་པར་འགྱུར་བའི་དུས། །དེ་ནི་གདོན་མི་ཟ་བར་འབྱུང་། །ཞེས་པ་ལྟར་བསྒོམ་པ་དང་། ཀླུ་སྒྲུབ་ཀྱི་ཞལ་ནས། །འཆི་བའི་རྐྱེན་ནི་མང་བ་སྟེ། །གསོན་པ་ཡི་ནི་ཉུང་ཟད་ཅིག །དེ་དག་ཉིད་ཀྱང་འཆི་བའི་རྐྱེན། །དེ་བས་རྟག

ཏུ་ཆོས་མཛོད་ཅིག །ཅེས་གསུངས་པ་ལྟར། ཕྱིའི་རྐྱེན་མི་དང་དུད་འགྲོ་དང་གདོན་ལ་སོགས་པ་སེམས་ཅན་དུ་གཏོགས་པ་དང་གཡང་ས་དང་མེ་ཆུ་ལ་སོགས་པ་སྣོད་དང་འབྱུང་བར་གཏོགས་པ། ནང་ལུས་ལ་ནད་རིགས་བཞི་བརྒྱ་རྩ་བཞི་ལ་སོགས་པ་མདོར་ན་འཆི་རྐྱེན་ལ་འདེངས་མི་བྱེད་བྱ་བ་མེད། མི་འཆི་བ་འཚོ་བའི་རྐྱེན་དུ་འདོད་པ་ཟས་གོས་གནས་མལ་སྨན་ལ་སོགས་པ་ཡིན་ན། ཁ་ཟས་མ་འཕྲོད་པ་དང་། སྨན་ལོག་པ་སོགས་འཚོ་བའི་རྐྱེན་དེ་ཀུན་ཡང་ནམ་ཞིག་ན་འཆི་རྐྱེན་དུ་འགྱུར་ཏེ། ལུས་སྲོག་ལ་ཀོལ་བའི་རྐྱེན་ངན་བུ་ཡུག་འཚུབས་པ་ལྟ་བུའི་དབུས་ན་བདག་གནས་པ་ཡིན་ན། ནམ་འཆི་ཆ་མེད་སྙམ་དུ་བསྒོམ། དམིགས་སྐོར་དྲུག་པའོ།

དོན་ཚན་གསུམ་པ་འཆི་བ་ལ་ཆོས་མ་ཡིན་པ་ཅིས་ཀྱང་མི་ཕན་པར་བསམ་པ་ནི། ཇི་སྐད་དུ། ཞི་བ་ལྷས། གཤིན་རྗེའི་སྐྱེས་བུས་ཟིན་པ་ལ། །གཉེན་གྱིས་ཅི་ཕན་བཤེས་ཅི་ཕན། །ཅེས་པ་ལྟར་འཆི་བའི་དུས་ན་ནོར་རྫས་མང་ཡང་ཏིལ་འབྲུ་ཙམ་ཡང་འཁྱེར་དབང་མེད། གཉེན་གྲོགས་གཡོག་འཁོར་རྗེ་དཔོན་སོགས་རྩ་འཛིང་ཆེ་ཡང་ཕྲན་གྱི་ཐ་མ་ཁྱེའུ་གཅིག་ཙམ་ཞིག་རང་ལ་འཁྲིད་དབང་ཡང་མེད་ཁོ་ལ་རྗེས་སུ་འབྲང་དབང་ཡང་མེད། འདི་ཐམས་ཅད་བྱེ་བྲལ་བྱེད་པའི་ཆོས་ཉིད་ཡིན་ཅིས་ཀྱང་ཕན་པ་མེད་སྙམ་སྒྲུག་ལོག་གེ་བ་བསྒོམ། དགྲ་གཉེན་བདེ་སྡུག་གཏམ་བཟང་ངན་ཐམས་ཅད་ལ་དེ་བཞིན་དུ་སྦྱར། འོན་འདི་དག་རྗེས་སུ་མི་འབྲང་ན་སུ་རྗེས་སུ་འབྲང་སྙམ་ན། རང་གིས་བསགས་པའི་ལས་དགེ་སྡིག་གཉིས་པོ་རྗེས་སུ་འབྲང་། སྡིག་པ་བྱས་ཟིན་པ་དེ་ཡང་ཤུལ་དུ་བཞག་ཐབས་མེད་ཧག་ཏུ་གནོད་པ་ཡིན། དགེ་བ་གང་བསགས་པ་དེས་ཀྱང་བདག་ལ་ཕན་པ་ཡིན་ཤུལ་དུ་ནི་མི་ལུས། ཆོས་ལྡན་རབ་འབྱོར་གྱི་ཞལ་ནས་ཀྱང་། དགེ་དང་སྡིག་པ་མ་གཏོགས་པ། །འགྲོ་བ་ཐམས་ཅད་ཕྱིར་ལྡོག་ནས། །འགའ་ཡང་ཁྲིད་རྗེས་མི་འབྲང་བར། །མཁྱེན་པར་གྱིས་ལ་ལེགས་པར་དཔྱོད། །ཅེས་གསུངས་པ་ལྟར་བསམ་པ་དང་། དེ་ལྟར་ན་ངེས་

པར་འཆི། ཕྱུར་དུ་འཆི། ནམ་འཆི་ཆ་མེད། འཆི་བ་ལ་གཞན་ཅིས་ཀྱང་མི་ཕན། འཆི་ཁ་ཕན་ཆད་སྐྱེ་བ་མཐའ་མེད་དུ་ཕན་ནུས་པ་ནི་དམ་པའི་ཆོས་ཁོ་ན་ཡིན་ན། ད་ལྟ་ཉིད་དུ་ཆོས་ལ་འབད་པར་བྱའོ་སྙམ་དུ་བསྒོམ། དམིགས་སྐོར་བདུན་པའོ།

ད་ནི་འཆི་བ་མི་རྟག་པའི་ཐུན་ཆོས་འདི་བསྒོམ་སྟེ། འདི་ལ་རྒྱ་བའི་ཚིག་ལྔ་ཞེས་བྱ། དང་པོ་མི་སྡོད་འགྱུར་བ་བསམ། །གཞན་དག་ཤི་བ་མང་དུ་བསམ། །འཆི་རྐྱེན་མང་པོ་ཡང་ཡང་བསམ། །འཆི་ཁར་ཇི་ལྟར་འགྱུར་སྙམ་བསྒོམ། །ཤི་ནས་ཇི་ལྟར་འགྱུར་བ་བསམ། །བྱ་བ་ཡིན་ཏེ་རང་རེ་སྐྱེས་ནས་མ་ཤིའི་བར་དུ་ཡང་ཕུང་པོའི་རྒྱུན་འདི་རྟག་ཏུ་འགྱུར་ཞིང་འགྲོ། བདག་དང་པོ་བུ་ཆུང་གི་དུས་ན་དེ་འདྲ། བྱིས་པའི་དུས་ན་དེ་འདྲ། ལང་ཚོ་ཅན་དེ་འདྲ། ད་ནི་འདི་འདྲ་སྙམ་པ་དང་། འཆི་བ་ལ་ཇེ་ཉེ་ཇེ་ཉེར་འགྲོ་བ་དེར་འདུག། ཅེས་ཀྱང་མ་ཕན་སྙམ་དུ་རིག་པ་བཙུན་ལ་སྐྱོ་ལྷང་ལྷང་བ་ལ་བཞག།

རང་རེས་དྲན་ནས་ད་ལྟ་ཡན་ཆད་ལ་ཡུལ་འདི་ན་མི་འདི་འདྲ་ཅིག་ཡོད་པ་ཡང་ཤི་འདུག། དེ་ན་དེ་འདྲ་ཞིག་ཡོད་པ་ཡང་ཤི་འདུག་སྙམ་དུ་རེ་རེ་ནས་ཞིབ་ཏུ་བགྲངས། རང་བས་རྒན་པ་ཡང་ཇི་ཙམ་ཞིག་ཤི་འདུག། མཉམ་པ་དང་གཞོན་པ་ཡང་ཇི་ཙམ་ཞིག་ཤི་འདུག་བསམམས་ན། ད་ལྟ་ཡོད་པ་བས་ཤི་བ་མང་། དེ་དག་ཀྱང་ཚེ་ཚད་དུ་ཐུབ་ནས་ཤི་བ་ཙམ་ཆེར་མི་འདུག། ཕལ་ཆེར་དུས་མིན་བར་མ་དོར་ཤི། བདག་ཀྱང་དེ་ལྟ་བུའི་ཆོས་ཉིད་ཡིན། དེ་ལྟ་བུའི་རང་བཞིན་ལས་མ་འདས། སྔར་དེ་དག་གི་སེབ་ཏུ་མ་སོང་བ་ཁར་རྗེ་ཆེ། མ་ཤི་གོང་དུ་ཆོས་གཤའ་མ་ཞིག་མི་བྱེད་པའི་ཐབས་མེད་སྙམ་དུ་བསམ། གཞན་མི་དང་དུད་འགྲོ་ཤི་བ་ཐོས་སམ། མཐོང་ངམ། བྱིས་པ་ནས་རྒན་པོའི་བར་དུ་ལང་ཚོ་འགྱུར་བ་མཐོང་ངམ། མ་ཤི་བ་ཉིད་ལ་ཡང་ཁ་དྲག་པོ་ཁ་ཞན་པོར་སོང་བ་དང་། ཞན་པོ་དྲག་པོར་སོང་བ་དང་། ཕྱུག་པོ་སྤྲང་པོར་སོང་བ་སོགས་གང་མཐོང་གང་ཐོས་ཀྱང་མི་རྟག་པ་ལྷང་གིས་དྲན་ཏེ། བདག་གམ་བདག་གི་ཕྱོགས་དང་། བདག་གི་ལོངས་སྤྱོད་

སོགས་ཀྱང་འདི་ལྟ་བུའི་རང་བཞིན་ཡིན། འདི་ལྟ་བུའི་ཆོས་ཉིད་ཡིན་སྙམ་དུ་བསམ། དེ་ནས་གོང་བཞིན་འཆི་བའི་རྐྱེན་མང་བ་བསམས་ཏེ། རང་གི་གདོང་དུ་བྱུང་བའི་དངོས་པོ་ཐམས་ཅད་ལ་འདི་ཀུན་གྱིས་ཀྱང་བདག་འཆི་བའི་རྐྱེན་ཇི་ལྟར་བྱེད་མི་ཤེས། ད་ལྟ་རང་ཡང་ཇི་ལྟར་འགྱུར་མི་ཤེས་སྙམ་དུ་བསམ། འཆི་བའི་ཚེ་མི་དགེ་བའི་སེམས་ཀྱི་འཆི་ན་ནི་གནད་གཅོད་ཀྱི་ལས་ལ་སོགས་པ་སྡུག་བསྔལ་འཇིགས་སུ་རུང་བ་ཡོད། འཆི་བ་དེ་འདོད་བཞིན་དགའ་བཞིན་དུ་ཡོང་བ་མིན། མི་འདོད་བཞིན་དུ་ཐོག་ཏུ་འབབ་པ་ཡིན། དགའ་བཞིན་སྐྱིད་བཞིན་དུ་འཆི་བ་མ་ཡིན། སྡུག་བསྔལ་ཤུགས་དྲག་པོ་དང་བཅས་ཏེ་འཆི་བ་ཡིན། འཇིག་རྟེན་ཕ་རོལ་ཆ་རྒྱུས་ཡོད་ནས་མ་ཡིན། ཆ་མེད་ཀྱི་ཡུལ་དུ་རྒྱུས་མེད་འཁྱམ་པ་ཡིན་སྙམ་པ་དང་། བདག་ཤི་ཟིན་པའི་གནས་སྐབས་ན། ལུས་སེམས་གཉིས་ནི་བྲེ་བྲལ་དུ་སོང་། ལུས་འདི་ནི་ཡང་ན་ས་ལ་སྐྱུངས་ནས་སྲིན་འབུའི་ཕུང་པོ་གཅིག་གམ། ཡང་ན་ཆུ་ལ་སྐྱུར་ནས་ཉ་སྲམ་གྱི་ཟས་གཅིག་གམ། མེ་ལ་བསྲེགས་ནས་རུས་པ་སྤུར་གང་ངམ། རིའམ་ཐང་ལ་བསྐྱལ་ནས་བྱ་ཁྱིའི་ཁ་ན་ཕར་ཡེར་རེ་རེ་བ་གཅིག་གམ། མཐར་ཞག་ཤས་ནས་ཤུལ་ཙམ་ཡང་མི་ལུས། ད་ལྟ་གཅེས་གཅེས་མོར་བྱས་པའི་ལུས་ཀྱི་ཐ་མ་ནི་དེ་འདྲ། སེམས་ནི་ལས་ཀྱི་ཁུར་ཐོགས་ནས་གར་སྐྱེ་ངེས་པ་མེད་པའི་གནས་སུ་འགྲོ་དགོས་ན། ད་ལྟ་ཆོས་མི་བྱེད་པའི་ཐབས་རང་འདུག་གམ། བྱས་ནས་ཕྱི་བཤོལ་དུ་འཇོག་པའི་ཐབས་རང་འདུག་གམ་སྙམ་དུ་བསམ། དེ་རྣམས་ཀྱི་གཞུག་སྡོམས་ཏེ། ད་ལྟ་རང་ཆོས་གཤའ་མ་ཞིག་བྱེད་སྙམ་པའི་གོ་ཆ་ཡོད་པ་བཞིན་ཆོས་ཀྱི་མགོ་ཐོན་གཞུག་འཁྱོངས་ནས། རང་ཡང་དགའ་བཞིན་དུ་ཆེའི་དུས་བྱེད། གཞན་ཀུན་གྱིས་ཀྱང་ཁོ་ལ་ཆོས་གཤའ་མ་ཞིག་བྱུང་ཟེར་ནས་སྨོན་བཞིན་དུ་ཆེའི་དུས་བྱེད་པ་ཅིག་ལ་གཏད་སོ་འཆོལ་དགོས། དེ་ལ་ཆོས་བསྒོམ་དགོས་བརྟན་པ་ཐོབ་དགོས། གོམས་དགོས་ལྷོངས་སུ་གྱུར་དགོས་པ་འདུག། བརྟན་པ་ནི་མ་ཐོབ། གལ་ཏེ་ན་རྐྱེན་ངན་དང་ཕྲད། རང་གི་བློ་ལས་སུ་མ་རུང་། ཆོས་ཀྱི་གཞུག

མ་འཁྱོངས། ཆོས་དང་འགལ། རང་ཡང་འགྱོད། གཞན་ཀུན་གྱིས་ཀྱང་སྨད་ར་དེར་རེ་འཆི་བ་ཞིག་ཡོང་ཉེན་ཡོད་ན། དེ་ལྟར་སོང་བའི་ཐབས་མི་འདུག་པས་ཆོས་གཤའ་མ་ཅིག་ལ་ད་ལྟ་རང་ཞུགས་ཏེ་མ་ཤི་བར་དུ་འཁྱོངས་པ་ཅིག་གཞན་སློན་ལ་རང་བདེ་བ་ཅིག་མི་བྱེད་རི་སྐམ་དུ་ཞེ་མནའ་ཡང་ཡང་བསྐྱལ། དེང་སང་གི་ཆོས་པ་ཀུན་ལ་གཉེན་པོ་འདི་ཁ་གནད་དུ་ཆེ། དེས་མི་རྟག་པའི་ཁྲིད་ཚར་བ་ལགས། དམིགས་སྐོར་བརྒྱད་པའོ།།

གསུམ་པ་ངན་སོང་གི་སྡུག་བསྔལ་བསམ་པ་ལ། དམྱལ་བའི་སྡུག་བསྔལ་བསམ་པ། ཡི་དྭགས་ཀྱི་སྡུག་བསྔལ་བསམ་པ། དུད་འགྲོའི་སྡུག་བསྔལ་བསམ་པ་གསུམ་ལས། དང་པོ་ནི། སྔོན་འགྲོ་དང་རྗེས་སྦྱར་ལྟར་ལས། བདག་མི་ཡུལ་དུ་ཡུན་རིང་བསྡད་དབང་མི་འདུག །འཆི་བ་འདིས་འཇིགས་སོ་བསམ། ནན་ཏར་ན་འཆི་བ་ཁོན་ལ་ཏ་ཆེས་འཇིགས་རྒྱུ་ཡང་མེད་ཏེ། ཤི་བས་མི་ཆོག་དབང་མེད་དུ་སྐྱེ་བ་ལེན་དགོས་པས་འདི་ཁོན་སྐྲག །དགེ་བ་ནི་མ་བྱས་སྡིག་པ་ནི་མང་ན་ངན་སོང་གསུམ་དུ་སྐྱེ་སྙེ་འོང་། ཅི་རང་གྲག་སྐམ་དུ་བསམ། འདི་ངན་སོང་གི་སྡུག་བསྔལ་བསམ་པའི་དམིགས་པ་ཐམས་ཅད་ཀྱི་སྒོ་ཡིན། དེ་ནས་ཚ་དམྱལ་གྱི་སྡུག་བསྔལ་བསམ་པ་ལ། སྡོམ་ནི། ཡང་གསོས་ཐིག་ནག་བསྡུས་འཇོམས་དང་། །ངུ་འབོད་ངུ་འབོད་ཆེན་པོ་དང་། །ཚ་བ་རབ་ཚ་མནར་མེད་པའོ། །དེ་ལ་ཚ་དམྱལ་ཐམས་ཅད་ཀྱི་གནས་ས་གཞི་རི་མེད་གླིང་མེད་ལྕགས་སྲེགས་ཡིན་པ། མེ་ལྕེ་ཁྲུ་གང་ཙམ་རྟག་ཏུ་འབར་བ། རི་རྫོང་ངམ་གྲོག་སལ་སུལ་ཁོ་ནས་ཁྱབ་པ། ཟངས་ཞུན་ནམ་ཁྲོ་ཆུ་འམ་ཞ་ཉེ་བཞུ་བ་དང་། ལན་ཚྭ་རྡོན་པོ་སོགས་འགྱུར་བྱེད་ཀྱི་ཆུ་ཚན་ཤིན་ཏུ་ཚ་བ་དང་། དེ་འདྲའི་རིགས་ཀྱི་འབབ་ཆུ་དང་མཚོ་ཡོད་པ། ཤིང་རྣམས་ཀྱང་ལྕགས་སྲེགས་སོགས་ལས་གྲུབ་པ། གདུག་པའི་བྱ་དང་གཅན་གཟན་དང་ལས་ཀྱི་སྲིན་པོ་དང་གཤེད་རྗེ་དུ་མས་གང་བ་ཞིག་ཡོད་དོ། །དེར་སྐྱེ་བའི་བར་དོ་རྣམས་ཆར་རླུང་གིས་བདས་པ་སོགས་གྲང་བའི་རྣམ་པ་ཆེར་བྱུང་ནས་ལས་ཀྱི་དབང་གིས་ཚ་དམྱལ་གྱི་གནས་མཐོང་

བས། དེ་དྲོ་བར་ཤེས་ནས་སྲིད་པས་རྒྱུགས་པས་གནས་དེར་ཚུད་ནས་སྐྱེ་བ་ལེན་པར་བཤད།
དེ་ཡང་མི་ཕལ་པ་བས་ཙན་དན་གྱི་མི་བདུན་འགྱུར་གྱིས་ཚ། དེ་བས་ཀྱང་ཡང་གསོས་
ཀྱི་མི་བདུན་འགྱུར་གྱིས་ཚ། དེ་བཞིན་དུ་གོང་མ་གོང་མ་ལས་འོག་མ་འོག་མ་བདུན་འགྱུར་
གྱིས་ཚ་བར་གྲགས། དམྱལ་བའི་འགྲོ་བ་ཐམས་ཅད་རིག་པ་ཚོར་ངས་རྐྱེན་ཅིང་སྒྲིན་པ།
ལུས་འདམ་ཞིང་མཉེན་ལ་གཞོན་ཤ་ཆགས་པ། ལུས་སེམས་གཉིས་ཀའི་ཆ་ནས་བཟོད་
སྲན་ཆུང་བ་ཞིག་ཡོད། དེས་ཀྱང་ལྷག་པར་སྡུག་བསྔལ་ཆེ། གནས་དེ་དག་ཏུ་བཞིན་ལག་
དབང་པོ་ཐམས་ཅད་ཚང་བ་སྐད་ཅིག་ལ་ཁྲིང་གིས་སྐྱེ་སྟེ། གཉིད་སད་པ་འདྲ་བ་ཞིག་ཡོད་
པར་གདའ། དམྱལ་བ་ཐམས་ཅད་རྫུས་སྐྱེས་ཡིན། རྫུས་སྐྱེས་ཕལ་ཆེར་གྱི་ལུགས་ལ་
དེ་བཞིན་དུ་འབྱུང་། སྡུག་བསྔལ་མི་འདྲ་བ་སོ་སོའི་ཁྱེད་པར་ནི། ཡང་གསོས་ན་ཕན་
ཚུན་དགྲ་མི་ཤ་བོ་མཐོང་བ་བཞིན་ཞེ་སྡང་སྐྱེ་ལ། ལག་ཏུ་བླངས་ཚད་མཚོན་ཆ་རྣོན་པོར་
སོང་ནས་གཅིག་ལ་གཅིག་གིས་བསྣུན་པས་དུམ་བུ་མང་པོར་སོང་བ་ན། རི་ཞིག་ཤི་བ་
བཞིན་དུ་བརྒྱལ་ཞིང་འགྱེལ་འགྲོ །ནམ་མཁའ་ལས་རླུང་གྲང་མོ་དང་། ཡང་གསོས་པར་
གྱུར་ཅིག་ཅེས་པའི་སྒྲ་བྱུང་བ་ན་གསོས་པར་འགྱུར་ཞིང་། ཡང་སྔོན་བཞིན་འཐབ་པ་སོགས་
ཡང་ཤི་ཡང་གསོས་ལ་ཟད་པ་མེད་པའི་ཚུལ་དུ་ཡོད། ཐིག་ནག་ནི། གཤེན་རྗེ་རྣམས་
ཀྱིས་དམྱལ་བའི་སེམས་ཅན་དེའི་ལུས་ལ་ཐིག་ནག་པོ་མང་པོ་བཏབ་སྟེ་སོག་ལེས་གཅོད་
པ་དང་། སྟེ་འུས་གཞོག་པ་དང་། མཚོན་ཆ་རྣོན་པོས་འབྲ་བ་སོགས་ཡོད་ཏེ། དེ་ཡང་
སྟོད་བཏུབས་ཙ་ན་སྨད་འགྲིག། སྨད་བཏུབས་ཙ་ན་སྟོད་འགྲིག། ཚུལ་དེ་ཀས་གྲུབ་ཟིན་
མེད་པ་ལ་དུས་འདའ་བའོ། བསྡུས་འཇོམས་ནི། ལུག་ཐུག་སོགས་སྒྲིག་ཆགས་ཆེན་པོ་
མི་བཟད་པ་འཐབ་པའི་བར་དུ་གཙེར་བ་དང་། ཡང་ན་བྲག་རི་ལུག་གི་གདོང་ངམ་རའི་
གདོང་ངམ་མ་ཧེ་དང་སེང་གེ་ལ་སོགས་པ་འཇིགས་སུ་རུང་བའི་རྣམ་པ་ཅན་གྱིས་བར་དུ་
གཙེར་བ་དང་། རི་ཆེན་པོས་སྟེང་ནས་བཙིར་ཞིང་འཇོམས་པ་དང་། ལྕགས་ཀྱི་གཏན་

པ་དཔག་ཚད་མང་པོ་ཅན་གྱི་སྟེང་དུ། དམྱལ་བའི་སེམས་ཅན་མང་པོ་ཕྱོགས་གཅིག་ཏུ་བསྡུས་ནས་རི་བོ་ཙམ་གྱི་གཏུན་ནམ་ཐོ་བས་འཛོམས་ཤིང་འཐག་པར་བྱེད་དོ། རི་ཁ་གྱེས་པའམ་གཏུན་ཤིང་སོགས་བཏེག་ན། ཡང་སྔར་བཞིན་གསོས་པར་འགྱུར་ལ། ཡང་བསྣུན་ཅིང་བཙིར་བ་ན། ལུས་ཕྱེ་མར་འཐག་པ་ཡིན་ནོ། །ངུ་འབོད་ནི། སྲོག་ཆགས་འཛེགས་སུ་རུང་བ་དུ་མས་བདས་པ་ན། རྒྱང་རིང་པོ་ནས་ཁང་པ་དཀར་པོ་ཞིག་མཐོང་ནས། དེ་བདེའོ་སྙམ་ནས་དེར་རྒྱུགས་ཏེ་ནང་དུ་ཕྱིན་པ་ན། ལྕགས་ཀྱི་ཁང་པ་སྒོ་མེད་དུ་གྱུར་ནས་ཕྱི་ནང་ཀུན་དུ་མེ་འབར་ཞིང་བསྲེགས་པས་ཐར་བའི་གོ་སྐབས་མེད་ཅིང་དྲག་ཏུ་ངུ་བར་བྱེད་པའོ། ངུ་འབོད་ཆེན་པོ་ཡང་དེ་དང་འདྲ་བ་ལས་ལྕགས་ཀྱི་ཁང་པ་ཉིས་རིམ་དུ་ཡོད་པའོ། །ལྕགས་ཀྱི་བུམ་པའི་ནང་དུ་འཚོད་པ་དང་། ཟངས་ཆེན་པོར་འཚོད་པ་སོགས་ཀྱང་དེ་དག་ན་ཡོད་དོ། ཚ་བ་ནི། ལྕགས་ཀྱི་གསེལ་ཤིང་ངམ་མདུང་ཐུང་རྣོན་པོ་མེ་འབར་བས། སྤྱི་བོ་ནས་བཤང་ལམ་མམ། བཤང་ལམ་ནས་སྤྱི་བོར་ཐལ་ཕྱུང་དུ་ཕུག་པས་ནང་ཁྲོལ་ཐམས་ཅད་ནི་ཚིག། བུ་ག་དགུ་ནས་མེ་དང་དུད་པ་བཏུད་མར་འབྱུང་བའོ། རབ་ཏུ་ཚ་བ་ཡང་དེ་དང་འདྲ་བ་ལས་མདུང་རྩེ་གསུམ་པ་ལ་སོགས་པས་བསྣུན་པའོ། །གོང་མ་གོང་མའི་སྡུག་བསྔལ་ཐམས་ཅད་འོག་མ་འོག་མ་ལ་ཡོད་ཅིང་། འོག་མ་འོག་མའི་སྡུག་བསྔལ་དུ་བཤད་པ་རྣམས་ལྷག་པོའོ། མནར་མེད་ཀྱི་གནས་ན་ནི་སྡུག་བསྔལ་ཚད་བཟུང་དུ་མེད་དོ། བདེ་བའི་གོ་སྐབས་ཙུང་ཟད་ཙམ་ཡང་མེད་དོ། །གནས་དེ་ན་ལྕགས་སྲེགས་ཀྱི་འདབ་མ་ལ་ལུས་ཐམས་ཅད་འགྲིལ་བ་དང་། ལྕགས་ཀྱི་ཞིབ་མ་ཆེན་པོར་བྱེ་ཚན་དང་ལྷན་ཅིག་འཁྲབ་པ་དང་། ལྕེ་ལ་རྨོས་དོར་ལྔ་བརྒྱས་རྨོད་པ་སོགས་ཀྱང་ཡོད་པར་བཤད་ལ། མར་མེའི་སྡོང་བུ་ལ་མེ་འབར་བ་ལྟར་ལུས་ཀྱི་ཕྱི་ནང་ཐམས་ཅད་ལ་མེ་འབར་བས་མེ་ལྕེ་དང་སྲོག་ཆགས་དབྱེ་བ་མི་ཕྱེད་དེ། སྨྲེ་སྔགས་འདོན་པ་ཙམ་ལས་སེམས་ཅན་ཡོད་པར་རྗེས་སུ་དཔོག་གོ། དེ་ལྟར་སྡུག་བསྔལ་དོས་དྲག་ཚུལ་དེ་བཞིན་ཡིན་ལ། ཡུན་ཚད་

རིང་བ་ནི། མདོན་པ་ལས། མི་རྣམས་ཀྱི་ལོ་ལྔ་བཅུ་ལ། །འདོད་པ་དག་གི་ལྷ་རྣམས་ལས། །འོག་མ་དག་གི་ཉིན་ཞག་གཅིག །དེས་ན་ཚེ་ལོ་ལྔ་བརྒྱའོ། །གོང་མ་གཉིས་ཀ་ཉིས་འགྱུར་རོ། །ཅེས་དང་། ཡང་གསོས་ལ་སོགས་དྲུག་རིམ་བཞིན། །འདོད་ལྷའི་ཚེ་དང་ཉིན་ཞག་མཉམ། །ཅེས་གསུངས་ཏེ། མི་ལོ་ལྔ་བཅུ་ལ་རྒྱལ་ཆེན་བཞིའི་རིགས་ཀྱི་ཞག་གཅིག །དེས་རྩིས་པའི་རང་ལོ་ལྔ་བརྒྱ་ཐུབ། དེ་ཡོངས་རྫོགས་ཡང་གསོས་པའི་ཞག་གཅིག་ཏུ་བྱས། དེའི་ལོ་ལྔ་བརྒྱ་ནི། ཡང་གསོས་པའི་ཚེ་ཚད་ཡིན་ལ། འོག་མ་རྣམས་ལོ་གྲངས་ཡང་ཉིས་འགྱུར་ཉིས་འགྱུར་དུ་འཕེལ་ཞིང་། ཞག་གྲངས་ཀྱང་ཉིས་འགྱུར་ཉིས་འགྱུར་གྱི་རིང་བས་གོང་མ་གོང་མའི་བཞི་འགྱུར་འོག་མ་འོག་མ་ལ་ཡོད་པར་ཤེས་པར་བྱའོ། །དམིགས་པའི་མཇུག་སྡོམས་ནི། དེ་ལྟར་སྡུག་བསྔལ་དོས་ནི་དྲག །ཡུན་ནི་རིང་། ད་ལྟ་མེ་ཕྲ་མོ་གཅིག་ལ་སོར་མོའི་རྩེ་མོ་ཙམ་ཡང་ཡུད་ཙམ་རེ་ཡང་འཛོག་ཏུ་མི་བཏུབ་ན་ནམ་ཞིག་དེ་ལྟ་བུ་རང་གི་ཐོག་ཏུ་བབས་ན། བཟོད་པའི་གོ་སྐབས་ཙུང་ཟད་ཀྱང་མི་འདུག་སྟེ། ལན་ཅིག་དེར་སྐྱེས་ཟིན་ནས་ཐར་པའི་ཐབས་མེད། ད་ལྟ་ཐར་པའི་ཐབས་ཡོད་དེ་དེར་སྐྱེ་བའི་རྒྱུ་ལས་ངན་སྡིག་པ་དག་སྤྱངས་ན་ཐར་པའི་ཐབས་དེ་ཁོ་ན་ཡིན། དེར་མི་སྐྱེ་བའི་ཕྱིར་ཆོས་ལ་འབད་དགོས་སྙམ་དུ་བསམ་མོ། དམིགས་སྐོར་དགུ་པའོ།།

ཡང་སྐྲོའི་རིམ་པ་དང་བསྟུན་ནས་སོ་སོར་ཕྲལ་ཏེ་དམིགས་སྐོར་འགའ་རེ་བྱས་ཀྱང་མི་རུང་བ་མེད་པ་ལགས། ད་ནི་གྲང་དམྱལ་གྱི་སྡུག་བསྔལ་བསམ་པར་བྱ་སྟེ། སྡོམས་ནི། ཆུ་བུར་ཆུ་བུར་བརྡོལ་བ་ཅན། །ཨ་ཆུ་ཀྱི་ཧུད་སོ་ཐམ་པ། །ཨུཏྤལ་པདྨ་པད་ཆེར་གས། །ཅེས་སོ། གྲང་དམྱལ་ཐམས་ཅད་མཐུན་པར་ས་གཞི་རི་གླུང་ཐམས་ཅད་གངས་དང་ཆུ་འཁྱགས་ཀྱི་རང་བཞིན་སྐྱབས་སྐྱིབས་སལ་སུལ་ཉུང་བ། རླུང་དང་བུ་ཡུག་འདྲེས་པ་ཆེས་ཤིན་དུ་གྲང་བས་ཏག་ཏུ་ཁྱབ་པ། རླུང་གྲང་མོ་རྣམས་ཤ་སྦུགས་ཕུག་ནས་རུས་པའི་གཏིང་དུ་ཡང་འགྲོ་བ་ཡོད། བརྒྱད་པོ་ཡང་གོང་མ་གོང་མ་ལས་འོག་མ་འོག་མ་བདུན་

འགྱུར་གྱིས་གྲང་བར་བཤད། དེར་སྐྱེ་བའི་སེམས་ཅན་དེ་ཡང་བར་དོའི་སྐབས་སུ་ཐོག་མར་མེ་ནང་དུ་ཞིག་པ་ལྟ་བུའི་ཉམས་བྱུང་ནས་གྲང་བ་འདོད་པའི་སྐབས་སུ་གྲང་དམྱལ་གྱི་གནས་མཐོང་། དེ་ཕྱོགས་སུ་རྒྱུགས་པས་དེར་ཚུད་ནས་སྐྱེ་བ་ལེན་པར་བཤད། དེ་ལ་ཆུ་བུར་ཅན་ནི། ཆེས་གྲང་བས་ལུས་ཀྱི་ཕྱི་ནང་ཐམས་ཅད་ཆུ་བུར་གྱིས་གང་བའོ། ཆུ་བུར་བརྡོལ་བ་ཅན་ནི། དེ་བས་ཀྱང་གྲང་བས་ཆུ་བུར་བརྡོལ་ཏེ། ཆུ་སེར་གྱི་ལུས་ཡོག་པ་རྣམས་ཀྱང་འཁྱག་པར་འགྲོ་བ་ཡིན་པར་བཤད་ལ། སློབ་སྤྲིང་ལས་ནི་ཆུ་སེར་ལས་སྐྱེས་པའི་སྲོག་ཆགས་ཀྱི་ལུས་འབུགས་ཤིང་ཟ་བར་ཡང་བཤད་དོ། ཨ་ཆུ་ཟེར་བ་ནི། སྐད་ཤིབ་ཤིབ་པོར་འབྲུ་ངག་ཅན་ཙུང་ཟད་ཐོན་ཙམ་གྱི་སྨྲེ་སྔགས་འདོན་པ་དང་། ཀྱི་ཧུད་ཟེར་བ་ནི་དེ་བས་ཀྱང་གྲང་བས་འབྲུ་དག་མི་ཐོན་ཏེ། ཉེན་སྐད་ཕྲ་མོ་ཙམ་འབྱིན་པའོ། སོ་ཐམ་ཐམ་པ་ནི། དེ་བས་ཀྱང་ཤིན་དུ་གྲང་བས་སྐད་མི་ཐོན་པར་ལུས་འདར་བས་སྐྱོས་ཐག་ཅིང་སོ་འདར་རྡབ་པའོ། །ཨུཏྤལ་ལྟར་གས་པ་ནི་ལུས་དུམ་བུ་བཞི་འམ་བརྒྱད་ལ་སོགས་པར་གས་པ་ཡིན་ལ། པདྨ་ལྟར་གས་པ་ནི། ལུས་དུམ་བུ་བརྒྱ་ལ་སོགས་པར་གས་པ་དང་། པདྨ་ལྟར་ཆེར་གས་པ་ནི། གྲང་བའི་མཐར་ཐུག་པས་ལུས་ཀྱི་ཆ་ཤས་རེ་རེ་ཡང་དུམ་བུ་བརྒྱ་ཚ་ལ་སྟོང་ཚལ་དུ་གས་པའོ། །ཚེ་ཚད་ནི་ཆུ་བུར་ཅན་ལ་ཁལ་བརྒྱད་ཅུ་འགྲོ་བའི་སྟོང་ཆེན་པོ་སྦྲངས་ཞེས་ཟེར་བ་ཅིག་ཏིལ་གྱིས་ཕྱུར་བུར་བཀང་། ལོ་བརྒྱ་རེ་ནས་ཏིལ་འབྲུ་རེ་ཕྱིར་བསྐྱུར་ན་དེ་ནམ་ཟད་པ་ཙམ་ཆུ་བུར་ཅན་གྱི་ཚེ་ཐུབ་པར་བཤད། འོག་མ་རྣམས་ལ་ཉི་ཤུ་ཉི་ཤུ་འགྱུར་གྱི་འགྲེས་རྩི་བ་ཡིན། འདི་ལ་ཡང་དམིགས་པའི་གཞི་དང་མཇུག་སྡོམས་ཚ་དམྱལ་གྱི་སྐབས་དང་འདྲ། དམིགས་སྐོར་བཅུ་པའོ།

ད་ནི་ཉེ་འཁོར་བའི་སྡུག་བསྔལ་བསམས་ཏེ། འདི་ནི་མངོན་པ་ལས། བརྒྱད་པོ་ཀུན་ལས་ལྷག་བཅུ་དྲུག །དེ་དག་གི་ནི་ངོས་བཞི་ན། །མེ་མ་མུར་དང་རོ་མྱགས་དང་། །སྤུ་གྲི་ལམ་སོགས་ཆུ་བོ་ཡིན། །ཅེས་འབྱུང་། དེ་ཡང་དམྱལ་བའི་དངོས་གཞི་ཚ་དམྱལ་

བརྒྱད་པོ་རེ་རེ་ལ་ཡང་སོ་སོའི་ཕྱོགས་བཞི་པོ་རྣམས་སུ་ཉེ་འཁོར་བ་བཞི་པོ་འདི་རྣམས་ཆ་ཚང་བ་རེ་རེ་ཡོད་པ་ཡིན། དེ་ཡང་མི་མ་མྱུར་གྱི་འོབས་ནི། འོབས་མི་འདུག་གིས་གང་བ་ཁ་ཞེང་ཤིན་ཏུ་ཆེ་བ་ཡོད་དེ། དེར་དང་པོ་ནས་སྐྱེས་པའམ་ཚ་དམྱལ་དངོས་གཞི་ནས་འཁྲུམས་པ་ཡིན་ཀྱང་རུང་། དམྱལ་བའི་སེམས་ཅན་རྣམས་ནི་སྡུག་བསྔལ་ཆེ་དྲག་པས་གཅིག་ཏུ་བློ་ཆགས་ནས་སྡོད་པའི་གནས་མེད། སྐབས་དེར་ཡང་གར་བབ་བབ་ཏུ་བྲོས་པས་མི་འདུག་གི་འོབས་དེར་ལྟུང་། ལས་ཆེ་ཆུང་གི་མཐུ་ལས་པུས་ནུབ་ཙམ་མམ། སྐེད་པ་ནུབ་ཙམ་སོགས་མ་ངེས་པར་འབྱུང་། འབྲོས་པར་འདོད་ན་ཡང་མགོ་འཁོར་བས་ལྡོག་གིན་ཡོང་བ་དང་། དམྱལ་སྲུངས་འཇིགས་པ་རྣམས་ཀྱིས་འགྲམ་ནས་བསྲུངས་ཏེ་འབྲོས་སུ་མི་སྟེར་རོ། །རོ་མྱགས་ཀྱི་འདམ་ནི། ཡང་བྲོས་པ་ན་རོ་མྱགས་ཞེས་བྱ་བ་མི་གཙང་བ་བཙོག་དགུའི་འདམ་ལ་ཐེབས་ཏེ། དྲི་མི་བཟད་པ་ཚོར་བས་མགོ་འགས་པ་ཙམ་དྲན་མེད་དུ་བརྒྱལ་བ་ཙམ་འབྱུང་། འདམ་གྱི་དབུས་ན་སྲིན་བུ་ལྕགས་མཆུ་ཅན་དང་ཟངས་མཆུ་ཅན་མང་པོ་བྱུང་སྟེ། ཤིན་སྲིན་གྱིས་ཤིང་ལ་ཟ་བ་བཞིན་དུ་ལུས་འབུགས་ཤིང་ཟ་བར་བྱེད་དོ། །སྤུ་གྲིས་གཏམས་པའི་ལམ་ལ་སོགས་པ་ནི། རྒྱང་རིང་པོ་ནས་ནི་གསེར་ཡིད་དུ་འོང་བ་ལྟར་མཐོང་ནས། དེར་རྒྱུགས་པ་ན་ས་གཞི་ཐམས་ཅད་སྤུ་གྲི་སོར་བཞི་པས་གཏམས་པ་ཡིན་ཏེ། རྐང་པ་གཅོད་པ་ལ་སོགས་པས་སྡུག་བསྔལ་བའོ།། སོགས་ཁོངས་ནས་བསྟུས་པ་རལ་གྲི་ལོ་མའི་ནགས་ཚལ་ཅེས་པ་ནི། ཚ་བས་གདུངས་པ་ན་རྒྱང་རིང་པོ་ནས་ནགས་ཚལ་སྔོན་པོ་མཐོང་སྟེ། དགའ་བས་རྒྱུགས་ནས་དེར་ཕྱིན་པ་ན། ལོ་འདབ་ཐམས་ཅད་རལ་གྲི་ལ་སོགས་པའི་མཚོན་ཆར་ཡོད་པ་དེ་རླུང་གིས་བསྐྱོད་པས་ཆར་ལྟར་བབས་ཏེ་ལུས་དུམ་བུ་མང་པོར་བྱེད་པའོ། །ཤལ་མ་ལིའི་སྡོང་པོ་ནི། སྦྲོག་ཆགས་གདུག་པ་ཅན་མང་པོས་བདས་པས་ཤལ་མ་ལིའི་སྡོང་པོ་ཆེན་པོ་མཐོང་ནས་དེ་ལ་འཛེགས་པ་ན། ལྕགས་ཀྱི་ཆེར་མ་སོར་བཅུ་དྲུག་པ་ཁ་འཐུར་དུ་ལྟས་པ་མང་པོ་ཡོད་པས། ལུས་

ཐལ་ཕྱུང་དུ་ཕྱུག་རིམ་པས་རྩེ་མོར་ཕྱིན་པ་ན། བྱ་གུདག་པ་ཅན་གྱི་ཚོགས་ཀྱིས་མིག་འབྱིན་པ་དང་ཤ་འཐོག་པ་ལ་སོགས་པ་འཇིགས་པ་དུ་མ་བྱུང་སྟེ། ཡང་འབྲུར་དུ་བབས་པ་ན། ཚེར་མ་ཁ་གྱེན་དུ་ལྷས་ཏེ་ལུས་འབུགས་པ་ལ་སོགས་པའོ། གསུམ་པོ་དེ་མཚོན་ཆའི་གནོད་པ་ཡིན་པས་གཅིག་ཏུ་སྡོམས་སོ། བཞི་པ་ཐལ་ཚན་གྱི་ཆུ་བོ་རབ་མེད་ནི་ཤིན་དུ་ཚ་བས་གདུངས་པ་དེ་རྒྱང་རིང་པོ་ན་ཆུ་ཀླུང་འབབ་པ་མཐོང་སྟེ། དེར་ཕྱིན་ནས་ཚམ་ཚོམ་མེད་པར་མཆོངས་པ་ན། དེ་ནི་མེ་ཆུ་འདྲེས་མ་ཤིན་དུ་ཚ་བ་གཏིང་ཟབ་ལ་རྒྱ་ཆེ་བ་ཞིག་ཡོད་དེ། དེའི་ལུས་ཆུ་ནང་དུ་ནུབ་པ་ན་ཤིན་དུ་ཚོས་པས་ཤ་རུས་བྲལ་ཏེ། ཤ་རྣམས་བུད་སྒྲོག་ནི་རུས་པ་ལ་གནས་ཏེ། ཀེང་རུས་སུ་ཟང་གིས་སོང་བ་དེ་ཆུའི་སྟེངས་སུ་ཐོན་ཡོང་། དེ་མ་ཐག་ཤ་སྔར་བཞིན་སྐྱེས་ནས་ཡང་ནུབ་པ་སོགས་སོ། དེ་དག་ལ་ཚེ་ཚད་ངེས་པ་མེད་ཀྱང་སོ་སོར་ལོ་བརྒྱ་སྟོང་དུ་མ་གནས་དགོས་པས་དེས་ནི་དྲག་ཡུན་ནི་རིང་ངོ་། །དམིགས་པའི་གཞི་དང་། མཛུག་སྡོམས་སྔར་མ་བཞིན་ནོ། །དམིགས་སྐོར་བཅུ་གཅིག་པའོ།།

ད་ནི་དམྱལ་བ་ཉེ་ཚེ་བའི་སྡུག་བསྔལ་བསམ་པར་བྱ་སྟེ། དེ་ལ་གནས་ནི་ས་འོག་དང་ས་སྟེང་གི་རི་དང་ཐང་དང་ཆུ་ལ་སོགས་པ་ངེས་མེད་ལ་གནས། ཚེ་ཡང་ངེས་པ་མེད་དེ་འགའ་ཞིག་དངོས་གཞི་རྣམས་ལས་ཀྱང་ཚེ་རིང་བ་ཙམ་ཡང་ཡོད། ཁ་ཅིག་ཚེ་ཐུང་བའང་ཡོད། སྡུག་བསྔལ་མྱོང་ཚུལ་ཡང་མ་ངེས་པ་སྣ་ཚོགས་པ་སྟེ། མདོ་ལས། ཉིན་མོ་ལྷའི་བདེ་བ་མྱོང་མཚན་མོ་དམྱལ་བའི་སྡུག་བསྔལ་མྱོང་བ་སོགས་དང་། དམྱལ་བ་གདན་འདྲ་བ་དང་། རྩིག་པ་འདྲ་བ་དང་། གཏུན་བུ་འདྲ་བ་དང་། ཁྲུ་བ་འདྲ་བ་དང་། སྒོན་ཤིང་འདྲ་བ་དང་། ཕྱགས་ཤིང་འདྲ་བ་ལ་སོགས་པ་ལུས་ཀྱི་རྣམ་པ་ཡང་མ་ངེས་པ་སྣ་ཚོགས་པ་ཡོད་དོ། །དམིགས་པའི་གཞི་དང་ཛུག་སྡོམས་སྔར་དང་འདྲ། དམིགས་སྐོར་བཅུ་གཉིས་པའོ།

སྐབས་འདི་དག་ཏུ་རྣ་བ་བྱེ་བ་རི་པ་དང་། འཕགས་པ་དགེ་འདུན་མཚོའི་རྟོགས་བརྗོད་ལ་སོགས་པས་ཀྱང་ངེས་ཤེས་བསྐྱེད་པར་བྱའོ། གཉིས་པ་ཡི་དྭགས་ཀྱི་སྡུག་བསྔལ་

བསམ་པ་ནི། སྨོན་འགྲོ་དང་དམིགས་པའི་གཞི་སྔར་ལྟར་བྱས། ཡང་འདི་ལྟར་བསམ་སྐྱེ་བདག་དམྱལ་བར་མ་སྐྱེས། ཡི་དྭགས་སུ་སྐྱེས་པའི་ཚེ་བདེ་བ་ཡོད་དམ་སྙམ་ན། དེ་ན་ཡང་བདེ་བ་མེད་དེ་ཡི་དྭགས་ལ་གནས་ན་གནས་པ་དང་ཁ་འཐོར་བ་རིགས་གཉིས་ཡོད། དང་པོ་ནི་ས་འོག་དཔག་ཚད་ལྔ་བརྒྱ་འདས་པ་ན། ཡི་དྭགས་ཀྱི་གྲོང་ཁྱེར་སེར་སྐྱ་བྱ་བ་ན། ཡི་དྭགས་ཐམས་ཅད་ཀྱི་གཙོ་བོ་གཤིན་རྗེ་ཆོས་ཀྱི་རྒྱལ་པོའི་རྒྱལ་ཁབ་ཡོད། དེའི་ཉེ་སྐོར་ན་ཡི་དྭགས་བགྲང་བ་ལས་འདས་པ་ཞིག་གནས། ཁ་འཐོར་བ་ནི་བར་སྣང་ལ་རྒྱུ་བ་དང་། ས་སྟེང་ན་རྒྱུ་བ་དང་། ས་འོག་ན་རྒྱུ་བ་བགྲང་བ་ལས་འདས་པ་ཞིག་ཡོད་དེ། གལ་ཏེ་མངོན་ཤེས་དང་ལྡན་པས་ལྟས་ན། ཕྱོགས་གང་ལ་ཕྱིན་ཀྱང་ཡི་དྭགས་ཀྱི་འགྲོ་བས་ཁྱབ། འགྲོ་སྡོད་ཀྱི་ས་ཙམ་ཡང་མི་རྙེད་པའི་ཚུལ་ཙམ་དུ་ཡོད་པར་གདའ། དེ་དག་ལས་ཡི་དྭགས་རྫུ་འཕྲུལ་ཆེ་བ་རེ་རེ་ཙམ་ཙུང་ཟད་སྲིད། གཞན་ཐམས་ཅད་ཆེས་སྡུག་བསྔལ་བ་ཡིན། མདོ་སྡེ་ཆེན་པོ་དྲན་པ་ཉེར་གཞག་ལས། ཡི་དྭགས་ལ་རིགས་སུམ་ཅུ་སོ་དྲུག་གསུངས། འདིར་བསྡུ་ན། ཕྱིའི་སྒྲིབ་པ་ཅན། ནང་གི་སྒྲིབ་པ་ཅན། ཟས་སྐོམ་གྱི་སྒྲིབ་པ་ཅན་གསུམ་དུ་འདུས། ཕྱིའི་སྒྲིབ་པ་ཅན་ནི། ལོ་མང་པོར་ཟས་སྐོམ་ཡེ་མི་རྙེད། རྒྱང་རིང་པོ་ནས་ཟས་ཀྱི་ཕུང་པོ་མཐོང་ཡང་དྲུང་དུ་ཕྱིན་ན་ཤུལ་ཙམ་ཡང་མེད་པར་སོང་བ་ལྟར་མཐོང་བ་དང་། ཆུ་ཀླུང་ཆེན་པོའི་འགྲམ་དུ་ཕྱིན་ན། གསེག་མ་དང་བྱེ་མའི་གྲོག་པོར་འགྲོ་བ་དང་། ལྗོན་ཤིང་འབྲས་བུ་རྒྱས་པའི་དྲུང་དུ་གཏུགས་ནའང་། ཤིང་སྐམ་པོར་འགྱུར་བ་སོགས་ཡོད། འགའ་ཞིག་ལ་སྲིན་པོ་མང་པོས་བསྲུངས་ཏེ་མི་གཏོང་བ་ཡང་ཡོད། ནང་གི་སྒྲིབ་པ་ཅན་ནི། ཁ་ཁབ་མིག་ཙམ་དུ་ཕྲུར་ནས་དང་པོར་བཟའ་བཏུང་ཁར་མི་ཆུད། ཙུང་ཟད་ཆུད་ན་ཡང་ཟས་རྣམས་འགྲམ་ཤུགས་ཡངས་པོ་དེར་སྟོར། སྐོམ་རྣམས་ཁའི་དུགས་ཆེན་པོས་སྐམ། གལ་ཏེ་བཟའ་བཏུང་མིད་ཀྱང་མགྲིན་པ་གཞུ་རྒྱུད་ལྟར་ཕྲ་བ་ནས་མི་འགྲོ། སོང་ཡང་ལྟོ་བ་རིའི་གཏོས་ཙམ་ཡོད་པས་ལྟོ་ཁངས་པའི་དུས་མེད་པ་ཡིན། ཟས་

སྐོམ་གྱི་སྒྲིབ་པ་ཅན་ནི། བཟའ་བཏུང་ཟོས་ཚད་ཁོང་ནང་དུ་མི་འབར་བར་སོང་ནས་ཚིག་པ་དང་། དང་པོ་ཉིད་ནས་ཀྱང་མི་མདག་དང་བཤང་གཅི་དང་རྣག་ཁྲག་ལ་སོགས་པ་ངན་པ་དང་སྡུག་བསྔལ་སྐྱིད་པ་ཁོ་ན་ཟ་དགོས་ཀྱི། བཟང་པོ་ཡི་མི་སྙེད་པ་ཡིན། ཡི་དྭགས་དེ་ཐམས་ཅད་སྤྱིར་ན་དུས་རྟག་ཏུ་བཀྲེས་པ་དང་སྐོམ་པའི་སྡུག་བསྔལ་བཟོད་གླགས་མེད་པ་ཡིན། གོས་དང་བྲལ་ཏེ་ཚད་པས་ཚིག་པ་དང་། གྲང་བས་སྦྲིབས་པའི་སྡུག་བསྔལ་དཔག་ཏུ་མེད། དགུན་གྲང་དུས་ཉི་མའི་འོད་ཀྱིས་ཀྱང་གྲང་རེགས་བྱེད། གསོས་ཀ་ཚད་དུས་སུ་ཟླ་བའི་འོད་ཀྱིས་ཀྱང་ཚིག་སྐོ་འོང་། ཆར་བབ་ན་མེ་ཆར་བབས་ཏེ་ཚིག་པའི་སྣང་བ་འབྱུང་། དུས་རྟག་ཏུ་འཚོལ་འགྲོས་ཀྱི་བྲེལ་བས་ངལ་ཞིང་ཐང་ཆད་པའི་སྡུག་བསྔལ་དང་། ཟས་སྐོམ་ཡེ་མ་བྱུང་བས་ལུས་སྐམས་པ་ལྟ་བུར་གྱུར། རུས་ཚིགས་སུམ་བརྒྱ་དྲུག་ཅུ་འཁྲིགས་པས་རྡོ་ངར་མ་འཐབས་པ་ལྟར་མེ་ལྕེ་ཤུག་ཤུག་པ་འབྱུང་། ཕན་ཚུན་དགྲར་གྱུར་པས་བརྡུང་པ་དང་འཆིང་བ་དང་། བརྡེག་པ་དང་། ཆད་པས་གཅོད་པའི་འཇིགས་པ་ཡང་ཡོད། ཞར་བ་རང་འགྲིགས་ཟེར་བའི་ཚུལ་གྱིས་བསྐྱད་པ་མེད་པར་ཡང་འཇིགས་སྐྲག་ཆེན་པོས་འབྲོས། དེ་འདྲ་བའི་སྡུག་བསྔལ་རྣོས་དྲག་པ་དང་། ཡི་དྭགས་ཕལ་མོ་ཆེའི་ཚེ་ཚད་མི་ལོ་སྟོང་ཕྲག་བཅོ་ལྔ་ཐུབ་པས་ཡུན་རིང་དམིགས་པའི་འཇུག་སྟོམས་དང་། རྗེས་ཀྱི་བྱ་བ་སྔར་དང་འདྲ། དམིགས་སྐོར་བཅུ་གསུམ་པའོ།།

དེར་མ་འདུས་པ་མིན་ཀྱང་ད་ལྟའི་ཡི་དྭགས་ཁ་འཐོར་བ་མཁའ་ལ་རྒྱུ་བའི་འདྲེ་བཀྲེན་འདི་རྣམས་ལ་སྨོས་སུ་བསྒོམ་པའི་དམིགས་སྐོར་གཅིག་མཛད་པའི་སྲོལ་ཡོད། དེ་ལྟ་ན་གཞན་ལ་གནོད་པ་བྱས་པས་སླར་ཡང་ངན་སོང་དུ་འགྲོ་བ་དང་། ཤུགས་ལ་མ་བསམས་ཀྱང་དུགས་ཆེན་པོས་གཞན་ལ་གནོད་པ་འབྱུང་བ་དང་། མཐུ་བོ་ཆེས་རྡུང་རྡེག་བྱེད་པ་དང་། མ་ཉེས་མ་ལན་པ་ལ་འདྲེས་བྱས་སོ་ཞེས་ཁག་ངན་བྱུང་བའི་ཚེ། སེམས་ལ་སྡུག་བསྔལ་སྐྱེ་བ་སོགས་ཡོད་གསུང་། འདི་དམིགས་སྐོར་ལོགས་པར་མ་བྱས་ཀྱང་རུང་སྟེ་

མ་དེའི་ནང་དུ་བལྟབ་པས་ཚོག་གོ། གསུམ་པ་དུད་འགྲོའི་སྡུག་བསྔལ་བསམ་པ་ནི། དུད་འགྲོ་ལ་བྱིངས་དང་ཁ་འཐོར་བ་གཉིས། བྱིངས་ན་གནས་པ་རྒྱ་མཚོ་ཆེན་པོ་ན་ཡོད། སྐྱིབ་པའི་གནས་མེད། རླབས་ཀྱིས་བདས་ཏེ་འགྲོ་བས་ངེས་མེད་དུ་འཁྱམས། ཕན་ཚུན་གཅིག་ལ་གཅིག་ཟ། རྟག་ཏུ་དགྲ་བྱུང་གི་དོགས་པས་འཇིགས་ཤིང་སྐྲག། གསོན་བཞིན་དུ་ཟ་བ་སོགས་ཀྱིས་སྡུག་བསྔལ་ལ་བཟོད་ཐབས་མེད། ཁ་འཐོར་བ་མི་དང་ལྷའི་ཡུལ་ན་ཡོད་པ་འདི་རྣམས་ཡིན། མེས་བདག་ཏུ་མ་བཟུང་བ་རྣམས་ནི་དགྲ་བྱུང་གི་དོགས་པས་རྟག་ཏུ་སེམས་ལ་བདེ་བ་མེད། མེས་བདག་ཏུ་བཟུང་བ་རྣམས་ཀྱང་སྨྱུ་འཇིད་པ་དང་། སྣ་འབིགས་པ་དང་། བརྡེག་པ་དང་། ཁུར་ལྕི་བས་དལ་བ་སོགས་དང་། ཤ་དང་ཁྲག་དང་ལྤགས་པ་དང་རུས་པའི་ཕྱིར་གསོད་པ་སོགས་གསོད་གཅོད་བཀོལ་སྤྱོད་ཀྱི་སྡུག་བསྔལ་མང་པོ་དང་། གཞན་ཡང་བཀྲེས་སྐོམ་ཚ་གྲང་ངལ་དུབ་ལ་སོགས་པ་དམྱལ་བའམ། ཡི་དྭགས་རྣམས་དང་སྡུག་བསྔལ་འདྲ་རུང་དུ་ཡོད། གཙོ་བོར་སྡུག་བསྔལ་གྱི་གཙོ་བོ་ཤིན་ཏུ་རྨོངས་པ་དང་གཅིག་ལ་གཅིག་ཟ་བ་ཡིན་ཏེ། མི་ཤ་ཆགས་པའི་དགྲ་ལ་ཟློན་བྱེད་པ་ལྟར་རྟག་ཏུ་གནས་དགོས་པ་ཡིན། དམིགས་པའི་གཞི་དང་མཇུག་སྡོམས་སྔར་དང་འདྲ། སྨོན་འགྲོ་དང་རྗེས་ཀྱང་སྔར་དང་འདྲ། དམིགས་སྐོར་བཅུ་བཞི་པའོ།།

དེ་རྣམས་ཀྱི་གནད་བསྡུས་པའི་ཐུན་ཆོས་ལ། དེ་ལྟར་ངན་སོང་གསུམ་གྱི་སྡུག་བསྔལ་བསམམས་ཙ་ན་བཟོད་པའི་ཐབས་མི་འདུག །དེ་ལས་སྐྱོབ་པའི་སྐྱབས་ཤིག་དགོས་པར་འདུག །སྐྱབས་སུས་ཐུབ་ན། ཚངས་པའམ། བརྒྱ་བྱིན་ནམ་འཁོར་ལོས་བསྒྱུར་བའི་རྒྱལ་པོས་ཀྱང་སྐྱོབ་མི་ཐུབ་ན། གཞན་འདི་པ་ཀུན་གྱིས་ག་ལ་ཐུབ། འོ་ན་སུས་ཐུབ་ན་དཀོན་མཆོག་གསུམ་གྱིས་ཐུབ། བདག་ལྷ་རྗེ་བོ་དཀོན་མཆོག་རིན་པོ་ཆེ་གསུམ་ལ་སྐྱབས་སུ་འགྲོ། སངས་རྒྱས་ལ་སྟོན་པ་ཞུ། ཆོས་ལ་ནི་ཉམས་ལེན་ཞུ། དགེ་འདུན་ལ་ནི་དེ་སྒྲུབ་པའི་གྲོགས་ཞུ་བ་ཡིན་སྙམ་དུ་བསམ། ཡང་སྐྱབས་པ་སངས་རྒྱས་ལ་བསྐྱབས་ཀྱང་།

སྐྱོབ་པ་ཆོས་ཀྱིས་སྐྱོབ་བྱ་བ་ཡིན། སངས་རྒྱས་ཀྱིས་ཀྱང་མི་ཆུས་ཁྲིར་བ་སྒྲ་ནས་འཛིན་པ་ལྟར་སྐྱབ་ཏུ་མི་བཏུབ། ཆོས་བཤད་ཆོས་བཞིན་བྱེད་དུ་བཅུག་ནས་སྐྱོབ་པ་ཡིན། སངས་རྒྱས་ལ་དད་པ་བསྒོམས་ཏེ། དེས་གསུངས་པའི་ཆོས་ནས་ཇི་སྐད་བཤད་པ་བཞིན་བྱ། འཕགས་པའི་དགེ་འདུན་རྣམས་ཀྱིས་ཇི་འདྲ་མཛད་འདུག་པ་དེ་བཞིན་དུ་རང་རེ་ཡང་དེའི་ལད་མོ་བཟློས་ཏེ་བྱེད་སྙམ་པ་རྒྱུན་དུ་བསྒོམ། ཐུན་གྱི་འགོ་ཞབས་ལ། སྐྱབས་འགྲོ་དང་འབྲེལ་བའི་ངག་འདོན་གྱི་དགེ་སྦྱོར་དེ་ཀུན་ཡང་འགྲུལ་པར་བྱེད་པ་གནད་ཆེ། སྐྱེས་བུ་ཆུང་ངུའི་ལུགས་ཀྱི་སྐྱབས་འགྲོ་རྣམ་དག་དེ་འཚམས་འདི་ནས་སྐྱེ་བ་ལགས་སོ། །ཞེས་གདམས་ཏེ་དམིགས་སྐོར་བཅོ་ལྔ་པའོ།།

སྐབས་འདིར་སྐྱབས་འགྲོའི་གོ་བ་རགས་རིམ་ཞིག་སློབ་མ་ལ་ངེས་པོར་འཆད་པ་གལ་ཆེ། སློབ་མས་ཀྱང་བློ་ལ་བཅགས་པ་གལ་ཆེ་འོ། །ལམ་རིམ་གྱི་ཡིག་རྙིང་འགའ་ཞིག་ཏུ་སྐྱེས་བུ་ཆུང་ངུའི་རིམ་པ་དེ་ཡན་གྱིས་ཚར་བར་མཛད། ལས་འབྲས་སེབ་ཚགས་སུ་གཏོང་བའི་ལུགས་ཀྱང་འདུག་སྟེ། ལམ་རིམ་གྱི་ཡི་གེ་ཕལ་ཆེར་གྱི་ལུགས་ལྟར་ལས་འབྲས་ལ་ཡང་ཁྲིད་ཡོགས་པ་སྐྱོང་པ་ཉིད་ལེགས་སོ། བཞི་པ་ལས་འབྲས་ཀྱི་འཁྲིད་ནི། ལས་འབྲས་སྤྱིར་བསམ་པ་དང་། བྱེད་བྲག་ཏུ་བསམ་པའོ། དང་པོ་ནི། ལས་དཀར་པོ་དགེ་བ་ལས་འབྲས་བུ་བདེ་བ་ཁོ་ན་འབྱུང་། ལས་ནག་པོ་སྡིག་པ་ལས་འབྲས་བུ་སྡུག་བསྔལ་ཁོ་ན་འབྱུང་སྟེ། དཀར་ནག་ལས་འབྲས་སོ་སོར་ངེས་པས་ཀྱང་སྤང་བླང་བྱེད་དགོས། ལས་དགེ་སྡིག་གང་ཡིན་ཡང་རུང་། རྒྱུ་ལས་ཀྱི་དུས་ན་ཆུང་ངུ་ལས་མེད་ཀྱང་འབྲས་བུ་རྣམ་སྨིན་གྱི་དུས་ན་འཕེལ་ཆེ་སྟེ། འགྱུར་ཆུང་ཤོས་རང་ལ་ཡང་བརྒྱ་འགྱུར་སྟོང་འགྱུར་དུ་འཕེལ། འགྱུར་ཆེ་བ་ལ་ཚད་བཟུང་དུ་མེད་པས་སྤང་བླང་གལ་ཆེ། རང་གིས་བྱས་པའི་ལས་དཀར་ནག་རྣམས་ནི་གཉེན་པོས་མ་བཅོམ་ན། འབྲས་བུ་མ་སྨིན་གྱི་བར་ཆུད་འཛའ་བ་མི་སྲིད། རང་གིས་མ་བྱས་ན་ལས་དཀར་ནག་གང་ཡང་རང་རྒྱུད་ལ་འབྱུང་བ་མི་སྲིད་

པས། རང་ཉིད་བླང་དོར་གྱི་གནས་ལ་བཟབ་པ་གལ་ཆེ་སྙམ་དུ་བསྒོམ། དམིགས་སྐོར་བཅུ་དྲུག་པའོ།།

གཉིས་པ་སོ་སོར་བསྒོམ་པ་ལ། ནག་པོའི་རྒྱུ་འབྲས་བསམ་པ་དང་། དཀར་པོའི་རྒྱུ་འབྲས་བསམ་པའོ། དང་པོ་ནི། སྔོན་འགྲོ་དང་རྗེས་སྦྱོར་ལྷར་ལས། ཡན་ལག་བདུན་པའི་མཇུག་ཏུ་སྐྱབས་འགྲོ་རེ་ཡང་ངེས་པར་བྱ། འདི་ལྟར་ངན་སོང་གསུམ་དང་། མཐོ་རིས་ཀྱི་སྡུག་བསྔལ་ཐམས་ཅད་ཀྱང་རྒྱུ་མེད་རྐྱེན་མེད་པ་ལས་བྱུང་བ་མ་ཡིན། རྒྱུ་མི་དགེ་བའི་ལས་ལས་བྱུང་ངོ་སྙམ་དུ་དམིགས་པའི་གཞི་བཅས་ནས། མི་དགེ་བ་དེ་ཡང་རྣམ་གྲངས་མང་མོད་ཀྱི་བླང་དོར་གྱི་གནས་ལ་གལ་ཆེ་བ་རགས་པ་ཆེ་ལོང་ཙམ་དུ་བསྡུས་ན། མི་དགེ་བ་བཅུ་སྟེ། དེ་ལ་ལུས་ཀྱི་ལས་རྣམ་པ་གསུམ་གྱི་སྲོག་གཅོད་པ་ནི། སྲོག་གཅོད་འདོད་ཀྱིས་བསམ་བཞིན་དུ་གསད་བྱ་མ་ནོར་བར་བསད་ལ། གསད་བྱ་དེ་མ་ཤི་བར་དུ་གསོད་སེམས་རྒྱུན་མ་ལྡོག་པའོ། མ་བྱིན་པར་ལེན་པ་ནི། གཞན་གྱི་ནོར་རང་ལ་མ་བྱིན་པ་འཕྲོག་པའམ་བརྐུས་པ་སོགས་ཇི་ལྟར་ཡིན་ཡང་རུང་སྟེ། རང་གིས་ཐོབ་པོ་སྙམ་པའི་བློ་སྐྱེས་པའོ། འདོད་པས་ལོག་པར་གཡེམ་པ་ནི། ཡུལ་བགྲོད་པར་བྱ་བ་མ་ཡིན་པ་ལ་མི་ཚངས་པར་སྤྱོད་པ་འཁྲིག་པའི་ཆོས་བསྟེན་པ་སྟེ། གཞན་གྱིས་བདག་ཏུ་བཟུང་བའི་བུད་མེད་དང་། བདུན་རྒྱུད་ཚུན་ཆད་ཀྱི་གཉེན་ཉེ་དུར་གྱུར་པ་དང་། ཕ་མ་ཉེ་དུ་རྒྱལ་པོ་ཡུལ་དཔོན་སོགས་གཞན་གྱིས་བསྲུངས་པ་དང་། ཚངས་སྤྱོད་ཀྱི་སྡོམ་པ་བླངས་པ་སྡོམ་པས་བསྲུངས་པ་སྟེ། དེ་དག་ལ་སོགས་པ་ཡུལ་གྱི་སྐྱོན་ནས་བགྲོད་བྱ་མ་ཡིན་པ་དང་། ནད་པ་ཅན་དང་མྱ་ངན་ཅན་དང་སྦྲུམ་པ་ལ་སོགས་པ་དུས་ཀྱི་སྐྱོན་ནས་བགྲོད་བྱ་མ་ཡིན་པ་དང་། ལྷ་ཁང་དང་ཀུན་དགའ་ར་བ་དང་མཆོད་རྟེན་གྱི་གནས་དང་བླ་མའི་གནས་སོགས་སུ་བསྟེན་པ་གནས་ཀྱི་སྐྱོན་ནས་བགྲོད་བྱ་མ་ཡིན་པ་དང་། ནམ་ཡང་འདོད་པས་ཚིག་མི་ཤེས་ཤིང་། སྐྱེ་གནས་ལས་གཞན་པའི་སྒོར་བསྟེན་པ། ལམ་གྱི་སྐྱོན་ནས་བགྲོད་བྱ་མ་ཡིན་

པ་སྟེ། དཔེ་ན་བཞིའོ། དེ་ཙམ་ནི་ཁྲིམ་པའི་དབང་དུ་བྱས་པ་སྟེ། ཚངས་པར་སྤྱོད་པའི་བརྟུལ་ཞུགས་ཁས་བླངས་པས་ནི། མི་ཚངས་པར་སྤྱོད་པ་ཅི་འདྲ་ཞིག་བསྟེན་ཀྱང་ལོག་གཡེམ་ཁོ་ན་ཡིན་ནོ། །ངག་གི་ལས་བཞི་ལས་རྫུན་དུ་སྨྲ་བ་ནི་འདུ་ཤེས་བསྒྱུར་ནས་ཤེས་བཞིན་དུ་མི་བདེན་པར་སྨྲས་ལ། སྨྲ་བའི་ཡུལ་མིའི་འགྲོ་བར་གྱུར་པ་དེས་གོ་བ་ནའོ། ཕྲ་མ་ནི་མི་མཐུན་པ་མེད་པའི་འགྲོ་བ་གཉིས་འཕོན་པར་བྱ་བའི་ཕྱིར་དུ་དཀྲུགས་ཀྱི་ཚིག་སྨྲས་ཤིང་ཕ་རོལ་གྱིས་གོ་བ་ནའོ། ཚིག་རྩུབ་པོ་ནི་དངོས་སུ་ཐོས་པར་དེའི་སྐྱོན་བརྗོད་པ་སོགས་ཞེ་ལ་འཕོག་པའི་ཚིག་སྨྲས་ཤིང་དེས་གོ་བའོ། ངག་འཁྱལ་ནི། དེ་གསུམ་མ་ཡིན་པ་གཞན་ཉོན་མོངས་ཅན་གྱི་ཚིག་ཐམས་ཅད་ཏེ་ཁ་གསག་དང་གཞོགས་སློང་དང་གླུ་དང་ཟློས་གར་དང་དམག་གི་གཏམ་དང་སྨད་འཚོང་མའི་གཏམ་དང་ཚོང་གི་གཏམ་ལ་སོགས་པ་དང་། ལྟ་བ་ལོག་པའི་ཆོས་ཀྱི་གཏམ་ལ་སོགས་པའོ། །ཡིད་ཀྱི་ལས་གསུམ་ལ་བརྣབ་སེམས་ནི། གཞན་གྱི་ནོར་དང་བུད་མེད་དང་ཁྱིམ་དང་འཁོར་གཡོག་དང་ཡུལ་ལ་སོགས་པ་རང་གིར་བྱེད་འདོད་པའི་བསམ་པ་གཏིང་ཚུགས་པར་བྱེད་པའོ། །གནོད་སེམས་ནི། གཞན་ལ་གནོད་པ་བྱེད་འདོད་དང་སྡུག་བསྔལ་འབྱུང་བར་གྱུར་ཅིག་པའི་བསམ་པ་གཏིང་ཚུགས་པའོ། །ལོག་ལྟ་ནི་ལས་འབྲས་མི་བདེན་པ་དང་། ཚེ་སྔ་ཕྱི་དང་། དཀོན་མཆོག་གསུམ་སོགས་མེད་པར་འཛིན་པ་དམ་པོ་འཆང་བ་ཡིན་ཏེ། དེ་ལྟར་བཅུ་པོ་དེ་ནི་ལས་ལམ་རྫོགས་པའི་དབང་དུ་བྱས་ལ། བསམ་བཞིན་མ་ཡིན་པ་ལ་ནོར་བར་བསད་པ་སོགས་བཅུ་པོའི་ཕྱོགས་མཐུན་ཐམས་ཅད་ཀྱང་ངེས་པར་སྤོང་དགོས་པའི་ལས་ནི་ཡིན་ནོ། །དེས་ན་བདག་གིས་ཐོག་མ་ཉིད་དུ་ངེས་པར་སྤོང་དགོས་པའི་ལས་ནི་འདི་དག་ཡིན་ནོ་སྙམ་དུ་ཡང་ཡང་བསྒོམ་སྟེ་དམིགས་སྐོར་བཅུ་བདུན་ནོ།།

ད་ནི་མི་དགེ་བ་དེ་དག་གི་འབྲས་བུ་བསམ་པར་བྱ་སྟེ། མི་དགེ་བ་བཅུ་པོ་འདི་རྣམས་རེ་རེ་ཡང་སྟོབས་ཆེན་པོ་བྱས་པ་དང་། ཡང་ཡང་བྱས་ན་དམྱལ་བར་སྐྱེ། འབྲིང་

དུ་བྱས་ན་ཡི་དྭགས་སུ་སྐྱེ། སྟོབས་ཆུང་བ་དང་ཉུང་ངུར་སྤྱད་པས་དུད་འགྲོར་སྐྱེ། སྡུག་
བསྔལ་ཅན་གྱི་འགྲོ་བ་དེ་དག་ཏུ་སྐྱེ་བ་ནི་རྣམ་སྨིན་གྱི་འབྲས་བུའོ། སྲོག་བཅད་པས་ཚེ་ཐུང་
བ་དང་། མ་བྱིན་པར་བླངས་པས་ལོངས་སྤྱོད་ཆུང་བ་དང་། ལོག་གཡེམ་གྱིས་དགྲ་མང་
བ་དང་། རྫུན་གྱིས་རང་ལ་སྐུར་བ་མང་པ་དང་། ཕྲ་མས་གྲོགས་དང་འཁོན་པ་དང་།
ཚིག་རྩུབ་ཀྱིས་གཏམ་མི་སྙན་པ་ཐོས་པ་དང་། ངག་འཆལ་སྨྲས་པས་རང་གི་ཚིག་ལ་གཞན་
གྱིས་མི་ཉན་པ་དང་། བརྣབ་སེམས་ཀྱིས་རེ་བ་མི་འགྲུབ་པ་དང་། གནོད་སེམས་ཀྱིས་
སེམས་ལ་སྡུག་བསྔལ་དང་འཇིགས་སྐྲག་འབྱུང་བ་དང་། ལོག་ལྟས་ཤིན་ཏུ་གླེན་ཅིང་གཏི་
མུག་པར་འགྱུར་བ་སྟེ། དེ་རྣམས་ནི་མྱོང་བ་རྒྱུ་མཐུན་གྱི་འབྲས་བུ་ཡིན་ལ། བྱེད་པ་རྒྱུ་
མཐུན་ནི། སྔར་ལས་དེ་དང་དེ་བྱས་པས་ཕྱིས་ཀྱང་དེ་དང་དེ་ལ་དགའ་བའོ།། བདག་
པོའི་འབྲས་བུ་ནི། ཕྱི་རོལ་སྣོད་ཀྱི་འཇིག་རྟེན་ལ་འབྱུང་སྟེ། སྲོག་གཅོད་ཀྱིས་ནི་འབྲུ་
དང་སྨན་ལ་སོགས་པ་མཐུ་ཆུང་བ་དང་། མ་བྱིན་ལེན་གྱིས་ལོ་ཉེས་པ་དང་། ལོག་གཡེམ་
གྱིས་ས་ཕྱོགས་རྡུལ་ཚུབ་ཆེ་ཞིང་དྲི་ང་བ་དང་། རྫུན་གྱིས་ནི་ས་ཕྱོགས་མཐོ་དམན་ཅན་
བསྒྲོད་མི་བདེ་བར་འགྱུར་བ་དང་། ཕྲ་མས་ས་ཕྱོགས་ཚ་སྒྲོ་ཅན་དུ་འགྱུར་བ་དང་། ཚིག་
རྩུབ་ཀྱིས་བྱེ་མ་དང་གསེག་མ་སོགས་འཕེལ་བ་དང་། ངག་འཆལ་གྱིས་དུས་ལོག་ཏུ་འགྱུར་
ཏེ། དགུན་ནི་རུ་ལ། དཔྱིད་ནི་རེངས། དབྱར་ནི་ཐན་སྟོན་ནི་ཞོད་པ་ལ་སོགས་པའོ།
།བརྣབ་སེམས་ཀྱིས་འབྲུ་ཕྲ་བར་གྱུར་པ་དང་། གནོད་སེམས་ཀྱིས་རོ་མ་ཞིམ་པར་འགྱུར་
བ་དང་། ལོག་ལྟས་ནི་འབྲུ་རྩ་བ་ནས་མི་ཆགས་པར་བྱེད་དེ། དེ་ལྟར་ན་རྒྱུ་མཐུན་པའི་
འབྲས་བུ་འདི་དག་དང་། བདག་པོའི་འབྲས་བུ་འདི་རྣམས་ལས་དེ་དང་དེ་བྱས་པའི་སྐྱེ་
བ་དེ་ཉིད་ལ་འབྱུང་བའང་ཡོད། སྐྱེ་བ་ཕྱི་མའི་གནས་སྐབས་མཐོ་རིས་སུ་སྐྱེས་པའི་སྐབས།
དུས་ངེས་མེད་སྣ་ཚོགས་པར་ཡང་འགྱུར་བའོ། དེ་ལྟར་ན་མི་དགེ་བ་བཅུ་པོ་འདི་ནི་སྡུག་
བསྔལ་མི་འདོད་པ་སྣ་ཚོགས་པའི་གཞིར་གྱུར་པའི་ཕྱིར། འདི་རྣམས་ཕྱིན་ཆད་སྲོག་ལ་

བབ་ཀྱང་མི་བྱ། སྔར་བྱས་པ་ཐམས་ཅད་ཀྱང་སྦྱོང་བའི་ཐབས་ལ་འབད་དགོས་སྙམ་དུ་ཡང་ཡང་བསྒོམ། དམིགས་སྐོར་བཅོ་བརྒྱད་པའོ།།

ད་ནི་དགེ་བའི་ལས་བསམ་པར་བྱ་སྟེ། མཐོ་རིས་ཀྱི་ལུས་རྟེན་ཐོབ་པ་དང་། གཞན་ཡང་འཁོར་བའི་བདེ་བ་གང་ཅི་ཡོད་པ་ཐམས་ཅད་དགེ་བའི་ལས་ལས་འབྱུང་། འཇིག་རྟེན་ལས་འདས་པ་བྱང་ཆུབ་རྣམ་པ་གསུམ་ཡང་དགེ་བ་ལས་འབྱུང་བ་ཡིན་ན། བདག་གིས་སྡིག་པ་ཐམས་ཅད་སྤངས་དགེ་བ་ཐམས་ཅད་ལ་ཅི་ནུས་སུ་སློབ་དགོས་པ་ལས་བསླབ་རྒྱུའི་དགེ་བ་ཡང་རིགས་མང་མོད་ཀྱི། དགེ་བ་ཐམས་ཅད་ཀྱི་ཐོག་མའི་འཇུག་སྒོ་ནི། ཆོས་དཀར་པོ་དགེ་བ་བཅུ་ཞེས་བྱ་བ་ཡིན་ན། དེ་ནི་སྔར་བསྟན་པའི་མི་དགེ་བ་བཅུ་པོ་དེ་རྣམས་ཡིད་ཀྱིས་སྤངས་ནས་ལུས་ངག་གིས་སླར་ལོག་པའི་སྤོང་བའི་སེམས་པ་སྦྱོར་ལམ་དང་བཅས་པ་དེ་ཡིན་ན། བདག་འདི་ལ་རྟག་ཏུ་གནས་པར་བྱའོ་སྙམ་དུ་བསྒོམ། དེ་ལ་མི་དགེ་བཅུ་ཡིད་ཀྱིས་སྤངས་པའི་གོ་དོན་ནི། དེ་རྣམས་ཉེས་དམིགས་ཅན་དང་སྐྱོན་ཆེན་པོར་ཤེས་ནས་ནམ་དུ་ཡང་མི་འདོད་པ་དེ་ཡིན་ལ། ལུས་ངག་གིས་སླར་ལོག་པ་ནི། བཅུ་པོ་དེ་དག་དུས་རྒྱུན་དུ་འམ། དལ་བར་འདུག་པའི་དུས་སུ་མི་བྱེད་པར་མ་ཟད། དེ་དག་བྱས་ན་ཁྲེ་ཡོད་པ་ལྟར་སྣང་ཞིང་། འབད་རྩོལ་མི་དགོས་པར་བྱེད་ཐུབ་པའི་སྐབས་བྱུང་ཡང་སྔར་ཡིད་ཀྱིས་སྤངས་པ་དེ་དྲན་པས་བྱ་བ་ངན་པ་དེ་ལ་ཡེ་ནས་འཇུག་པར་མི་ནུས་པ་སྟེ། ལུས་ངག་གི་བདུན་པོ་ལ་ནི་འདི་གཉིས་ཀར་ཚང་བ་དགོས་ལ། ཡིད་ཀྱི་ལས་གསུམ་ལ་ཡིད་ཀྱིས་སྤངས་པ་ཁོ་ནས་ཆོག་གོ །མི་དགེ་བ་ལ་མི་རུང་བར་སེམས་པ་དེ་ཀ་སྤོང་སེམས་ཡིན་ལ། དེ་ནི་མི་རུང་བ་ཡིན་པ་ལ་མི་རུང་བར་ཤེས་པའི་ཀུན་རྫོབ་ཤེས་པ་མ་འཁྲུལ་བ་ཡིན་པས་ལམ་གཉེན་པོའི་ཆོས་སུ་འགྱུར་ཞིང་། འདི་ཚུལ་ཁྲིམས་ཀྱི་ངོ་བོ་ཡིན། སྤོང་སེམས་ཤུགས་ཆེ་བ་ལན་འགའ་རེ་བྱུང་ན། གཉིད་རྨུགས་དང་རྣམ་གཡེང་ལ་སོགས་པས་བར་ཆོད་ཀྱང་། དེ་ལྟ་བུའི་རྐྱེན་དམིགས་པའི་ཚེ། ཉེས་སྤྱོད་དེ་སྐྱོན་དུ་ཤེས་ནས་མི་བྱེད་ཅིང་སྡོམ་པར་འགྱུར་

རོ། འདི་ནི་སྔར་གྱི་སེམས་པ་དེའི་ཤུགས་ལས་བྱུང་བ་ཡིན་པ་ཤུགས་དེ་ཡང་ས་བོན་གྱི་མཐུ་ལས་ཡིན་ཏེ། དེའི་ཕྱིར་མི་དགེ་བ་བཅུ་སྤྱོད་པའི་སེམས་པ་ས་བོན་དང་བཅས་པ་ནི་དགེ་བ་བཅུའོ། དམིགས་སྐོར་བཅུ་དགུ་པའོ།།

ད་ནི་དགེ་བ་བཅུའི་ཕན་ཡོན་བསམ་པར་བྱ་སྟེ། དེ་ཡང་ལས་དགེ་བ་བཅུ་ཆེར་སྤྱད་པ་ལས་རྣམ་སྨིན་གྱི་འབྲས་བུ་ལྷའི་སྐྱེ་བ་ལེན། ཆུང་ངུར་སྤྱད་པ་ལས་རྣམ་སྨིན་གྱི་འབྲས་བུ་མི་ལུས་ཐོབ། དགེ་བ་ཡིན་ཡང་བསམ་པ་མ་དག་པ་སོགས་སྲ་བསྲེ་ཅན་གྱིས་ནི་ལྷ་མིན་དུ་སྐྱེ་བར་མདོ་ལས་བཤད། རྒྱུ་མཐུན་པ་དང་བདག་པོའི་འབྲས་བུ་ཡང་སྔར་མི་དགེ་བཅུའི་སྐབས་སུ་བཤད་པ་དེ་ཉིད་ཕྱིན་ཅི་ལོག་ཏུ་འབྱུང་སྟེ། ཚེ་རིང་འབྱོར་པ་དགྲ་སྲུངས་དང་། །བསྟོད་དང་གྲོགས་མང་སྙན་པའི་གཏམ། །ཚིག་བཙུན་བསམ་པ་འགྲུབ་པ་དང་། །ཡིད་བདེ་བ་དང་བློ་གྲོས་འཕེལ། །འདི་དག་དགེ་བའི་རྒྱུ་མཐུན་བཅུ། །མཐུ་ཆེ་ལོ་ལེགས་ཉམས་དགའ་བ། །མཐོ་དམན་སྙོམས་དང་ཞིང་ས་གཤིན། །རྩ་ཤིང་རྒྱས་དང་དུས་ཚིགས་རན། །འབྲུ་སྨིན་རོ་ཞིམ་འབྲས་བུ་རྒྱས། །དགེ་བ་བཅུ་ཡི་བདག་འབྲས་ཡིན། །ཅེས་སོ། དེ་ལྟར་དགེ་བཅུ་ལ་གནས་པ་ནི། ཚེ་འདི་དང་ཕྱི་མར་རྟག་ཏུ་བདེ་བའི་རྒྱུ་ཡིན་པས་བདག་དགེ་བ་བཅུ་ལ་རྟག་ཏུ་གནས་པར་བགྱིའོ་སྙམ་དུ་ཡང་ཡང་བསྒོམ། དམིགས་སྐོར་ཉི་ཤུ་པའོ།།

འདི་དག་གི་སྐབས་སུ་ལས་འབྲས་ཀྱི་དབྱེ་བ་ཞིབ་མོར་ཤེས་པ་གལ་ཆེ་བས་ཡང་དང་ཡང་དུ་བླ་མས་བཤད་ཅིང་། སློབ་མས་བློ་ལ་སྦྱོང་བ་དང་། ཁ་ཕྱིར་ལྟས་སུ་མ་སོང་བར་རང་ཐོག་ཏུ་འགེལ་བ་ཁོ་ན་གནད་དུ་ཆེའོ། ད་ནི་ལས་འབྲས་བསམས་པའི་ཆོས་སྐོར་རྣམས་ཀྱི་སྙིང་པོའི་གྲུབ་དོན་ཐོན་ཆོས་འདི་ཡིན་ཏེ། སྔར་ཇི་སྐད་བསྟན་པའི་དཀར་ནག་གི་ལས་འབྲས་བསམ། སྡིག་པ་མི་དགེ་བའི་ལས་སྔར་བྱས་ཟིན་ལ། སྟོབས་བཞི་ཚང་བའི་བཤགས་པ་འབུལ་བ་གལ་ཆེ། རྟེན་གྱི་སྟོབས་སྐྱབས་འགྲོ་དང་སེམས་བསྐྱེད། གཉེན་

པོ་ཀུན་དུ་སྤྱོད་པའི་སྟོབས་སྡིག་སྤྱོང་གི་དགེ་བ་གང་འགྲུབ། སུན་འབྱིན་པའི་སྟོབས་སྔར་བྱས་ལ་འགྱོད་སེམས། སླར་ལྡོག་པའི་སྟོབས་ཕྱིན་ཆད་སྡོམ་སེམས་ཏེ། དེ་བཞི་ཚང་བའོ། དེས་ན་ཐུན་གྱི་འགོ་གཞུག་རྣམས་སུ་ཡང་དེ་ལྟ་བུའི་བཤགས་པ་ཚར་རེ་བྱ། ཐུན་མཚམས་སུ་ནི། མཁན་པོ་སློབ་དཔོན་བླ་མ་རྟེན་གསུམ་དགེ་འདུན་ལ་སོགས་པའི་དྲུང་དུ་འཐོལ་བཤགས་ཡང་ཡང་འབུལ་བ་དང་། དེ་དག་མ་འཛོམ་ཀྱང་། རྒྱལ་བ་སྲས་བཅས་མཁའ་དབྱིངས་གང་བ་ལ་དམིགས་ཏེ་བཤགས་པ་འབུལ། བཤགས་ཚིག་ཕུང་པོ་གསུམ་པའི་མདོ་དང་། གསེར་འོད་དམ་པའི་བཤགས་པ་སོགས་དང་། རང་གིས་སྡིག་པ་བགྱིས་པ་གང་ཡིན་པ་དེ་འདི་ལྟར་བགྱིས་སོ་ཞེས་མ་སྦྲས་མ་གསང་བར་བརྗོད་པ་ཉིད་གནད་ཆེ་བ་ཡིན་ནོ། མི་དགེ་བ་བཅུར་མ་ཟད་སྡིག་པ་མི་དགེ་བའི་ལས་སུ་གཏོགས་པ་ཆེ་ཆུང་ཐམས་ཅད་རང་ཡང་མི་བྱེད། གཞན་ཡང་བྱེད་དུ་མི་འཇུག་སྡིག་པ་ལ་ཡི་རང་བའམ་དགའ་བར་མི་བྱ། བསྟོད་ཅིང་བསྔགས་པར་ཡང་མི་བྱ་སྙམ་དུ་བསྒོམ། དཀར་པོ་དགེ་བའི་ལས་ནི་ལས་ལམ་བཅུ་པོ་དེ་ར་མ་ཟད་གཞན་གྱི་སྲོག་བསྐྱབས་པ་དང་། འཚོ་བ་སྟེར་བ་དང་། ཡོ་བྱད་སྦྱིན་པ་དང་། ཚུལ་ཁྲིམས་སྲུང་བ་དང་། དཀོན་མཆོག་མཆོད་པ་དང་། དད་པ་ལ་སོགས་པའི་དགེ་བར་གཏོགས་སོ་ཅོག་རང་གིས་ཀྱང་ཅི་ལྕོགས་སུ་སྒྲུབ་གཞན་ཡང་བྱེད་དུ་འཇུག། རང་གཞན་གྱིས་དགེ་བ་བྱས་པ་ལ་ཡི་རང་ཡང་བསྒོམ། བསྔགས་པ་ཡང་བརྗོད་པར་བྱའོ་སྙམ་དུ་བསམ། ཡང་དགེ་སྡིག་གཉིས་མ་ཡིན་པའི་ལས་ལུང་མ་བསྟན་ཅེས་བྱ་བ་འགྲོ་འཆག་ཉལ་འདུག་སོགས་ངེས་མེད་སྣ་ཚོགས་པ་ཞིག་འདུག་པ། དེ་དག་ལ་རྣམ་པར་སྨིན་པའི་འབྲས་བུ་མེད་ཀྱང་དོན་མེད་དུ་དུས་འདའ་བར་འདུག། ལེ་ལོ་དང་རྣམ་གཡེང་གི་རྒྱུ་ལས་དེ་དག་གི་དབང་དུ་འགྲོ་ཡིན་འདུག་པ་ལ། ཕྱིན་ཆད་ལེ་ལོ་རྣམ་གཡེང་གི་དབང་དུ་མི་བཏང་། ལས་ལུང་མ་བསྟན་འབྱུང་བའི་དོན་དུ་ཡང་དགེ་བ་འབའ་ཞིག་ལ་བློ་དང་བྱ་སྤྱོད་བསྒྱུར་བར་བྱའོ་སྙམ་དུ་བསྒོམ། ཞར་བྱུང་ཐུན་མཚམས་སུ་འདི་

ལྷར་ཡང་བསམ་དགོས་ཏེ། སྐྱེ་བ་ནས་སྐྱེ་བར་ཚོགས་ཁྱད་པར་ཅན་གསོག་པའི་རྒྱུར་མཐོ་རིས་ཀྱི་ལུས་ཡོན་ཏན་བརྒྱད་ལྡན་བསྒྲུབ་དགོས་པས། འཆི་བའི་བསམ་པ་སྤངས་པས་ཚེ་རིང་བ་དང་། མར་མེ་དང་གོས་ཀྱི་སྦྱིན་པ་སོགས་བྱས་པས་གཟུགས་བཟང་བ་དང་། བླ་མ་དང་གྲོགས་ཚངས་པ་མཚུངས་པར་སྤྱོད་པ་རྣམས་ལ་ང་རྒྱལ་མེད་ཅིང་གུས་པར་བྱས་པས་རིགས་ཕུན་སུམ་ཚོགས་པ་དང་། ཕན་ཐོགས་ཀྱི་ཞིང་དང་། སྡུག་བསྔལ་གྱི་ཞིང་དང་། ཡོན་ཏན་གྱི་ཞིང་ལ་སོགས་པ་དང་། གཞན་ཡང་སློང་བ་པོ་ལ་འདོད་དགུ་སྦྱིན་པས་དབང་ཕྱུག་རྗེ་ལོངས་སྤྱོད་ཕུན་སུམ་ཚོགས་པ་དང་། ངག་གི་དགེ་བ་ཁོ་ན་བྱས་པས་ཚིག་བཙུན་པ་དང་། བླ་མ་དང་དཀོན་མཆོག་དང་ཕ་མ་སོགས་མཆོད་ཅིང་། ཡོན་ཏན་སྣ་ཚོགས་སྒྲུབ་པར་སྨོན་ལམ་བཏབ་པས་དབང་ཐང་ཆེ་བ་དང་། སྐྱེས་པའི་དངོས་པོ་ལ་དགའ་ཞིང་། ཕོ་དབང་གཅོད་པ་ལས་བསྐྱབས་པས་སྐྱེས་པ་ཉིད་དུ་འགྱུར་བ་དང་། སྐྱེ་བོ་གཞན་གྱི་བྱ་བ་ཆོས་ལྡན་ལ་རེ་བ་མེད་པའི་བློ་ནས་ཕན་པའི་གྲོགས་བྱས་པས། སྟོབས་ཕུན་སུམ་ཚོགས་པ་ཐོབ་སྟེ། དེ་དག་ཀྱང་ཅི་རིགས་པར་སྒྲུབ་པ་ཡིན་ནོ། དམིགས་སྐོར་ཉེར་གཅིག་པའོ། དེ་ཡན་ཆད་ཀྱིས་སྐྱེས་བུ་ཆུང་ངུའི་རིམ་པ་ཚར་རོ།།

།།གཉིས་པ་སྐྱེས་བུ་འབྲིང་དང་ཐུན་མོང་གི་བསམ་པ་སྦྱང་བ་ལ། འཁོར་བའི་རྒྱུ་འབྲས་བསམ་པ་དང་། ཐར་པའི་རྒྱུ་འབྲས་བསམ་པའོ། དང་པོ་ལ་འབྲས་བུ་འཁོར་བའི་སྡུག་བསྔལ་བསམ་པ་དང་། རྒྱུ་ཀུན་འབྱུང་གི་རབ་དབྱེ་བསམ་པའོ། །དང་པོ་ལ་མཐོ་རིས་ཀྱི་སྡུག་བསྔལ་བསམ་པ་དང་། འཁོར་བ་སྤྱིའི་སྡུག་བསྔལ་བསམ་པའོ། །དང་པོ་ནི། ཕྱག་མཆོད་བཤགས་པ་གསུམ་ཙུང་ཟད་རྒྱས་པ་རེ་བྱས་ནས། ཡན་ལག་བདུན་པ་དང་སྐྱབས་འགྲོ་རྣམས་སྔོན་དུ་བཏང་། བདག་ལས་ཀྱི་དབང་གིས་འགྲོ་བ་རིགས་དྲུག་ཏུ་སྐྱེ་བ་ལེན་པར་འགྱུར་བ་ལས་ངན་སོང་གསུམ་དུ་སྐྱེས་ན་སྡུག་བསྔལ་ནི་དེ་འདྲ། མིར་སྐྱེས་ན་སྐྱིད་དོ་སྙམ་ན་ཡང་མི་སྐྱིད་ཏེ་མི་ཕལ་ཆེར་མངལ་སྐྱེས་ཡིན། མངལ་དུ་ཟླ་བ་

དགུ་འམ་བཅུའི་བར་དུ་གནས་དགོས་ན། མངལ་གནས་དེ་ལ་དོག་པའི་སྡུག་བསྔལ་དང་།
མུན་གནག་པའི་སྡུག་བསྔལ་དང་། དྲི་མི་ཞིམ་པའི་སྡུག་བསྔལ་གསུམ་རྟག་ཏུ་ཡོད། མ་
དེ་བཀྲེས་པའི་ཚེ། གཡང་ཟ་བའི་རྣམ་པ་དང་། འགྲངས་པའི་ཚེ་རིས་ནོན་པ་ལྟ་བུ་དང་།
བཟའ་བཏུང་དྲོན་མོ་ཟོས་འཐུངས་བྱས་ན་ཆུ་ཚན་དུ་བཙོས་པ་ལྟ་བུ་དང་། གྲང་མོ་ཟོས་
འཐུངས་བྱས་ན་འཁྱགས་རུམ་དུ་བསྐྱུར་བ་ལྟ་བུའི་སྡུག་བསྔལ་ཡོད། མངལ་ནས་ཕྱི་རུ་
བཙའ་བའི་ཚེ་ཡང་ཏིལ་མར་འཚིར་བའི་ཤིང་གི་བར་དུ་གཙེར་བ་ལྟ་བུ་དང་། ཚོགས་ཐམས་
ཅད་བྱེ་ཞིང་ཞིག་པ་ལྟ་བུའི་སྡུག་བསྔལ་ཡོད། བཙས་མ་ཐག་ཏུ་གང་ལ་རེག་ཀྱང་རྩུབ་
སྟེ། དར་འཇམ་པོས་དཀྲིས་ཀྱང་ཚེར་མའི་དོང་དུ་བསྐྱུར་བ་ལྟ་བུ་དང་། གཞན་གྱི་ལག་
ཏུ་བླངས་པ་ན། ཁྱིའུ་ཁྲས་ཁྱེར་བ་ལྟ་བུའི་སྡུག་བསྔལ་ཡོད། ད་ལྟ་རང་རེས་མ་དྲན་པར་
ཟད། དྲན་ན་གཞན་མི་དགོས། སྐྱེ་བའི་སྡུག་བསྔལ་གཅིག་བུ་ལ་བསམས་ཀྱང་མིར་སྐྱེས་
པ་ལ་གྲོག་ཅི་ཡང་མི་འདུག བདག་ལས་ཀྱི་དབང་གིས་འཁོར་བར་སྐྱེ་བ་མི་ལེན་པའི་ཆོས་
ཅིག་བྱ་དགོས། མིའི་འགྲོ་བ་མངལ་སྐྱེས་ཀྱི་སྡུག་བསྔལ་ནི་དེ་ལྟ་བུར་འདུག །སྤྱིར་ཁམས་
གསུམ་གང་དུ་སྐྱེས་ཀྱང་སྡུག་བསྔལ། འགྲོ་བ་གང་དུ་སྐྱེས་ཀྱང་སྡུག་བསྔལ། སྐྱེ་གནས་ཇི་
ལྟ་བུར་སྐྱེས་ཀྱང་སྡུག་བསྔལ་ཏེ། སྡུག་བསྔལ་རྣམ་པ་ལྔ་དང་ལྡན་པའོ། །དེ་ཡང་སྐྱེ་བ་སྡུག་
བསྔལ་དང་ལྡན་པ་ཞེས་བྱ་བ་ཚོར་བ་དྲག་པོ་དང་བཅས་ཏེ་སྐྱེ་དགོས། སྐྱེ་བ་གནས་ངན་ལེན་
དང་ལྡན་པ་བྱ་བ་ཉོན་མོངས་པ་བསྐྱེད་འཕེལ་གྱི་ས་བོན་དང་ལྡན་པར་སྐྱེ་དགོས། སྐྱེ་བ་སྡུག་
བསྔལ་གྱི་གནས་སུ་གྱུར་པ་བྱ་བ། སྐྱེས་པ་ལས་ན་ནད་འཆི་བ་སོགས་སྡུག་བསྔལ་གཞན་འབྱུང་
བ་ཡིན། སྐྱེ་བ་ཉོན་མོངས་ཀྱི་གནས་སུ་གྱུར་པ་བྱ་བ་སྐྱེ་བ་བླངས་པས་ཕྱིས་རྐྱེན་དང་ཕྲད་ནས་
ཉོན་མོངས་པ་མང་པོ་སྐྱེས་ཤིང་དེས་ཀུན་ནས་བླངས་པའི་ལས་དུ་མ་གསོག་པའོ། །སྐྱེ་བ་ཉིད་
དབང་མེད་དུ་འཇིག་པས་སྡུག་བསྔལ་བ་བྱ་བ་ནི། སྐྱེ་བ་ཉིད་སྐད་ཅིག་སྐད་ཅིག་གིས་འཇིག་
པའོ། །དེ་ལྟར་ན་སྐྱེ་བ་སྡུག་བསྔལ་བའོ་སྙམ་དུ་བསྒོམ། དམིགས་སྐོར་ཉེར་གཉིས་པའོ།།

།གཞན་ཡང་མི་རྣམས་ལ་རྒས་པའི་སྡུག་བསྔལ་ཡོད་དེ། རྒས་པའི་ཚེ་ཉམས་པའི་སྡུག་བསྔལ་ལྔ་ཡོད། ཁ་དོག་ཉམས་པ་བྱ་བ་ཤ་མདོག་དང་མདངས་ལེགས་པོ་རྣམས་ཉུབ་སྟེ་ཁ་དོག་མི་སྡུག་པ་ནག་སྲམ་པའམ། སྒོ་ཐལ་གྱིས་འགྲོ། མགོ་སྐྲ་བའི་མེ་ཏོག་ལྟར་སྐྱ་བ་དང་། དབང་པོ་ཀུན་གྱི་བཀྲག་ཤོར་བ་ཡིན། དབྱིབས་ཉམས་པ་བྱ་བ་སོ་ནི་ལྷུང་། ལུས་ནི་གུག་གུག་པར་སོང་། ཡན་ལག་རྣམས་ནི་འཁྱོགས། ཤ་ནི་སྐམས། པགས་པ་ནི་ལྷོད། གདོང་བྱད་ནི་གྲུས་གདན་རྙིང་པ་ལྟར་གཉེར་མས་ཁེངས་པ་ལ་གང་ལ་ལྟས་ཀྱང་མི་མཛེས་པའོ། མཐུ་སྟོབས་ཉམས་པ་བྱ་བ་ནི། ལྡང་བ་ན་སུག་བཞི་འཛུགས། འགྲོ་བ་ན་འཁྱོར། འདུག་པ་ན་ཚ་དོ་ཐག་པ་ཆད་པ་བཞིན་སྡོད། སྨྲ་བ་ན་ལྷབ་ལྷིབ་ལས་མེད་པ་ལ་སོགས་པའོ། །དབང་པོ་ཉམས་པ་བྱ་བ་ནི། མིག་མི་གསལ་རྣ་བ་འོན་པ་སོགས་གཞན་གྱིས་ལྟས་ན་རྫུས་འདེབས་པ་འདྲ་བར་འགྱུར། ལོངས་སྤྱོད་ཉམས་པ་བྱ་བ་ནི། ཁ་ཟས་ཉུང་ན་བཀྲེས། མངས་ན་མི་འཇུ་བ་ལ་སོགས་པ་འདོད་ཡོན་ལ་སྤྱོད་དུ་མེད་པའོ། །བདག་ཀྱང་རྒས་པའི་སྡུག་བསྔལ་མ་སྤངས་པས། ཚེ་རིང་རྒས་ལོང་བྱུང་ན་ཐ་མ་རྒས་པར་འགྱུར། གཉེན་བཤེས་དང་དགྲ་གཉེན་འགྲོ་བ་འདི་ཀུན་ཀྱང་དེ་དང་འདྲ་སྙམ་དུ་བསྒོམ། དམིགས་སྐོར་ཉེར་གསུམ་པའོ།།

ན་བའི་སྡུག་བསྔལ་བསམ་པ་ནི། སྡུག་བསྔལ་གཞན་ཡང་ཡོད་དེ། སྔོན་གྱི་ལས་དང་འཕྲལ་གྱི་རྐྱེན་ལས་ནད་རྣམ་པ་སྣ་ཚོགས་པ་འབྱུང་བ་ཡིན། དེ་ཡང་སྡུག་བསྔལ་ལྔ་སྟེ། སྡུག་བསྔལ་དང་ཡིད་མི་བདེ་འཕེལ་བ་ཞེས་བྱ་བ་ནི་ཟུག་རྔུ་དངོས་ཀྱི་སྡུག་བསྔལ་ཡིན། ལུས་ཀྱི་རང་བཞིན་འགྱུར་བ་ནི་ཤ་ཞུ་པགས་པ་བསྐམས་པ་ལ་སོགས་པའོ། །ཡུལ་ཡིད་དུ་འོང་བ་སྤྱད་དབང་མེད་པ་དང་། ཡིད་དུ་མི་འོང་བ་ངེས་པར་བསྟེན་དགོས་པ་གཉིས་ནི་ཟས་དང་སྤྱོད་ལམ་འདོད་པ་བྱེད་དུ་མེད་ཅིང་། མི་འདོད་པའི་སྨན་ཁ་བ་དང་མེ་གཏར་སོགས་བསྟེན་དགོས་པའོ། །སྲོག་གི་དབང་པོ་དང་འབྲལ་བ་ཞེས་བྱ་བ་ནི། འཆི་བའམ་

འཆིར་ངོགས་པས་སྡུག་བསྔལ་བ་སྐྱེ། ན་བ་རང་བས་ཀྱང་འཆི་བའི་སྡུག་བསྔལ་སྔོན་བསུ་བ་ཡིན། བདག་ཀྱང་ན་བ་ལས་མ་ཐར་ན་བར་འགྱུར་ཏེ་འོང་། བདག་གི་བཤེས་ལ་སོགས་པ་དགྲ་གཉེན་འགྲོ་བ་འདི་ཀུན་ཀྱང་དེ་དང་འདྲའོ་སྙམ་མོ། །དམིགས་སྐོར་ཉེར་བཞི་པའོ།།

ཡང་སྡུག་བསྔལ་གཞན་ཡོད་དེ། འཆི་བའི་སྡུག་བསྔལ་རྣམ་པ་ལྔ་ནི་ཡོངས་སྤྱོད་ཕུན་སུམ་ཚོགས་པ་དང་འབྲལ། རྗེ་འཛིང་ཕུན་སུམ་ཚོགས་པ་དང་འབྲལ། འཁོར་གྲོགས་ཕུན་སུམ་ཚོགས་པ་དང་འབྲལ། ཕངས་ཤིང་སྡུག་པའི་ལུས་དང་ཡང་འབྲལ། འཆི་བ་ཉིད་སྡུག་བསྔལ་དང་ཡིད་མི་བདེ་དྲག་པོ་དང་བཅས་པའོ། རང་རེ་མངོན་པར་ཞེན་ཅིང་ཆགས་པའི་ཡུལ་ཕྱོགས་སམ། ཁང་ཁྱིམ་མམ། ནོར་རྫས་སམ། ཡར་གྱི་དཔོན། མར་གྱི་གཡོག། ཐད་ཀའི་གྲོགས་པོ་ཐམས་ཅད་དང་བྲལ་ཞིང་། གནད་གཅོད་ཀྱི་སྡུག་བསྔལ་ཆེན་པོ་དང་བཅས་ཏེ་འཆི་དགོས། རྒྱུས་པར་གོང་འཆི་བ་མི་རྟག་པ་བཤད་པའི་སྐབས་སུ་བསྟན་པ་ལྟར་བསྒོམ། དམིགས་སྐོར་ཉེར་ལྔ་པའོ།།

སྡུག་བསྔལ་གཞན་ཡང་ཡོད་དེ། འདོད་པ་བཙལ་ཏེ་མ་རྙེད་པས་སྡུག་བསྔལ། དེ་ཡང་ཡོངས་སྤྱོད་དམ། ཁ་དྲག་གམ། མངའ་ཐང་འཕྲུན་བུ་བསྒྲུབ་པའི་ཕྱིར་དུ་སྲོག་ལ་མ་ལྟས་པར་འཁྲུག་པ་ལ་ཡང་འཇུག །ཡོ་བླ་མང་པོ་བགྲོད་དགོས་པའི་བྱེས་སུ་ཡང་འགྲོ །དུས་བཞིར་ཟིན་པ་དང་འཁོར་བ་མེད་པའི་ལས་ལ་རྟག་ཏུ་འཇུག །རྐང་ཁྲག་ནི་ཛོ། ལག་ཁྲག་ནི་ཤིང་། བྱིན་པ་ནི་རྟ། སྣལ་མ་ནི་ལྕུག་ཏུ་བྱས་ཀྱོ་བསླན་བྱུང་བཀུག་ཀྱང་འདོད་དོན་གང་ཡང་མ་བྱུང་། ལྟོགས་སྐོམ་ཐམས་ཅད་ནི་དང་དུ་བླངས། ཚ་གྲང་ཐམས་ཅད་ནི་ཁྱད་དུ་བསད། ཉིན་མཚན་ཀུན་དུ་ནི་དལ་བ་མེད། ཤ་ཁྲག་ལྷུ་བར་སོང་སོང་ལས་བྱས་ཀྱང་ལྟོ་རྒྱབ་ཙམ་ཡང་མ་འགྲོར། འབད་པ་བྱས་པ་དོན་མེད་དུ་སོང་བས་སེམས་ལ་ཡི་ཆད་སྐྱེ། གཞན་ཡང་མི་སྡུག་པ་དང་ཕྲད་པའི་སྡུག་བསྔལ་བྱ་བ་ཡོད། རང་ཉིད་དགྲ་བོའི་དབང་དུ་སོང་བའམ། ནད་དང་སྡུག་བསྔལ་དྲག་པོ་ཐོག་ཏུ་བབ་པའམ། གསོད་

པར་བྱེད་པའི་སྒྲིག་ཆགས་དང་འཕྲད་པའམ། གཡངས་སུ་ལྷུང་བའམ། ཆུས་ཁྱེར་བའམ། གཏམ་ངན་པ་ཐོས་པའམ། བཙོན་དུ་གཞུག་པ་དང་ཆད་པས་བཅད་པ་སྤྱོད་པ་ལ་སོགས་པ་ཡིན། གཞན་ཡང་སྡུག་པ་དང་བྲལ་བའི་སྡུག་བསྔལ་བྱ་བ་ཡོད། ཕ་མ་སྤུན་ཟླ་ཁྱིམ་ཐབ་གྲོགས་ལ་སོགས་པ་མེད་ཐབས་མེད་པ་དང་བྲལ་ཙ་ན་སེམས་ལ་བཟོད་ཐབས་མེད་པའི་སྡུག་བསྔལ་ལུས་ཚུན་ཆད་ཀྱང་རྒྱུད་ནས་འགྲོ་བ་ཡོད། དེ་བཞིན་དུ་ནོར་རྫོར་རླག་བྱུང་བའམ། མངའ་ཐང་ཉམས་པའམ། དབང་ཐང་ཤོར་བའམ། རང་གི་ཡིད་ཆགས་ཤིང་བློ་སྨོན་པའི་གནས་ཅི་འདྲ་ཞིག་ཉམས་ཀྱང་སེམས་ལ་མྱ་ངན་ཆེན་པོ་སྐྱེ་བ་ཡིན་ཏེ། དེ་ལྟར་ན་བདག་ཀྱང་སྡུག་བསྔལ་དེ་དག་ལས་མ་འདས། །ཞེས་སོགས་གོང་བཞིན་བསྒོམ། དེ་ལྟར་སྡུག་བསྔལ་བདུན་པོ་དེ་ནི་འགྲོ་བ་གཞན་རྣམས་ལ་ཡང་ཡོད་མོད་ཀྱི། མི་རྣམས་གཙོ་བོར་སྤྱོད་པའི་ཕྱིར་འདིར་སྨོས་པའོ། སྡུག་བསྔལ་བརྒྱད་པ་སྐབས་འདིར་བསམ་པའི་ལུགས་ཡོད་ཀྱང་འོག་ཏུ་བཤད་ན་བདེའོ། དམིགས་སྐོར་ཉེར་དྲུག་པའོ།།

ཡང་ལྷ་མིན་གྱི་འགྲོ་བ་ཞེས་བྱ་བར་སྐྱེས་ན་སྐྱིད་དམ་སྙམ་ན་མི་སྐྱིད་དེ། རང་བཞིན་གྱིས་ལྷའི་དཔལ་ལ་ཕྲག་དོག་པས་སེམས་ལ་མི་བདེ་བ་ཆེན་པོ་རྟག་ཏུ་ཡོད། དུས་དུས་ན་ལྷ་དང་འཐབ་པ་ལས་ལྷ་མིན་བསོད་ནམས་ཀྱི་སྟོབས་ཆུང་བས་གསོད་པ་དང་བཅག་པ་དང་ཡན་ལག་གཅོད་པ་དང་འདྲལ་བ་ལ་སོགས་པའི་སྡུག་བསྔལ་ཤིན་དུ་མང་། ཕལ་ཆེར་ནག་ཕྱོགས་ཡིན་པས་ཆོས་ལ་མི་དགའ། འགའ་ཞིག་མོས་སུ་ཆུག་ཀྱང་རྣམ་སྨིན་གྱི་སྒྲིབ་པ་ཅན་ཡིན་པས་ཁྱད་པར་རྟོགས་པའི་སྐལ་བ་མེད་དོ། འོ་ན་འདོད་པའི་ཁམས་ཀྱི་ལྷར་སྐྱེས་ན་བདེའོ་སྙམ་ན། དེར་ཡང་མི་བདེ་སྟེ་འདོད་ཡོན་ལ་བག་མེད་པར་སྤྱོད་པས་ཚེ་ཟད་དུ་མ་ཚོར་བ་ལ་ཟད། གཞན་ཡང་ལྷ་དབང་ཆུང་བ་རྣམས་དབང་ཆེ་བས་གནས་ནས་བསྐྲད་པས་སྡུག་བསྔལ། བསོད་ནམས་ཆུང་བ་འགའ་ཞིག་པེ་ཚེ་རེ་ཙམ་མ་གཏོགས་ལོ་བྱད་གང་ཡང་མེད་པས་ཤིན་དུ་འཕོངས་པའང་ཡོད། དེ་དག་གིས་ལྷ་གཞན་འབྱོར་

པ་ཆེན་པོ་རྣམས་མཐོང་བ་ན། རང་གི་བསོད་ནམས་ལ་ཡི་ཆད་པའི་སེམས་ཀྱི་སྡུག་བསྔལ་དཔག་ཏུ་མེད་པ་ཡོད། ཁྱད་པར་རྒྱལ་ཆེན་བཞིའི་རིགས་དང་སུམ་ཅུ་རྩ་གསུམ་པའི་གནས་ན། ལྷ་མ་ཡིན་དང་འཐབ་པའི་སྡུག་བསྔལ་ཤིན་དུ་ཆེ། འདོད་ཁམས་ཀྱི་ལྷ་ཐམས་ཅད་ལ་ཐུན་མོང་དུ་འཆི་འཕོ་བ་དང་ལྟུང་བའི་སྡུག་བསྔལ་ཞེས་བྱ་བ་ཡོད་དེ། དེ་ལ་ལྷ་རྣམས་འཆི་བའི་སྔོན་རོལ་ཞག་བདུན་ནས་འཆི་ལྟས་ལྔ་འབྱུང་སྟེ། ལུས་ཀྱི་ཁ་དོག་མི་སྡུག་པར་འགྱུར་བ་དང་། ཡིད་སྐྱོ་ཞིང་སྟན་ལ་མི་དགའ་བ་དང་མེ་ཏོག་གི་འཕྲེང་བའི་རྒྱན་རྣམས་རྙིངས་པ་དང་། གོས་ལ་དྲི་མ་ནག་པོ་ཆགས་པ་དང་། ལུས་ལས་རྔུལ་འབྱུང་བ་རྣམས་སོ། །དེ་རྣམས་བྱུང་བ་ན་རང་རང་གི་གཡོག་དང་གྲོགས་པོ་མོ་རྣམས་ཀྱིས་ཀྱང་སྤངས་ཏེ། ལྷ་གཞན་གྱི་དྲུང་དུ་འགྲོ་ལ། ལྷའི་འདོད་ཡོན་ལ་ནི་ཆགས་ཀྱང་དབང་མེད་དུ་འབྲལ་བར་ཤེས། ཟློག་ཐབས་ནི་མེད། ཛ་མོ་ཛེའུ་སྡོར་བ་ལྟ་བུ་དང་། ཀླུ་ནམ་མཁའ་ལྡིང་གིས་ཁྱེར་བ་ལྟ་བུ་དང་། ཉ་བྱེ་ཚན་ལ་བསྲེགས་པ་ལྟ་བུ་དང་། རྒྱ་མཚོ་ཆེན་པོའི་དབུས་སུ་གྲུ་ཞིག་པ་ལྟ་བུའི་སྡུག་བསྔལ་འབྱུང་། དུས་རིང་ཐུང་ནི་ལྷའི་ཞག་བདུན་ཡིན་ན་ཐུང་ཤོས་རྒྱལ་ཆེན་བཞི་རིགས་ཀྱི་དབང་དུ་བྱས་ཀྱང་མི་ལོ་ཕྱེད་དང་བཞི་བརྒྱ་ཡིན། དོས་ནི་དྲག། ཡུན་ནི་རིང་ལྟུང་བའི་སྡུག་བསྔལ་བྱ་བ་ལྷ་རྣམས་ཤི་བའི་འོག་ཏུ་ལྷར་སྐྱེ་བ་ནི་སྲིད་མཐའ་ཙམ། མིར་སྐྱེ་བ་ཡང་ཤིན་དུ་ཉུང་། ཕལ་ཆེར་ངན་སོང་དུ་སྐྱེ་བ་ཡིན། ཇི་སྐད་དུ། ལྷ་ཡི་འཇིག་རྟེན་དག་ནས་འཕོས་པ་ལ། །གལ་ཏེ་དགེ་བའི་ལྷག་མ་འགའ་མེད་ན། །དེ་ནས་དབང་མེད་དུད་འགྲོ་ཡི་དྭགས་དང་། །དམྱལ་བར་གནས་པ་གང་ཡང་རུང་བར་འགྱུར། །ཅེས་གསུངས། ལྷ་རྣམས་ཀྱི་མངོན་ཤེས་འོག་ཏུ་འཇུག་པས་འཆི་ཁར་གང་དུ་སྐྱེ་བ་ལེན་པ་ཤེས་ནས་མིར་སྐྱེ་ནའང་འདོད་ཡོན་གྱི་མིག་མི་ཁེངས་ཤིང་། སྡུག་བསྔལ་མང་པོ་ཅན་དུ་མཐོང་། གལ་ཏེ་ངན་སོང་གསུམ་དུ་སྐྱེ་ན། དེའི་སྡུག་བསྔལ་མྱོང་དགོས་པར་ཤེས་ནས་སེམས་ཀྱི་སྡུག་བསྔལ་ལ་བཟོད་གླགས་མེད་པ་འབྱུང་བ་ཡིན་ཏེ། ངན་སོང་གསུམ་

གྱི་ལུས་ཀྱི་སྡུག་བསྔལ་བས་དེའི་སེམས་ཀྱི་སྡུག་བསྔལ་ཆེ་བ་ཡོད་སྙམ་དུ་བསམ། དམིགས་སྐོར་ཉེར་བདུན་པའོ།།

འོ་ན་ཁམས་གོང་མའི་ལྷར་སྐྱེས་ན་བདེ་བ་ཡོད་དམ་སྙམ་ན། དེར་ཡང་བདེ་བ་མེད་ཏེ། ཁམས་གོང་མ་དེ་དག་ན། སོ་སོ་སྐྱེ་བོས་ལྟས་ན་སྡུག་བསྔལ་མངོན་འགྱུར་བ་མེད་ཀྱང་འཕགས་པས་གཟིགས་ན་འདུ་བྱེད་ཀྱི་སྡུག་བསྔལ་གྱི་ནའི་རང་བཞིན་ལས་མ་འདས་པ་དང་། ཏིང་ངེ་འཛིན་གྱིས་མྱོས་པ་ལྟར་གྱུར་པས་སོ་སོ་སྐྱེ་བོ་རྣམས་ཡོན་ཏན་གོང་ནས་གོང་དུ་འགྲོ་བ་མེད་ཅིང་། ཏིང་ངེ་འཛིན་གྱི་རོ་མྱངས་པས་རོ་མྱང་ཅན་གྱི་ཏིང་ངེ་འཛིན་དང་འབྲལ་མི་འཕོངས་ཤིང་། དེས་རང་རང་གི་ཏིང་ངེ་འཛིན་ཉམས་ནས་འཆི་བར་འགྱུར་བའང་ཡོད། སྔོས་སུ་དེ་ན་གནས་པའི་འགྲོ་བ་སོ་སོ་སྐྱེ་བོ་ཐམས་ཅད་སྔོན་གྱི་ལས་ཀྱིས་འཕེན་པ་ཟད་པ་ན། སླར་ཡང་འདོད་པའི་ཁམས་སུ་སྐྱེ་བ་ལེན་ཏེ། སྔོན་མའི་རྟེན་ལ་འཇིག་རྟེན་པའི་ཏིང་ངེ་འཛིན་བསྒོམས་པའི་སྐབས་དང་། སྐབས་དེར་བསམ་གཏན་གཟུགས་མེད་ཀྱི་ཏིང་ངེ་འཛིན་ལ་ཉམས་བདེ་བདེ་འདྲ་བ་གསོས་དལ་དལ་འདྲ་བར་འདུག་ཀྱང་ཡིད་བརྟན་ཅི་ཡང་མ་བྱུང་བར་སྐྱེ་བོ་ཕལ་པར་ཉམས་ཏེ། ཉོན་མོངས་དྲག་ལ་སྡུག་བསྔལ་ཆེ་བར་སོང་བ་དེ་འདྲ་བ་ལ་སྙིང་པོ་ཅི་ཞིག་ཡོད་སྙམ་དུ་བསམ། དམིགས་སྐོར་ཉེར་བརྒྱད་པའོ།།

གཉིས་པ་འཁོར་བ་མཐའ་དག་སྡུག་བསྔལ་དུ་བསམ་པ་ནི། སྔོན་འགྲོ་སོགས་སྔར་བཞིན་ལས་དམྱལ་བའི་གནས་ན་ནི་སྡུག་བསྔལ་དེ་འདྲ་སྙམ་པ་ནས། ཡི་དྭགས་དང་དུད་འགྲོ་དང་མི་དང་ལྷ་མ་ཡིན་དང་འདོད་ཁམས་ཀྱི་ལྷ་དང་གཟུགས་དང་གཟུགས་མེད་པའི་ལྷའི་བར་དུ་སྡུག་བསྔལ་དེ་འདྲ་ན། ཁམས་གསུམ་འཁོར་བ་འདི་ཀུན་སྡུག་བསྔལ་གསུམ་མམ་དྲུག་གམ་བརྒྱད་ལ་སོགས་པ་སྡུག་བསྔལ་གྱི་རང་བཞིན་ཅན་དང་། སྡུག་བསྔལ་གྱི་ཁོང་འཚངས་ཅན་དང་། སྡུག་བསྔལ་གྱིས་ཀུན་དུ་བསྐོར་བ་ཡིན། སྡུག་བསྔལ་མི་

ལྟར་འབར། ཆུ་ལྟར་འཁྱུག རླུང་ལྟར་གཡེངས། རི་ལྟར་ནོན་པ་ཡིན། གནས་གང་དུ་གནས་ཀྱང་སྡུག་བསྔལ་གྱི་གནས། ལུས་ཅི་འདྲ་བླངས་ཀྱང་སྡུག་བསྔལ་གྱི་ལུས། གྲོགས་སུ་དང་འགྲོགས་ཀྱང་སྡུག་བསྔལ་གྱི་གྲོགས། ལོངས་སྤྱོད་ཅི་ལ་ལོངས་སྤྱད་ཀྱང་སྡུག་བསྔལ་གྱི་ལོངས་སྤྱོད་ཡིན། སྡུག་བསྔལ་དེ་ཡང་རྣམ་པ་གསུམ་སྟེ། སྡུག་བསྔལ་གྱི་སྡུག་བསྔལ་ཞེས་བྱ་བ། ཚ་གྲང་ནད་ལ་སོགས་པ་ཚོར་བ་སྡུག་བསྔལ་ཐམས་ཅད་ཡིན། འགྱུར་བའི་སྡུག་བསྔལ་ཞེས་བྱ་བ། ཚེ་དང་ལོངས་སྤྱོད་ལ་སོགས་པ་ཐ་ན་བསམ་གཏན་གྱི་བདེ་བ་ཕུན་ཆད་ཏེ་ཚོར་བ་བདེ་བ་ཐམས་ཅད་ཡིན། འདུ་བྱེད་ཀྱི་སྡུག་བསྔལ་ཞེས་བྱ་བ་སྡུག་བསྔལ་དེ་གཉིས་ཀའི་གཞི་འདུ་བྱེད་ཉེ་བར་ལེན་པའི་ཕུང་པོ་ཙམ་འདི་སྡུག་བསྔལ་ཐམས་ཅད་ཀྱི་འབྱུང་གནས་དང་ཞིང་ས་ཡིན། འདི་ཚོར་བ་བཏང་སྙོམས་ཕོ་ན་དང་ལྡན་པའི་ཚེ་འདུ་བྱེད་ཀྱི་སྡུག་བསྔལ་ཕོ་ནའི་མིང་ཐོགས་པ་ཡིན། འདི་ལས་མ་ཐར་ན་གཞན་གཉིས་ལས་ཐར་བ་མེད་པས་ཅིས་ཀྱང་སྡུག་བསྔལ་གསུམ་ལས་ཐར་བར་བྱ་སྙམ་དུ་བསྒོམ། དམིགས་སྐོར་ཉེར་དགུ་པའོ།།

ད་ནི་གོང་དུ་བཤད་པ་ལྟར་སྐྱེ་བ་སྡུག་བསྔལ། རྒས་པ་སྡུག་བསྔལ། ན་བ་སྡུག་བསྔལ། འཆི་བ་སྡུག་བསྔལ། མི་སྡུག་པ་དང་ཕྲད་པས་སྡུག་བསྔལ། སྡུག་པ་དང་བྲལ་བས་སྡུག་བསྔལ། འདོད་པ་བཙལ་གྱིས་མ་རྙེད་པས་སྡུག་བསྔལ་ཅེས་སྡུག་བསྔལ་བདུན་དང་། བརྒྱད་པ་ནི་མདོར་ན་ཉེ་བར་ལེན་པའི་ཕུང་པོ་ལྔ་སྡུག་བསྔལ་ཏེ། དེ་ཡང་རྣམ་པ་ལྔས་སྡུག་བསྔལ་བ་སྟེ་མངོན་པར་འགྲུབ་པའི་སྡུག་བསྔལ་གྱི་སྣོད་དུ་གྱུར་པ་ནི། སྐྱེ་བ་ཕྱི་མ་ཕན་ཆད་ཀྱི་སྡུག་བསྔལ་གསོས་འདེབས་པ་ཡིན། མངོན་པར་གྲུབ་པ་ལ་བརྟེན་པའི་སྡུག་བསྔལ་གྱི་སྣོད་ནི་ཕུང་པོ་ཉིད་གྲུབ་པ་ལ་བརྟེན་ནས། སྐྱེ་རྒ་ན་འཆི་སོགས་གཞན་ཐམས་ཅད་འབྱུང་དུ་རུང་བ་ཡིན། སྡུག་བསྔལ་གྱི་སྡུག་བསྔལ་གྱི་སྣོད་དང་། འགྱུར་བའི་སྡུག་བསྔལ་གྱི་སྣོད་ཅེས་བྱ་བ་གཉིས་ནི། ཕུང་པོ་ལ་བརྟེན་ནས་དེ་དག་འབྱུང་བ་ཡིན།

འདུ་བྱེད་ཀྱི་སྡུག་བསྔལ་གྱི་རང་བཞིན་དུ་གྱུར་པ་ནི། ཕུང་པོ་རང་ཉིད་འདུ་བྱེད་ཀྱི་སྡུག་བསྔལ་ཡིན་པར་ཤེས་པ་སྟེ། ཁམས་གསུམ་འཁོར་བ་ཐམས་ཅད་སྡུག་བསྔལ་བརྒྱད་ཀྱི་ངོ་བོ་འོ་སྙམ་དུ་སྒོམ་པའོ། །སྡུག་བསྔལ་བརྒྱད་ལ་བསམ་པ་སྟེ་དམིགས་སྐོར་སུམ་ཅུ་པའོ། འཁོར་བ་འདི་ལ་སྡུག་བསྔལ་གྱི་རྣམ་གྲངས་གཞན་ཡང་ཡོད་ཏེ། དང་པོ་ངེས་པ་མེད་པས་སྡུག་བསྔལ་བའི་ཉེས་པ་ནི། དགྲ་གཉེན་དང་ཕ་བུ་དང་། གནས་ལུས་ལོངས་སྤྱོད་ཐམས་ཅད་མ་ངེས་པ་ཁོ་ནར་འགྲོ་བ་སྟེ། ཇི་སྐད་དུ། ཕ་ནི་བུ་ཉིད་མ་ནི་ཆུང་མ་ཉིད། །ཅེས་པ་ལ་སོགས་པ་བ་ལྟ་བུའོ། །གཉིས་པ་ངོམས་མི་ཤེས་པའི་ཉེས་པ་ནི། འདོད་ཡོན་ཇི་ཙམ་སྤྱད་ཀྱང་ངོམས་པ་མེད། སྡུག་བསྔལ་ཇི་ཙམ་མྱོང་ཡང་སུན་ཆུ་མེད་པའོ། །རེ་རེས་རྒྱ་མཚོ་བཞི་བས་ལྷག་པ་ཡི། །ཞེས་སོགས་སྦྱར། གསུམ་པ་ལུས་ཡང་ཡང་འདོར་བའི་ཉེས་པ་ནི། ཡང་ཡང་འཆི་བ་མྱོང་དགོས་པ་སྟེ། རེ་རེས་བདག་ཉིད་རུས་པའི་ཕུང་པོ་ནི་སོགས་སོ། །བཞི་པ་ཡང་ཡང་ཉིང་མཚམས་སྦྱོར་བའི་ཉེས་པ་ནི། སྐྱེ་བ་མཐའ་མེད་པ་ལེན་དགོས་པ་སྟེ། མ་ཡི་ཐུག་མཐའ་རྒྱུ་ཤུག་ཚི་གུ་གུ་ཙམ་སོགས་སོ། །ལྔ་པ་ཡང་ཡང་མཐོ་དམན་དུ་འགྱུར་བའི་ཉེས་པ་ནི། བརྒྱ་བྱིན་དུ་གྱུར་ཀྱང་ས་སྟེང་དུ་ལྷུང་། འཁོར་ལོས་བསྒྱུར་རྒྱལ་དུ་གྱུར་ཀྱང་བྲན་གྱི་ཐ་མར་སྐྱེ། ཚེ་གཅིག་པོ་དེ་ཉིད་ལ་ཡང་བདེ་སྡུག་མཐོ་དམན་འགྱུར་རྒྱུད་གང་ལ་ཡང་ཡིད་བརྟན་ཅུང་ཟད་ཀྱང་མེད་པ་སྟེ། བརྒྱ་བྱིན་འཇིག་རྟེན་མཆོད་འོས་གྱུར་ནས་ཀྱང་། །ཅེས་པ་ལ་སོགས་པ་ལྟར་རོ། །དྲུག་པ་གཅིག་པུ་གྲོགས་མེད་པས་སྡུག་བསྔལ་བའི་ཉེས་པ་ནི། སྐྱེ་ན་ཡང་གཅིག་པུར་སྐྱེ། འཆི་ན་ཡང་གཅིག་པུར་འཆི། རྒས་པ་དང་ན་བ་ཡང་གཅིག་གཅིག་པུར་མྱོང་། བར་དོར་འགྲོ་བ་ཡང་གཅིག་པུར་འགྲོ་དགོས་ན། འགྲོགས་བཤེས་མཛའ་བ་ཐམས་ཅད་སྙིང་པོ་མེད་ཏེ། དེ་ལྟར་ཉོངས་པར་འགྱུར་འཚལ་བསོད་ནམས་ནི།། ཞེས་སོགས་དང་སྦྱར་རོ། དེ་ལྟར་ན་འཁོར་བ་ཐམས་ཅད་སྡུག་བསྔལ་དྲུག་གི་རང་བཞིན་གྱིས་སྡུག་བསྔལ་ཏེ། ཡ་གི་སྲིད་པའི་རྩེ་མོར་

སྐྱེས་ཀྱང་མཐར་མེད་ཀྱི་འཁྲམ་ཇོར་འགྲོ་བ་ལ་ཚོགས་མེད། སྡུག་བསྔལ་ཡང་ལ་ཡང་བསྲིངས་ཁོ་ན་ཡིན། ཁང་པ་མེ་འབར་བའི་ནང་དུ་ཚུད་པ་དང་འདྲ། ཚོང་པ་སྲིན་མོའི་གླིང་དུ་ཚུད་པ་དང་འདྲ། འབྲོག་དགོན་ལམ་མེད་པར་འཁྱམས་པ་དང་འདྲ་བས། ཅེས་ཀྱང་མྱུར་དུ་འདི་ལས་ཐར་བར་བྱ་སྙམ་དུ་ཡང་ཡང་བསམ། སྡུག་བསྔལ་དྲུག་ལ་དམིགས་པ་སྟེ། དམིགས་སྐོར་སོ་གཅིག་པའོ།།

གཉིས་པ་རྒྱུ་ཀུན་འབྱུང་བསམ་པ་ནི། འོ་ན་དེ་ཙམ་དུ་སྡུག་བསྔལ་ཆེ་བའི་འཁོར་བ་དེ་ཐམས་ཅད་ཀྱང་རྒྱུ་མེད་རྐྱེན་མེད་པ་མ་ཡིན་པས། རྒྱུ་སྤངས་ཏེ་འཁོར་བ་དེ་ལྡོག་དགོས་པ་འདུག་ན། རྒྱུ་གང་ཡིན་སྙམ་ན་སྡུག་བསྔལ་དེ་རྣམས་ལས་བསགས་པ་ལས་བྱུང་། ལས་དེ་ཐམས་ཅད་དང་པོར་ཉོན་མོངས་ཀྱིས་ཀུན་ནས་ལེན་དགོས་ཤིང་། ཉོན་མོངས་མེད་ན་ནི་ཕྱིས་ནས་ཀྱང་ལས་ལ་འབྲས་བུ་མི་འབྱུང་བས་རྩ་བ་ཉོན་མོངས་པ་ལ་ཐུག། བདག་དང་སེམས་ཅན་འཁོར་བར་འཁྱམས་པའི་རྒྱུའི་རྩ་བ་ཉོན་མོངས་དེ་ཡང་འདོད་ཆགས་དང་། ཁོང་ཁྲོ་དང་། ང་རྒྱལ་དང་། མ་རིག་པ་དང་། ལྟ་བ་ངན་པ་དང་། ཐེ་ཚོམ་སྟེ་དྲུག་ཏུ་ཡང་ཡོད། ཀུན་དུ་སྦྱོར་བ་དགུ་སོགས་རྣམ་གྲངས་དུ་མར་ཡོད་ཀྱང་ཀུན་གྱི་རྩ་བ་འདོད་ཆགས་ཞེ་སྡང་གཏི་མུག་སྟེ་དུག་གསུམ་དུ་འདུས། ལས་ཀྱི་རྣམ་གྲངས་ཤིན་ཏུ་མང་ཡང་འཁོར་བར་འཕེན་བྱེད་ཀྱི་ལས་རྣམས་གསུམ་དུ་འདུས། བསོད་ནམས་མ་ཡིན་པའི་ལས་ཅེས་བྱ་བ་སྡིག་པ་སྟེ་ངན་འགྲོར་འཕེན་ནུས། བསོད་ནམས་ཀྱི་ལས་ནི་སེམས་མཉམ་པར་མ་བཞག་པ་འདོད་ཁམས་ཀྱི་དགེ་བ་སྟེ་ཐར་པའི་ལམ་དུ་མ་སོང་བའི་སྦྱིན་པ་དང་། འདོད་པའི་ཚུལ་ཁྲིམས་ལ་སོགས་པ་སྟེ། འདོད་ཁམས་ཀྱི་ལྷ་དང་མིའི་རྒྱུ་ཡིན། མི་གཡོ་བའི་ལས་ནི། བསམ་གཏན་བཞི་འམ་གཟུགས་མེད་བཞིའི་ཏིང་ངེ་འཛིན་གྱི་ལས་དགེ་བ་ཉག་གཅིག་སྟེ། གཟུགས་ཁམས་དང་གཟུགས་མེད་ཁམས་སུ་འཕེན་ནུས་པའོ། །དེ་ཐམས་ཅད་གནས་ལུགས་མ་རྟོགས་པའི་མ་རིག་པས་བསྒྲིབས། འཁོར་བའི་ཕུང་པོ་ལ་ཞེན་ནས་

བདག་ཏུ་འཛིན་པ་དང་། བདག་གཉིས་པར་འཛིན་པས་ཀུན་ནས་བླངས་པས་འཁོར་བའི་རྒྱུར་སོང་བ་ཡིན། དེ་ལ་ཉོན་མོངས་པ་མ་རིག་པའམ། གཉིས་མུག་ནི་རང་རེའི་བློ་ལ་རང་གིས་བརྟགས་དུས་འཁོར་བའི་རང་བཞིན་དང་འཁོར་བ་གང་ལས་བྱུང་བ་ཡང་མི་ཤེས། ཐར་པའི་རང་བཞིན་དང་དེ་ཐོབ་བྱེད་ཀྱི་ཐབས་ཇི་ལྟར་ཡིན་པའང་མི་ཤེས། དེ་དག་དེས་ཇི་ལྟར་འགྲུབ་ཀྱང་མི་ཤེས། ཐོས་བསམ་གྱི་གོ་བ་ཙམ་ཞིག་ཡོད་པ་སྲིད་ན་འང་རང་བློའི་འཆར་ཚུལ་ལ་བརྟགས་ན། དེ་དག་གང་ལ་ལྟས་ཀྱང་ཆ་རྒྱུས་མེད་པའི་ལ་ཕར་རྒྱབ་ཀྱི་ཡུལ་ལ་སེམས་གཏད་པ་བཞིན་གང་ཡང་མི་ཤེས་པའི་མུན་སྨོམ་མེ་བའི་རྣམ་རྟོག་གཅིག་འདུག་པ་འདི་ཀ་ཡིན། འདིས་གནས་ཚུལ་མ་ཤེས་པས་བདེན་པའི་དོན་ལ་ཐེ་ཚོམ་སྐྱེ། ང་ཞེས་བྱ་བ་མེད་པ་ལ་ངར་བཟུང་ལྟ་བ་ངན་པ་ཐམས་ཅད་བྱུང་སྟེ། ལྟ་བ་ངན་པ་ཐམས་ཅད་གཉིས་མུག་གི་རྗེས་འབྲང་ཡིན། ཡང་དེ་ཡོད་པ་དང་། དང་པོར་རང་གི་ལུས་སེམས་ལ་ཆགས། དེ་ལ་བརྟེན་ནས་བུད་མེད་ཉེ་དུ་འཁོར་གཡོག་སོགས་ནང་སེམས་ཅན་ལ་ཆགས་པ་དང་། ཟས་གོས་ལོངས་སྤྱོད་ཁང་ཞིང་ནོར་རྫས་ཡུལ་ཕྱོགས་སོགས་ཕྱི་ཉེར་སྤྱོད་ལ་ཆགས་པ་རྣམས་འབྱུང་སྟེ། ད་ལྟ་རང་རེའི་ལུས་ལོངས་སྤྱོད་ལ་དགའ་ལྷང་ངེ་སེམས་གནས་པ་འདི་ཀ་ཉོན་མོངས་པ་འདོད་ཆགས་ཡིན། འདི་ལ་བརྟེན་ནས་ང་རྒྱལ་དང་སེར་སྣ་དང་ཕྲག་དོག་ཐམས་ཅད་འབྱུང་། ཡང་རང་ངམ་རང་ཕྱོགས་ལ་གནོད་ན་དེ་ལ་ཞེ་སྡང་འབྱུང་སྟེ། རང་ངམ་རང་གིས་ཡོངས་སུ་བཟུང་བ་ལ་གནོད་པ་བྱས་སམ་བྱེད་པར་དོགས་པ་ཡོད་པའི་སེམས་ཅན་དེ་རང་གི་བློ་ཡུལ་དུ་མ་བདེ་ཀར་རེ་འབྱུང་བ་དེ་ཁོ་ན་ཁོང་ཁྲོ་འམ། ཞེ་སྡང་ཡིན། དེར་མ་ཟད་སེམས་མེད་ལ་ཡང་ཁོང་ཁྲོ་འདི་སྐྱེ་སྟེ། དགྲ་བོའི་ཡུལ་མཁར་བློ་ཡུལ་དུ་མི་བདེ་བ་དང་། རང་གི་ཞིང་ལ་གནོད་པའི་ཆུ་རྒྱུན་ཚུན་ཆད་ལ་ཡང་ཚིག་པ་ཟ་བ་སོགས་འབྱུང་བས་མཚོན་ནོ།། ཁོང་ཁྲོ་འདི་སྟོབས་ཆེར་རྒྱས་པ་ལས་གནོད་སེམས་རགས་པ་དང་། ཁྲོ་བ་དང་། འཚིག་པ་དང་། འཁོན་དུ་འཛིན་པ་ལ་སོགས་ཞེ་སྡང་གི་

རྣམ་འགྱུར་སྣ་ཚོགས་པ་འབྱུང་ངོ་། །དུག་གསུམ་པོ་འདི་རྣམས་བདག་དང་སེམས་ཅན་གང་ཅི་ཡང་རུང་བ་ཐམས་ཅད་འཁོར་བར་འཁྱམས་བྱེད་ཀྱི་རྒྱུའི་གཙོ་བོ་ཡིན་པས་ད་རེས་འདི་ཙམ་ཀྱང་སྤྱོང་ཐུབ་པ་ཞིག་བྱའོ་སྙམ་རང་གི་རྒྱུད་ཐོག་ཏུ་བཀར་གྱིན་རང་རྒྱུད་ལ་སྐྱེས་པའི་ཉོན་མོངས་དང་། དེས་ཀུན་ནས་བླངས་པའི་ལས་ངོ་ཤེས་པར་བྱས་ཀྱིན་བསྒོམ་དགོས་སོ། །དམིགས་སྐོར་སོ་གཉིས་པའོ།།

འདི་དག་གི་སྐབས་སུ་ལས་དང་ཉོན་མོངས་ཀྱི་རྣམ་གཞག་ཇི་ལྟར་རིགས་པ་ཤེས་ན་ཕོགས་ཆེ་བར་ཡོང་ངོ་།། གཉིས་པ་ཐར་པའི་རྒྱུ་འབྲས་བསམ་པ་ནི། ཡང་བདག་འཁོར་བ་སྤངས་ནས་ཐར་པ་ཐོབ་དགོས་པར་ནི་འདུག་ན། ཐར་པ་དེའི་རང་བཞིན་ཇི་ལྟ་བུ་ཞེས་དཔྱོད་ཏེ། ཐར་པ་ཞེས་བྱ་བ་ཡུལ་ཕྱོགས་གཞན་ཞིག་ཏུ་བྲོས་ཏེ་འགྲོ་ས་ཡོད་པ་མ་ཡིན། རང་གི་རིག་པའི་སྟེང་གི་ཉོན་མོངས་རྣམས་ས་བོན་རྩ་བ་ནས་སྤངས། ཕྱིན་ཆད་གཏན་དུ་མི་སྐྱེ་ཞིང་དབྱིངས་སུ་དག། དེ་དག་པས་ལས་རྣམས་ཀྱང་ཆེད་དུ་སྤང་མ་དགོས་པར་འབྲས་བུ་འབྱུང་བའི་ནུས་པ་མེད་ཏེ། དོན་ལ་དབྱིངས་སུ་ཡལ་བ་ཡིན། སྡེ་སྣོད་ཀྱི་ཆོས་སྐད་ལྟར་ན་འགའ་ཞིག་ས་བོན་སྤངས། འགའ་ཞིག་འབྲས་བུ་འབྱིན་མི་ནུས་པར་བྱས་པ་ཡིན། ལས་དང་ཉོན་མོངས་སྤངས་པས་འཁོར་བ་གསར་པ་ནི་མི་སྐྱེད། རྙིང་པའི་འཕྲོས་རྣམས་མྱུར་དུ་དེངས་བར་འགྱུར། ཁམས་གསུམ་འཁོར་བའི་སྡུག་བསྔལ་ཐམས་ཅད་ཟད་པའི་མཐའ་རིག་པ་དྲི་མ་མེད་པར་གནས་པ་ལ་ཐར་པ་ཞེས་བྱ་སྟེ། སྤངས་པ་སླར་མི་ལྡོག་པ་ཞེས་བྱ་བ་ལན་གཅིག་ཐར་པ་ཐོབ་ནས་སླར་གོ་འཕང་ཉམས་པ་མི་སྲིད་པ་ཡིན། ཐར་པ་དེ་ཐོབ་པའི་རྒྱུ་ཟག་མེད་ཀྱི་ཤེས་རབ་ཀྱིས་བདག་མེད་ལ་སོགས་པའི་གནས་ལུགས་རྟོགས་ཤིང་སྒྲིབ་པ་སྤངས་པས་ཐོབ་པ་ཡིན། དེའི་རྒྱུར་སེམས་རྩེ་གཅིག་པའི་ཏིང་ངེ་འཛིན་དགོས། སེམས་རྩེ་གཅིག་ཐོབ་པ་ལ་ཚུལ་ཁྲིམས་རྣམ་པར་དག་པ་དགོས། ཚུལ་ཁྲིམས་དེ་ཡང་ངེས་འབྱུང་གི་བསམ་པ་རྣམ་པར་དག་པ་དང་། བདག་མེད་ཀྱི་ལྟ་བས་ཟིན་ན་ཐར་པའི་རྒྱུ་

གྲུང་པོ་ཡིན། ད་ནི་འཁོར་བ་ལས་ཐར་བའི་ཕྱིར་ཚུལ་ཁྲིམས་བསྲུང་བར་བྱ། ཏིང་ངེ་འཛིན་བསྒོམ་པར་བྱ། སྒོམ་བྱུང་གི་ཤེས་རབ་བསྐྱེད་ནས། མི་རྟག་སྡུག་བསྔལ་སྟོང་པ་བདག་མེད་ཀྱི་དོན་རྟོགས་པར་བྱའོ་སྙམ་དུ་ཡང་ཡང་བསམས། དམིགས་སྐོར་སོ་གསུམ་པའོ།

སྐབས་འདིར་འབྲས་བུ་ཞི་བ་མྱང་འདས་ཐུན་མོང་བའི་རྣམ་གཞག་དང་། བསླབ་པ་གསུམ་པོ་སོ་སོའི་རྣམ་གཞག་རགས་པ་ཙམ་བཤད་ན་ལེགས་སོ། །ཞི་གནས་ཀྱི་འཁྲིད་དང་གང་ཟག་གི་བདག་མེད་སྒོམ་པའང་སྐབས་འདིའི་ཐོབ་ཐང་ཡིན་མོད་ཀྱང་། ཉམས་ལེན་གྱི་མཐིལ་སྐྱེས་བུ་འབྲིང་གི་ལམ་ལ་མི་བྱེད་ཅིང་། སྐྱེས་བུ་ཆེན་པོའི་བསམ་པ་ལ་བསྒྲིལ་བ་ཡིན་པས། སྐབས་འདིར་ཐར་པའི་ལམ་ལ་སློབ་འདོད་ཀྱི་དམིགས་པ་སྦྱོང་བའི་རིམ་པ་ཙམ་ལ་ལག་ལེན་མཛད་དོ། དེ་ཡན་ཆད་ཀྱི་སྐྱེས་བུ་འབྲིང་གི་ཉམས་ལེན་ཚར་བ་ལགས།།

།།ད་ནི་གསུམ་པ་སྐྱེས་བུ་ཆེན་པོའི་ཐུན་མོང་མ་ཡིན་པའི་བསམ་པ་ལ་བསླབ་པ་ལ། བསམ་པའི་འཇུག་སྒོ་ལ་བསླབ་པ་དང་། དེ་ཉིད་མཐའ་རྒྱས་སུ་བྱེད་པའི་རྣམ་གྲངས་སོ། །དང་པོ་ནི་སྔ་མ་དང་སྦྲེལ་ཏེ་འཁོར་བའི་ཉེས་དམིགས་བསམས་ཙ་ན། འཁོར་བ་སྤངས་པའི་མྱ་ངན་ལས་འདས་པ་ཞིག་ཐོབ་དགོས་པ་འདུག། དེ་ཐོབ་པའི་ཕྱིར་བདག་བསླབ་པ་གསུམ་ལ་སློབ་དགོས་ན། ཐོབ་བྱ་མྱང་འདས་དེ་ལ་བྱང་ཆུབ་གསུམ་དུ་དབྱེ། ཉན་ཐོས་ཀྱི་བྱང་ཆུབ། རང་རྒྱལ་གྱི་བྱང་ཆུབ། རྫོགས་པའི་བྱང་ཆུབ་གསུམ་ཡིན། དེ་གསུམ་ལས་ཉན་རང་གི་བྱང་ཆུབ་གཉིས་པོ་དེ་རང་དོན་སྤངས་རྟོགས་མ་རྫོགས། གཞན་དོན་སེམས་ཅན་ལ་ཕན་འདོགས་རྒྱ་ཆེན་པོ་དང་བྲལ། སྤངས་པ་མ་རྫོགས་ཏེ་ཉོན་མོངས་པའི་སྒྲིབ་པ་ཁོ་ན་སྤངས་ཀྱི་ཤེས་བྱའི་སྒྲིབ་པ་མ་སྤངས། རྟོགས་པ་མ་རྫོགས་ཏེ་གང་ཟག་གི་བདག་མེད་དང་། གནས་སྐབས་ཀྱི་རྟེན་འབྲེལ་ཉེ་ཚེ་ཙམ་རྟོགས་ཀྱི་ཆོས་ཀྱི་བདག་མེད་དང་རྟེན་འབྲེལ་མཐར་ཐུག་མ་རྟོགས།། ཡོན་ཏན་གྱི་ཁྱད་པར་ཡང་ཐོར་བུ་ཐོར་བུ་མ་གཏོགས་མཐའ་མེད་དུ་འཕེལ་བ་མེད། དྲིན་ཅན་གྱི་འགྲོ་བ་རྣམས་སྡུག་བསྔལ་ལས་མི་

འདྲེན་པར་རང་གཅིག་པུ་གྲོལ་བའི་ཐབས་སྒྲུབ་པ་དེ་ཁྲེལ་མེད་གདོང་ཚུང་ཕྱི་ཐག་མེད་པ་
གཞན་དོན་སྤངས་བའི་ཐར་པར་འདུག་པ། འཕགས་པ་དེ་དག་འཁོར་བར་མི་ལྡོག་ཅིང་
སྙོམས་མེད་ལ་སེམས་ངང་གིས་གནས་པ། ཡོན་ཏན་ཡང་དུ་མ་དང་ལྡན་པ་ཡིན་པས། རང་
ཅག་སོ་སོ་སྐྱེ་བོ་ལ་བལྟོས་ན་ཏ་བློས་མི་འཁྱུད་པའི་ཇམ་ཆེན་ཡིན་མོད་ཀྱི། སངས་རྒྱས་
བྱང་སེམས་རྣམས་ཀྱིས་སྒྲིབ་པ་གཉིས་སྤངས་ཚུལ་དང་། ཇི་ལྟ་བ་དང་ཇི་སྙེད་པ་མཁྱེན་
པའི་ཡེ་ཤེས་རྒྱས་ཚུལ་དང་། ཡོན་ཏན་མུ་མཐའ་མེད་པ་མངའ་ཚུལ་དང་། ཐུགས་རྗེའི་
ཤུགས་དང་ནུས་མཐུའི་རྩལ་རྫོགས་པར་དཀའ་བ་བཞུགས་ཚུལ་དང་། ཕྱོགས་ཐམས་
ཅད་ལ་དུས་ཐམས་ཅད་དུ་སེམས་ཅན་གྱི་དོན་སྤྱོད་པའི་འཕྲིན་ལས་འཇུག་ཚུལ་བསམ་གྱིས་
མི་ཁྱབ་པ་རྣམས་དང་བསྒྲུན་ན། ཉན་རང་གི་རྣམ་གྲོལ་དེ་ཆེས་ཆུང་བར་འདུག་སྟེ། དཔེར་
ན་རི་རབ་དང་ཉུངས་ཀར་གྱི་ཁྱད་ལས་ཀྱང་ཁྱད་པར་ཆེ། དེས་ན་རང་དོན་སྤངས་རྟོགས་
ཐམས་ཅད་ཡོངས་སུ་རྫོགས་ནས་གཞན་དོན་འཕྲིན་ལས་ཟད་པ་མེད་པའི་རང་བཞིན་ཅན་
ཐར་བའི་མཆོག་རྫོགས་པའི་བྱང་ཆུབ་ཐོབ་པར་བྱ། ཇི་ལྟར་བྱས་ན་བདག་སངས་རྒྱས་
ཐོབ་པར་འགྱུར་ཞིག་གུ། སྙམ་དུ་ཡང་ཡང་བསམ། དམིགས་སྐོར་སོ་བཞི་པའོ།།

གཉིས་པ་དེ་ཉིད་མཐའ་རྒྱས་སུ་བྱེད་པའི་རྣམ་གྲངས་ལ། རྒྱུ་འབྲས་ཀྱི་འབྲེལ་
བ་བསམ་པ་དང་། རྒྱུ་འབྲས་ཀྱི་དོན་བསམ་པ་གཉིས་སོ། །དེ་ཡང་འདི་ལྟར་དམིགས་
པ་སྔ་མ་དང་སྦྲེལ་ནས་བསྒོམ་སྟེ། བདག་སངས་རྒྱས་ཐོབ་དགོས་པ་དེ་སངས་རྒྱས་ཀྱི་
རྒྱུར་བྱང་ཆུབ་ཀྱི་སེམས་དགོས་པར་འདུག དེའི་རྒྱུར་སྙིང་རྗེ་དགོས་པར་འདུག དེའི་
རྒྱུར་བྱམས་པ་དགོས་པ་འདུག དེའི་རྒྱུར་བྱས་པ་ཤེས་ཤིང་དྲིན་དུ་གཟོ་བ་དགོས་པར་
འདུག དེའི་རྒྱུར་སེམས་ཅན་ཐམས་ཅད་ཕ་མར་ཤེས་པ་དགོས་པར་འདུག། འདི་རྣམས་
བདག་གིས་རིམ་ཅན་དུ་བསྒོམ་དགོས། སེམས་ཅན་ཐམས་ཅད་ཕ་མ་ཡིན་དྲིན་རེ་ཆེ། འདི་
རྣམས་སྡུག་བསྔལ་དང་བྲལ་ན་ཅི་མ་རུང་། བདེ་ཞིང་སྐྱིད་ན་ཅི་མ་རུང་། འདི་རྣམས་

བདེ་བ་ལ་འགོད་པའི་ཕྱིར་སངས་རྒྱས་ཐོབ་པར་བྱའོ། སངས་རྒྱས་ཐོབ་ནས་ཀྱང་སེམས་ཅན་ཐམས་ཅད་སངས་རྒྱས་ཀྱི་ས་ལ་བཞག་པར་བྱའོ་སྙམ་དུ་ཡང་ཡང་བསྒོམ། དམིགས་སྐོར་ས་ལྔ་པའོ།།

འདིར་བཤེས་གཉེན་ཤར་བ་པའི་སློབ་མ་དགེ་བཤེས་གཏུམ་སྟོན་པ་བློ་གྲོས་གྲགས་ནས་བརྒྱུད་པའི་མན་ངག་ལ། རྒྱུ་འབྲས་རིམ་པ་ལྔར་མཛད་པ་འདི་ཁར་འདུག། ཡང་བྱ་ཡུལ་བའི་སློབ་མ་གཙང་བ་རིན་པོ་ཆེ་ནས་བརྒྱུད་པ་དགེ་བཤེས་མུས་སྨན་པས་བཀོད་པའི་ཐེག་པ་ཆེན་པོ་བློ་སྦྱོང་གི་རིམ་པ་ཟེར་བའི་བསྟན་རིམ་གྱི་ཡི་གེ་ན། འདི་སྐད་ཅེས་སྣང་སྟེ་ཐུན་མོང་མ་ཡིན་པ་ཐེག་པ་ཆེན་པོ། ཨ་ཏི་ཤའི་རྒྱུ་འབྲས་བདུན་ལ། བློ་སྣ་རིམ་གྱིས་སྦྱོང་དགོས་གསུང་། དེ་ཡང་རྒྱུ་འབྲས་རྣམ་པ་བདུན་གྱི་དབང་དུ་བྱས་ན། རྒྱུ་མེད་རྐྱེན་མེད་མ་ཡིན་ཏེ་རྒྱུ་བྱང་ཆུབ་ཀྱི་སེམས་ལས་སྐྱེ། དེ་ལྷག་པའི་བསམ་པ་རྣམ་པར་དག་པ་ལས་སྐྱེ། དེ་སྙིང་རྗེ་ཆེན་པོ་ལས་སྐྱེ། དེ་བྱམས་པ་ཆེན་པོ་ལས་སྐྱེ། དེ་ཡིད་དུ་འོང་བ་ལས་སྐྱེ། དེ་བྱས་པ་ཤེས་ཤིང་དྲིན་དུ་གཟོ་བ་ལས་སྐྱེ། དེ་མའི་འདུ་ཤེས་བསྒོམས་པ་ལས་སྐྱེ་སྐད་པ། དེ་རྣམས་རྒྱུ་འབྲས་བདུན་ཡིན་བྱ་བ་ཡོད་པས། རྒྱུ་འབྲས་བདུན་གྱི་ཐ་སྙད་ཀྱང་ཕྱིས་ཀྱི་གསར་བྱུང་རང་མིན་པ་གོ་དགོས་སོ། །གཉིས་པ་རྒྱུ་འབྲས་ཀྱི་དོན་བསམ་པ་ལ། བྱམས་པ་སྒོམ་པ། སྙིང་རྗེ་སྒོམ་བ། བྱང་ཆུབ་ཀྱི་སེམས་སྒོམ་པ་གསུམ་མོ། དང་པོ་ནི་རྩ་བའི་མ་བྱ་བ། ཚེ་འདི་བསྐྱེད་པའི་མ་ལ་ཟེར་བ་ལགས་ཏེ་འདི་བདག་ལ་དྲིན་ཆེ་བར་འདུག། དང་པོར་ཟླ་བ་དགུ་འམ་བཅུའི་བར་དུ་ཁོང་དུ་བཟུང་། དེའི་བར་དུའང་རང་གི་སྲོག་ལས་གཅེས་པར་བསྲུངས། མིའི་ལུས་དང་སྲོག་དང་ཚེ་སྦྱིན་པ་ཡིན། བཙས་པ་ནས་བརྩམས། ལུས་ཀྱིས་ཕན་བཏགས་ཏེ་སོར་བཅུའི་རྩེ་ལ་བླངས། ཤའི་དྲོད་ལ་བཅར། ནུ་མ་བསྣུན། ཟས་ལྕེས་སྟོད། མི་གཙང་བ་ལག་པས་ཕྱིས། རང་ཅག་བྱ་བྱེད་གང་ཡང་མི་ནུས་པ་འབུ་འདྲ་བ་ཞིག་ནས་བསྐྱངས་པ་ཡིན། དག་གི་སྣ་ནས་ཀྱང་ཕན་

བཏགས་ཏེ། མིང་སྨན་པ་ནས་བོས། བསྟོད་རྒྱུ་མེད་ཀྱང་བསྟོད་ར་གཏོང་། ཡོན་ཏན་མེད་ཀྱང་ཡོན་ཏན་བརྗོད། འབྲིད་ཐབས་སྣ་ཚོགས་ཀྱིས་ཀྱང་སེམས་དགའ་བར་བྱས། ཡིད་ཀྱིས་ཀྱང་ཕན་བཏགས་ཏེ། བདག་གི་བུ་འདི་ཇི་ལྟར་བྱས་ན་ཚེ་རིང་བར་འགྱུར། ཅི་འདྲ་བྱས་ན་ནད་མེད་པ་ཡོང་། ག་འདྲ་ཞིག་བྱས་ན་མིས་ཕུ་དུད་དུ་འཁུར་བ་ཞིག་ཡོང་། གཏམ་སྙན་པ་ཞིག་ཨེ་འོང་། མགོ་ཐོན་པ་ཞིག་ཨེ་ཡོང་ཁོ་ན་བསམ། དང་པོ་ཅོག་ཐུབ་པ་དང་། འགོག་ཤེས་པ་དང་། གཏམ་ཚིག་རེ་ཙམ་སྨྲ་ཤེས་པ་ལ་ཡང་དགའ་བ་དཔག་ཏུ་མེད་པ་བྱས། ཆེར་སྐྱེས་ནས་རང་ལ་ཡོད་ཚད་བུ་ལ་འབོགས་པ་ལ་ཉམས་ང་ཙམ་ཡང་མེད་ཀྱི་སྟེང་དུ་དགའ་བ་བསྒོམ། སྟོང་གསུམ་ནོར་དང་གཡོག་གིས་བཀང་བ་བྱིན་ཀྱང་ཆེས་སྐམ་པ་མེད། ངའི་མ་འདི་དེ་ཙམ་དུ་བདག་ལ་ཕན་འདོགས་པ་ཡིན། བདག་ལ་བྱམས་པ་དྲིན་ཆེ་བ་ཨང་། མ་འདི་དུས་དང་གནས་སྐབས་ཐམས་ཅད་དུ་བདེ་ན་ཅི་མ་རུང་། སྐྱིད་ན་ཅི་མ་རུང་། ངས་མ་འདི་བདེ་སྐྱིད་ལྡན་མེད་པ་ལ་དགོད་པར་བྱ་སྙམ་དུ་བསྒོམ། དམིགས་སྐོར་སོ་དྲུག་པའོ།།

རྩ་བའི་མ་ལ་བྱམས་པ་བསྒོམ་པ་འདི་བྱམས་པའི་སྐོར་གྱི་དམིགས་པའི་རྩ་བ་ཡིན། སྐྱེ་ཡང་བླ་སྟེ་འདི་ལ་སྐྱོང་བ་ཐོན་པ་གལ་ཆེ་གསུང་ངོ་། དེ་ནས་བདག་གི་མ་འདིས་ཚེ་འདི་ལ་ཕན་བཏགས་ཚུལ་དེ་ལྟར་ཡིན་ལ། འདིས་སྐྱེ་བ་གཅིག་མིན་གཉིས་མིན་སྐྱེ་བ་ཤིན་ཏུ་མང་པོར་མ་ཁོ་ནར་གྱུར་ནས་ཚེ་འདིའི་དངོས་ཀྱི་མ་བཞིན་དུ་ཕན་བཏགས་པ་རང་ལའང་གྲངས་མེད། དེ་བཞིན་དུ་ཕར་གྱུར་ནས་ཕན་བཏགས་པ་རང་ཡང་དཔག་ཏུ་མེད། དེ་བཞིན་དུ་ཉེ་དུ་གཉེན་མདུན་གྲོགས་མཛའ་བཤེས་ལ་སོགས་པར་གྱུར་ནས་ཀྱང་ཕན་བཏགས་པ་རང་ཡང་མཐའ་མེད། གོས་བསྐོན་པ་དང་རྒྱན་བཏགས་པ་རང་ཡང་ཕྱོགས་གཅིག་ཏུ་སྤུངས་ན། རི་བོ་མཆོག་རབ་ཀྱི་སྤུངས་ (དཔངས་) ལས་ཀྱང་ཐལ། ནུ་ཞོ་འཐུངས་པ་གཅིག་པུ་བསགས་ཀྱང་རྒྱ་མཚོ་ཆེན་པོ་བཞིས་ཀྱང་མི་ཚད། མ་འདི་རང་ཅག་

གི་ཕ་མ་བུ་ཚ་ཉེ་དུར་གྱུར་ནས་རང་རེ་སྟོན་ལ་ཞི་བ་ལ་གདུང་བའི་སེམས་ཀྱིས་དུས་པའི་མཆི་མ་ཕྱོགས་གཅིག་ཏུ་བསགས་ན་རྒྱ་མཚོ་ཆེ་བ་ཕྲག་བརྒྱས་མི་བསྒྲུན། བདག་གི་དོན་དུ་སྡིག་པ་ལ་མ་ལྟོས། སྡུག་བསྔལ་ལ་མ་ལྟོས། གདམ་ངན་ལ་མ་ལྟོས་པར་བདག་གི་དོན་ཁོ་ན་བསྒྲུབས་པ་ཡིན། འདི་ཙམ་དུ་ཕན་འདོགས་པ་ཨང་སྐམ་པ་ལ་སོགས་པ་གོང་བཞིན་བསྒོང་། དམིགས་སྐོར་སོ་བདུན་པའོ།།

དེ་ནས་དེའི་སྟེང་དུ་ཕ་དང་སྤྱུན་ཟླ་ཉེ་དུ་འདྲེས་པ་ལྔ་དྲུག་བསྟན་ཏེ། འདི་དག་གིས་ཀྱང་ཚེ་འདིར་ནི་ལ་ལས་ཕན་ཆེར་བཏགས། ལ་ལས་འབྲིང་དུ་བཏགས། ལ་ལས་ཆུང་དུ་བཏགས་པ་ཡིན་མོད། འཁོར་བ་ཐོག་མ་མེད་པ་ནས་བསམས་ན། རྩ་བའི་མ་བཞིན་དུ་ཕན་བཏགས་པ་ལ་མང་ཉུང་མེད། དྲིན་ལ་ཆེ་ཆུང་མེད་པས་འདི་ཙམ་དུ་ཕན་འདོགས་པ་འདི་བདེ་ན་ཅི་མ་རུང་། སྐྱིད་ན་ཅི་མ་རུང་། ངས་བདེ་སྐྱིད་མཐར་ཐུག་ལ་འགོད་དགོས་སྙམ་པ་སོགས་གོང་བཞིན་བསྒོམ། དེ་བཞིན་དུ་རིམ་གྱིས་སྦྱར་ནས་བསྒོམ་དགོས་ཏེ། དེ་ལ་ཡང་བཤེས་གཉེན་བྱེ་ཡུལ་བ་དང་། སྔར་ཐང་བའི་ལུགས་ཀྱིས་ཡུལ་ཕྱོགས་སོགས་རེ་རེ་ནས་བསྟན་གྱིན་བསྒོམ་པའི་ལུགས་ཡོད་དེ། ལས་དང་པོ་པའི་དམིགས་པ་བསྒོམ་ཚུལ་ལ། ལུགས་འདི་ཁོ་ན་གནད་ཆེ་བར་མཐོང་། དེའི་རྗེས་ནས་རང་ཉིད་གང་དུ་གནས་པའི་ཡུལ་ཕྱོགས་དེའི་མིའི་འགྲོ་བ་དགྲ་གཉེན་བར་མ་གསུམ། དུད་འགྲོ་ས་འོག་ས་སྟེང་ས་བར་སྣང་ལ་སྤྱོད་པ་གསུམ། ཡི་དྭགས་འདྲེ་བགྲེན་ཡང་མཆོག་དམན་བར་གསུམ་ཇི་ཙམ་ཅིག་ཡོད། དེ་ཐམས་ཅད་སྐྱེ་བ་དཔག་ཏུ་མེད་པའི་ཕ་དང་མ་ཡིན་པ་དང་། ཕན་བཏགས་ཚུལ་དང་། དྲིན་དུ་གཟོ་བ་དང་བྱམས་པ་བསྒོམ་པ་གོང་བཞིན་སྦྱར། དེ་བཞིན་དུ་རྒྱལ་ཁམས་རྒྱ་ཇེ་ཆེ་ཇེ་ཆེར་བསྟན་ཏེ། མཐར་རང་རེ་བོད་པའི་དབང་དུ་བྱས་ན་བོད་རི་ལ་བོ་ཙམ་གྱི་འགྲོ་བ་རིགས་གསུམ་ལ་བསྒོམ། དེ་ནས་དེ་བཞིན་དུ་བོད་ཀྱི་ཤར་ན་རྒྱ་ནག་ལྷོ་ན་རྒྱ་གར་ནུབ་ན་ཁ་ཆེ་བྱང་ན་ཧོར་དང་སྟག་གཟིག་སྟེ་རྒྱལ་ཁམས་ཆེན་པོ་

དེ་རྣམས་ལ་གནས་པའི་འགྲོ་བ་རིགས་གསུམ་ལ་བསྒོམ། དེ་ནས་འཛམ་བུ་གླིང་རིལ་པོའི་འགྲོ་བ་རིགས་གསུམ་ལ་བསྒོམ། དེ་ནས་འཛམ་བུ་གླིང་གི་འོག་ན་ཡི་དྭགས་ཀྱི་གནས་དང་། ཚ་དམྱལ་བརྒྱད་དང་གྲང་དམྱལ་བརྒྱད་ཀྱི་གནས་ཡོད་དེ། དེ་རྣམས་ལ་སྔར་བཞིན་བསྒོམ། དེ་བཞིན་དུ་ཤར་ལུས་འཕགས་པོ་དང་། ནུབ་བ་ལང་སྤྱོད་དང་། བྱང་སྒྲ་མི་སྙན་ཏེ་གླིང་བཞི་ལ་སྟེང་ན་གོང་བཞིན་འགྲོ་བ་རིགས་གསུམ་གྱིས་གང་བ་དང་། འོག་ན་ངན་སོང་གསུམ་གྱི་འགྲོ་བ་སྣ་ཚོགས་དང་བཅས་པ་ལ་ཡང་གོང་བཞིན། རི་རབ་ཀྱི་བང་རིམ་བཞི་ལ་རྒྱལ་ཆེན་བཞི་རིགས་ཀྱི་ལྷ་ཡོད། རྩེ་མོ་ན་སུམ་ཅུ་རྩ་གསུམ་པའི་ལྷ་རྣམས་ཡོད། རི་རབ་ཀྱི་ཁོར་སེང་ཆུ་མཚམས་མན་ཆད་ན། ལྷ་མ་ཡིན་གྱི་གཙོ་བོ་རྣམས་གནས་པའི་གྲོང་ཡོད། དེ་དག་ན་གནས་པ་ལ་སྔར་བཞིན་བསྒོམ། དེ་ནས་གསེར་གྱི་རི་བདུན་དང་ཕྱི་ལྕགས་རི་ཁོར་ཡུག་ཆུན་ཆད་ལ་ཆུ་མཚམས་ཡན་ཆད་ལ་ལྷ་དང་། གནོད་སྦྱིན་དུད་འགྲོའི་འགྲོ་བ་དག་གནས། ཆུ་མཚམས་མན་ཆད་ལྷ་མིན་དང་ཡི་དྭགས་དང་དུད་འགྲོ་སྣ་ཚོགས་རྣམས་གནས། དེ་དག་གི་བར་བར་གྱི་རོལ་མཚོ་བདུན་དང་ཕྱིའི་རྒྱ་མཚོ་ལ་ཀླུ་དང་ལྷ་མ་ཡིན་དང་། དུད་འགྲོའི་འགྲོ་བ་ཕལ་པ་གོ་མཚམས་མེད་པ་ཙམ་དུ་གནས། དེ་ཐམས་ཅད་ལ་སྔར་བཞིན་བསྒོམ། དུད་འགྲོའི་ནང་ན་དུད་འགྲོ་རྫུ་འཕྲུལ་ཅན་གསུམ་ཡོད་ཏེ། ནམ་མཁའ་ལ་སྤྱོད་པའི་བྱ་ཁྲུང་། ས་སྟེང་ན་སྤྱོད་པའི་མི་འམ་ཅི། ས་འོག་གམ་ཆུ་ལ་སྤྱོད་པའི་ཀླུ་རྣམས་སོ། དེ་དག་ལ་ཡང་སྙོམས་སུ་བསྒོམ། དམིགས་སྐོར་དེ་ཡན་ཆད་ཀྱི་ས་འོག་དབང་ཆེན་གསེར་གྱི་ས་གཞི་ཡན་ཆད། ཐད་ཀར་ཕྱི་ལྕགས་རི་ཆུན་ཆད། སྟེང་དུ་སུམ་ཅུ་རྩ་གསུམ་མན་ཆད་ལ་བསྒོམས་ཚར། དེའི་སྟེང་དུ་འཐབ་བྲལ་དང་། དགའ་ལྡན་དང་། འཕྲུལ་དགའ་དང་། གཞན་འཕྲུལ་དབང་བྱེད་རྣམས་རིམ་པས་བསྣན་ཏེ་སྔར་བཞིན་བསྒོམ། དེ་ནས་གླིང་བཞི་པའི་འཇིག་རྟེན་གྱི་ཁམས་ཀྱི་ཚད་དང་མཉམ་པའི་ཚངས་རིས། ཚངས་པ་མདུན་ན་འདོན། ཚངས་ཆེན་ཏེ་བསམ་གཏན་དང་པོའི་གནས་གསུམ་བསྣན། སྐབས་

འདིར་འདི་སྐད་ཅེས་བྱ་སྟེ། འདི་ནས་བཟུང་སྟེ་གཟུགས་ཁམས་ཀྱི་གནས་འདི་ཀུན་ན་ལྷའི་འགྲོ་བ་གཟུགས་ཁམས་པ་རང་ཁོ་ན་མ་གཏོགས། འགྲོ་བ་གཞན་ལྷ་པོ་གང་ཡང་མེད་ཏེ། ལྷ་འདོད་ཁམས་པ་ཡང་མེད། གནས་སོ་སོ་རང་རང་གི་ལྷ་ཁོ་ན་གནས་པ་ཡིན། སྤྱིར་ན་ཚངས་པའི་འཇིག་རྟེན་མན་ཆད་གླིང་བཞི་པའི་འཇིག་རྟེན་གྱི་ཁམས་གཅིག་ན་གནས་པའི་འགྲོ་བ་རིགས་དྲུག་པོ་ཐམས་ཅད་ལ་གོང་བཞིན་བསྒོམ། ད་ནི་དེ་ཀ་འདྲ་བ་འཕྲེང་ལ་སྟོང་ཕྲག་གཅིག་བཤིབས་པའི་མཐའ་ལྕགས་རི་གཅིག་གིས་བསྐོར་བ། སྟེངས་ན་འོད་ཆུང་། ཚད་མེད་འོད། འོད་གསལ་ཏེ་བསམ་གཏན་གཉིས་པའི་གནས་གསུམ་ཡོད་པའི་ནང་ནས། འོད་གསལ་བའི་གནས་ཆེན་པོ་གཅིག་གིས་སྟེངས་ནས་ཁེབས་པ་ནི་སྟོང་སྤྱི་ཕུད་ཀྱི་འཇིག་རྟེན་གྱི་ཁམས་ཏེ། དེ་ན་གནས་པའི་རིགས་དྲུག་ལ་སྔར་བཞིན་བསྒོམ། ད་སྟེ་དེ་འདྲ་བ་སྟོང་ཕྲག་གཅིག་ཐད་ཀར་བསྒྲིགས་པའི་མཐའ་སྐོར་དུ། སླར་ཡང་ཁོར་ཡུག་གཅིག་གིས་བསྐོར་ཏེ། སྟེང་དུ་ནི་དགེ་ཆུང་དང་། ཚད་མེད་དགེ་དང་། དགེ་རྒྱས་ཏེ་བསམ་གཏན་གསུམ་པའི་གནས་གསུམ་ཡོད་ལ། དེ་ཀུན་གྱི་སྟེང་ནས་དགེ་རྒྱས་ཀྱི་གནས་གཅིག་གིས་ཁེབས་པ་ཡིན་ཏེ། སྟོང་གཉིས་པ་བར་མའི་འཇིག་རྟེན་གྱི་ཁམས་གཅིག་གི་འགྲོ་བ་རིགས་དྲུག་ལ་སྔར་བཞིན་བསྒོམ། ཡང་དེ་འདྲ་བ་ཐད་ཀར་སྟོང་ཕྲག་གཅིག་བསྒྲིགས་པའི་ཐ་མ། སླར་ཡང་ཁོར་ཡུག་ཆེན་པོ་གཅིག་གིས་བསྐོར། འཇིག་རྟེན་གྱི་ཁམས་རེ་རེ་ལ་འོག་གཞི་གསེར་གྱི་ས་གཞི་རེ་རེ་ཡོད། དེ་རེ་རེའི་འོག་ན་ཆུའི་དཀྱིལ་འཁོར་རེ་རེ་ཡོད། ཆུའི་དཀྱིལ་འཁོར་བྱེ་བ་ཕྲག་བརྒྱ་རླུང་གི་དཀྱིལ་འཁོར་གཅིག་ལ་བརྟེན། འོག་ཏུ་ནི་རླུང་གི་དཀྱིལ་འཁོར་ཡན་ཆོད། སྟེང་དུ་ནི། སྤྲིན་མེད། བསོད་ནམས་སྐྱེས། འབྲས་བུ་ཆེ་བ་སྟེ་བསམ་གཏན་བཞི་པའི་གནས་ཕལ་པ་གསུམ། དེ་བཞིན་དུ་མི་ཆེ་བ། མི་གདུང་བ། གྱ་ནོམ་སྣང་། ཤིན་ཏུ་མཐོང་། འོག་མིན་པ་རྣམས་བསྣན། འོག་མིན་པའི་གནས་གཅིག་པོ་དེ་སྟེང་ནས་སྟོང་གསུམ་ཁེབས། དེ་ལ་སྟོང་གསུམ་གྱི་སྟོང་ཆེན་པོའི་འཇིག་རྟེན་

ཀྱི་ཁམས་ཞེས་ཟེར། གཟུགས་མེད་ཁམས་ཀྱི་སེམས་ཅན་ཡང་དཔག་ཏུ་མེད་པ་ཞིག་ཡོད་པ་དེ་དག་ཀྱང་བསྟན་ཏེ། ཁམས་གསུམ་འགྲོ་བ་རིགས་དྲུག་གི་སེམས་ཅན་རྣམས་ལ་གོང་བཞིན་བསྒོམ་མོ། དེ་ནས་ཡང་སྟོང་གསུམ་འདིའི་ཤར་ཕྱོགས་ན་ཕར་ལ་སྟོང་གསུམ་གྲངས་མེད་གཞལ་དུ་མེད། དཔེར་ན་སྟོང་གསུམ་གཅིག་ཡུངས་འབྲུས་མེར་ཏེ་བཀང་ནས། ཡུངས་འབྲུ་དེ་ལས་གཅིག་བླངས་ཏེ་འདིའི་ཤར་ཕྱོགས་ཀྱི་སྟོང་གསུམ་གཅིག་ལ་བཞག། དེ་བཞིན་དུ་སྟོང་གསུམ་རེ་རེ་ལ་ཡུངས་འབྲུ་རེ་རེ་བཞག་ན་མཐར་ཡུངས་འབྲུ་ནི་ཟད་འགྲོ། ཤར་ཕྱོགས་ཀྱི་སྟོང་གསུམ་མི་ཟད་དོ། ཡང་དེ་ཀ་བཞིན་བྱས་ཀྱང་ཡུངས་འབྲུ་འཛད། སྟོང་གསུམ་མི་ཟད། ཡང་བསྒྱུར་ཏེ་བྱས་ཀྱང་དེ་དང་འདྲ། དེ་འདྲ་བ་བསྐལ་པ་མཐའ་མེད་དུ་བྱས་ཀྱང་འཇིག་རྟེན་གྱི་ཁམས་ལ་ཟད་པ་མེད། དེ་དག་ཐམས་ཅད་འགྲོ་བ་རིགས་དྲུག་གིས་གང་བ་ཡིན་ཏེ། དེ་ཐམས་ཅད་ལ་མར་ཤེས་པ་ནས་བྱམས་པ་བསྒོམ་པའི་བར་གོང་བཞིན། ད་ནི་ཤར་ཕྱོགས་སུ་མ་ཟད། ཕྱོགས་བཅུ་རབ་འབྱམས་ཐམས་ཅད་ཀྱང་དེ་དང་འདྲ་སྟེ། ཕྱོགས་བཅུའི་ནམ་མཁའ་ལ་མཐའ་གཏན་ནས་མེད། ནམ་མཁས་གར་ཁྱབ་སྣོད་ཀྱི་འཇིག་རྟེན་གྱིས་ཁྱབ། སེམས་ཅན་ཐམས་ཅད་དྲིན་ཅན་གྱི་ཕ་མ་ཡིན། ཕ་མ་བྱམས་པ་ལན་གྲངས་དཔག་ཏུ་མེད། བྱམས་རེས་ནས་ཕན་སྣ་ཚོགས་ནི་བཏགས། གནོད་པ་སྣ་ཚོགས་ནི་བསལ། མ་རྒན་སེམས་ཅན་འདི་རྣམས་བདེ་བར་གྱུར་ཅིག། སྐྱིད་པར་གྱུར་ཅིག། བདག་གིས་འདི་རྣམས་བདེ་སྐྱིད་བླ་ན་མེད་པ་ལ་འགོད་པར་བྱའོ་སྙམ་དུ་བསྒོམ། དེ་རྣམས་ལ་ནང་ཚན་དམིགས་སྐོར་ཤིན་ཏུ་མང་བར་འགྱུར་མོད། བློ་རིགས་དང་བསྟུན་ནས་ངེས་མེད་དུ་འཁྲིད་དགོས་པས་ཚད་ཀྱི་དབྱེ་བ་ཙུང་ཟད་དཀའ་བ་དང་། བྱམས་པའི་སེམས་རྒྱ་བསྐྱེད་པར་རིགས་གཅིག་པས་དམིགས་ཆེན་གཅིག་ཏུ་བསྡུས་ཏེ། དམིགས་སྐོར་སོ་བརྒྱད་པའི་ཐ་སྙད་བྱེད་དོ།

སྐབས་འདིར་སྣོད་བཅུད་འཇིག་རྟེན་ཁམས་ཀྱི་རྣམ་གཞག་ཞིག་ཤེས་ན་གནད་

ཆེའོ། དེས་བྱམས་པའི་ཁྲིད་ཚར་བ་ལགས།། གཉིས་པ་སྙིང་རྗེ་བསྒོམ་པ་ནི། སྔོན་འགྲོ་དང་རྗེས་སོགས་སྔར་དང་འདྲ་བ་ལས། སེམས་ཅན་འདི་རྣམས་བདེ་ཞིང་སྐྱིད་པ་ལ་འགོད་དགོས་པ་འདུག་པ་ལ་སེམས་ཅན་གྱི་ཁམས་ལ་ལྟས་ན། སེམས་ཅན་འདི་རྣམས་བདེ་བ་དང་བདེ་བའི་རྒྱུ་ལ་མི་གནས། སྡུག་བསྔལ་དང་སྡུག་བསྔལ་གྱི་རྒྱུ་ལ་གནས། འདོད་པ་ནི་བདེ་བ་འདོད། སྡུག་བསྔལ་མི་འདོད་ཀྱང་ཡོང་བ་ནི་བདེ་བ་མི་འབྱུང་སྡུག་བསྔལ་ཁོ་ན་འབྱུང་། ཕལ་ཆེར་ནི་སྡུག་བསྔལ་དངོས་ལ་གནས། དམྱལ་བ་ན་ཚ་གྲང་། ཡི་དྭགས་ན་བཀྲེས་སྐོམ། དུད་འགྲོ་ན་གཅིག་ལ་གཅིག་ཟ། མཐོ་རིས་ན་ཡང་ཚེ་ཐུང་བ་དང་། ནད་མང་བ་དང་། དབང་ཆུང་བ་དང་། བཀྲེན་ཅིང་འཕོངས་པ་དང་ལས་ལ་འཁོལ་བ་དང་ཆད་པས་བཅད་པ་སོགས་དངོས་སུ་རང་ཡང་སྡུག་བསྔལ་འདི་མི་སྤྱོད་བྱ་བ་མེད་པ་དེར་འདུག། འགྲོ་བ་ཐམས་ཅད་སྤྱིར་ན་སྡུག་བསྔལ་གྱི་རྒྱུ་དཔག་ཏུ་མེད་པ་ལ་སྤྱོད་པ་དེ་ཡིན། སྙོམས་སུ་འགའ་ཞིག་ད་ལྟ་རང་མི་འདོད་པའི་སྡུག་བསྔལ་དྲག་པོ་ནི་མེད་དུ་ཆུག་ཀྱང་སྡིག་པའི་ལས་ཧམ་པོ་ཆེ་བསགས་པས་དབུགས་ཁ་གང་པོ་འགགས་པ་དང་མཉམ་དུ་དམྱལ་བར་ཁྲིད་ཁྲིད་སྐྱེ་དགོས་པ་འདི་རྣམས་དངོས་སུ་ད་ལྟ་སྡུག་བསྔལ་སྤྱོད་བ་རྣམས་ལས་ཀྱང་སྙིང་རྗེ་བར་འདུག། སྣང་བ་རེ་འཁྲུལ་ན་ཨ་ཙ་མ་ཙ་རིང་དྲག་སྙམ་དུ་བསམ། དཔེར་ན་རང་གི་རྒྱ་བའི་མ་དེ་མིག་ནི་ལོང་། རྐང་པ་ནི་ཆག ལོང་ཁྲིད་ནི་མེད། མཁར་བ་ནི་བོར། གད་ཁ་གཡང་ཁ་གཅིག་ནས་མར་ལྷུང་ལ་ཁད་ཁད་འདུག་ན། བདག་ཇི་ཙུག་བྱེད། གཞན་གང་ལ་ཡང་མ་ལྟས་པར་ཏབ་རྒྱུགས་སུ་ཕྱིན་ནས་མ་དེ་གཡང་ཁ་ནས་འཛིན་དགོས། དཔེ་དེ་བཞིན་དུ་མ་རྒན་འགྲོ་བ་འདི་རྣམས་ཤེས་རབ་ཀྱི་མིག་ནི་ལོང་། ཐབས་ཀྱི་རྐང་བ་ནི་ཆག། དགེ་བའི་བཤེས་གཉེན་ནམ་གྲོགས་བཟང་པོའི་ལོང་ཁྲིད་ནི་མེད། བསོད་ནམས་ཀྱི་མཁར་བ་དང་ནི་བྲལ། ཡིད་ལ་དྲན་དུ་ཡང་མི་རུང་བའི་སྡིག་པ་ཐམས་ཅད་ནི་ལག་ལེན་དུ་ཡང་ཡང་བཏབ། མཐོ་རིས་ཀྱི་ལམ་ནས་བདེག་འཚོས་ཏེ། ངན་སོང་གསུམ་གྱི་

གཡང་ལ་ལྷུང་ལ་ཁད་ཁད་པ་སྡུག་བསྔལ་གྱི་རྒྱུ་མི་བཟད་པ་ལ་གནས་པ་འདི་རྣམས་སྙིང་རེ་རྗེ། ད་ནི་འདི་རྣམས་ངས་སྡུག་བསྔལ་ལས་དངོས་སུ་མ་སྐྱབས་པའི་ཐབས་མེད། དེས་ན་ངན་སོང་གསུམ་ན་ནི་ཚོར་བ་སྡུག་བསྔལ་དངོས་ལ་གཙོ་བོར་སྤྱོད། བདེ་འགྲོ་གསུམ་ན་ནི་ཚོར་བ་སྡུག་བསྔལ་གྱི་རྒྱུ་ལ་གཙོ་བོར་སྤྱོད། དེ་དག་གི་སྡུག་བསྔལ་སྐྱེས་བུ་ཆུང་འབྲིང་གི་སྐབས་སུ་བཤད་པ་ལྟར་དྲན་པར་བྱ། སྡུག་བསྔལ་དེ་བདག་གི་ཐོག་ཏུ་བབས་ན་ཆ་ཤས་ཙམ་ཡང་བཟོད་པའི་གླགས་མི་འདུག། བདག་གིས་མི་བཟོད་པ་ཞིག་འདི་རྣམས་ཀྱིས་ཀྱང་ག་ལ་བཟོད། དེ་འདྲ་བའི་སྡུག་བསྔལ་དངོས་སུ་ཡང་མྱོང་ཞིང་། སྡུག་བསྔལ་གྱི་རྒྱུ་ཟད་མི་ཤེས་པ་ལ་རིམ་གྱིས་རིམ་གྱིས་སྤྱད་པས། སྡུག་བསྔལ་ནས་སྡུག་བསྔལ་བརྒྱུད་མར་འབྱུང་བ་འདི་རྣམས་སྙིང་རེ་རྗེ། འདི་རྣམས་སྡུག་བསྔལ་ཐམས་ཅད་དང་བྲལ་བར་གྱུར་ཅིག། སྡུག་བསྔལ་གྱི་རྒྱུ་ལས་དང་ཉོན་མོངས་ཐམས་ཅད་དང་བྲལ་བར་གྱུར་ཅིག། མ་རྒན་འགྲོ་དྲུག་གི་སེམས་ཅན་འདི་རྣམས་སྡིག་པ་དང་སྡུག་བསྔལ་ཐམས་ཅད་ལས་བདག་གིས་བསྐྱབ་པར་བྱ། སྡུག་བསྔལ་གྱི་གནས་འཁོར་བ་ལས་འདྲེན་པར་བྱ་སྙམ་དུ་ཡང་ཡང་བསམ། དམིགས་སྐོར་སོ་དགུ་པའོ།།

ཡང་ན་འདི་ལ་སྡུག་བསྔལ་དངོས་ལ་སྤྱོད་པ་ལ་དམིགས་སྐོར་གཅིག། སྡུག་བསྔལ་གྱི་རྒྱུ་ལ་སྤྱོད་པ་ལ་དམིགས་སྐོར་གཅིག། གཉིས་ཀ་བསྡོམས་པ་ལ་གཅིག་སྟེ་གསུམ་བྱེད་པའི་ལུགས་ཀྱང་ཡོད། སྔར་བྱམས་པའི་སྐབས་སུ་བཤད་པ་བཞིན་རིམ་གྱིས་ཐམས་ཅད་ལ་རྒྱ་བསྐྱེད་དེ་བསྒོམས་ན་ཡང་ལེགས་པར་འོང་ངོ་། །ཡང་བྱམས་སྙིང་རྗེའི་ཁྲིད་ལན་ཅིག་བསྐྱངས་པའི་རྗེས་སུ་འདི་གཉིས་འབྲེལ་བ་ཅན་ཁོ་ན་འབྱུང་བས། བྱམས་པ་རེ་ལ་སྙིང་རྗེ་རེ་འཐུད་ཀྱིན་བསྒོམས་པས་ཆོག་ཚན་པ་སོ་སོར་མ་བཅད་ཀྱང་རུང་བ་ལགས་སོ། །གསུམ་པ་བྱང་ཆུབ་ཀྱི་སེམས་བསྒོམ་པ་ལ། སྨོན་པ་བྱང་ཆུབ་ཀྱི་སེམས་བསྒོམ་པ་དང་། འཇུག་པ་བྱང་ཆུབ་ཀྱི་སེམས་བསྒོམ་པ་གཉིས་སོ། །འདི་གཉིས་ལ་བསམ་པ་བྱང་ཆུབ་ཀྱི་སེམས་

དང་། སྦྱོར་བ་ཕ་རོལ་ཏུ་ཕྱིན་པ་ལ་བསླབ་པ་ཞེས་ཟེར་བའང་ཡོད་དོ། དེའི་དང་པོ་ལ་བྱང་ཆུབ་ཀྱི་སེམས་དངོས་ལ་བསླབ་པ། ཕན་ཡོན་དྲན་པ་ལ་བསླབ་པ། བསླབ་བྱ་ལ་དམ་འཆའ་བ་སྟེ་གསུམ་མོ། དང་པོ་ནི། སྔར་གྱི་བྱམས་སྙིང་རྗེ་གཉིས་དང་འབྲེལ་བར་བསྒོམ་སྟེ། མ་འདི་རྣམས་བདེ་དགོས་པར་འདུག སྐྱིད་དགོས་པར་འདུག་པ་ལ། མི་བདེ་མི་སྐྱིད་སྡུག་བསྔལ་བར་འདུག་པ་སྙིང་རེ་རྗེ། བདག་གིས་འདི་རྣམས་ཀྱི་སྡུག་བསྔལ་མི་སེལ་བའི་ཐབས་མེད། འདི་རྣམས་བདེ་བ་ལ་མི་འགོད་པའི་ཐབས་མེད་ཏོ། འོན་ཀྱང་དེའི་ནུས་པ་བདག་ལ་མི་འདུག དེར་མ་ཟད་ཚངས་པ་བརྒྱ་བྱིན་འཁོར་ལོས་བསྒྱུར་རྒྱལ་རྣམས་ལའང་མེད། འོ་ན་སུ་ལ་ཡོད་ན་རྫོགས་པའི་སངས་རྒྱས་ཁོ་ན་ལ་ཡོད། དེ་ལྟ་ན་ཡང་སངས་རྒྱས་དེ་བསྒྲུབས་ན་ཐོབ་ཡོང་བ་ཡིན་པས་བདག་གིས་སངས་རྒྱས་ཐོབ་པར་བྱ། ཐོབ་ནས་སེམས་ཅན་འཁོར་བ་ལས་འདྲེན་པར་བྱ། སེམས་ཅན་ཐམས་ཅད་ལ་ཕན་པའི་ཕྱིར་སངས་རྒྱས་ཐོབ་དགོས་པ་འདུག་སྙམ་པ་ཡང་ཡང་བྱ། དམིགས་སྐོར་བཞི་བཅུ་པའོ།།

གོང་དུ་དམིགས་སྐོར་སོ་བཞི་པ་བསམ་པའི་འཇུག་སྒོ་ལ་བསླབ་པའི་སྐབས་སུ་ནི། སངས་རྒྱས་ཀྱི་ཡོན་ཏན་ཤེས། ཐེག་པ་ཆེ་ཆུང་གི་ཁྱད་པར་ཤེས་པའི་སྒོ་ནས་རྫོགས་བྱང་དོན་གཉེར་ཙམ་བསྒོམ་པ་ཡིན་ལ། དེ་ཙམ་གྱིས་བྱང་ཆུབ་སེམས་ཀྱི་མཚན་ཉིད་རྫོགས་པར་མི་འགྱུར་ཞིང་། འདིར་གཞན་དོན་ཁོ་ནར་རྫོགས་བྱང་དོན་གཉེར་གྱི་བསམ་པ་བསྒོམས་པས་སྨོན་པ་བྱང་ཆུབ་སེམས་ཀྱི་མཚན་ཉིད་ཚང་བར་འགྱུར་རོ། །གོང་དུའང་གཞན་དོན་བསམ་པ་ཙམ་ཡོད་མོད། བྱམས་སྙིང་རྗེ་མཐར་མ་ཕྱིན་པས་གཞན་དོན་དུ་གཙོ་བོར་དམིགས་པ་མི་འབྱུང་ངོ་། དེ་ནས་གཉིས་པ་ཕན་ཡོན་བསམ་པ་ལ་བསླབ་པ་ནི། རང་གི་དོན་ཐམས་ཅད་སྒྲུབ་པའི་ཕན་ཡོན་ནི་མདོ་ལས་བྱང་ཆུབ་ཀྱི་སེམས་ནི་སངས་རྒྱས་ཀྱི་ཆོས་ཐམས་ཅད་བསྐྱེད་པའི་ཕྱིར་ས་བོན་ལྟ་བུའོ། །ཞེས་གསུངས། གཞན་དོན་བསྒྲུབ་པའི་ཕན་ཡོན་ནི། འགྲོ་བ་རྣམས་ཀྱི་ཆོས་དཀར་པོ་འཕེལ་བས་ཞིང་ས་ལྟ་བུའོ། །ཞེས་

སོ། ཉེས་པ་ཐམས་ཅད་སེལ་བའི་ཕན་ཡོན་ནི། ཉེས་པར་སྤྱོད་པ་ཐམས་ཅད་ཟད་པས་སའི་འོག་ལྷ་བུའོ། །ཞེས་སོ། ཡོན་ཏན་ཐོབ་པའི་ཕན་ཡོན་ནི། ཡོན་ཏན་ཐམས་ཅད་འདུ་བས་རྒྱ་མཚོ་ཆེན་པོ་ལྟ་བུའོ། །ཞེས་འབྱུང་བ་ལྟར་ཕན་ཡོན་བཞི་སྟེ། ད་ལྟ་བྱང་ཆུབ་ཀྱི་སེམས་བསྒོམ་པ་ཉིད་ནས་རང་རྒྱུད་ཀྱི་ཐར་པའི་ས་བོན་གསོས་ཐེབས་ཤིང་དགེ་བའི་བག་ཆགས་ཐམས་ཅད་སད། བསམ་པ་བཟང་པོ་དེས་དངོས་སུ་སེམས་ཅན་ལ་ཕན་པ་བྱེད་ཅིང་། ཕན་འདོགས་པའི་ནུས་པ་ཡང་ཉེད་འོང་། འདི་བསྒོམ་ཙམ་ཉིད་ནས་སྡིག་པ་མང་པོ་འདག་ཅིང་། ཆགས་སྡང་ང་རྒྱལ་ཕྲག་དོག་སོགས་ཉོན་མོངས་ཀྱི་དཔལ་འཛོམས། རྒྱུད་འཛམ་པོར་སོང་བས་ཡོན་ཏན་ཐམས་ཅད་སྐྱེ་ཞིང་། སངས་རྒྱས་བསྒྲུབ་པར་དམ་བཅས་ཕྱིན་ཡོན་ཏན་གཞན་མང་པོ་བསྒྲུབ་དགོས་པ་ཅིག་ཀྱང་ཤུགས་ལ་འོང་། དེ་ནས་མཐར་ཐུག་གི་བར་དུ་རང་དོན་རྟོགས་པ་དང་། གཞན་དོན་འཕྲིན་ལས་དང་། སྤང་བྱ་སྤོང་བ་དང་། ཡོན་ཏན་སྒྲུབ་པ་ཐམས་ཅད་འདིས་བྱེད་པ་ཡིན། མདོར་ན་རྣམ་པ་ཐམས་ཅད་མཁྱེན་པ་ཉིད་ལ་ཡོན་ཏན་ཇི་ཙམ་ཡོད་པ། བྱང་ཆུབ་ཀྱི་སེམས་ལའང་ཡོད་པ་ཡིན། སངས་རྒྱས་ལ་ཇི་ཙམ་རི་བ་འདི་ལའང་རི་སྙམ་དུ། བྱང་ཆུབ་ཀྱི་སེམས་ལ་སྤྲོ་སེང་ངེ་བ་བསྐྱེད་ལ། སླར་ཡང་བྱང་ཆུབ་ཀྱི་སེམས་སྔར་བཞིན་བསྒོམ། དེ་ཀ་ཡང་ཡང་བསྐྱར། ཐུན་མཚམས་སུ་སེམས་བསྐྱེད་རང་གིས་ལེན་པའི་ཚིགས་ཀྱང་ཡང་ཡང་ལེན་པའི་དམིགས་པ་སྤྱོད། ཡང་སྔར་སེམས་བསྐྱེད་མ་ཐོབ་ན། རྒྱན་བཤགས་ཀྱི་འགྲོ་ལ་ཕན་ཕྱིར་སངས་རྒྱས་འགྲུབ་པར་ཤོག །ཅེས་འབྱུང་བ་དེ་ཁ་སེམས་བསྐྱེད་ཡིན་པས་ཡན་ལག་བདུན་པ་ཡང་ཡང་བྱ། དམིགས་སྐོར་ཞི་གཅིག་པའོ།།

གསུམ་པ་བསླབ་བྱ་ལ་དམ་འཆའ་བ་ནི། བསླབ་བྱ་དང་པོ་སེམས་ཅན་བློས་མི་སྤང་བ་ལ་བསླབ་དགོས་ཏེ། སེམས་ཅན་བློས་སྤོང་བ་ལ་གཉིས་ཡོད། ཁྱུ་རིལ་དུ་བློས་སྤོང་བ་དང་། སོ་ཐད་དུ་བློས་སྤོང་བའོ། དང་པོ་ནི་ཆོས་ལ་འཇུག་པའི་བློ་ལོག་པ་སྟེ། ངས་

རང་དོན་གཞན་དོན་གང་ཡང་མི་ཡོང་འཇིག་རྟེན་ཕལ་པ་བྱ་སྐམ་པ་དང་། ཐེག་ཆེན་ལ་བློ་ལོག་པ་སྤྱི་སེམས་ཅན་གྱི་དོན་སྒྲུབ་མི་ནུས་པས་བདག་ཉན་རང་གི་ཐེག་པར་སེམས་བསྐྱེད་དགོས་སྐམ་པ་ལྟ་བུ་ཡིན། སྨྲ་ཐད་དུ་བློས་སྤངས་བ་ནི། རང་དང་འགལ་བ་ཁ་ཅིག་ལ་ཁྲོད་ལ་ཕན་ཐོགས་པའི་དུས་བྱུང་ཀྱང་གནས་སྐབས་མཐར་ཐུག་གང་ལ་ལྟོས་ཀྱང་ཕན་མི་འདོགས་སྐམ་དུ་སྙིང་བརྩེ་ལྡན་གྱིས་བྲལ་བ་དེ་ཡིན། དེ་ལྟར་ཁྲུ་རིལ་གྱི་བློས་སྤངས་སམ། སྨྲ་ཐད་ཀྱི་བློས་སྤངས་ཀྱང་རུང་སྟེ། གཉེན་པོས་མ་སླེབ་བར་ཐུན་ཚོད་གཅིག་འདས་ན་སེམས་བསྐྱེད་གཏོང་བ་ཡིན་པར་འདུག། བདག་གིས་སེམས་ཅན་སྤྱོང་བའི་བློ་ནམ་དུ་ཡང་མ་སྐྱེས་བ་ཞིག་བྱ། གལ་ཏེ་དབང་མེད་དུ་སྐྱེས་ཀྱང་འཕྲལ་དུ་གཉེན་པོས་སླེབ་ནས་དེ་མ་ཐག་བཤགས་པ་བྱ། ད་ལྟ་དངོས་སུ་ཕན་གདགས་མ་ནུས་པ་ལ་ཡང་ཞུགས་སུ་ཕན་པར་བྱ་སྐམ་དུ་བསྒོམ། དམིགས་སྐོར་ཞི་གཉིས་པའོ།།

བསླབ་བྱ་གཉིས་པ་ཚོགས་བསག་པ་ལ་འབད་དགོས། བདག་རིམ་པས་ཡོན་ཏན་གོང་ནས་གོང་དུ་སོང་ན། ཚོགས་གཉིས་རྒྱ་ཆེ་ཆེ་ལ་བསླབ་དགོས། ཉི་མ་དེ་རིང་རང་ནས་ཚོགས་གཉིས་ལ་བསླབ་དགོས་ཏེ། བསོད་ནམས་ཀྱི་ཚོགས་ནི། མདོ་བསྟན་བཅོས་རྣམས་ལས་ཕན་ཡོན་ཆེ་བར་བཤད་པའི་དཀོན་མཆོག་གི་མཆོད་པ། དགེ་འདུན་གྱི་བསྙེན་བཀུར། འབྱུང་པོའི་གཏོར་མ། ཕྱག་མཆོད་བསྐོར་བ་གཟུངས་སྔགས་བཟླས་པ་དད་པ་བསྒོམ་པ་བྱམས་སྙིང་རྗེ་བསྒོམ་པ། བཟོད་པ་བསྒོམ་པ་ལ་སོགས་པ་ལ་བསླབ་དགོས་སྐམ་པ་དང་། ཡེ་ཤེས་ཀྱི་ཚོགས་ཆོས་ཉན་པ། ཚིག་འཛིན་པ། དོན་སེམས་པ། འགལ་འབྲེལ་གྱི་སྒོ་ནས་རིག་པས་ཐེ་ཚོམ་གཅོད་པ། འཁོར་གསུམ་རྣམ་པར་མི་རྟོག་པར་རྒྱས་འདེབས་པ་ཞེས་བྱ་བ། འཁོར་འདས་ཐམས་ཅད་བདེན་མེད་དུ་ཐོས་པའི་སྒོ་ནས་གོ་ཞིང་ཤེས། བསམ་པའི་སྒོ་ནས་ངེས་པ་རྙེད། སྒོམ་པའི་སྒོ་ནས་མངོན་སུམ་དུ་རྟོགས་པ་ཅིག་དགོས་པས་དོན་འདི་ལ་བསླབ་དགོས་སྐམ་པ་དང་། མཆོད་པ་ལ་སོགས་པ་ཟླདེན་

མེད་ཀྱི་ལྟ་བས་ཟིན་པ་དང་། ལྟ་བ་དེའི་ངང་ནས་དེ་ལྟར་བསླབས་པས་བསོད་ནམས་ཀྱི་ཡེ་ཤེས། ཡེ་ཤེས་ཀྱི་བསོད་ནམས་སུ་སོང་ནས་ཚོགས་གཉིས་ཟུང་དུ་འཇུག་པ་ཅིག་བྱའོ་སྙམ་དུ་ཡང་ཡང་བསམ། ཐུན་མཚམས་ཀུན་དུ་དེ་དག་ལས་ཅི་ལྟར་འོས་འོས་ལག་ལེན་དུ་ཐེབས་པར་ཡང་བྱ། དམིགས་སྐོར་ཞེ་གསུམ་པའོ།།

བསླབ་བྱ་གསུམ་པ་ཟུང་བཞི་ཡ་བརྒྱད་ལ་བསླབ་དགོས་ན། ནག་པོའི་ཆོས་བཞི་སྤྱིར་ཡང་ཉེས་པ་ཆེ། སྒོས་སུ་སྐྱེ་བ་འཕོས་ན་སེམས་བསྐྱེད་བརྗེད་པའི་རྒྱུ་ཡིན། དཀར་པོའི་ཆོས་བཞི་སྤྱིར་ཡང་ཕན་ཡོན་ཆེ། སྒོས་སུ་སྐྱེ་བ་ཐམས་ཅད་དུ་སེམས་བསྐྱེད་དྲན་པའི་རྒྱུ་ཡིན། དེས་ན་ནག་པོའི་ཆོས་བཞི་སྤང་། དཀར་པོའི་ཆོས་བཞི་ལ་བསླབ་དགོས། དེ་ལ་ཟུང་དང་པོ་བླ་མ་དང་སྦྱིན་གནས་དང་། མཆོད་འོས་བསླུ་བ་ནག་པོའི་ཆོས་ཡིན། བསླུ་བ་ཞེས་བྱ་བ་དེ་དག་ལ་རྫུན་གྱིས་མགོ་སྐོར་གཏོང་བ་ལ་ཟེར། དེའི་གཉེན་པོར་ཤེས་བཞིན་གྱི་རྫུན་སྨྲ་བ་མཐའ་དག་སྤངས་པ་ཡིན། སྐྱེ་བོ་ཐ་མལ་པ་ལ་ཤེས་བཞིན་གྱི་རྫུན་ཕྲ་མོ་ཡང་མི་སྨྲ་ན། མཆོད་འོས་བསླུ་བ་ལྟ་ག་ལ་ཞིག། ཟུང་གཉིས་པ་གཞན་འགྱོད་པའི་གནས་མ་ཡིན་པ་ལ་འགྱོད་པ་ནག་པོའི་ཆོས་ཟེར། འགྱོད་པའི་གནས་སྡིག་པ་བྱས་པ་ལ་འགྱོད་པ་བསྐྱེད་དགོས་ཀྱང་། གནས་མ་ཡིན་པ་དགེ་བ་བྱས་པ་ལ་འགྱོད་པ་བསྐྱེད་པའི་ཐབས་བྱས་ན། དེ་འགྱོད་རུང་མ་འགྱོད་རུང་ནག་པོའི་ཆོས་ཡིན། འགྱོད་པ་བསྐྱེད་ཚུལ་ནི། སྦྱིན་པ་འདི་ཆེས་ཏེ་འདི་ཙམ་སྦྱིན་ན་ཅི་ཟ། ཅེས་པ་དང་། ཁྱོད་སྡོམ་པ་བླངས་ན་བུ་སྨད་འདི་ཀུན་ཁ་ཞན་པོར་འགྲོ་ཅེས་པའམ། དཀའ་ལ་ལན་པོ་མ་བྱས་པ་དེས་ཁྱེད་ལྟངས་ཆག་པར་འགྱུར་ཅེས་པ་ལྟ་བུའོ། དེའི་གཉེན་པོར་སེམས་ཅན་རྣམས་ཐེག་པ་གསུམ་གྱི་དགེ་བ་ལ་སྦྱིན་པར་བྱ་བ། དཀར་པོའི་ཆོས་ལ་བསླབ་སྟེ། སེམས་ཅན་རྣམས་ཐེག་པ་གསུམ་པོ་གང་མོས་མོས་ལ་སེམས་བསྐྱེད་དུ་གཞུག། སྒོས་སུ་ཐེག་ཆེན་ལ་ཅི་ནུས་ནུས་སུ་དགོད། དགེ་བའི་རིགས་ཅི་འགྲུབ་བྱེད་དུ་བཅུག། དེ་ཡང་བྱང་ཆུབ་ཏུ་སྨོན་ལམ་འདེབས་སུ་འཇུག་

དགོས་ཏེ། དགེ་བ་མི་བྱེད་པ་ཚོ་ཡང་སླར་ནས་དགེ་བ་ལ་འགོད་གང་ཐུབ་བྱེད་དགོས་ན་འགྱོད་པ་བསྐྱེད་པ་ག་ལ་འོང་། ད་ནི་ཟུར་གསུམ་པ་ལ་སློབ་སྟེ། སེམས་བསྐྱེད་པའི་གང་ཟག་ལ་ཚིགས་སུ་བཅད་པ་མ་ཡིན་པ་བརྗོད་པ་ནག་པོའི་ཆོས་ཟེར། ཚིགས་བཅད་མ་ཡིན་པ་ནི་དངོས་སམ་ཤོག་ཏུ་སྐྱོན་བརྗོད་པ་ཡིན། སེམས་བསྐྱེད་སྐྱེས་རུང་མ་སྐྱེས་རུང་ཉམས་རུང་མ་ཉམས་རུང་འདྲ། སེམས་བསྐྱེད་བླངས་སོ་ཟེར་བ་ཙམ་ཚོད་སྨད་དུ་མི་རུང་། དེའི་གཉེན་པོར་སེམས་ཅན་ཐམས་ཅད་ལ་སྟོན་པའི་འདུ་ཤེས་བསྒོམ་པ་ལ་བསླབ་པ་དཀར་པོའི་ཆོས་ཡིན། སེམས་ཅན་ཐམས་ཅད་སངས་རྒྱས་ཀྱི་སྙིང་པོ་ཅན་ཡིན་པ་དང་། ཚོགས་གསོག་སྒྲིབ་སྦྱོང་གི་ཡུལ་ལ་སངས་རྒྱས་དང་འདྲ། ཇི་སྐད་དུ། སེམས་ཅན་རྣམས་དང་རྒྱལ་བ་ལ། །སངས་རྒྱས་ཆོས་འགྲུབ་འདྲ་བ་ལ། །ཅེས་གསུངས་པ་ལྟར་ཡིན། དེས་ན་སྟོན་པའི་འདུ་ཤེས་བསྐྱེད་ནས། རྟག་ཏུ་བསྔགས་པ་དང་བསྟོད་ར་བརྗོད་པར་བྱ། སེམས་ཅན་ཕལ་པ་ལ་ཡང་མི་སྨོད་ཅིང་བསྔགས་པ་བརྗོད་ན། སེམས་བསྐྱེད་པ་ལ་མི་སྨོད་པ་ལྟ་ཅི་སྨོས། ཟུར་བཞི་པ་སེམས་ཅན་ལ་གཡོ་སྒྱུས་ཀུན་དུ་སྤྱོད་པ་ནག་པོའི་ཆོས་ཟེར། རང་གི་དོན་བསྒྲུབ་པའི་ཕྱིར་དུ་གཞན་ལ་ཁྲམ་དང་གྱབ་སྐོར་བྱེད་པ། ཐ་ན་བྲེ་སྲང་ཚུན་ཆད་ལ་གཡོ་སྒྱུ་བྱས་ཀྱང་རུང་སྟེ། ནག་པོའི་ཆོས་ཡིན། དེའི་གཉེན་པོར་སེམས་ཅན་ཐམས་ཅད་ལ་ཕན་པ་དང་བདེ་བ་དང་ལྷག་པའི་བསམ་པས་གནས་པ་དཀར་པོའི་ཆོས་ཡིན། ཕན་པ་དང་བདེ་བ་ནི་ཚེ་འདི་ཕྱི་གཉིས་ཀྱི་བདེ་བ་ལ་འགོད་པ་དང་། ལྷག་པའི་བསམ་པ་ནི། གཞན་དོན་གྱི་ཁུར་རང་གིས་ཁྱེར་བ་ལ་ཡང་ཟེར། ཡང་གཡོ་ཐབས་ཀྱི་ཀྱ་ཀྱུ་མི་བྱེད་པར་བསམ་པ་དྲང་པོས་ཚིག་གསོང་པོར་སྨྲ་བ་ཕ་མ་བུ་ཚ་ལྟར་ཕྱི་ནང་མེད་པ་ལའང་ཟེར་བས་དེ་ལྟ་བུ་ལ་བསླབ་དགོས། སེམས་ཅན་ཐམས་ཅད་ལ་ཕན་བདེ་ལྷག་བསམ་དུ་གནས་དགོས་ན། ཕར་ལ་གཡོ་སྒྱུ་འཚོང་བའི་གོ་སྐབས་ག་ལ་ཡོད། དཀར་པོའི་ཆོས་འདི་རྣམས་ལ་ཤིན་དུ་ནན་ཏན་སྙིང་པོར་བྱ་རྒྱུ་ཡིན་པ་འདུག། བདག་དེང་ནས་གཟུང་སྟེ་ནག་པོའི་ཆོས་

བཞི་ནམ་དུ་ཡང་མ་བྱེད། དཀར་པོའི་ཆོས་བཞི་ལ་ཅི་ནུས་ཅི་སྟོབས་ཀྱིས་བསླབ་པར་བྱའོ་སྙམ་དུ་བསམ། དམིགས་སྐོར་ཞེ་བཞི་པའོ།།

འདིར་བྱུང་བཞི་རེ་རེ་ལ་དམིགས་སྐོར་རེ་རེ་མཛད་པའི་ལུགས་ཀྱང་ཡོད། བློ་འཕོབས་ཆུང་བ་ལ་དེ་ལྟར་བྱས་ན་ངེས་ཤེས་སྐྱེ་ཞིང་ལེགས་པར་འོང་ཡང་འོང་ངོ་། །ཡང་སེམས་བསྐྱེད་ཀྱི་ཕན་ཡོན་དྲན་པ་དང་། ཉིན་མཚན་དུས་དྲུག་ཏུ་སེམས་བསྐྱེད་ལེན་པ་ཡང་བསླབ་བྱར་བསྡུས་ཏེ། སེམས་ཅན་མི་སྤང་བ། ཚོགས་གཉིས་ལ་བསླབ་པ། བྱང་བཞི་ལ་རེ་རེ་སྟེ་བསླབ་བྱ་བརྒྱད་ཟེར་བའང་ཡོད་པས་ཇི་ལྟར་འོས་པར་སྦྱར་བར་བྱའོ། །སློང་རྗེའི་ཁྲིད་སོང་བའི་མཚམས་སུ་སེམས་བསྐྱེད་བླངས་ནས། དེ་རྗེས་སྨོན་སེམས་ཀྱི་ཁྲིད་འདི་རྣམས་བསྐྱངས་ན་གོ་རིམ་འགྲིག་མདོག་ཁ་ཞིང་ལེགས་པར་འགྱུར་ལ། ཡང་ཐོག་མར་དམིགས་པ་འདི་རྣམས་བྱང་བར་བྱས་ཏེ། བར་འདིར་སེམས་བསྐྱེད་བླངས་ན་ཚོགས་ལེན་པའི་སྐབས་དེར་ངེས་ཤེས་སྐྱེ་ཚབས་ཆེ་བས། སྐབས་འདིར་བྱས་ན་ཡང་ལེགས་པར་འགྱུར། ཡང་ཁྲིད་ཡོངས་སུ་རྫོགས་པའི་མཐར་བྱང་སྡོམ་ལེན་པའི་སྔོན་དུ་སེམས་བསྐྱེད་བླངས་ཀྱང་རུང་སྟེ། ཇི་ལྟར་སྐབས་སུ་བབ་པ་དེ་ལྟར་བྱའོ། །གཉིས་པ་འཇུག་པ་བྱང་ཆུབ་ཀྱི་སེམས་ལ་བསླབ་པ་ནི་འདི་ཡིན་ཏེ། སངས་རྒྱས་ཐོབ་པར་འདོད་པས་བྱང་ཆུབ་སྤྱོད་པ་ལ་བསླབ་དགོས། སངས་རྒྱས་འགྲུབ་པར་འདོད་ཀྱང་སྤྱོད་པ་ལ་མི་སློབ་ན། ལོ་ལེགས་པར་འདོད་སྐད། བསོ་ནམ་མི་བྱེད་པ་དང་འདྲ། སྤྱིར་བྱང་ཆུབ་ཏུ་སྨོན་པ་ཙམ་ལའང་ཕན་ཡོན་མང་མོད་ཀྱི་བྱང་ཆུབ་སྤྱོད་པ་ཉམས་སུ་མ་བླངས་ན་ཡོན་ཏན་གོང་འཕེལ་དུ་མི་འགྲོ་བས་སྤྱོད་པ་ལ་བསླབ་དགོས། སྤྱོད་པའི་ངོ་བོ་ཡང་ཕ་རོལ་ཏུ་ཕྱིན་པ་དྲུག་དང་བསྡུ་དངོས་བཞི་ཡིན། ཕར་ཕྱིན་དང་བསྡུ་དངོས་བྱ་བ་ཡང་ལོགས་ལོགས་སུ་མེད། ཕྱིན་དྲུག་རང་གིས་ཉམས་སུ་ལེན། གཞན་ལ་ཚིག་གི་སྒོ་ནས་སྟོན། གཞན་རྣམས་བྱེད་དུ་འཇུག་པ་དེ་ཁ་ཕར་ཕྱིན་ཀྱང་ཡིན། བསྡུ་དངོས་ཀྱང་ཡིན། བདག་གིས་ཕ་རོལ་ཏུ་

ཕྱིན་པ་བཅུ་ལ་ནན་ཏན་སྙིང་པོར་བསྒྲུབ་པར་བྱའོ། །དེ་ཡང་ཕྱི་དུས་ཕྱི་དུས་ན་མ་ཡིན་པར་ད་ལྟ་ཉིད་དུ་འཇུག་པར་བྱའོ་སྙམ་པ་ཡང་ཡང་སྦྱོང་བ་ཡིན། འདི་སྐབས་དམ་བཅའ་དང་ལག་ལེན་མ་འཛོལ་བར་ཅི་ནུས་ཅི་ལྕོགས་ཀྱིས་ལག་ལེན་དུ་ཐེབས་པ་ཉི་མ་དེ་རིང་ནས་བྱེད་དགོས་པ་ཡིན་ནོ། །ཅེས་བྱ་སྟེ་འཇུག་སེམས་སྦྱིར་བསྒོམ་པ་ཡིན། དམིགས་སྐོར་ཞེ་ལྔ་པའོ།།

བདག་གིས་བྱང་ཆུབ་སེམས་དཔའི་སྤྱོད་པ་སྤྱོད་དགོས་ན། དང་པོར་སྦྱིན་པའི་ཕ་རོལ་ཏུ་ཕྱིན་པ་ལ་བསླབ་དགོས། སྦྱིན་པ་དེ་ལ་དབྱེ་ན་གསུམ། ཟང་ཟིང་གི་སྦྱིན་པ། མི་འཇིགས་པའི་སྦྱིན་པ། ཆོས་ཀྱི་སྦྱིན་པ་གསུམ་མོ། བདག་གིས་སེམས་ཅན་ཐམས་ཅད་ལ་ཟང་ཟིང་གི་སྦྱིན་པ་བྱིན་ལ་ཚིམས་པར་བྱ། ད་ལྟ་དེ་ཙམ་གྱི་ནུས་པ་མེད་ཏེ། ཕྱིས་འཁོར་ལོས་བསྒྱུར་བའི་རྒྱལ་སྲིད་ཕུན་ཚོགས་བཟུང་ལ་སྦྱིན་དགོས་སྙམ་པ་བསམ་པའི་སྒོ་ནས་བསླབ། ད་ལྟ་རང་ཡང་རང་གི་ནུས་པ་དང་སྦྱར་ལ་ཆོས་ཀྱི་འགལ་རྐྱེན་དུ་མི་འགྲོ་ཙམ་གྱི་སྒོ་ནས། ཟས་གོས་ལ་སོགས་པ་ཅི་ནུས་ཅི་ལྕོགས་སུ་སྦྱིན། མ་ཐ་རང་ལ་ཡང་སློང་མོ་བ་ཁ་སྟོང་དུ་མི་གཏོང་བ་ཙམ་རེ་མི་བྱེད་པའི་ཐབས་མི་འདུག་བསམ་ཞིང་། འདི་དམིགས་པ་ཙམ་མ་ཡིན་པ་ལག་ལེན་དུ་ཡང་ཁེལ་ངེས་པ་དགོས་ཏེ། སྦྱོར་བ་ལ་བསླབ་པ་ཡིན། མི་འཇིགས་པའི་སྦྱིན་པ། བདག་གིས་སེམས་ཅན་ཐམས་ཅད་ནད་ཀྱི་འཇིགས་པ་དང་། མཚོན་གྱི་འཇིགས་པ་དང་། ཆོམ་རྐུན་གྱི་འཇིགས་པ་དང་། དུག་གི་འཇིགས་པ་དང་། གཅན་གཟན་དང་དུག་སྦྲུལ་ལ་སོགས་པ་སྲོག་ཆགས་གདུག་པ་ཅན་གྱི་འཇིགས་པ་དང་། གཡང་སའི་འཇིགས་པ་དང་། ལམ་འཕྲང་གི་འཇིགས་པ་དང་། མེའི་འཇིགས་པ་དང་། ཆུའི་འཇིགས་པ་དང་། ཆད་པས་གཅོད་པའི་འཇིགས་པ་ལ་སོགས་པ་ངན་འགྲོའི་འཇིགས་པའི་བར་ཐམས་ཅད་ལས་བསྐྱབ་པར་བྱ་སྙམ་དུ་བསམ་པས་སྦྱངས། ད་ལྟ་ཡང་དངོས་སུ་ནད་དང་གདོན་དང་དགྲ་དང་འབྱུང་བཞིའི་འཇིགས་པ་སོགས་ལ་ཅི་ནུས་ཅི་ལྕོགས་ཀྱིས་སྐྱོབ་པའི་ཐབས་བྱའོ་སྙམ་དུ་བསྒོམ་ཞིང་། དམིགས་པར་མ་ཟད་ལག་ལེན་གྱི་སྒོ་ནས་ཀྱང་ཚུལ་

ཁྲིམས་དང་། སྒྲུབ་པའི་བར་ཆད་དུ་མི་འགྱུར་བ་རྣམས་ཅི་འགྲུབ་ཏུ་བྱ་ཞིང་། ཐ་ན་ཁ་ཕན་ཚིག་ཕན་ཚུན་ཚོད་བྱ། སྦྱོར་བའི་སྒོ་ནས་བསླབ་པ་ཡིན། མི་འཇིགས་པའི་སྦྱིན་པ་བྱས་ཀྱང་སེམས་ཅན་སྡུག་བསྔལ་བ་ལ་ཕན་འདོགས་པའི་མིང་ཡིན། སྐབས་སུ་མ་བབ་པ་དང་སྡིག་རྐྱེན་དུ་འགྲོ་ན་ཁྲེ་ཡིས་གྲོང་མི་སུབས་པ་འབྱུང་ཉེན་ཆེ་བས། བསམ་པས་སྦྱོང་དགོས་ཀྱང་སྦྱོར་བ་བཏང་སྙོམས་སུ་འཇོག་པའི་སྐབས་ཡིན་ནོ། །ཆོས་ཀྱི་སྦྱིན་པ་བདག་གིས་སེམས་ཅན་ཐམས་ཅད་ཆོས་ཀྱི་སྦྱིན་པས་ཚིམས་པར་བྱ། བདག་གིས་ཆོས་བསྟན་ཏེ། སེམས་ཅན་མ་སྨིན་པ་རྣམས་སྨིན་པར་བྱ། སྨིན་པ་རྣམས་གྲོལ་བར་བྱ། མ་གོ་བ་རྣམས་གོ་ར་གཞུག མ་རྟོགས་པ་རྣམས་རྟོགས་སུ་གཞུག མ་ཐོབ་པ་རྣམས་ཐོབ་ཏུ་གཞུག་སྙམ་དུ་བསམ་པའི་སྒོ་ནས་སྦྱངས། ད་ལྟ་ཡང་རང་ལ་ཆོས་བཤད་པའི་ནུས་པ་ཡོད་ན་རྙེད་བཀུར་དང་ཁེངས་གྲགས་ལ་མི་ལྟ་བར་གཞན་ལ་ཆོས་བཤད་པས་ཕན་འདོགས་དགོས། དེ་ལྟར་མི་ནུས་པ་ཞིག་ཡིན་ནའང་། མི་དང་མི་མ་ཡིན་ལ་ཆོས་བཤད་པར་མོས་ཏེ། མདོ་འདོན་པའམ་གསུང་རབ་སྒྲོག་པའི་ཐུན་མ་ཆག་པར་བྱའོ་སྙམ་དུ་བསམ་པས་སྦྱང་བར་བྱ་ཞིང་། དེ་དམིགས་པར་མ་ཟད་ལག་ལེན་དུ་ཡང་ཁེལ་བར་བྱེད་པ་ནི། སྦྱོར་བའི་སྒོ་ནས་བསླབ་པ་ཡིན་ཏེ། དེ་ལྟར་ན་སྦྱིན་པ་གསུམ་ལ་བསམ་སྦྱོར་གཉིས་གཉིས་ཀྱི་བསླབ་ཚུལ་ཏེ་དྲུག་ཡོད། ཡོངས་རྫོགས་ནས་སྦྱིན་པའི་ཕ་རོལ་ཏུ་ཕྱིན་པ་ལ་བསླབ་པ་ཡིན་ཏེ། དམིགས་སྐོར་ཞེ་དྲུག་པའོ།།

བསམ་སྦྱོར་སོ་སོ་ལ་བསླབ་ཚུལ་འདི་ཕྱི་མ་རྣམས་ལ་ཡང་རིགས་འགྲེ། དེ་གཞན་ཡང་ཚུལ་ཁྲིམས་ཀྱི་ཕར་ཕྱིན་ལ་བསླབ་དགོས། ཚུལ་ཁྲིམས་ལ་གསུམ། ཉེས་སྤྱོད་སྡོམ་པའི་ཚུལ་ཁྲིམས། དགེ་བ་ཆོས་སྡུད་ཀྱི་ཚུལ་ཁྲིམས། སེམས་ཅན་དོན་བྱེད་ཀྱི་ཚུལ་ཁྲིམས་གསུམ་མོ། །ཉེས་སྤྱོད་སྡོམ་པའི་ཚུལ་ཁྲིམས་ནི། སྤྱིར་མི་དགེ་བ་བཅུ་སོགས་རང་བཞིན་གྱི་ཁ་ན་མ་ཐོ་བ་ཐམས་ཅད་སྤངས་པ་ཅིག་དང་། སྒོས་སུ་དགེ་བསྙེན་ནམ། དགེ་སློང་

ངམ། དགེ་ཚུལ་ལམ། བྱང་སྡོམ་གྱི་བསླབ་བྱ་འམ། སྔགས་ཀྱི་དམ་ཚིག་སོགས་རང་གིས་གང་བླངས་པའི་སྡོམ་ཁྲིམས་ཀྱི་བསྲུང་བྱ་དང་མ་འགལ་བ་ཞིག་དགོས། མདོར་ན་མདོ་དང་བསྟན་བཅོས་ལས་མི་རུང་བར་གསུངས་པ་ཐམས་ཅད་ལས་ལྡོག་པ་སྟེ། བདག་གིས་འདི་ལ་འཕྲུལ་དུ་བསླབ་པར་བྱ་སྙམ་དུ་བསམ། དགེ་བ་ཆོས་སྡུད་ཀྱི་ཚུལ་ཁྲིམས་ནི། དགེ་བ་སྣ་རེ་དང་ཕྱོགས་རེར་མ་སོང་བར་ཕར་ཕྱིན་དྲུག་གིས་བསྡུས་པ་ཐམས་ཅད་ལ་རྟག་ཏུ་བསླབ་དགོས་པའི་དོན་ཡིན། དེ་ལའང་ད་ལྟ་རང་ནས་ཅི་ནུས་ཅི་ལྕོགས་སུ་བསྒྲུབ། སེམས་ཅན་དོན་བྱེད་ཀྱི་ཚུལ་ཁྲིམས། སེམས་ཅན་རྣམས་བདེ་བ་དང་། དགེ་བ་སྣ་ཚོགས་པ་ལ་འགོད་པའི་སྒོ་ནས་ཕན་པ་སྒྲུབ་པ་ལ་ཟེར། དེ་ཡང་བདག་གིས་ཅི་ནུས་ཅི་ལྕོགས་ཀྱིས་ད་ལྟ་རང་ནས་ཀྱང་སེམས་ཅན་རྣམས་ཕན་པ་དང་བདེ་བ་ལ་འགོད་གང་ཐུབ་བྱ་སྙམ་དུ་བསམ། ཉེས་སྤྱོད་སྡོམ་པ་ལ་ཕྱི་དུས་འདེབས་སུ་མེད། ཐོས་མ་ཐག་ནས་བཅག་སྟེ་ལྡོག་དགོས། ཕྱི་མ་གཉིས་ལ་ཕྱི་དུས་ཅིག་ཀྱང་འདེབས་སུ་ཡོད་དེ། རང་གི་བློ་སྟོབས་དང་བསྟུན་ནས་ད་ལྟ་གང་ནུས་གང་ལྕོགས་བྱས། ད་ལྟ་མི་ཐུབ་པ་རྣམས་ཕྱིས་སྨོན་ལམ་གྱི་ཡུལ་དུ་བཞག་པས་ཆོག་པ་ཡིན། སྤྱིར་བྱང་ཆུབ་སེམས་དཔའ་གཞན་དོན་མ་བྱས་ན་དེ་ཉིད་ཉེས་པ་ཆེ་ཤོས་ཡིན་ཏེ། སེམས་ཅན་དོན་བྱེད་ཀྱི་ཚུལ་ཁྲིམས་དགོས། གཞན་དོན་བྱེད་པ་ལ་རང་རྒྱུད་སྨིན་དགོས་པས། དགེ་བ་ཆོས་སྡུད་དགོས་པ་ཡིན། རང་ཉེས་ལྟུང་གིས་མ་གོས་པ་གཅིག་པོས་ཀྱང་མི་ཆོག་པ་ཅིག་ཡིན་པར་འདུག་ནའང་། ཐོག་མའི་གཞི་ལ་ཉེས་སྤྱོད་སྡོམ་པ་རང་གལ་ཆེ་སྟེ། འདི་མེད་ན་གཞན་གཉིས་ཀྱང་ཇི་བཞིན་མི་ཡོང་བ་ལགས། དམིགས་སྐོར་ཞེ་བདུན་པའོ།།

ད་ནི་བཟོད་པའི་ཕར་ཕྱིན་ལ་གསུམ། གནོད་པ་ལ་ཇི་མི་སྙམ་པའི་བཟོད་པ། སྡུག་བསྔལ་དང་ལེན་གྱི་བཟོད་པ། ཆོས་ལ་ངེས་པར་སེམས་པའི་བཟོད་པ་སྟེ་གསུམ་མོ། །དེའི་དང་པོ་ནི། གཞན་གྱིས་བདག་ལ་བརྡེག་པ་དང་། ནོར་འཕྲོག་པ་ལ་སོགས་པའི་

གནོད་པ་བྱས་པའི་ཚེ་མི་བཟོད་ཅིང་ཞེ་སྡང་སྐྱེ་བའི་རྣམ་འགྱུར་ཡོང་བས། བདག་སངས་རྒྱས་བསྒྲུབ་རྒྱུ་ཡིན་པ་ལ་གནོད་པ་འདི་ཙམ་མ་བཟོད་པས་ག་ན་འོང་། ཁམས་གསུམ་སེམས་ཅན་དགྲར་གྱུར་ནས་གནོད་པ་སྣ་མི་འདྲ་བ་ཐམས་ཅད་ནས་བྱེད་ཀྱང་བཟོད་སྲན་ཆུགས་པར་བྱ། གནོད་པ་འདི་ཙམ་ཡང་མི་བཟོད་པར་སངས་རྒྱས་ཐོབ་ཏུ་རེ་བ་དང་། ཆོས་པ་ཡིན་དུ་རེ་བ་ང་རང་འཁྲུལ་སྙམ་དུ་བསྒོམ། སྡུག་བསྔལ་དང་ལེན་གྱི་བཟོད་པ་ནི་ཆོས་སྒྲུབ་པའི་དུས་ན་ཚ་གྲང་ལྟོགས་སྐོམ་ལ་སོགས་པའི་སྡུག་བསྔལ་བྱུང་བའམ། ལམ་བགྲོད་དཀའ་བ་དང་། མཐུན་རྐྱེན་མ་འཛོམས་པ་དང་། ངལ་དུབ་ཐང་ཆད་ཉི་ལྷགས་ཆར་གསུམ་སོགས་གང་བྱུང་ཀྱང་ཡོངས་བདག་ཆོས་ཀྱི་ཕྱིར་དུ་དཀའ་སྤྱད་ཕྲ་མོ་འདི་ཙམ་མ་བཟོད་པས་ག་ལ་ཡོད། ནོར་དང་བུ་སྨད་ཀྱི་ཕྱིར། འདི་འདྲ་བས་བརྒྱ་འགྱུར་སྟོང་འགྱུར་གྱི་སྡུག་བསྔལ་ཆེ་བ་ཀུན་ལའང་ཚམ་ཚོམ་མེད་པར་འཇུག་གིན་གདའ་བ། བདག་སངས་རྒྱས་བསྒྲུབ་དགོས་པ་ལ། སྔོན་གྱི་བྱང་ཆུབ་སེམས་དཔའི་རྣམ་ཐར་ལ་སློབ་དགོས་ན། ཆོས་ཕྱིར་དཀའ་བ་འདི་ཙམ་ཡང་མི་བཟོད་པར་ཐེག་ཆེན་པར་ཁས་འཆེ་བ་རེ་བླུན་ན་སྙམ་དུ་གཉེན་པོ་བརྟན་ཐང་གིས་བཏང་། ཆོས་ལ་ངེས་པར་སེམས་པའི་བཟོད་པ་ནི་ཐབས་ཟབ་མོ་དང་། ཐབས་མཁས་ཀྱི་ཁྱད་པར་དང་། མཛད་པ་རླབས་པོ་ཆེ་དང་། ཡོན་ཏན་མཐའ་ཡས་པ་དང་གནས་ལུགས་སྤྲོས་བྲལ་སོགས་གང་ལའང་བློར་མི་ཤོང་བ་མེད་པ་ཅིག་ལ་ཟེར། སྟོང་ཉིད་ལ་སེམས་ཡུན་རིང་དུ་གནས་ཐུབ་པ་ཅིག་ལའང་ཟེར། ད་རེས་འདིར་གནོད་པ་དང་སྡུག་བསྔལ་ཐམས་ཅད་སྒྱུ་མ་ལྟ་བུ་མི་ལམ་ལྟ་བུ་བདེན་པས་སྟོངས་པ་མེད་བཞིན་དུ་སྣང་བ་ཡིན་ན་མི་བཟོད་རྒྱུ་ཅི་ཡོད་སྙམ་དུ་སྒོམ་པ་ལ་བྱའོ། དམིགས་སྐོར་ཞེ་བརྒྱད་པའོ།།

ད་ནི་གཞན་ཡང་བརྩོན་འགྲུས་ཀྱི་ཕ་རོལ་ཏུ་ཕྱིན་པ་ལ་བསླབ་དགོས་ཏེ། དེ་ལ་གསུམ་གོ་ཆའི་བརྩོན་འགྲུས། སྦྱོར་བའི་བརྩོན་འགྲུས། སླར་མི་ལྡོག་པའི་བརྩོན་འགྲུས་སོ། །གོ་ཆའི་བརྩོན་འགྲུས་ནི། ཆོས་དགེ་བ་ཐམས་ཅད་ལ་འདི་ལྟ་བུ་བྱེད་མི་དགོས་སྙམ་

པའི་ཁྲིད་གསོད་དང་། ཆེན་པོ་རྣམས་ལ་འདི་ཙམ་སྒྲུབ་མི་ནུས་སྙམ་པའི་ཞུམ་པའི་སེམས་གཉིས་ཀར་མི་བྱེད་པར་བདག་གིས་འདི་དག་ཐམས་ཅད་བསྒྲུབ་ཀྱང་དགོས། བསྒྲུབ་ནུས་པ་ཡང་ཡིན། ད་ལྟ་ཉིད་དུ་བསྒྲུབ་པར་བྱའོ། །རྒྱུན་མི་འཆད་པར་བསྒྲུབ་པར་བྱའོ། །ཅེས་སེམས་ཀྱི་དམ་བཅའ་དང་འབྲེལ་བའི་དགེ་བ་ལ་སྤྲོ་སེམས་དཔའ་མ་ཞུམ་པ་དེ་ཡིན། དེ་རང་གི་རྒྱུད་ཐོག་ཏུ་སྦྱར་ནས་ཡང་ཡང་བསྒོམ་པར་བྱ། སྦྱོར་བའི་བརྩོན་འགྲུས་ནི་དངོས་སུ་ལག་ལེན་ལ་སྦྱོར་བའི་སྐབས། ལེ་ལོ་དང་རྣམ་གཡེང་གི་དབང་དུ་མི་གཏོང་བར་སྤྲོ་བ་དང་བཅས་པས་འཕྲལ་དུ་དགེ་བ་ལ་འཇུག་ཅིང་། དེ་ཉིད་སྤྲོ་བཞིན་དུ་རྒྱུན་བསྲིང་བའོ། །སླར་མི་ལྡོག་པའི་བརྩོན་འགྲུས་ནི། དྲོད་རྟགས་དང་ཕན་ཡོན་འཕྲལ་དུ་མ་བྱུང་ནའང་། དང་པོར་གང་ལ་ཞུགས་པ་དེའི་འབྲས་བུ་མངོན་དུ་མ་གྱུར་བར་ཡུན་ཇི་ཙམ་འགོར་ཡང་རུང་། དཀའ་བ་ཇི་ཙམ་སྤྱོད་དགོས་ཀྱང་རུང་སྤྲོ་བ་ཡི་མི་ལྡོག་པའོ། །ཡང་བསྟན་རིམ་གྱི་མན་ངག་འགའ་ཞིག་ལས། ལུས་ཀྱི་བརྩོན་འགྲུས་ཕྱག་དང་བསྐོར་བ་སོགས། ངག་གི་བརྩོན་འགྲུས་བཟླས་བརྗོད་ཁ་བཏོན་སོགས་། ཡིད་ཀྱི་བརྩོན་འགྲུས་སྤྱིར་དགེ་བ་དང་སྒོས་སུ་ཆོས་འདི་ལ་སྤྲོ་ཞིང་བརྩོན་པ་སྟེ། ཅེས་པའང་ཡོད་པས། གང་ལྟར་ཡང་རུང་བརྩོན་འགྲུས་ནི་དེ་རྣམས་ཡིན་ན། བདག་ཀྱང་བརྩོན་འགྲུས་དང་ལྡན་པར་བྱ། ལེ་ལོ་ཕྱི་བཤོལ་གྱི་དབང་དུ་མ་བཏང་བར་དགེ་བ་ལ་སྤྲོ་བར་བྱའོ་སྙམ་དུ་བསྒོམ། དམིགས་སྐོར་ཞེ་དགུ་པའོ།།

ད་ནི་གཞན་ཡང་བསམ་གཏན་གྱི་ཕ་རོལ་ཏུ་ཕྱིན་པ་བྱ་བ་ཡོད་དེ། དེའི་རྒྱུ་ཚོགས་ལ་ད་ལྟ་ནས་གནས་དགོས། ཏིང་ངེ་འཛིན་གྱི་རྒྱུར་སེམས་དབེན་པ་གཅིག་དགོས། དེའི་རྒྱུར་ལུས་དབེན་པ་དགོས། དེའི་རྒྱུར་དོན་ཉུང་ལ་བྱ་བ་ཉུང་བ་དགོས། དེའི་རྒྱུར་འདོད་པ་ཆུང་ཞིང་ཆོག་ཤེས་པ་དགོས། དེའི་རྒྱུར་ཟས་གོས་གནས་མལ་ངན་ངོན་ཙམ་གྱིས་ཆོག་ཤེས་པ་དགོས། བདག་ཀྱང་ཅི་སྟེ་འབྱོར་པ་དང་ལྡན་ན་དེ་ལ་མ་ཆགས་པར་ཏིང་ངེ་འཛིན་བསྒོམ། གལ་ཏེ་མ་འབྱོར་ན་ཡང་མ་འབྱོར་བ་ཉིད་བཟང་སྟེ། ཆོས་ཀྱི་བར་ཆད་མེད་

པ་ཡིན། གང་བྱུང་དེ་ཀས་ཚིག་སྨམ་པ་ཡང་ཡང་བསམ་ཞིང་བསྒོམ། དེས་ཏིང་ངེ་འཛིན་གྱི་རྒྱུ་བསམ་པ་སོང་། དམིགས་སྐོར་ལྔ་བཅུ་བའོ།།

དངོས་ནི་བསམ་གཏན་ལ་དབྱེ་ན། དབྱེ་སྒོ་མི་འདྲ་བ་དུ་མ་ཡོད་ཀྱང་། མཐོང་ཆོས་ལ་བདེ་བར་གནས་པའི་བསམ་གཏན་ཞེས་བྱ་བ། ལུས་སེམས་ཤིན་དུ་སྦྱངས་པའི་བདེ་བ་སྒྲུབ་པ་ཡིན། ཡོན་ཏན་མངོན་པར་སྒྲུབ་པའི་བསམ་གཏན་ཞེས་བྱ་བ། སྤྱི་ཇོག་ནས་མངོན་ཤེས་དང་རྫུ་འཕྲུལ་ལ་སོགས་པ་སྒྲུབ་པར་བྱེད་པ་རྣམས་ཡིན། སེམས་ཅན་གྱི་དོན་བྱེད་པའི་བསམ་གཏན་ཞེས་བྱ་བ། ཏིང་ངེ་འཛིན་གྱི་སྟོབས་ལ་བརྟེན་ནས། གཞན་རྒྱུད་བྱིན་གྱིས་རློབ་པར་བྱེད་པའམ། མངོན་ཤེས་ཀྱི་ཁྱད་པར་ལ་བརྟེན་ནས་སེམས་ཅན་གྱི་དོན་སྤྱོད་པ་ཡིན། དེ་ཐམས་ཅད་ཀྱང་ཞི་གནས་སྐྱོན་དང་བྲལ་ཞིང་མཚན་ཉིད་རྫོགས་པ་ཅིག་ལ་བརྟེན་དགོས། བདག་གིས་ཐོག་མ་ཞི་གནས་ལ་སེམས་མཉམ་པར་བཞག་པར་བྱ། དེ་ནས་ཏིང་ངེ་འཛིན་གྱི་ཁྱད་པར་གཞན་ཐམས་ཅད་ཀྱང་བསྒྲུབ་པར་བྱའོ་སྙམ་དུ་ཡང་ཡང་བསྒོམ། དམིགས་སྐོར་ང་གཅིག་པའོ།།

སྐབས་འདིར་ཞི་གནས་ཀྱི་རྣམ་གཞག་ཞིབ་ཙམ་བཤད་ཅིང་ངེས་པོར་བྱུང་ན་ལེགས། ཞི་གནས་ཀྱི་འཁྲིད་ཀྱང་འདིར་སྟོན་པ་ཐོབ་ཐང་ཡིན་མོད་ཀྱང་ལྟ་བ་ལ་ངེས་པ་དང་ཉམས་མྱོང་སྐྱེད་པར་འགྱུར་བ་ཙམ་ལ། ཞི་གནས་བརྟན་པོ་མེད་ཀྱང་ཆོག་པ་དང་། ཞི་གནས་བརྟན་པོ་ལེགས་པོ་བསྒྲུབས་ནས། དེའི་འོག་ཏུ་ལྟ་བ་བསྐྱངས་ཏེ་ལྷག་མཐོང་སྒྲུབ་པ་གཞུང་ཆེན་ཀུན་གྱི་དགོངས་པ་དང་། གཞུང་ལམ་ཆེན་མོ་ཡིན་མོད་ཀྱང་། དེང་སང་གི་གང་ཟག་དབང་པོ་རྟུལ་པོས་སེམས་གནས་སྐྱོན་མེད་བརྟན་པོ་ཞིག་སྒྲུབ་པ་ལ་ཡུན་རིང་དུ་འགོར་བས་ཤེར་ཕྱིན་སྒོམ་པའི་སྐལ་བ་ཆད་ཀྱི་དོགས་པ་དང་། ལྟ་བའི་མྱོང་བ་སྐྱེད་པའི་སྟེང་དུ་སེམས་གནས་བསྒྲུབས་ན། ཞི་ལྷག་ལྷན་ཅིག་ཏུ་འགྲུབ་སྟེ། སློབ་མ་འཁྲིད་བླ་མྱོང་བ་སྐྱེད་བླ་བའི་གནད་ཡོད་པར་དགོངས་ནས་ཕྱག་ལེན་ལ་སྐབས་འདིར་མི་མཛད་

པ་ཡིན་པར་སྣང་ངོ་། ད་ནི་དེ་ཐམས་ཅད་ཀྱི་ནང་ནས་ཆེས་མཆོག་ཏུ་གྱུར་པ་བསླབ་བྱ་ཀུན་གྱི་གཙོ་བོ་ཡང་ཡིན། ཉམས་ལེན་ཀུན་གྱི་མཐར་ཐུག་ཀྱང་ཡིན། ཤེས་རབ་ཀྱི་ཕ་རོལ་ཏུ་ཕྱིན་པ་སྟོན་པར་བྱེད། དེ་ལ་ཤེས་རབ་ནི་གསུམ་ཡོད་དེ། དོན་དམ་ཤེས་པའི་ཤེས་རབ་དང་། ཀུན་རྫོབ་ཤེས་པའི་ཤེས་རབ་དང་། གཞན་དོན་ཤེས་པའི་ཤེས་རབ་སྟེ་གསུམ་མོ། དང་པོ་ནི་གནས་ལུགས་སྟོང་ཉིད་རྟོགས་པའི་ཤེས་རབ་ཡིན། གཉིས་པ་ནི། ཤེས་བྱ་ཐམས་ཅད་ཀྱི་ངོ་བོ་དབྱེ་བ་རྒྱུ་འབྲས་རྟེན་འབྲེལ་མ་ནོར་བར་ཤེས་པའི་ཤེས་རབ་ཡིན། གསུམ་པ་ནི། བསྡུ་བའི་དངོས་པོ་བཞིའི་སྒོ་ནས་འགྲོ་དོན་ཤེས་པའི་ཤེས་རབ་སྟེ། དེ་ལ་ཟང་ཟིང་གི་སྦྱིན་པ་བཏང་སྟེ། སྐྱེ་བོ་རྣམས་མགུ་ནས་ཆོས་ལ་འགོད་ཐུབ་པ་ཤེས། བསམ་པ་དང་མཐུན་པར་ཆོས་སྟོན་པའི་སྙན་པར་སྨྲ་བ་ཤེས། དོན་སྤྱོད་པ་གཞན་ཕྱིན་དྲུག་ལ་འགོད་ཐབས་ཤེས། དོན་མཐུན་པ་རང་ཡང་ཕྱིན་དྲུག་ལས་མི་འདའ་བར་སྤྱོད་ཤེས་པ་སྟེ། དེའི་ནང་གི་གཞན་ཕྱིན་དྲུག་ལ་འགོད་པ་ནི། གདུལ་བྱ་གང་ལ་གང་འདུལ་གྱི་ཐབས་ཤེས་པའི་སྒོ་ནས་ཡིན་ནོ། །ཡང་ན་ཐོས་པ་དང་། བསམ་པ་དང་། སྒོམ་པའི་ཤེས་རབ་སྟེ། ཐོས་པས་གོ། བསམ་པས་སྒྲོ་འདོགས་ཆོད། སྒོམ་པས་མངོན་སུམ་དུ་རྟོགས་པའི་ཤེས་རབ་སྟེ་གསུམ་པོ་འདི་རྣམས་བདག་གིས་ཅི་ནས་ཀྱང་རྒྱུད་ལ་བསྐྱེད་པར་བྱའོ། འདི་ཤེར་ཕྱིན་གྱི་བསམ་པ་ལ་བསླབ་པ་ཡིན། དམིགས་སྐོར་ང་གཉིས་པའོ།།

ད་ནི་ཤེས་རབ་ཀྱི་ཕ་རོལ་ཏུ་ཕྱིན་པའི་སྦྱོར་བ་ལ་བསླབ་དགོས་ཏེ། དེ་ལ་གང་ཟག་གི་བདག་མེད་བསྒོམ་པ། ཆོས་ཀྱི་བདག་མེད་བསྒོམ་པ། སྟོང་ཉིད་སྙིང་རྗེའི་སྙིང་པོ་ཅན་ལ་བསླབ་པ་སྟེ་གསུམ་མོ། དང་པོ་ནི། སྟོན་འགྲོ་དང་རྗེས་སོགས་སྔར་བཤད་པ་ལྟར་ལས། དངོས་གཞིའི་སྐབས་འདིར་ཁང་པ་སྐྱིལ་ཀྱང་ལག་པ་མཉམ་གཞག་སྐྱིལ་ཚིགས་བསྒྲང་། མཁྲིན་པ་དཀུག དཔུང་པ་ཕྱིར་བསྐྱེད། སོ་མཆུ་རང་སར་བཞག་ཅིང་ལྕེ་རྩེ་ཁན་ལ་སྦྱར། མིག་སྣ་རྩེར་ལྟ། དེ་ནས་རླུང་སྣ་ནས་ལན་གསུམ་ཕྱི་ལ་སང་སང་

བ་འབྱུང་། དེ་རྗེས་དབུགས་རང་སོར་བཞག ངེས་འབྱུང་སྐྱོ་ཤས་དུང་ཙམ་དང་། བྱམས་སྙིང་རྗེ་རྒྱུད་འགྱུར་ཙམ་བསྒོ།། དེ་ནས་རང་གི་ལུས་ངག་ཡིད་གསུམ་ལ་སེམས་གཏད། གཞིག་འགྲོལ་བཙུག། འཁོར་བ་ཐོག་མ་མེད་པ་ནས་ང་བདག་ཏུ་འཛིན་པ་གོམས་པས་བདག་ཡོད་ཡོད་ལྟར་སྣང་བ་མ་གཏོགས། ང་བདག་ཅེས་པ་གནས་ཚུལ་ལ་གྲུབ་པ་ཡེ་མེད་པར་འདུག་སྙམ་དུ་བསམ། འདི་དམིགས་པའི་གཞི་ཡིན། དེ་ལ་ངའམ་བདག་ཅེས་བྱ་བ། གནས་ལུགས་ལ་ཡོད་ན་ཏ་དེ་གང་ཟག་གི་བདག་ཡིན་མོད། དེ་འདྲ་དངོས་པོ་ལ་ཡེ་མ་གྲུབ་པས་གང་ཟག་གི་བདག་དེ་འདྲ་ངོ་བོའི་སྒོ་ནས་སྟོན་རྒྱུ་མེད། འོན་ཀྱང་མེད་པ་ལ་ཡོད་པར་འཛིན་པའི་བདག་འཛིན་གྱི་འཛིན་སྟངས་ཚོམ་ཚུལ་དང་བསྟུན་ན་རྟག་པ་གཅིག་པུ་རང་དབང་ཅན་དུ་འཛིན་པ་ཡིན། དེ་ཡང་ན་ཉིང་ངས་འདི་བྱས། ང་ད་བཟོད་འདི་བྱེད་སྙམ་པ། ན་ཉིང་གི་ང་དེ་ད་ལྟའི་ང་འདི་ཡིན། འདི་ད་གཟོད་ཡང་འགྲོ་སྙམ་པ་དེ་ལ་རྟག་པར་འཛིན་པ་ཟེར། ང་སྙམ་པ་ཤར་དུས་ཕྱི་ནང་གི་དངོས་པོ་གཞན་སུ་དང་ཡང་མ་འདྲེས་པའི་ཁོ་རང་གི་ངོ་བོ་ཚུགས་ཐུབ་ཅིག་ཡོད་པའི་ཁྲུངས་སུ་སྣང་བ་དེ་གཅིག་པུར་འཛིན་པ་ཡིན། ཇི་ལྟར་རིགས་པའི་ཡོངས་སྤྱོད་དམ། རྫས་སམ་འཁོར་ལ་རང་ཉིད་བདག་པོའི་ཚུལ་དུ་ཡོད་པ་ལྟར་སྣང་བ་དེ་རང་དབང་ཅན་དུ་འཛིན་པ་ཞེས་བྱ་བ་ཡིན། འཛིན་སྟངས་ཀྱིས་དེ་ལྟར་བཟུང་ཡང་དེ་ལྟ་བུར་མ་གྲུབ་སྟེ། གལ་ཏེ་བདག་དེ་རྟག་ན་ནི་བདག་དེ་ལན་ཅིག་བདེ་བ་སྐྱོང་ན་རྟག་ཏུ་བདེ་དགོས་པ་དང་། ལན་ཅིག་སྡུག་བསྔལ་སྐྱོང་ན་རྟག་ཏུ་སྡུག་དགོས་པ་དང་། དུས་དང་པོ་འཁོར་བར་བཅིངས་ན་ཕྱིས་གྲོལ་བའི་དུས་མི་སྲིད་པ་དང་། ཕྱིས་གྲོལ་བའི་གནས་སྐབས་སུ་ཡོད་ན། སྔོན་འཁོར་བ་མ་སྐྱོང་བར་ཐལ་བ ལས་བདེ་སྡུག་སྤེལ་མ་དང་། བཅིངས་གྲོལ་གྱི་གནས་སྐབས་སོ་སོར་འབྱུང་བས་རྟག་པའི་བདག་མེད་པར་ཐག་ཆོད། གཅིག་པུ་ཡང་མི་འཐད་དེ་བདག་ཅེས་བྱ་བ། རང་གི་ལུས་སེམས་ཀྱི་ཕུང་པོ་ལ་ཡོད་པ་ལྟར་སྣང་ན། མིག་ཀྱང་བདག་མ་ཡིན། རྣ་བ་དང་། སྣ་

དང་། ལྟེ་དང་། ཡིད་ཀྱང་བདག་མ་ཡིན། དེ་དག་རེ་རེ་བཞིན་བདག་ཡིན་ན་དུ་མར་འགྱུར། རེ་རེ་ནས་བདག་མ་ཡིན་ན་བདག་མ་རྙེད། གཞན་ཡང་བདག་ཕུང་པོ་ཡིན་ན་བདག་མི་རྟག་པར་ཐལ། བདག་ཕུང་པོ་ལས་གཞན་ཡིན་ན་མིག་ཤེས་ཀྱིས་མཐོང་བ་ལ་བདག་གིས་མཐོང་། ལུས་ཀྱིས་རེག་པ་ལ་བདག་གིས་རེག་ཅེས་པའི་འདུ་ཤེས་འབྱུང་བ་འགལ། དེའི་ཕྱིར་གཅིག་པུའི་རང་བཞིན་ཅན་གྱི་ང་བདག་མ་གྲུབ། གཅིག་པུ་མ་གྲུབ་པས་རང་དབང་ཅན་མི་འགྲུབ། ཁྱད་པར་དུ་ཡང་བྱ་བྱེད་ཐམས་ཅད་རྐྱེན་ལ་རག་ལུས་པར་མངོན་སུམ་དུ་མཐོང་བས། རང་དབང་ཅན་གྱི་བདག་མི་སྲིད། གཞན་ཡང་ཕུང་པོའི་ཕྱི་རོལ་ན་ཡང་བདག་མ་གྲུབ། ཕུང་པོའི་ནང་ནའང་བདག་མི་གནས། ཕུང་པོ་རེའང་བདག་མིན། ཕུང་པོ་བསལ་བའི་ཤུལ་ནའང་བདག་མེད། ཕུང་པོའི་སྤྱི་ལའང་བདག་མེད་དེ། རེ་རེ་ལས་གཞན་པའི་སྤྱི་མ་གྲུབ་པའི་ཕྱིར་རོ། །དེས་ན་བདག་ཅེས་བྱ་བ་ནི་བློས་བཏགས་པ་ཙམ། འཁྲུལ་ངོ་ཙམ། ཕྱིན་ཅི་ལོག་ཁོ་ན་ཡིན་གྱི། ངོ་བོས་གྲུབ་པ་ནི་འགའ་ཡང་མེད་དོ་སྙམ་དུ་བསྒོམ། དམིགས་སྐོར་ང་ག་སུམ་པའོ།།

གང་ཟག་གི་བདག་མེད་སྒོམ་པ་འདི་ལ་བློའི་འཕོབས་དང་བསྟུན་པའི་དམིགས་སྐོར་དུམ་བུ་འགའ་ཤས་སུ་བཅད་ཀྱང་རུང་བ་ལགས། ད་ནི་ཆོས་ཀྱི་བདག་མེད་སྟོན་ཏེ་ཆོས་ཞེས་པ་ཕུང་ཁམས་སྐྱེ་མཆེད་ལ་ཟེར། དེ་རྣམས་ལ་བློས་བཏགས་བ་ཙམ་མ་ཡིན་པར་རང་ཚུགས་ཐུབ་པའི་དངོས་པོ་ཅིག་ཡོད་སྲིད་ན། དེ་ཆོས་ཀྱི་བདག་ཡིན་མོད་ཀྱང་། དེ་འདྲ་ཡེ་མི་སྲིད་པས་ཆོས་ཐམས་ཅད་ཆོས་ཀྱི་བདག་མེད་པ་ཡིན་ནོ། །དེ་ལྟར་ཡིན་ཡང་འཁོར་བ་ཐོག་མ་མེད་པ་ནས་ཕུང་ཁམས་སྐྱེ་མཆེད་རྣམས་རང་ཚུགས་སུ་གྲུབ་པར་འཛིན་པའི་རྣམ་རྟོག་འདི་སྤོང་བའི་ཕྱིར་ཆོས་ཀྱི་བདག་མེད་བསྒོམ་དགོས་པ་ཡིན་ནོ། དེ་ལ་དང་པོར་རང་རྒྱུད་ཀྱི་ཕུང་པོ་རང་བཞིན་མེད་པར་བསྒོམ་དགོས། དེའི་ཡང་ཐོག་མ་རང་རྒྱུད་ཀྱིས་བསྡུས་པའི་གཟུགས་ཕུང་ལུས་ཀྱི་ཆོས་ལ་ལྟོས་ན། དངོས་པོ་སྣ་ཚོགས་ཚོགས་པ་

ལྟར་སྣང་བ་གཅིག་ལ་ལུས་ཞེས་སྤྱི་མིང་ཅིག་ཏུ་བཏགས་ནས། མིང་དང་མཚུངས་པའི་དངོས་པོ་ཞིག་ཡོད་དོ་སྙམ། བློ་ཕྱིན་ཅི་ལོག་གིས་བཟུང་བ་མ་གཏོགས། དེ་ལྟར་མ་གྲུབ་སྟེ། དང་པོར་ལུས་འདི་ལ་མིག་དང་རྣ་བ་དང་སྣ་དང་ལྕེ་དང་ལུས་ཀྱི་དབང་པོ་རྣམས་ཀྱང་ཐ་དད་དབང་པོ་རྣམས་དང་མི་གཅིག་པའི་དབང་རྟེན་ཁོག་པ་ཡང་སོ་སོ་རེ་འདུག མགོ་བོ་དང་མཁྲིན་པ་དང་བྲང་དང་རྒྱབ་དང་སྙིད་པ་དང་ཕོ་བ་དང་ལྟོ་བ་དང་ཕྲག་པ་གཉིས་དང་དཔུང་པ་གཉིས་དང་བར་ལྷུ་གཉིས་དང་ལག་ངར་གཉིས་དང་ལག་མགོ་གཉིས་དང་དཔྱི་གཉིས་དང་བྱིན་པ་གཉིས་དང་རྐང་མགོ་གཉིས་དང་དོན་ལྔ་སྣོད་དྲུག་སོགས་ནང་ཁྲོལ་རྣམས་དང་བུ་ག་དགུ་ལ་སོགས་པ་སྣ་ཚོགས་པ་འདུས་པའི་ཕུང་པོ་ཡིན་སྙམ་དུ་བསམ། དེས་ན་ལུས་ཞེས་བྱ་བ་བློས་བཏགས་པ་མ་གཏོགས་བདེན་པར་མི་འདུག། དེ་རྣམས་རེ་རེ་ནས་ལུས་ཡིན་ན་ལུས་མང་པོ་ཅན་དུ་འགྱུར། རེ་རེ་ནས་མིན་ན་ནི་ལུས་མ་རྙེད། ཚོགས་པ་ཙམ་ཡིན་ནོ་སྙམ་ན། རེ་རེ་ལས་གཞན་པའི་ཚོགས་པ་མེད་པའི་ཕྱིར་བློས་བཏགས་པ་ཙམ་མ་གཏོགས་མེད་པར་སོང་ངོ་། དམིགས་སྐོར་ང་བཞི་པའོ།།

ཡང་གཟུགས་ཀྱི་ཕུང་པོས་བསྡུས་པའི་ལུས་འདི་བདེན་པར་མ་གྲུབ་སྟེ། རྐང་ལག་བཞི་སྟོད་སྨད་མགོ་བྲང་ཞོལ་ནང་ཁྲོལ་ཏེ་གཟུག་དགུར་འགྲོ། གཟུག་རེ་རེ་ནས་གྲུབ་བམ་སྙམ་ན་མ་གྲུབ་སྟེ། རེ་རེ་བཞིན་ལྷུ་གསུམ་གསུམ་ལ་སོགས་པར་འགྲོ། ལྷུ་རེ་རེ་ནས་བདེན་ནམ་སྙམ་ན་མི་བདེན་ཏེ། སོར་ཚིགས་ཙམ་དུ་མར་འགྲོ། སོར་ཚད་རེ་རེ་ནས་གྲུབ་བམ་སྙམ་ན་མ་གྲུབ་སྟེ། རེ་རེ་ནས་ནས་ཙམ་བདུན་བདུན་དུ་འགྲོ། དེ་རེ་རེ་ནས་ཀྱང་མི་བདེན་ཏེ། ཤིག་གི་ཚད་ཙམ་བདུན་བདུན་མཛར་སྦྲོ་མ་དང་། ཉི་ཟེར་རྡུལ་དང་། གླང་རྡུལ་དང་། ལུག་རྡུལ་དང་། རི་བོང་རྡུལ་དང་། ཆུ་རྡུལ་དང་། ལྕགས་རྡུལ་གྱི་བར་དུ་ཧ་མ་ཧ་མའི་དཀྲུམ་ཀྱི་ཚད་བདུན་བདུན་དུ་བཏུབས་པས་ཕྱི་མ་ཕྱི་མའི་ཚད་དུ་འགྱུར། ལྕགས་རྡུལ་རེ་རེ་ནས་བདེན་ནམ་སྙམ་ན་མི་བདེན་ཏེ། ལྕགས་རྡུལ་གྱི་དཀྲུམ་

ཀྱི་ཚད་ལ་རྟུལ་ཕྲན་བདུན་ཡོད། དེར་ཡང་མ་གྲུབ་སྟེ་རྡུལ་ཕྲན་རེ་རེ་ལ་རྡུལ་ཕྲ་རབ་བདུན་ཡོད་དོ། བདུན་འགྱུར་འདི་རྣམས་ལ་དཀྲུས་ཤིང་རྒྱ་སྒྲངས་(དཔངས་)ཐམས་ཅད་བསྡོམས་ན། སྟོ་མ་སྟོ་མ་གསིལ་བས་ཕྱི་མ་ཕྱི་མ་སུམ་བརྒྱ་བཞི་བཅུ་ཞེ་གསུམ་རེ་ཡོད། དཀྲུས་ལ་བདུན་ཡོད་པ་ཞིང་ལའང་དེ་ཙམ་ཡིན་པས་བཞི་བཅུ་ཞེ་དགུར་འགྱུར་ལ། དེ་ཙམ་སྒྲངས་(དཔངས་)སུ་ཡང་བདུན་ཡོད་པས་སོ། །དམིགས་སྐོར་ང་ལྔ་པའོ།།

རྡུལ་ཕྲ་རབ་རེ་རེ་བཞིན་བདེན་པར་གྲུབ་བམ་སྙམ་ན་མ་གྲུབ་སྟེ། རེ་རེ་བཞིན་ཕྱོགས་རེ་དང་། སྟེང་འོག་ཏུ་ལྷ་བའི་ཆ་རེ་སྟེ་དྲུག་ཏུ་སྣང་ལ། དབུས་ཀྱི་ཆ་གཅིག་ཀྱང་ཡོད་དགོས་ཏེ། དེ་མེད་ན་ཤར་ནུབ་སོགས་ལ་ལྟ་བ་རྩོམ་མི་ཐུབ་པས་སོ། །དེ་ལྟར་ཆ་བདུན་པོ་རེ་རེ་ལ་ཡང་དེ་བཞིན་དུ་ཕྱེ་བས་དེ་ཡང་མ་གྲུབ། དེ་ལྟར་ཐུག་མེད་དུ་ཕྱེ་བས་མཐའ་མེད་དེ། ལུས་ཞེས་བྱ་བ་བློས་བཏགས་པ་ཙམ་མ་གཏོགས། གནས་ཚུལ་ལ་མ་གྲུབ་པ་ཁོ་ནའོ། །དེས་ན་སྣང་བ་ཙམ་མ་འགགས་པ་སྒྱུ་མ་ལྟ་བུ་ལ། རང་བཞིན་གདོད་ནས་གང་དུའང་མ་གྲུབ་སྟེ། དངོས་པོ་འདི་རྣམས་དེ་ལྟར་ན་གཅིག་ཏུ་མ་གྲུབ། དེ་མ་གྲུབ་པས་དུ་མར་ཡང་མི་འགྲུབ་སྟེ། གཅིག་གཅིག་པོར་གྲུབ་པ་མང་པོར་བསགས་པ་ལས་དུ་མ་སྒྲུབ་དགོས་པའི་ཕྱིར་རོ།། དམིགས་སྐོར་ང་དྲུག་པའོ།།

འོ་ན་གཟུགས་ཕུང་མི་བདེན་ཡང་སེམས་སུ་བདེན་པ་ཡིན་སྙམ་ན། སེམས་ལ་དབྱེ་ནའང་། གཟུགས་མཐོང་བ་དང་སྒྲ་ཚོར་བ་ལ་སོགས་པ་གཙོ་བོ་རྣམ་པར་ཤེས་པ། རྣམ་ཤེས་ཚོགས་བརྒྱད་སོ་སོར་འདུག་སྟེ། རྣམ་ཤེས་ཀྱི་ཕུང་པོ་ཡང་དུ་མར་ཞིག་སྟེ་ཐལ། བདེ་སྡུག་བཏང་སྙོམས་སྨྱོང་བ་སོགས་ཚོར་བར་འདུག་སྟེ། ཚོར་བ་ཡང་གཅིག་ཏུ་མ་གྲུབ། མཐོ་དམན་བཟང་ངན་མིང་དོན་སྦྲ་ཚོགས་འཛིན་པ་སོགས་འདུ་ཤེས་སུ་འདུག་སྟེ། དེ་ལའང་གཅིག་ཏུ་ངེས་བཟུང་མ་བྱུང་ལྷག་མ་འདོད་ཆགས་ཞེ་སྡང་དད་པ་ལ་སོགས་པ་རྣམ་རྟོག་མི་འདྲ་བ་ཇི་སྙེད་ཅིག་ལ་བློས་བསྡོམས་ནས་འདུ་བྱེད་ཅེས་བཏགས་པར་ཟད་ཀྱི། སེམས་

ཞེས་བྱ་བ་ཡང་གཅིག་ཏུ་མ་གྲུབ། གཅིག་མ་གྲུབ་པས་དུ་མར་ཡང་མ་གྲུབ་བོ་ཅེས་བསྒོམ་སྟེ། དམིགས་སྐོར་ང་བདུན་པའོ།།

ད་ཤེས་པའི་རྣམ་གྲངས་དེ་ཐམས་ཅད་ཀྱང་རིག་རིག་ཏུར་ཏུར་པོ་འདིའི་རྣམ་འགྱུར་མ་གཏོགས་ཚུགས་ཐུབ་ཏུ་མི་འདུག དཔེར་ན་རྒྱ་ལ་རི་བྲག་གི་གཟུགས་བརྙན་ཤར་བ་དང་འདྲ། རིག་རིག་པོ་འདི་ལ་ལྟས་ན། འདས་པའི་སེམས་ནི་འགགས་ནས་མེད། མ་འོངས་པའི་སེམས་ནི་མ་སྐྱེས་ནས་མེད། ད་ལྟའི་རིག་པ་སྐད་ཅིག་མ་བྱས་ཀྱང་རང་ངོས་ནས་བདེན་པར་གྲུབ་པ་མེད་ཏེ། སྐད་ཅིག་གཅིག་པོ་དེ་ལའང་སྔ་མ་དང་འབྲེལ་བ་སྐྱེ་བའི་ཆ་ཅིག་དང་། ཕྱི་མ་དང་འབྲེལ་བ་འགགས་པའི་ཆ་ཅིག་དང་། དབུས་ན་གནས་པའི་ཆ་ཅིག་སྟེ་གསིལ་བུར་འགྲོ། དེའི་དབུས་ཀྱི་ཆ་ལ་ལྟས་ན་ཆ་གསུམ་སོགས་ཐུག་མེད་དུ་དཔྱད་ན་མཐའ་མེད་དུ་སོང་ནས་གང་ཡང་གཅིག་པུའི་ངོ་བོ་མ་གྲུབ་པ་དེར་གདའ། གཅིག་མ་གྲུབ་པས་དུ་མ་མ་འགྲུབ་པ་སོགས་གོང་བཞིན། དམིགས་སྐོར་ང་བརྒྱད་པའོ།།

དེས་རང་རྒྱུད་ཀྱི་ཕུང་པོ་བདེན་མེད་དུ་གཏན་ལ་ཕབ་ཟིན། ད་ནི་རང་གི་ལུས་སེམས་ཀྱིས་བསྡུས་པའི་ཕུང་པོ་ལྔ་པོ་བདེན་མེད་དུ་གཏན་ལ་ཕབས་ཟིན་པ་དེ་བཞིན་དུ། སེམས་ཅན་ཐམས་ཅད་ཀྱི་ལུས་སེམས་ཕུང་པོ་ལྔ་ཡང་དེ་དང་འདྲ། ཁྱད་པར་དུ་དགྲ་སྡང་བའམ། གཉེན་བྱམས་པ་ལྟ་བུ་ཉོན་མོངས་དྲག་ཏུ་སྐྱེ་བའི་ཡུལ་ཅིག་ལ་ཆེད་གཏད་དུ་དམིགས་ནས། རང་གི་ལུས་ལ་དཔྱད་པ་བཞིན་དེའི་ལུས་ལ་ཡང་དཔྱད། རང་གི་སེམས་མིང་གཞིའི་ཕུང་པོ་ལ་དཔྱད་པ་བཞིན་དུ། དེའི་སེམས་ལ་ཡང་དཔྱད་དེ་དེས་ན་སྐྱེ་བོ་ཆེ་གེ་མོ་དང་། ག་གེ་མོ་ཅེས་བྱ་བ་འདི་ཀུན་ཡང་བློས་བཏགས་ནས་སེམས་ཅན་དེ་དང་དེའོ་ཞེས་ཕྱིན་ཅི་ལོག་ཏུ་བཏགས་པར་ཟད་ཀྱི་ངེས་པར་ན་གང་ཡང་མ་གྲུབ་པས་སྒྱུ་མ་ལྟ་བུའོ་ཞེས་སྒྲུངས་ནས། དེས་ཐམས་ཅད་ལ་རིགས་བསྒྲེས་ཏེ་བསྒོམ་དགོས་སོ། འདི་བཙུད་ཀྱི་སེམས་ཅན་ཐམས་ཅད་སྟོང་པར་བསྒོམ་པ་ཞེས་བྱ་སྟེ། དམིགས་སྐོར་ང་དགུ་པའོ།།

ཡང་བཅུད་ཀྱི་སེམས་ཅན་དུ་མ་ཟད། ཕྱི་སྣོད་ཀྱི་འཇིག་རྟེན་ཡང་མི་བདེན་ཏེ། སྟོང་གསུམ་བཤིག་པས་སྟོང་བར་མ་དང་། དེ་བཞིན་དུ་སྟོང་སྤྱི་ཕུད་དང་། གླིང་བཞི་པ་དང་། ཛམ་བུ་གླིང་ལྷ་བུ་དང་། རྒྱལ་ཁམས་གཅིག་དང་། དཔག་ཚད་ཙམ་དང་། རྒྱང་གྲགས་ཙམ་དང་། འདོམ་གང་ཙམ་དང་། ཁྲུ་གྲུ་བཞི་པ་དང་། སོར་གཅིག་ཙམ་དང་། ནས་ཙམ་ནས་རྡུལ་ཕྲ་རབ་ཀྱི་བར་དུ་བཤིག་ན་ཕྲ་མ་ཕྲ་མ་མ་གྲུབ་ཅིང་། རྡུལ་ཕྲན་ཡང་སྔོན་བཞིན་དུ་བཤིག་པས་མཐར་གང་ཡང་མ་གྲུབ། གཅིག་ཏུ་མ་གྲུབ་པས་དུ་མ་མི་འགྲུབ་པས་སོགས་གོང་བཞིན་ཏེ། མདོར་ན་འདི་དང་འདི་ལྷ་བུའོ། འདི་ནི་ཁང་ཁྱིམ་མོ། །འདི་ནི་ཞིང་ངོ་། །འདི་ནི་འབྲུའོ། འདི་ནི་ནོར་རྫས་སོ། འདི་ནི་ལོ་ཐོག་གོ། དེ་བཞིན་དུ་རི་དང་ཐང་དང་ཆུ་དང་རྒྱལ་ཁམས་ལ་སོགས་པར་འཛིན་པ་དག་ཀྱང་བདེན་དངོས་སུ་མ་གྲུབ་པའི་ཚོགས་པར་སྣང་བ་ཙམ་ལ་བློས་མིང་འདོགས་ཐ་དད་བཏགས་ནས་བདེན་དངོས་སུ་འཛིན་པ་ཙམ་དུ་ཟད་ཀྱི། དོན་དུ་ན་ཅུང་ཟད་ཙམ་ཡང་གྲུབ་པ་མེད་དོ་སྙམ་དུ་འདུན་པ་སྦྱངས། སྣོད་ཀྱི་འཇིག་རྟེན་སྟོང་པར་བསྒོམ་པ་སྟེ། དམིགས་སྐོར་དྲུག་ཅུ་པའོ།།

ཡང་རང་གཞན་སྣོད་བཅུད་མཐོང་ཐོས་གཟུགས་ཅན་ཐོགས་བཅས་ཐམས་ཅད་ནི། ས་ཆུ་མེ་རླུང་ནམ་མཁའ་སྟེ་ཁམས་ལྔས་བསྡུས། རིག་ཙམ་འགྱུ་བ་ཐམས་ཅད་ནི་རྣམ་པར་ཤེས་པས་བསྡུས། དེ་ལ་འབྱུང་བ་བཞི་པོ་ནི། ཕྲ་མོར་ན་རང་ཚུགས་མ་ཐུབ་སྟེ་འདྲེས་ཤིང་གནས། སའི་རྡུལ་ཕྲན་ཡང་མ་གྲུབ་སྟེ་འབྱུང་བ་གཞན་དང་འདྲེས་པའི་ཕྱིར་དང་། ཕན་ཚུན་གཅིག་ལ་གཅིག་བརྟེན་ཏེ་གནས་པ་མ་གཏོགས། རང་ཚུགས་ཐུབ་པར་སྡོད་པའི་སྐབས་གང་ཡང་མི་སྣང་བའི་ཕྱིར་རོ། །ནམ་མཁའ་ཞེས་བྱ་བ་ནི་གཟུགས་ཅན་དེ་རྣམས་མེད་པའི་ཤུལ་ལ་བློས་བཏགས་པ་མ་གཏོགས་བྱ་བྱེད་མེད་ཅིང་། བདེན་དངོས་མེད་ལ། རྣམ་པར་ཤེས་པ་ཡང་རྐྱེན་གློ་བུར་བའི་སྣང་ཆ་ཙམ་མ་གཏོགས། དངོས་བཟུང་དུ་མེད་པས་རང་གཞན་སྣོད་བཅུད་ཐམས་ཅད་གནས་ཚུལ་ལ་ཡེ་མ་གྲུབ་ལ། རེ་

ཞིག་འཁྲུལ་པ་ཅན་གྱི་བློ་ལ་སྣང་ཆ་མ་འགགས་ཀྱང་རང་བཞིན་མེད་པས་སྒྱུ་མ་ལྟ་བུའི་སྣམ་དུ་བསྒོམ། སྣོད་བཅུད་ཐམས་ཅད་སྟོང་པར་བསྒོམ་པ་སྟེ། དམིགས་སྐོར་དྲུག་ཅུ་རེ་གཅིག་པའོ།།

གཞན་ཡང་དངོས་མེད་ཅེས་བྱ་བ་ནི་དངོས་པོ་ལ་བརྟེན་ནས་བློས་བཞག་པ་ཙམ་ཡིན་གྱི་དོན་དམ་པར་ལྟ་ཅི་སྨོས། ཀུན་རྫོབ་བླང་དོར་གྱི་ཡུལ་དུ་ཡང་མ་གྲུབ་སྟེ་གང་ཡང་ཡོད་པ་མ་ཡིན་ལ། གོང་དུ་སྣང་གྲགས་ཀྱི་ཆོས་འདི་དག་ཐམས་ཅད་ཡེ་ནས་མ་གྲུབ་པོ་ཞེས་བསམས་མོད། གདོད་ནས་རྒྱ་བ་དང་བྲལ་བ་ལ་སྟོང་པའི་ཆོས་ཞེས་བྱུང་བ་ཡང་མེད་དེ། མོ་གཤམ་གྱི་བུ་དང་པོ་ནས་བྱུང་བ་མ་སྲིད་པས་མོ་གཤམ་གྱི་བུ་མེད་ཅེས་པའང་མི་སྲིད་དེ། དེ་འདྲ་བའི་སྟོང་པ་ཡང་མི་སྟོང་བ་ལ་ལྟོས་ཏེ་བློས་བཞག་པ་ཡིན་པའི་ཕྱིར་ཡོད་མེད་ཡིན་མིན་སོགས་ཅིར་ཡང་མ་གྲུབ་པ་ལ་བློས་གང་དུའང་མི་འཛིན་པར་གསལ་ལ། རྟོག་མེད་ཀྱི་ངང་དུ་ལྷན་ནེ་འཇོག ཡང་རྟོག་པ་སྐྱེས་བྱུང་ན། དེའི་ངོ་བོ་ལ་ལྟས་ཏེ་ངོས་བཟུང་དང་བྲལ་བ་དེ་ཀ་བསྒོམ། དམིགས་པ་སྔམ་དང་འདི་གཉིས་སྤྲེལ་ནས་གསལ་ལ་ཡུན་ཐུང་བ་ཡང་ཡང་བསྒོམ་པ་གནད་དུ་ཆེ། མཐར་ཐུག་སྤྲོས་བྲལ་བསྒོམ་པའི་དམིགས་པ་སྟེ། དམིགས་སྐོར་རེ་གཉིས་པའོ།།

དེ་ནས་དེ་ཐམས་ཅད་བསྡོམས་ནས་བསྒོམ་སྟེ། སྔར་གྱི་གོ་བ་རྣམས་ཡུད་ཅིག་དྲན་པར་བྱས་ནས། རང་གཞན་སྣོད་བཅུད་འདི་དག་ཐམས་ཅད་ལ་ང་བདག་ཞེས་བྱ་བ་ཡང་མ་གྲུབ། བྱེད་པ་པོ་གང་ཡང་མེད་དེ། རྟེན་འབྲེལ་ཚོགས་པ་ཙམ་ལས་སྣང་བ་ཡིན། འདི་ཐམས་ཅད་གཅིག་དང་དུ་མ་གང་ཡང་མ་གྲུབ་པས་འཁྲུལ་ངོར་སྣང་ཙམ་མ་གཏོགས། གནས་ལུགས་ལ་ཅི་ཡང་མ་གྲུབ་ཅིང་། ལེགས་པར་བརྟགས་ན་མ་གྲུབ་པ་དང་མེད་པ་ཞེས་བྱ་བ་ཡང་བློས་ཡོད་པའི་མཚན་ཉིད་གཅིག་གསར་དུ་བཅོས་ནས་དེ་དང་འགལ་བར་སྣང་བ་ལ་མེད་པ་དང་མ་གྲུབ་པའི་ཐ་སྙད་བཏགས་པ་ཙམ་དུ་ཟད་དོ།། དེ་ལྟར་ཕན་ཚུན་བརྟགས་པས་དམིགས་གཏད་ཡལ་བ་དེ་ལ་ཅི་ཡང་མི་བསམ་པར་མཉམ་པར་

བཞག་ཅིང་། སྣང་གྱི་དམིགས་གཏད་སངས་པའི་ངོས་བཟུང་ཐམས་ཅད་དང་བྲལ་བའི་རྣམ་ཆ་དེ་མ་ཡལ་བར་དུ་མི་རྟོག་པ་དེ་ལ་བཞག། ཡང་དེ་ཡལ་སོང་ན་སྟོང་ཉིད་ཀྱི་རྣམ་པ་ཉུབ་པའི་མི་རྟོག་པ་ཙམ་ལ་མི་འཇུག་སྟེ། སྣང་གྱི་དེ་བསྐྱར་གྱིན་བསྒོམ་དགོས་པས་ཡལ་མ་ཡལ་གྱི་ས་མཚམས་ཤེས་པ་གལ་ཆེ་གསུང་། ཐོག་མའི་སྐབས་སུ་སྟོང་པའི་རྣམ་པ་ཡུན་རིང་མི་སྡོད་པ་འདྲ་ཞིག་ཡོང་ཡང་ཉམས་མྱོང་གི་སྣེ་ཞིག་རྙེད་པའི་མཚམས་ནས་ཇེ་རིང་ཇེ་རིང་ལ་འགྲོ། འདི་ཀ་དམིགས་པ་ལ་སེམས་གཏད་པའི་འཛིན་པ་དང་། དེའི་རྒྱུན་བསྲིང་བ་ཉེ་བར་འཛོག་པ་ཡིན། རྣམ་རྟོག་བྱུང་ཚད་འཕྲོ་གཅོད་པ་དེ་བསླན་ཏེ་འཛོག་པ་ཡིན། དེ་ནས་ཡུན་ཇེ་རིང་ཇེ་རིང་ལ་འགྲོ་བ་དེ་ཉེ་བར་འཛོག་པ་ཡིན། དེ་ནས་ཏིང་ངེ་འཛིན་གྱི་ཡོན་ཏན་དྲན་ནས་དགའ་བ་བསྒོམས་པས་ལྷག་པར་བསྒོམ་པ་ལ་སྤྲོ་བ་འབྱུང་སྟེ། འདུལ་བར་བྱེད་པ་ཡིན། རེས་འགའ་རྣམ་གཡེང་ལ་སོགས་པའི་ཉེས་དམིགས་དྲན་པས་རྣམ་གཡེང་སོགས་རང་འགགས་ལ་འགྲོ་སྟེ། ཞི་བར་བྱེད་པ་ཡིན། དེ་གཉིས་སྤྲོ་བ་བསྐྱེད་པ་དང་སྐྱོ་ཤས་བསྐྱེད་པའི་རྣམ་གྲངས་ཡིན། རེ་དོགས་དང་ཆགས་སྡང་གི་རྣམ་རྟོག་གང་བྱུང་བ་ཐམས་ཅད་གང་སྐྱེས་ཀྱི་ངོ་བོ་ལ་ཆེར་རེ་ལྟས་པས། སྣང་ཤེས་པ་བདེན་མེད་དུ་བསྒོམས་པ་དེས་རྒྱུས་ཐེབས་ནས། རང་བབས་སུ་ཞི་བ་ནི་ཉེ་བར་ཞི་བ་ཡིན། རེ་ཞིག་བར་ལ་རྒྱུད་ལང་ཤོར་ཙན་དེ་ཐབས་དེ་དག་གིས་ཡང་ཡང་འཆོ་དགོས་ཤིང་། དེ་ནས་ཇི་ཞིག་ལྟར་ན་སེམས་བསྲིམས་ན་བྱིང་རྒོད་ཀྱི་སྐྱོན་མེད་ཅིང་། དམིགས་ཡུལ་སྟོང་པའི་རྣམ་པ་དེ་ལ་སེམས་ཡུན་རིང་དུ་གནས་པ་འབྱུང་། དེ་སྐབས་བསྲིམ་དགོས་ཏེ། སེམས་ཀྱི་རྒྱུད་གཅིག་ཏུ་བྱེད་བྱ་བ་དེ་ཡིན། མཐར་སྣང་གྱི་ལྟ་བའི་ཉམས་མྱོང་དྲན་ཙམ་བྱས་ནས་བཞག་པ་ཁོ་ནས་སྟོང་པའི་རྣམ་པ་ཙན་དེ་ཡུན་རིང་དུ་གནས་པ་འབྱུང་སྟེ། དེའི་ཚེ་རྩོལ་བ་ཀློད་དེ་རང་བབས་སུ་འཇོག་དགོས་པས་མཉམ་པར་བཞག་པ་ཞེས་བྱ་བ་གྲུབ་པ་ཡིན་ནོ། །སྒོམ་སྐྱོང་ཚུལ་འདི། ཆོས་མངོན་པ་ལས། ལྷག་མཐོང་སྔོན་དུ་སོང་བའི་ཞི་

གནས་སྐོམ་ཚུལ་གཅིག་ཀྱང་ཡོད་པ་དེའི་ལུགས་ཡིན། འདི་ཀ་མ་ལ་ཤཱི་ལའི་སྐོམ་རིམ་
ལ་སོགས་པའི་ལུགས་དང་མཚུངས་པར་དཔྱད་པ་སྟོན་སོང་གི་མི་རྟོག་པ་སྐོམ་ཚུལ་ཡིན།
བཤེས་གཉེན་པོ་ཏོ་བ་ཆེན་པོའི་བེའུ་བུམ་ལས། དཔལ་ལྡན་ཨ་ཏི་ཤའི་ལུགས་ལ་དཔྱད་
པ་སྟོན་སོང་ཁོ་ན་དགོས་པར་གསུངས། འོན་ཀྱང་ཨ་ཏི་ཤའི་བློ་སྦྱོང་གི་གདམས་ངག་འགའ་
རེ་སོགས་མདོ་ལུགས་དང་། ཕྱག་ཆེན་སོགས་སྔགས་ཀྱི་གདམས་ངག་མང་པོ་ལ་དཔྱད་
པ་སྤངས་པའི་གདམས་ངག་ཀྱང་ཤིན་ཏུ་མང་མོད་རེ་ཞིག་བསྟན་རིམ་གྱི་མན་ངག་སྟོན་
པའི་སྐབས་འདིར། བཤེས་གཉེན་ཆེན་པོ་པོ་ཏོ་བས་གསུངས་པ་ལྟར་བྱེད་དགོས་སོ།
།དམིགས་སྐོར་རེ་གསུམ་མོ།

ལྟ་བ་སྐྱོང་ལུགས་འདིའི་རིགས་ལ་སེམས་གནས་པ་ནམ་གྲུབ་པ་ན་ལྷག་མཐོང་
ཡང་གྲུབ་སྟེ། ཐོག་མ་ཉིད་ནས་ཞི་ལྷག་ཟུང་དུ་འདུག་པ་ཉིད་ཡོད་པར་བཞེད་དོ།། གསུམ་
པ་སྟོང་ཉིད་སྙིང་རྗེའི་སྙིང་པོ་ཅན་ནི། དེ་ལ་སྟོང་རྐྱང་གིས་ཤེས་རབ་ཀྱི་ཕ་རོལ་ཏུ་ཕྱིན་
པའི་སྒྲུབ་པར་མི་འགྲོ་བས་སྟོང་ཉིད་སྙིང་རྗེ་ཟུང་འདུག་ཅིག་དགོས་པ་ཡིན། དེ་ལྟར་ན་
དོན་དམ་པར་སྣང་ཞིང་སྲིད་པས་བསྡུས་པའི་ཆོས་གང་ཡང་མ་གྲུབ་པར་འདུག། དཔེ་
ནམ་མཁའ་དང་འདྲ། དེ་ལྟར་མ་གྲུབ་པ་ལ་མ་གྲུབ་པར་མངོན་སུམ་དུ་རྟོགས་ན། སྡུག་
བསྔལ་མྱོང་བ་པོའི་སེམས་ཅན་ཡང་མེད། མྱོང་རྒྱུའི་སྡུག་བསྔལ་ཡང་མེད། མྱོང་ཚུལ་
ལས་ཉོན་སྡུག་བསྔལ་གསུམ་ཕན་ཚུན་གཅིག་ནས་གཅིག་ཏུ་འཁོར་འགྲོ་རྒྱུ་ཡང་གདོད་ནས་
མ་གྲུབ་པར་འདུག་མོད། དེ་ལྟར་མ་རྟོགས་ཙ་ན། སྡུག་བསྔལ་མྱོང་བ་པོའི་སེམས་ཅན་
གྱི་སྣང་བ་ཡང་ཤར། མྱོང་བྱ་སྡུག་བསྔལ་གྱི་སྣང་བ་ཡང་ཤར། མྱོང་ཚུལ་དང་འཁོར་
ཚུལ་ཡང་ཤར། དེ་ཐམས་ཅད་མེད་བཞིན་དུ་སྣང་བ་ཡིན་ཀྱང་སྒྱུ་མས་བསླུས་པའི་སེམས་
ཅན་ལྟར་སྡུག་བསྔལ་སྣ་ཚོགས་མྱོང་བ་སྙིང་རེ་རྗེ། འདི་རྣམས་འཁྲུལ་པ་སངས་ཏེ། གནས་
ལུགས་རྟོགས་པའི་སངས་རྒྱས་ལ་འགོད་པར་བྱ། དོན་དམ་པར་བདག་ཀྱང་མ་གྲུབ། སེམས་

ཅན་དེ་རྣམས་ཀྱང་མ་གྲུབ། འཁྲུལ་བ་ཡང་མ་གྲུབ། འཁྲུལ་བ་སེལ་བར་བྱེད་པའི་ལམ་ཡང་མ་གྲུབ་མོད་ཀྱི། ཀུན་རྫོབ་འཁྲུལ་པའི་སྣང་བ་ཙམ་དུ་སྡུག་བསྔལ་དང་སྒྲིབ་པ་ཡོད་པར་སྣང་བ་བཞིན་དུ། ལམ་ཡང་ཡོད་པར་སྣང་། ལམ་བསྒོམས་པས་འཁྲུལ་བ་སངས་ཏེ། གནས་ལུགས་ལ་ངང་གིས་གནས་པའི་སངས་རྒྱས་སུ་འགྱུར་བའང་ཡིན་པ་ལ། སྒྱུ་མ་ལྟ་བུའི་བདག་གིས་སྒྱུ་མ་ལྟ་བུའི་སེམས་ཅན་རྣམས་ལ། སྒྱུ་མ་ལྟ་བུའི་ལམ་མམ་ཆོས་བསྟན་པས་སྒྱུ་མ་ལྟ་བུའི་སྡུག་བསྔལ་གྱིས་ཤ་ཐང་ཆད་པ་འདི་དབྱིངས་སུ་གྲོལ་བར་བྱའོ། །སྡུག་བསྔལ་ལ་སྐྱོང་བྱ་སྐྱོང་བྱེད་ཐམས་ཅད་བདེན་པར་མ་གྲུབ་ལ། སྣང་གྲགས་ཀྱི་ཆོས་གང་ཡང་བདེན་པར་གྲུབ་པ་མི་སྲིད་མོད་ཀྱི། རྟག་པ་མཐར་བཟུང་སྟེ། ཅི་སྟེ་བདེན་གྲུབ་ཀྱི་སྡུག་བསྔལ་ཞིག་སྲིད་དུ་ཆུག་ཀྱང་། བདེན་མེད་ཀྱི་སྡུག་བསྔལ་སྐྱོང་བ་འདི་ལས་ལྷག་པོའི་སྡུག་བསྔལ་སྐྱོང་རྒྱུ་མེད། འདི་མེད་པར་རྟོགས་ན་རང་གྲོལ་དུ་འདུག་པ་ལ་དེ་ལྟར་མ་རྟོགས་པ་སྙིང་རེ་རྗེ། ཞེས་ཡང་ཡང་བསམ་ཞིང་བསྒོམ། དམིགས་སྐོར་དྲུག་ཅུ་རེ་བཞི་པའོ།།

ད་ནི་དེའི་ཐོགས་འདོན་དུ་ཞག་གཅིག་སྟོང་ཉིད་འབའ་ཞིག་བསྒོམ། ཞག་གཅིག་སྙིང་རྗེ་འབའ་ཞིག་བསྒོམ། ཞག་གཅིག་སྤར་གྱི་སྟོང་ཉིད་སྙིང་རྗེ་ཟུང་འཇུག་དེ་བསྒོམ། དེ་འདྲ་ཡང་ཡང་བྱས་པས་ཐོགས་ཅིག་ཐོན་ནས་འོང་། ཡང་རེས་འགའ་ཐུན་གཅིག་སྟོང་ཉིད་རྐྱང་པ་བསྒོམ། ཐུན་གཅིག་སྙིང་རྗེ་རྐྱང་པ་བསྒོམ། ཐུན་གཅིག་གམ་གཉིས་སྟོང་ཉིད་སྙིང་རྗེ་ཟུང་འཇུག་བསྒོམ། དེ་ལྟར་སྐབས་སྐབས་སུ་ཡང་ཡང་བྱས་པས་ཀྱང་ཐོགས་ཅིག་ཐོན་ནས་ཡོང་། ཐུན་གཅིག་གོ། ད་འདི་ལ་ལེགས་སེལ་གྱི་ཐ་སྙད་གསུང་བར་གདའ། སྟོང་ཉིད་སྙིང་རྗེ་ཟུང་འབྲེལ་དེ་སྒོམ་གྱི་མཐིལ་ཡིན། དེ་ལ་ཚེ་འདིའི་བདེ་བ་ལ་ཞེན་པའི་གེགས་འབྱུང་སྟེ། ཚེ་འདིར་ལོངས་སྤྱོད་ཆེ་བ་དང་། གཏམ་སྙན་པ་དང་། ཁ་དྲག་པ་ཅིག་འདོད་དམ། མི་གཞན་རྣམས་ཀྱིས་ཀྱང་ཆོས་པ་བཟང་པོར་འཛིན་དུ་རེ། གཞན་

པས་རང་ལྷག་པ་ཅིག་ཡོད་དུ་རེ། སྙིང་ནས་འདོད་ཞེན་མ་ལོག་པར་གཞན་སུན་འབྱིན་པའི་ཕྱིར་དང་། རང་ཕྱོགས་འཁྱོངས་པའི་ཕྱིར་དུ་བྱ་བཏང་བྱེད། ཚིག་རིའམ། འདག་སྦྱར་རམ། དཀའ་ཐུབ་བམ། ལྟུམ་བུའམ། ལྟོ་འདོད་ཀྱི་བརྩུན་པ། གྲགས་ཕྱིར་གྱི་བསྙེན་རྫོགས། ཁེངས་དྲེགས་ཀྱི་ཚུལ་འཆོས། ཕྱུགས་མི་ཐམས་ཅད་རང་ལ་དད་པ་སྐྱེས་ཏེ། རང་རྒྱལ་བ་ཅིག་ཡོད་དུ་རེ་བས་འཕྲལ་ཕམ་ཁ་ལེན་པ་ལྟར་བྱེད་པ་སོགས་ཀྱང་ཆོས་ལ་སྣང་ནས་འཇིག་རྟེན་གྱི་ཆེ་ཐབས་སྒྲུབ་པར་གདའ། སྟོང་ཉིད་སྙིང་རྗེ་དང་རྒྱབ་འགལ་ཡིན། དེ་དག་དུག་དང་འདྲེས་པའི་ཟས་བྱ་བ་ལགས། ཐོག་མ་ཉིད་ནས་འཇིག་རྟེན་ཕལ་པ་བཞིན་དུ་བསམ་པ་དང་སྤྱོད་གཉིས་ཀར་ནག་ཀྱང་དུ་སོང་བ་དེ་ཆེས་སྨད་པ་གཞིར་བཞག་མོད་ཀྱང་། དེ་ལ་དགེ་སྦྱོར་དང་འདྲེས་པ་ལྟར་བཟང་རྫུའི་ཡུལ་དུ་ཡང་མ་བྱུང་། དེ་རྣམས་ཀྱི་གཉེན་པོར་སྐྱེས་བུ་ཆུང་ངུའི་བསམ་པ་ཡང་ཡང་དྲན་དགོས། ཕྱི་མ་ལྷ་མིའི་བདེ་བ་ལ་ཞེན་པའི་གེགས་བྱ་བ། འཁོར་བའི་བདེ་བ་ལ་སྲེད་པ་མ་ལོག་པས་སྦྱིན་པ་འདྲ་གཏོང་། ཚུལ་ཁྲིམས་འདྲ་སྲུང་། ཁྲིགས་ཆགས་ཀྱི་དགེ་སྦྱོར་བག་རེ་བྱེད་ཀྱང་སྐྱེ་བ་ཕྱི་མའི་ཟས་གོས་ལོངས་སྤྱོད་གནས་ཁང་། བུ་སྨད་འཁོར་གཡོག དབང་ཐང་འཇོམས་པས་སྐྱིད་པ་ཅིག་ཀ་སྨོན་ན། སྟོང་ཉིད་སྙིང་རྗེའི་མི་མཐུན་ཕྱོགས་སུ་སོང་། དེའི་གཉེན་པོར་སྐྱེས་བུ་འབྲིང་གི་བསམ་པ་རྣམས་བསྐྱར་གྱིན་བསྒོམ་དགོས། བློ་ཆོས་སུ་སོང་ཡང་རང་དོན་ཡིད་བྱེད་ཁོ་ན་འདུག་ན། སྟོང་ཉིད་སྙིང་རྗེ་དང་རྒྱབ་འགལ་ཡིན་པས། དེའི་གཉེན་པོར་བདག་གཞན་མཉམ་པ་དང་བརྗེ་བ་བསྒོམ་དགོས། དེ་ཡང་གོ་ཡུལ་ཙམ་ལ་མ་ལུས་པའི་རང་གི་ལུས་སེམས་ཀྱི་ཐོག་ཏུ་དམིགས་གཏད་ཁེལ་ངེས་ཤེས་པ་གལ་ཆེ། དེའི་གདམས་ངག་བློ་སྦྱོང་ན་གསལ། སྤྱོད་འཇུག་དང་བསླབ་བཏུས་ཀུན་ན་ཡང་རྒྱས་པར་ཡོད། རྒྱལ་ཚབ་བྱམས་པས། བདག་དང་གཞན་དུ་མཉམ་པའི་སེམས་ཉིད་དམ། བདག་པས་གཞན་གཅེས་སྡུག་པ་རྙེད་ནས་ནི། དེ་ལྟར་བདག་པས་གཞན་དོན་མཆོག་ཏུ་ཤེས། རང་གི་དོན་གང་

གཞན་གྱི་དོན་གང་ཡིན། ཅེས་གསུངས། སྟོང་ཉིད་སྒོམ་པའི་གོ་ཡུལ་ཡང་ཡང་བྱས་ཀྱང་། བདེན་པར་མེད་དོ། །སྒྱུ་མ་ལྟ་བུའི་བྱ་བ་དེ་ཡལ་ཡུལ་དུ་སོང་ནས་གནད་དུ་མ་འགྱོར། དགྲ་གཉེན་ཡོངས་སྤྱོད་གཏམ་སོགས་ཀྱི་རྣམ་རྟོག་རགས་པ་དེ་ཀ་འདུག་ན། སྟོང་ཉིད་སྙིང་རྗེའི་མི་མཐུན་ཕྱོགས་ཡིན་པས་རང་གི་ལུས་སེམས་ཟས་ཡོ་བྱད་དགྲ་གཉེན་རྣམས་ཀྱི་སྙིང་དུ། སྒྱུ་མ་ལྟ་བུའི་བློ་དེ་ཁེལ་ངེས་ཤེས་པ་སྙིང་ཐག་པ་ནས་སྐྱོང་བ་གལ་ཆེ། དེ་ཡང་ཐུན་གཅིག་གོ། ཡང་དལ་འབྱོར་རྙེད་དཀའ། འཆི་བ་མི་རྟག་པ། འཁོར་བའི་སྡུག་བསྔལ། ལས་རྒྱུ་འབྲས། ཆོས་ལ་དད་པ། བྱམས་པ་སྙིང་རྗེ་བྱང་ཆུབ་ཀྱི་སེམས། བདག་མེད་གཉིས་བསྒོམ་པ་རྣམས་ཞག་རེའམ། ཐུན་རེའི་ནང་དུ་རེས་འགའ་བསྐྱར་ཆགས་སུ་བསྒོམ། རེས་འགའ་ལུགས་ཟློག་ཏུ་བསྒོམ། རེས་འགའ་ཐང་འཐོན་དུ་བསྒོམ། རེས་འགའ་དཀྲུགས་པ་དང་འཆོལ་པར་བསྒོམ། རེས་འགའ་སེམས་ལ་གང་གནོད་པའི་སྲུང་བྱ་ཤེས་ཆེ་བ་དེའི་སྙིང་དུ་བསྒོམ། རེས་འགའ་འདི་སྒོམ་བདེ་བར་འདུག་སྙམ་པ་དེ་བསྒོམ། འདི་ཡང་ཐུན་གཅིག་གོ། རྒྱུན་གྱི་ཉམས་ལེན་ལ་མི་རྟག་པ་ངུར་ངུར་དྲན་པ་དང་། ལས་འབྲས་ཀྱི་དོན་བསམ་པའི་འཛེམ་བག་དང་། ཁམས་གསུམ་འཁོར་བ་པ་ཐམས་ཅད་ལ་སྙིང་རྗེ་དང་། སྤྲོས་བྲལ་གྱི་གནས་ལུགས་ལ་མཉམ་པར་འཇོག་པ་སྟེ། བཞི་པོ་འདི་གཙོ་བོར་བསྒོམ། གཞན་རྣམས་འཁོར་གྱི་ཚུལ་དུ་བསྒོམ་མོ། །ཆོས་འདི་སྤྱོད་པའི་བླ་མ་དམ་པའམ། གྲོགས་བཟང་པོ་དང་འགྲོགས། ཐུན་མཚམས་སུ་མདོ་སྡེ་རྣམས་ཀློག་པའམ། ཉན་པས་ཀྱང་སྒོམ་གྱི་བོགས་འབྱིན། ཆོས་ལ་ངེས་པ་རྙེད། དད་པ་གསོས་འདེབས་པ་ཡིན། ཁྱད་པར་བཀའ་གདམས་གོང་མའི་གསུང་བསྟན་རིམ་དང་འབྲེལ་བའི་བེའུ་བུམ་དེ་ལའང་ལྟ་རྟོག་དང་ནན་ཆགས་དང་དོན་སེམས་ཐོག་ཏུ་འཇོག་པ་ཁོ་ན་གནད་དུ་ཆེ་བ་ལགས། འདི་ལའང་ཐུན་གཅིག་སྟེ། ཕྱི་མ་བཞི་པོ་འདི་རྒྱུན་གྱི་ཉམས་ལེན་དང་། གེགས་སེལ་བོགས་འདོན་ལ་སློབ་པ་ཡིན། དམིགས་སྐོར་དུ་བཅད་ནི་མི་དགོས། ཡང་དམིགས་

སྐོར་དུ་བྱས་ཀྱང་འགལ་བ་ཡང་མེད་དོ།། །།རྩ་བའི་ས་བཅད་གསུམ་པ། དེ་ལས་འབྲས་བུ་བླ་ན་མེད་པའི་བྱང་ཆུབ་འགྲུབ་ཚུལ་ནི། རྒྱས་པར་གཞུང་ལུགས་ཆེན་པོ་རྣམས་ཉན་པས་གོ་བར་འགྱུར། འདིར་བཤད་ཀྱི་ཡང་མི་ལང་བ་ལགས། སྙིང་པོ་ནི། ཇི་སྐད་དུ། སློབ་དཔོན་འཕགས་པས། ཚུལ་ཁྲིམས་སྦྱིན་པ་གཞན་གྱི་དོན། །བརྩོན་འགྲུས་བཟོད་པ་བདག་ཉིད་ཀྱི། །བསམ་གཏན་ཤེས་རབ་ཐར་པའི་རྒྱུ། །སྙིང་རྗེ་བས་ནི་དོན་ཀུན་འགྲུབ། །ཅེས་དང་། བདུན་པོ་འདི་དག་མ་ལུས་པར། །གཅིག་ཅར་ཕ་རོལ་ཕྱིན་པ་ཡིས། །ཡེ་ཤེས་བསམ་གྱིས་མི་ཁྱབ་ཡུལ། །འཇིག་རྟེན་མགོན་པོ་ཉིད་ཐོབ་འགྱུར། །ཅེས་གསུངས་པ་ལྟར་ཡིན་ཏེ། བསམ་པ་བྱང་ཆུབ་ཀྱི་སེམས་དང་། སྤྱོད་པ་སྦྱིན་སོགས་དྲུག་ལ་སྦྱངས་པས། རང་ལུགས་ཀྱིས་ཆོས་ལས་གཞན་དུ་བློ་མི་འགྲོ་ཞིང་། དཀོན་མཆོག་ལ་དད་པ་དང་། ལས་འབྲས་ལ་འཛེམ་བག་དང་། འཁོར་བ་ལ་སྐྱོ་ཤས་རྣམས་ངང་གིས་སྐྱེ། ཆོས་རྩེ་གཅིག་ཏུ་བསྒོམ་པ་ལ་སུན་པ་མེད་པར་སྤྲོ་བ་ངང་གིས་འཕེལ་ན། ཏིང་ངེ་འཛིན་བརྟན་པོ་སྐྱེས་རུང་མ་སྐྱེས་རུང་ལམ་སྔ་ཟིན་པ་དང་། ཚོགས་ལམ་ཆུང་ངུ་རྒྱུད་ལ་སྐྱེས་པ་ཡིན་ནོ། །དེ་ནས་ཚོགས་ལམ་དུ་མི་རྟག་སྡུག་བསྔལ། སྟོང་པ་བདག་མེད་ཀྱི་དོན་ལ་གསལ་སྣང་ཙུང་ཟད་སྐྱེད་པ་ནི། བྱིས་པ་ཉེར་སྤྱོད་ཀྱི་བསམ་གཏན་ཞེས་བྱའོ། །དེ་ནས་བསྒོམས་པའི་སྟོབས་དང་ཚོགས་བསགས་པའི་སྟོབས་གཉིས་འཛོམས་པ་ལས། གཟུགས་ནི་དབུ་བ་རྡོས་པ་འདྲ། །ཅེས་སོགས་ལྟར་ཕུང་པོ་ལྔ་སྒྱུ་མ་ལྟར་རྟོགས་ཤིང་། ཆོས་ཀྱི་བདག་མེད་ལ་གསལ་སྣང་རིམ་པས་སྐྱེད་པ་ནི། དོན་རབ་འབྱེད་པའི་བསམ་གཏན་ཞེས་བྱའོ། །མཐོང་ལམ་ནས་བརྩམས་ཏེ། བྱང་ཆུབ་སེམས་དཔའི་ས་བཅུ་ལ་སྤྲོས་བྲལ་མངོན་སུམ་དུ་རྟོགས་པའི་ཡེ་ཤེས་སྐྱེས་པ་ནི། དེ་བཞིན་ཉིད་ལ་དམིགས་པའི་བསམ་གཏན་ཞེས་བྱའོ།། ས་དང་པོ་ནས་བདུན་པའི་བར་དུ་དེ་བཞིན་གཤེགས་པ་དགེ་བའི་བསམ་གཏན་ཆ་ཕྲ་བ་ཙམ་ཡོད་ལ། ས་བརྒྱད་པ་དགུ་པ་བཅུ་པ་རྣམས་ལ། ཆུང་ངུ་དང་འབྲིང་དང་ཆེན་པོ་དག་

ཡོད་དོ། །རྫོགས་པའི་སངས་རྒྱས་ཀྱི་སར་ནི། དེ་བཞིན་གཤེགས་པ་དགེ་བའི་བསམ་གཏན་མཐར་ཐུག་པ་ཡོད་དེ། བསམ་གཏན་བཞི་པ་འདི་ནི་སྙིང་པོ་མངོན་སུམ་དུ་རྟོགས་པའི་ཡེ་ཤེས་ཏེ་རྒྱས་པར་གཞན་དུ་རྟོགས་པར་བྱའོ། བསམ་གཏན་བཞི་པོ་འདི་གོང་མའི་ཡི་གེ་ན་མ་བྲིས་ཀྱང་མདོ་ནས་འབྱུང་བ་ལྟར་བཀོད་པ་ཡིན་ནོ། །དང་པོར་ལམ་སྣ་མ་ཟིན་གྱི་བར་དུ་ཅུང་དཀའ་བ་ཡིན་པས་བྱ་བ་གཞན་ཐམས་ཅད་བོར་ལ་གཅིག་ཏུ་འབད་པ་གལ་ཆེ། དེ་ནས་ཀྱང་འབད་རྩོལ་གོང་འཕེལ་དུ་གཏོང་དགོས་མོད་ཀྱི་ཅུང་ཟད་བླ་བར་འོང་། ཚོགས་ཀྱི་སྒོ་དུ་མ་ནས་བསགས། སྨོན་ལམ་ཕྱོགས་སྣ་ཚོགས་ནས་བཏབ་སྟེ་རྒྱུད་སྦྱངས་པས་སྦྱོར་ལམ་གྱི་ཡེ་ཤེས་སྐྱེས་པ་ན། རང་ཤུགས་ཀྱིས་གོང་འཕེལ་དུ་འགྲོ་ཞིང་འཇུག་པ་བདེ་བ་ཡིན། དེར་ཡང་བདུད་ཀྱི་ལས་ཕྲ་མོ་སྤྱོང་བ་དང་། གེགས་སེལ་བ་དང་། བོགས་དབྱུང་བ་མང་དུ་དགོས་པར་ཡོད། དེ་ནས་རིམ་པས་ཆོས་ཉིད་མངོན་སུམ་དུ་རྟོགས་པའི་ཡེ་ཤེས་སྐྱེ་བར་འགྱུར་ཏེ། དེ་ནས་བདེ་བ་ནས་བདེ་བར་སྤྱོད་པ་འབའ་ཞིག་གོ། འབྲས་བུའི་སངས་རྒྱས་ནི། ངོ་བོ་ཉིད་སྐུ་རང་བཞིན་འོད་གསལ་སྤྲོས་བྲལ་གྱི་ཡེ་ཤེས་དང་། ལོངས་སྐུ་འོག་མིན་དུ་དག་པའི་འཁོར་ལ་ཆོས་འཁོར་ལ་ཆོས་འཁོར་མཐར་ཐུག་བསྐོར་བ་པོ་དང་། སྤྲུལ་པའི་སྐུ་མ་དག་པའི་ཞིང་རྣམས་སུ་གང་ལ་གང་འདུལ་གྱིས་འགྲོ་བའི་དོན་མཛད་པ་དང་། འཕྲིན་ལས་ནི་མཁྱེན་བརྩེ་ནུས་གསུམ་གྱི་སྒོ་ནས། སེམས་ཅན་ཐམས་ཅད་སྐལ་བ་དང་འཚམས་པར་ཕན་པ་དང་བདེ་བ་བླ་ན་མེད་པ་ལ་འགོད་པའོ། །འདི་ལ་ཐུན་གྱི་ངེས་པ་མེད་དེ་ལྟར་འཚམས་པར་བཤད་པར་བྱའོ། །དེས་བསྟན་པ་ལ་འཇུག་པ་ཞེས་བྱ་བའི་ཁྲིད་ལེགས་པར་ཆར་རོ།། །།

ད་ནི་ཀྱབ་འབྲས་སེམས་བསྐྱེད་དང་། བྱང་སྡོམ་ལེན་པའི་ཆོ་ག་བཤད་པར་བྱ་སྟེ། དེ་ལ་གཉིས་སེམས་བསྐྱེད་ཀྱི་ཆོ་ག་དང་། བྱང་སྡོམ་གྱི་ཆོ་གའོ། །དང་པོ་ནི། རྟེན་དང་མཆོད་པ་བཤམས། མཚལ་ཕུལ་ཏེ། ཕྱོགས་བཅུ་ན་བཞུགས་པའི་སངས་རྒྱས་

དང་བྱང་ཆུབ་སེམས་དཔའ་ཐམས་ཅད་བདག་ལ་དགོངས་སུ་གསོལ། སློབ་དཔོན་བདག་ལ་དགོངས་སུ་གསོལ། ཇི་ལྟར་སྔོན་གྱི་དེ་བཞིན་གཤེགས་པ་དགྲ་བཅོམ་པ་ཡང་དག་པར་རྫོགས་པའི་སངས་རྒྱས་རྣམས་དང་། ས་ཆེན་པོ་ལ་བཞུགས་པའི་བྱང་ཆུབ་སེམས་དཔའ་རྣམས་ཀྱིས་དང་པོར་བླ་ན་མེད་པ་ཡང་དག་པར་རྫོགས་པའི་བྱང་ཆུབ་ཏུ་ཐུགས་བསྐྱེད་པ་དེ་བཞིན་དུ་བདག་མིང་འདི་ཞེས་བགྱི་བ་ཡང་སློབ་དཔོན་གྱིས་བླ་ན་མེད་པ་ཡང་དག་པར་རྫོགས་པའི་བྱང་ཆུབ་ཏུ་སེམས་བསྐྱེད་དུ་གསོལ། ཅེས་ལན་གསུམ་རྗེས་བཟླས་བྱ། དེ་ནས་དགོངས་གསོལ་གོང་བཞིན་ལ། བདག་མིང་འདི་ཞེས་བགྱི་བ་དུས་འདི་ནས་གཟུང་སྟེ། ཇི་སྲིད་བྱང་ཆུབ་སྙིང་པོ་ལ་མཆིས་ཀྱི་བར་དུ། རྐང་གཉིས་རྣམས་ཀྱི་མཆོག་སངས་རྒྱས་བཅོམ་ལྡན་འདས་རྣམས་ལ་སྐྱབས་སུ་མཆིའོ། །ཆོས་རྣམས་ཀྱི་མཆོག ཞི་བ་འདོད་ཆགས་དང་བྲལ་བའི་ཆོས་ལ་སྐྱབས་སུ་མཆིའོ། །ཚོགས་རྣམས་ཀྱི་མཆོག་འཕགས་པ་བྱང་ཆུབ་སེམས་དཔའ་ཕྱིར་མི་ལྡོག་པའི་དགེ་འདུན་རྣམས་ལ་སྐྱབས་སུ་མཆིའོ། །ཅེས་པའི་རྗེས་བཟླས་ལན་གསུམ་བྱ། སྐྱབས་འགྲོ་རེ་རེ་བཞིན་དགོངས་གསོལ་རེ་བྱེད་པ་དེ་རྒྱས་པའི་ལུགས་ཡིན། བསྡུ་ན་འདི་ཙམ་གྱིས་ཆོག བར་འདིར་བཟང་སྤྱོད་ནས་འབྱུང་བའི་ཡན་ལག་བདུན་པ་ཚར་གསུམ་བྱ་སྟེ་ཚོགས་གསག་པའོ། དངོས་གཞིའི་ཚོ་ག་ནི་དགོངས་གསོལ་གོང་དང་འདྲ། བདག་མིང་འདི་ཞེས་བགྱི་བས། སྐྱེ་བ་འདི་དང་སྐྱེ་བ་གཞན་དང་གཞན་དག་ཏུ་སྦྱིན་པའི་རང་བཞིན་དང་། ཚུལ་ཁྲིམས་ཀྱི་རང་བཞིན་དང་། སྒོམ་པའི་རང་བཞིན་གྱི་དགེ་བའི་རྩ་བ་བདག་གིས་བགྱིས་པ་དང་། བགྱིད་དུ་སྩལ་བ་དང་། བགྱིད་པ་ལ་རྗེས་སུ་ཡི་རང་བའི་དགེ་བའི་རྩ་བ་དེས། ཇི་ལྟར་སྔོན་གྱི་དེ་བཞིན་གཤེགས་པ་དགྲ་བཅོམ་པ་ཡང་དག་པར་རྫོགས་པའི་སངས་རྒྱས་རྣམས་དང་། ས་ཆེན་པོ་ལ་རབ་ཏུ་བཞུགས་པའི་བྱང་ཆུབ་སེམས་དཔའ་ཆེན་པོ་རྣམས་ཀྱིས་ཐུགས་བསྐྱེད་པར་མཛད་པ་དེ་བཞིན་དུ། བདག་མིང་འདི་ཞེས་བགྱི་བས་ཀྱང་དུས་འདི་ནས་གཟུང་ནས། ཇི་སྲིད་བྱང་ཆུབ་སྙིང་

པོ་ལ་མཆིས་ཀྱི་བར་དུ། བླ་ན་མེད་པ་ཡང་དག་པར་རྫོགས་པའི་བྱང་ཆུབ་ཆེན་པོར་སེམས་བསྐྱེད་པར་བགྱི་སྟེ། སེམས་ཅན་མ་བསྒྲལ་བ་རྣམས་བསྒྲལ་བར་བགྱིའོ། །མ་གྲོལ་བ་རྣམས་དགྲོལ་བར་བགྱིའོ། །དབུགས་མ་ཕྱུང་བ་རྣམས་དབུགས་དབྱུང་བར་བགྱིའོ། །ཡོངས་སུ་མྱ་ངན་ལས་མ་འདས་པ་རྣམས་ཡོངས་སུ་མྱ་ངན་ལས་འདའ་བར་བགྱིའོ། །ཅེས་ལན་གསུམ་རྗེས་བཟླས་བྱར་གཞུག སྨོན་སེམས་ཀྱི་བསླབ་བྱ་གོང་དུ་བཤད་པ་རྣམས་ལས་ཅི་རིགས་པའམ་རྒྱས་བསྡུས་ཇི་ལྟར་རིགས་པ་བཤད། འཕགས་པ་སྤྱན་རས་གཟིགས་ཀྱིས་ཞུས་པ་ཆོས་བདུན་པ་ཞེས་བྱ་བའི་མདོ་དང་། སྡོང་པོ་བཀོད་པ་ལ་སོགས་པའི་མདོ་ནས་བསླབ་བྱ་དང་ཕན་ཡོན་དུ་མ་འབྱུང་བ་རྣམས་རྒྱས་པར་མདོ་སྡེ་དེ་དག་ལས་ཤེས་པར་བྱའོ་ཞེས་བརྗོད། དེ་ནས་སྨོན་ལམ་ཇི་ལྟར་འོས་པ་གདབ་ཅིང་། བསྔོ་ན་དགེ་བ་འདི་ཡིས་སྐྱེ་བོ་ཀུན། །ཞེས་སོགས་བརྗོད། སླར་ཡང་དཀོན་མཆོག་མཆོད། སློབ་དཔོན་ལ་ཡོན་དབུལ། འདི་ནི་སེམས་བསྐྱེད་ཀྱི་ཆོ་གར་གྲགས་པ་སྨོན་སེམས་ཀྱི་ཆོ་ག་སྟེ། འདི་ལ་སྣོད་བརྟག་པ་དང་། སོ་ཐར་རིགས་བརྒྱད་སྔོན་དུ་འགྲོ་བ་སོགས་གང་ཡང་མི་དགོས་པས་དོན་དུ་གཉེར་བ་ཐམས་ཅད་ལ་སྦྱིན་དུ་རུང་ངོ་། འདི་ནི་བྱམས་པ་ནས་བརྒྱུད་པའི་སེམས་བསྐྱེད་ཏེ། སློབ་དཔོན་འཕགས་པ་ཐོག་མེད་ཀྱིས་མཛད་པའི་སེམས་བསྐྱེད་ཀྱི་ཆོ་ག་ལོགས་པ་ཞིག་འཕགས་ཡུལ་ན་ཡོད་པར་གྲགས་ལ། དེ་ནི་དཀོན་བརྩེགས་ཀྱི་ནང་གི་འདི་མ་ཡིན་པའི་བྱང་ཆུབ་སེམས་དཔའི་སྡེ་སྣོད་ཅེས་བྱ་བའི་མདོ་ལོགས་པ་ཞིག་ལས་བསྡུས་པ་སྟེ། དེའི་དགོངས་དོན་ཕྱོགས་འདིར་ཡོད་པ། དཔལ་ལྡན་ཨ་ཏི་ཤས་མཛད་པའི་སེམས་བསྐྱེད་ཀྱི་ཆོ་ག་ན་གསལ་བར་བཞུགས་པ་བཞིན་བཀོད་པ་ཡིན་ནོ། །གཉིས་པ་བྱང་སྡོམ་ལེན་པའི་ཆོ་ག་ནི། རབ་ཏུ་བྱང་ཆུབ་སེམས་དཔའི་བསླབ་གཞི་རྒྱས་པར་སྟོན་པ་ནི་ཐེག་པ་ཆེན་པོའི་མདོ་སྡེ་རྣམས་ཡིན་པས་མདོ་སྡེ་མང་དུ་ཐོས་པར་བྱ། ཡང་ན་བྱང་ཆུབ་སེམས་དཔའི་སའམ། བསླབ་པ་ཀུན་ལས་བཏུས་པ་ལྟ་བུ་ཉན་ནའང་། ཐེག་ཆེན་ཀུན་གྱི་སྙིང་

པོ་འདུས་པ་ཡིན་པས་ཤིན་ཏུ་ལེགས། འཕགས་པ་དཀོན་མཆོག་སྤྲིན་ནམ་ནམ་མཁའི་སྙིང་པོའི་མདོ་ལྟ་བུ་ཅིག་གི་བཀླགས་ལུང་ཙམ་མ་མཐའ་ཡང་ངེས་པར་ཐོབ་པར་བྱའོ། སྔར་བསྟན་རིམ་གྱི་ཁྲིད་ཞིབ་པར་བསྐྱངས་པས་ཀྱང་ཐེག་ཆེན་གྱི་སྙིང་པོ་ཐོས་པ་ཡིན་མོད་ཀྱི། བརྗོད་བྱེད་ཚིག་གི་སྒོ་ནས་ཐེག་ཆེན་གྱི་མདོ་སྡེ་གཅིག་མ་ཐོས་པའི་ཐབས་མེད། དེ་ནས་བྱང་སྡོམ་བླང་བ་དངོས་ནི། རྟེན་གསུམ་གྱི་དྲུང་དུ་མཆོད་པ་བཤམས། སློབ་དཔོན་ལ་ལན་གསུམ་དུ་ཕྱག་བྱས་ནས་ཐལ་མོ་སྦྱར་ཏེ། སློབ་དཔོན་ཁྱོད་ལས་བདག་བྱང་ཆུབ་སེམས་དཔའི་ཚུལ་ཁྲིམས་ཀྱི་སྡོམ་པ་ཡང་དག་པ་ལེན་པར་འཚལ་གྱི། དེ་ལ་གནོད་པ་མ་མཆིས་ན། བདག་ལ་ཐུགས་བརྩེ་བའི་སླད་དུ་ཉུང་ཟད་ཅིག་གསན་ཅིང་སྩལ་བའི་རིགས་སོ། །ཅེས་ལན་གསུམ་གསོལ་བ་གདབ་དགོས་ཏེ། ཚིག་དེ་བློ་ལ་ཡོད་ན་སློབ་མ་ཉིད་ཀྱིས་གསོལ་བ་གདབ། དེ་མིན་སློབ་དཔོན་ནམ་གྲོགས་ཀྱི་རྗེས་བཟློས་བྱའོ། དེ་ནས་སློབ་དཔོན་གྱིས་འདི་སྐད་ཅེས། རིགས་ཀྱི་བུ་ཁྱོད་ཉོན་ཅིག། ཁྱོད་འདི་ལྟར་སེམས་ཅན་མ་བསྒྲལ་བ་རྣམས་བསྒྲལ་བ་དང་། མ་གྲོལ་བ་རྣམས་དགྲོལ་བ་དང་། དབུགས་མ་ཕྱུང་བ་རྣམས་དབུགས་དབྱུང་བ་དང་། ཡོངས་སུ་མྱ་ངན་ལས་མ་འདས་པ་རྣམས་ཡོངས་སུ་མྱ་ངན་ལས་འདའ་བ་དང་། སངས་རྒྱས་ཀྱི་གདུང་རྒྱུན་མི་འཆད་པར་འདོད་དམ། སློབ་མས་ཀྱང་འདོད་ལགས། ཞེས་བརྗོད། སློབ་དཔོན་གྱིས་འདི་སྐད་ཅེས་བྱ་སྟེ། དེ་ལ་ཁྱོད་ཀྱིས་སེམས་བསྐྱེད་པ་བརྟན་པ་དང་། ཡི་དམ་བརྟན་པར་བྱའོ། ཅེས་དང་། གཞན་དང་འགྲན་པའི་ཆེད་དུ་མ་ཡིན་ནམ། མ་ལགས། གཞན་གྱི་ནན་གྱིས་ལེན་དུ་བཅུག་པ་མ་ཡིན་ནམ། མ་ལགས། ཅེས་དྲི་བ་དང་ལན་བྱ། དེ་ནས་མཆོད་ཡོན་ཕལ་ཆེར་ལ་སོགས་པའི་ཚིགས་བཅད་ཀྱིས་མཆོད་པ་རྣམས་ཕུལ། མགོན་པོ་ཐུགས་རྗེ་ཆེ་ལྡན་པ། ཅེས་པ་ལ་སོགས་པ་ཇི་ལྟར་འོས་པས་བསྟོད་ཅིང་ཕྱག་ཀྱང་འབུལ། དེ་ནས་སློབ་དཔོན་ལ་གུས་པ་དང་བཅས་པས་བསྐུལ་མའི་གསོལ་བ་གདབ་ནི་འདི་སྐད་ཅེས། སློབ་དཔོན་གྱི་བྱང་ཆུབ་སེམས་དཔའི་

ཚུལ་ཁྲིམས་ཀྱི་སྡོམ་པ་ཡང་དག་པར་བླངས་པ་བདག་ལ་མྱུར་དུ་སྩལ་དུ་གསོལ། ལན་གསུམ། སློབ་དཔོན་གྱིས་འདི་སྐད་ཅེས། མིང་འདི་ཞེས་བྱ་བའམ། རིགས་ཀྱི་བུ་ཁྱོད་བྱང་ཆུབ་སེམས་དཔའ་ཡིན་ནམ། དེས་ཀྱང་ཡིན་ལགས། བྱང་ཆུབ་ཏུ་སྨོན་ལམ་བཏབ་བམ། བཏབ་ལགས། དེ་ནས་དངོས་གཞི་ནི་སློབ་དཔོན་གྱིས་འདི་སྐད་ཅེས། རིགས་ཀྱི་བུ་ཁྱོད་ཉོན་ཅིག། བྱང་ཆུབ་སེམས་དཔའ་ཐམས་ཅད་ཀྱི་བསླབ་པའི་གཞི་ཐམས་ཅད་དང་། བྱང་ཆུབ་སེམས་དཔའ་ཐམས་ཅད་ཀྱི་ཚུལ་ཁྲིམས་དེ་དག་ཅི་བདག་ལས་ལེན་པར་འདོད་དམ། དེ་ལྟར་ལེན་པར་འཚལ་ལོ། །དེ་ནས་ཆོ་ག་དངོས་གཞི་ནི་སློབ་དཔོན་གྱིས་འདི་སྐད་ཅེས། ཚེ་དང་ལྡན་པའམ་རིགས་ཀྱི་བུ་མིང་འདི་ཞེས་བྱ་བ་ཁྱོད། བདག་བྱང་ཆུབ་སེམས་དཔའ་མིང་འདི་ཞེས་བྱ་བ་ལས། འདས་པའི་བྱང་ཆུབ་སེམས་དཔའ་རྣམས་ཀྱི་བསླབ་པའི་གཞིར་གྱུར་པ་གང་ཡིན་པ་དང་། ཚུལ་ཁྲིམས་སུ་གྱུར་པ་གང་ཡིན་པ་དང་། མ་བྱོན་པའི་བྱང་ཆུབ་སེམས་དཔའ་ཐམས་ཅད་ཀྱི་བསླབ་པའི་གཞིར་གྱུར་པ་གང་ཡིན་པ་དང་། ཚུལ་ཁྲིམས་སུ་གྱུར་པ་གང་ཡིན་པ་དང་། ད་ལྟར་ཕྱོགས་བཅུའི་འཇིག་རྟེན་ན་ད་ལྟར་བཞུགས་པའི་བྱང་ཆུབ་སེམས་དཔའ་ཐམས་ཅད་ཀྱི་བསླབ་པའི་གཞིར་གྱུར་པ་གང་ཡིན་པ་དང་། ཚུལ་ཁྲིམས་སུ་གྱུར་པ་གང་ཡིན་པའི་བསླབ་པའི་གཞི་གང་དག་དང་། ཚུལ་ཁྲིམས་གང་དག་ལ། འདས་པའི་བྱང་ཆུབ་སེམས་དཔའ་ཐམས་ཅད་ཀྱིས་བསླབས་པར་གྱུར་པ་དང་། མ་བྱོན་པའི་བྱང་ཆུབ་སེམས་དཔའ་ཐམས་ཅད་སློབ་པར་འགྱུར་བ་དང་། ཕྱོགས་བཅུ་དག་ན་ད་ལྟར་བཞུགས་པའི་བྱང་ཆུབ་སེམས་དཔའ་ཐམས་ཅད་ད་ལྟར་སློབ་བཞིན་པའི་བྱང་ཆུབ་སེམས་དཔའི་བསླབ་པའི་གཞི་ཐམས་ཅད་དང་། བྱང་ཆུབ་སེམས་དཔའི་ཚུལ་ཁྲིམས་ཐམས་ཅད་ཏེ། སྡོམ་པའི་ཚུལ་ཁྲིམས་དང་། དགེ་བ་ཆོས་སྡུད་ཀྱི་ཚུལ་ཁྲིམས་དང་། སེམས་ཅན་གྱི་དོན་བྱེད་པའི་ཚུལ་ཁྲིམས་ང་ལས་ཉོད་དམ། ཅེས་དྲིས་པ་ལ། སློབ་མས་རབ་ཏུ་ལེན་ལགས་སོ། །དེ་ལྟར་ལན་གསུམ་བརྗོད་པས་བྱང་ཆུབ་

སེམས་དཔའི་སྡོམ་པ་སྐྱེ་བ་ཡིན་ནོ། དེ་ནས་སློབ་དཔོན་གྱིས། སངས་རྒྱས་དང་བྱང་ཆུབ་སེམས་དཔའ་རྣམས་ལ་མཁྱེན་པར་གསོལ་བ་ནི། རིགས་ཀྱི་བུ་བྱང་ཆུབ་སེམས་དཔའ་མིང་འདི་ཞེས་བྱ་བས། བདག་བྱང་ཆུབ་སེམས་དཔའ་མིང་འདི་ཞེས་བྱ་བ་ལས། བྱང་ཆུབ་སེམས་དཔའི་ཚུལ་ཁྲིམས་ཀྱི་སྡོམ་པ་ཡང་དག་པར་བླང་བར་བྱ་བ་ལན་གསུམ་གྱི་བར་དུ་ཡང་དག་པར་མནོས་ལགས་ཏེ། བྱང་ཆུབ་སེམས་དཔའ་མིང་འདི་ཞེས་བྱ་བ་འདིས། བྱང་ཆུབ་སེམས་དཔའི་ཚུལ་ཁྲིམས་ཀྱི་སྡོམ་པ་ཡང་དག་པར་བླངས་པ་ལ། བདག་མིང་འདི་ཞེས་བགྱི་བ་དཔང་པོར་གྱུར་པས། འཕགས་པའི་མཆོག་ལྐོག་ཏུ་གྱུར་ཀྱང་། ཕྱོགས་བཅུའི་འཇིག་རྟེན་གྱི་ཁམས་མཐས་གཏུགས་པའི་ཆོས་ཐམས་ཅད་ལྐོག་ཏུ་མ་གྱུར་པའི་ཐུགས་མངའ་བ་ཐམས་ཅད་ལ་མཁྱེན་པར་གསོལ་ལོ། །ཅེས་ལན་གསུམ་མོ། །འདི་སློབ་དཔོན་ལངས་ཏེ་ཕྱོགས་བཅུར་མེ་ཏོག་གཏོར་ནས་ཐལ་མོ་སྦྱར་ཏེ་འདོན་པར་སྣང་ངོ་། །དེ་ནས་སློབ་མས་དཀོན་མཆོག་དང་། སློབ་དཔོན་ལ་ཕྱག་གསུམ་གསུམ་བྱས་ཏེ་ཡང་འདུག་པ་ལ་འདི་སྐད་ཅེས་ཁྱེད་ཀྱིས་བྱང་ཆུབ་སེམས་དཔའི་སྡོམ་པ་བླངས་པ་ལ། སངས་རྒྱས་དང་བྱང་ཆུབ་སེམས་དཔའ་ཐམས་ཅད་ཀྱིས་བུ་དང་སྤུན་ཟླའི་དགོངས་པ་མཛད་དེ། རྟག་ཏུ་སྲུང་ཞིང་སྐྱོང་བར་འགྱུར་རོ། ཁྱོད་ཀྱི་བསོད་ནམས་དང་ཡེ་ཤེས་ཀྱི་ཚོགས་ཐམས་ཅད་འཕེལ་བར་འགྱུར་རོ། ཁྱོད་ཀྱིས་བྱང་ཆུབ་སེམས་དཔའི་སྡོམ་པ་བླངས་པ་འདི། དད་པ་མེད་པའི་མི་རྣམས་ལ་མི་སྨྲ་ཞིང་གསང་བ་གལ་ཆེ། དེང་ཕྱིན་ཆད་ཕས་ཕམ་པ་བཞི་འམ་བརྒྱད། ཉེས་བྱས་བཞི་བཅུ་ཞེ་དྲུག་ལ་སོགས་པ་རྟག་ཏུ་སྲུང་བར་བྱ། བྱང་ཆུབ་སེམས་དཔའི་ཚུལ་ཁྲིམས་སྲུང་བའི་ཐབས་དང་། ལྟུང་བ་ཡང་ལྕིའི་ཁྱད་པར་དང་། དེ་དག་ཕྱིར་བཅོས་པ་ལ་ཡང་མཁས་པར་བྱའོ། །ཅེས་བརྗོད། རྒྱས་པ་ལ་སྦྱིན་བསླབ་བྱ་རགས་རིམ་ཙམ་སྐབས་འདིར་བརྗོད་ནའང་ལེགས་སོ། །སྤྱིར་བྱང་སྡོམ་ལེན་པའི་ལུགས་འདི་ལ། བསླབ་བྱ་རྣམས་སྔོན་དུ་ངེས་པར་བྱས་ནས་སྡོམ་པ་ཕྱིས་ལེན་པ་ཡིན་པས་སྐབས་

འདི་ར་མ་བརྗོད་ཀྱང་ཆོ་གའི་ཡན་ལག་ཉམས་པའི་སྐྱོན་དུ་མི་འགྱུར་རོ། །དེ་རྗེས་ཡོན་ཕུལ། དགེ་བ་བྱང་ཆུབ་ཏུ་བསྔོའོ། །དེས་བྱང་ཆུབ་སེམས་དཔའི་སྡོམ་པའི་ཆོ་ག་ལེགས་པར་སོང་། བསྟན་པ་ལ་འཇུག་པའི་རིམ་པའམ། སྐྱེས་བུ་གསུམ་གྱི་ཁྲིད་བསྐྱངས་པའི་གྲུབ་འབྲས་སེམས་བསྐྱེད་ལག་ལེན་དང་བཅས་པ་ཚར་པ་ལགས། ཆོས་འདོད་པ་གང་ཞིག་མདོ་ལུགས་ཁོ་ན་ལ་མོས་ན། མདོའི་ཉམས་ལེན་ཐམས་ཅད་འདིར་འདུས་ཤིང་། དེང་སང་གི་མདོ་ལུགས་པ་གཞན་ལ་མེད་པའི་བྱིན་རླབས་ཀྱི་བཀའ་བབས་དང་ལྡན་པ་ཡིན་པས། ཆོས་འདི་ཉིད་ཉམས་ལེན་གྱི་གཙོ་བོར་བྱེད་དགོས་ལ། སྔགས་ལ་མོས་པ་རྣམས་ཀྱང་འདི་ལ་མ་ཞུགས་ན། གསང་སྔགས་ལོག་པར་འགྲོ་ཉེན་ཡོད་པས། རྒྱལ་བ་སྲས་བཅས་ཀུན་གྱི་བཞེད་གཞུང་འདི་ལ་ལེགས་པར་འདོད་པ་ཐམས་ཅད་ཀྱིས་བསླབ་པར་བྱའོ།། །།ཐུགས་རྗེའི་དབང་ཕྱུག་རྒྱལ་བ་བཅོམ་ལྡན་འདས། །རྒྱལ་ཚབ་དམ་པ་རྒྱལ་སྲས་མི་ཕམ་མགོན། །ཆོས་ཀུན་བདག་པོ་འཕགས་པ་ཐོགས་མེད་ཞབས། །ཀུན་མཁྱེན་གཉིས་པ་རྒྱལ་སྲས་དབྱིག་གཉེན་ལ། །ཕྱག་འཚལ་སྐྱབས་སུ་མཆི་འོ་གསོལ་བ་འདེབས། །མཆོག་སྡེ་ལ་སོགས་གསེར་གླིང་རྒྱལ་པོའི་བར། རྒྱ་ཆེན་སྤྱོད་བརྒྱུད་བླ་མ་མཆོག་རྣམས་དང་། །རྒྱལ་སྲས་འཇམ་དཔལ་འཕགས་པ་ཀླུ་སྒྲུབ་སོགས། ཟབ་མོ་ལྟ་བའི་བརྒྱུད་པ་མཆོག་རྣམས་དང་། །གསང་བདག་རྣལ་འབྱོར་མ་དཔལ་ཏི་ལློ་སོགས། །ཉམས་ལེན་བྱིན་རླབས་བརྒྱུད་པ་མཆོག་རྣམས་ལ། །གུས་པས་གསོལ་བ་འདེབས་སོ་བྱིན་གྱིས་རློབས། །ཡིད་བཞིན་ནོར་འདྲའི་ཐུགས་མངའ་ཨ་ཏི་ཤ །རྒྱལ་བའི་འབྱུང་གནས་འབྲོམ་སྟོན་རིན་པོ་ཆེ། །མཁྱེན་པའི་དཀྱིལ་འཁོར་རབ་རྒྱས་པོ་ཏོ་བ། །གཞུང་ལུགས་རྒྱ་མཚོའི་མཐར་སོན་ཤ་ར་བ། །ཆོས་བཞིན་སྤྱོད་མཛད་གཏུམ་སྟོན་བློ་གྲོས་གྲགས། །བཀའ་གདམས་བསྟན་པའི་སྲོག་ཤིང་རྡོ་སྟོན་པ། །ཡེ་ཤེས་གཟི་འོད་འབར་བའི་དཔལ་ལྡན་གྲོ། །བསླབ་གསུམ་རྣམ་དག་སྐྱོ་སྟོན་སེང་གེ་སྐྱབས། །ཚེ་དགུའི་གཙུག་རྒྱན་འཆིམས་ཆེན་ནམ་མཁའ་གྲགས། །ནུས་མཐུའི་

མངའ་བདག་སྨོན་ལམ་ཚུལ་ཁྲིམས་ཞབས། །འགྲོ་དོན་དཔག་མེད་ཟེའུ་གྲགས་པའི་མཚན། །ཆོས་མངོན་རྒྱ་མཚོའི་མཐར་སོན་བློ་བཟང་འཆིམས། །རྣམ་དག་ཐུགས་མངའ་གྲོ་སྟོན་ཀུན་རྒྱལ་བ། །གྲུབ་པ་ཤེས་རབ་སྟང་སྟོན་ཆོས་ཀྱི་རྗེ། །བློ་མཆོག་དམ་པ་བསོད་ནམས་མཆོག་གྲུབ་དང་། ཟབ་དོན་སྲོལ་འཛིན་དཔལ་ལྡན་དོན་གྲུབ་ཞབས། །ཐུགས་ཀྱི་སྲས་གྱུར་གནས་བརྟན་བསོད་ནམས་གྲགས། །བྱང་ཆུབ་ཐུགས་ལྡན་ཀུན་དགའ་མཆོག་གྲུབ་ཞབས། །འཇམ་མགོན་གྲུབ་པའི་དཔའ་བོ་གྲོལ་མཆོག་རྗེ། །སྐྱེ་མེད་དོན་གཟིགས་ལུང་རིགས་རྒྱ་མཚོའི་ཞབས། །དེ་ལྟར་རྩ་བརྒྱུད་བླ་མ་ཐམས་ཅད་ལ། །གསོལ་བ་འདེབས་སོ་བྱིན་གྱིས་བརླབ་ཏུ་གསོལ། །ཡང་ན་རྒྱལ་བའི་འབྱུང་གནས་ཀྱི་རྗེས་སུ། །ཚུལ་ཁྲིམས་ཡེ་ཤེས་འབར་བའི་སྤྱན་མངའ་བ། །བླ་མ་དམ་པས་བྱིན་བརླབས་བྱ་ཡུལ་བ། །གནས་ལུགས་མངོན་གྱུར་གཙང་པ་རིན་པོ་ཆེ། །གདམས་ངག་རྒྱ་མཚོའི་མཐར་སོན་སྨུས་སླན་པ། །དེ་རྗེས་དཔལ་ལྡན་གྲོ་ནས་མཁན་ཆེན་བསོད་ནམས་མཆོག་གྲུབ་ཀྱི་བར་གོང་བཞིན། དེ་ནས། ཡོན་ཏན་མཆོག་གྱུར་མཁན་ཆེན་ཀུན་རྒྱལ་བ། །མཁྱེན་རབ་རྣམ་དག་ཡེ་ཤེས་རིན་ཆེན་དང་། །བརྩོན་པས་རྩེ་གཅིག་སྒྲུབ་མཛད་ལྷ་ཆུང་བ། །བྱམས་པའི་མཚན་ཅན་རྩ་བའི་བླ་མ་ལ། །གསོལ་བ་འདེབས་སོ་བྱིན་གྱིས་བརླབ་ཏུ་གསོལ། །གཞན་ཡང་སྔ་ཟུར་ནས་བརྒྱུད་པ་མི་འདྲ་བ་མང་དུ་བཞུགས་པས་ཇི་ལྟར་སྦྱར་ཀྱང་ཆོག་ལ། གཞུང་གདམས་ངག་གཉིས་ཀྱི་བརྒྱུད་པའི་ཐང་གོང་དུ་བཤད་པ་ཉིད་གཙོ་བོར་བྱའོ། དེ་ནས་འདི་སྐད་ཅེས་བྱ་སྟེ། དང་པོ་རྣམ་དག་སྐྱེས་བུ་ཆུང་ངུའི་ལམ། །ངེས་འབྱུང་རྣམ་དག་སྐྱེས་བུ་འབྲིང་གི་ལམ། །ལྷག་བསམ་རྣམ་དག་སྐྱེས་བུ་ཆེན་པོའི་ལམ། །རྣམ་དག་ལམ་གསུམ་ཐོབ་པར་བྱིན་གྱིས་རློབས། །མི་རྟག་འཆི་བ་རྒྱུད་ལམ་སྐྱེས་ན། །ཇི་ལྟར་འབད་ཀྱང་ཚེ་འདིའི་ཁ་འཛིན་ཅན། །རང་བློ་ཆོས་སུ་འགྲོ་སྐབས་མི་འདུག་པས། །ཆོས་བརྒྱད་འཆིང་བ་གྲོལ་བར་བྱིན་གྱིས་རློབས། །ལས་འབྲས་བསླུ་མེད་ཡིད་ཆེས་མ་སྐྱེས་ན། །ཆོས་སྤྱོད་

ཐམས་ཅད་བཟང་རྫུའི་ངང་དུ་འཚོར། །སྒྲུབ་པ་ལྷུར་ལེན་སྐད་ཀྱང་གཞན་ངོར་ཐལ། །ཆོས་ལ་ཡིད་ཆེས་སྐྱེ་བར་ར་བྱིན་གྱིས་རློབས། །བྱམས་དང་སྙིང་རྗེ་རྒྱུད་ལ་མ་སྐྱེས་ན། །སྒྲུབ་ལ་བརྩོན་ཡང་ཐེག་པ་དམན་པར་གོལ། །འགྲོ་བ་ཀུན་གྱི་སྡུག་བསྔལ་ཁུར་ཁྱེར་ནས། །བྱང་ཆུབ་སེམས་མཆོག་འབྱོངས་པར་བྱིན་གྱིས་རློབས། །སྤྲོས་ཀུན་རང་གྲོལ་སྟོང་ཉིད་མ་རྟོགས་ན། །ཆོས་ཀུན་སྒྱུ་མ་ལྟ་བུར་མི་ཤེས་ཤིང་། །མཚན་འཛིན་དབང་སོང་རང་སེམས་མི་གྲོལ་བས། །གནས་ལུགས་མཐར་ཐུག་རྟོགས་པར་བྱིན་གྱིས་རློབས། །ཅེས་གསོལ་བ་གདབ་པར་བྱའོ། བདག་གིས་ཆོས་སྐོར་འདིར་གདོགས་པ་ལ། ལམ་སྒྲོན་རྩ་འགྲེལ། བདེན་གཉིས་རྩ་འགྲེལ། དབུ་མའི་མན་ངག་རྩ་འགྲེལ་གྱི་བཤད་པ། སྨུས་སྨན་པའི་འཁྲིད་ཡིག། ལུམ་པ་པའི་ལམ་རིམ། པོ་ཏོ་བའི་དཔེ་ཆོས་རྩ་འགྲེལ་རྣམས་མཁས་མཆོག་བྱམས་པ་ལྷུན་གྲུབ་ལས་ཐོས། །པོ་ཏོ་བའི་བེའུ་བུམ་རྩ་འགྲེལ་དང་། སྣར་ཐང་པའི་ལམ་མཆོག་རྩ་འགྲེལ། འཆིམས་ཀྱི་གསུང་རྒྱུན་འཁྲིད་ཡིག་གི་ལུང་རྣམས་དང་། བསྟན་རིམ་གྱི་འཁྲིད་ཚུལ་རྒྱས་པ་གསུང་ངག་ནས་ཉམས་ཁྲིད་ཀྱི་ཚུལ་དུ་མཁན་ཆེན་ལུང་རིགས་རྒྱ་མཚོ་ལས་ཐོས་སོ། །ཐོར་བུ་ཐོར་བུ་དམ་པ་གཞན་འགའ་ཞིག་ལས་ཀྱང་ཐོས་མོད་ཀྱི། ཆོས་སྐོར་འདི་ལ་བརྒྱུད་པའི་གཙོ་བོ་གོང་དུ་སྨོས་པ་ཉིད་ཡིན་ནོ། །རྒྱལ་བ་སྲས་བཅས་ཀུན་གྱི་དགོངས་པ་འདི། །མདོ་ཙམ་བྲིས་ལས་བསོད་ནམས་གང་ཡོད་དེས། །མ་ལུས་ལུས་པ་མེད་པའི་སེམས་ཅན་རྣམས། །ཀུན་མཁྱེན་རྒྱལ་བའི་གོ་འཕང་མྱུར་ཐོབ་ཤོག །བསྟན་པ་ལ་འཇུག་པའི་རིམ་པ། སྐྱེས་བུ་གསུམ་གྱི་མན་ངག་གི་ཁྲིད་ཡིག་བདུད་རྩིའི་ཉིང་ཁུ་ཞེས་བྱ་བ། རྒྱལ་ཁམས་པ་ཏཱ་ར་ནཱ་ཐས་ངེས་པར་བརྗོད་པའོ། །འདི་ན་སྒོམ་ཚུལ་དམིགས་པའི་ཁྲིད་ཡིག་ཡིན་ལ། གོ་དོན་བློ་ལ་འགོད་པའི་བཤད་པ་ནི། དམ་པ་སྔ་མ་རྣམས་ཀྱིས་མཛད་པ་ལས་བཙལ་བར་བྱའོ། འདིས་ཀྱང་བསྟན་པ་རིན་པོ་ཆེ་རྒྱས་ལ་ཡུན་རིང་དུ་གནས་པར་གྱུར་ཅིག ཞུས་དག། བཀྲ་ཤིས།།

Glossary of Technical Terms and Proper Names

absorption	(Tib. *bsam gtan*, Skt. *dhyāna*): The fifth of the six perfections, absorption is the practice of tranquility meditation that leads to attainment of mental peace and stability. The four absorptions and nine stages of resting the mind (For the stages, see Glossary of Classifications) come under the category of absorption.
aggregate	(Tib. *phung po*, Skt. *skandha*): In this text, the term aggregate refers to the five components of sentient life—form, feeling, perception, mental formations and consciousness.
arhat	(Tib. *dgra bcom pa*): An individual who has attained freedom from the emotional afflictions but has not attained full buddhahood. The attainment of arhatship is the goal of hearers.
Atisha	(982-1054): A great Indian philosopher and teacher considered a founder of the Kadampa sect. His work *Lamp on the Path to Enlightenment* became the prototype for stages of the path literature.
awakening mind	(Tib. *byang chub kyi sems*, Skt. *Bodhicitta*): On the relative level, awakening mind is the wish to become enlightened in order to benefit sentient beings as well as the attitude of loving kindness and compassion. On the ultimate level, it is the non-conceptual insight into the nature of all phenomena.
bodhicitta	(Tib. *byang chub kyi sems*): *See "awakening mind".*
bodhisattva	(Tib. *byang chub sems dpa'*): A being who has engendered the wish to bring all beings to enlightenment and who practices the six paramitas. Sometimes this term refers to noble bodhisattvas, who have attained direct insight into emptiness.
buddha	(Tib. *sangs rgyas*): A being who has purified all obscurations of mind and perfected all qualities of enlightenment.

Buddha	(Tib. *Sangs rgyas*): The founder of Buddhism who lived around the 5th century B.C.E.
Brahma	(Tib. *tshangs pa*): King of the gods in the form realm.
demi-god	(Tib. *lha min,* Skt. *asura*): A type of being living in the demi-god realm. Demi-gods have subtle mental bodies, are afflicted by jealousy and experience the suffering of battling with the gods.
Dharma	(Tib. *chos*): The teaching of the Buddha.
hearer	(Tib. *nyan thos*, Skt. *shrāvaka*): A follower of the Hinayana who hears the words of the Buddha and aspires to enlightenment for his or her own peace and benefit.
Hinayana	(Tib. *theg pa chung ngu*): The "lesser vehicle" tradition that upholds the doctrine of personal discipline as a means to enlightenment.
hungry ghost	(Tib. *yi dwags*, Skt. *preta*): A kind of being living in the realm of hungry ghosts, afflicted with the suffering of hunger and thirst. The principal affliction leading to birth in this realm is greed.
Indra	(Tib. brgya byin): King of the god realm of the Thirty Three.
karma	(Tib. *las*): (1) action (2) the effects produced by past actions, including latent habitual tendencies.
Mahayana	(Tib. *theg pa chen po*): The "great vehicle" tradition practiced in Tibet that upholds the doctrines of awakening mind, compassion, wisdom and selflessness as its basic tenets.
Nagarjuna	(Tib. Klu sgrub): An Indian philosopher who lived in the 1st-2nd century, author of several seminal works of the middle way doctrine.
self of person	(Tib. *gang zag gi bdag,* Skt. *pudgalātman*): The inherent existence of a nominally existent person,[186] used to refer to the erroneous concept that imputes an inherent existence to sentient beings.
self of phenomena	(Tib. *chos kyi bdag,* Skt. *dharmātman*): The inherent existence of phenomena, used to refer to the erroneous concept that imputes an inherent existence to phenomena.
Shantideva	(Tib. Zhi ba lha) A great Indian poet and bodhisattva who lived in the 7th century, author of *The Bodhisattva's Way of Life.*
solitary realizer	(Tib. *rang sangs rgyas,* Skt. *pratyekabuddha*): Self-liberated Buddhas who have attained a state of peace but do not aspire to teach or directly help sentient beings.

Three Jewels	(Tib. *dkon mchog gsum,* Skt. *trisharaṇa*): The Buddha, Dharma and Sangha: the sources of refuge for Buddhists.
trance	(Tib. *ting nge 'dzin,* Skt. *samādhi*): The state of peaceful absorption that emerges from the practice of tranquility meditation.
Vajrayana	(or secret mantra) (Tib. *rdo rje thek pa*): The "diamond vehicle", tantric Buddhism, emphasizes the practices of deity visualization, mantra recitation and non-conceptuality as methods to attain enlightenment.

Glossary of Classificatory Terms with Tibetan

The two selflessnesses	**བདག་མེད་གཉིས།**
The selflessness of persons	གང་ཟག་གི་བདག་མེད།
The selflessness of phenomena	ཆོས་ཀྱི་བདག་མེད།
The three Jewels	**དཀོན་མཆོག་གསུམ།**
Buddha	སངས་རྒྱས།
Dharma	ཆོས།
Sangha	དགེ་འདུན།
The Three Vehicles	**ཐེག་པ་གསུམ།**
Hinayana	ཐེག་པ་ཆུང་ངུ།
Mahayana	ཐེག་པ་ཆེན་པོ།
Vajrayana	རྡོ་རྗེ་ཐེག་པ།
The three baskets	**སྡེ་སྣོད་གསུམ།**
The sutra	མདོ།
The vinaya	འདུལ་བ།
The abhidharma	མངོན་པ།
The three poisons	**དུག་གསུམ།**
Desire	འདོད་ཆགས།
Aversion	ཞེ་སྡང་།
Ignorance	གཏི་མུག

The three types of suffering	**སྡུག་བསྔལ་གསུམ།**
The manifest suffering	སྡུག་བསྔལ་གྱི་སྡུག་བསྔལ།
The suffering of change	འགྱུར་བའི་སྡུག་བསྔལ།
The suffering of conditioned existence	འདུ་བྱེད་ཀྱི་སྡུག་བསྔལ།
The three types of vows	**སྡོམ་པ་རྣམ་གསུམ།**
The vows of individual liberation (*pratimoksha*)	སོ་སོ་ཐར་པའི་སྡོམ་པ།
The bodhisattva vow	བྱང་ཆུབ་སེམས་པའི་སྡོམ་པ།
The vows of secret mantra	གསང་སྔགས་ཀྱི་སྡོམ་པ།
The three realms	**ཁམས་གསུམ།**
The desire realm	འདོད་ཁམས།
The form realm	གཟུགས་ཁམས།
The formless realm	གཟུགས་མེད་ཁམས།
The four kinds of birth	**སྐྱེ་གནས་བཞི།**
Birth from a womb	མངལ་ནས་སྐྱེས་པ།
Birth from an egg	སྒོང་ང་ལས་སྐྱེས་པ།
Miraculous birth	བརྫུས་ཏེ་སྐྱེས་པ།
Birth from warmth and moisture	དྲོད་གཤེར་ལས་སྐྱེས་པ།
The four powers	**སྟོབས་བཞི།**
The power of the support	རྟེན་གྱི་སྟོབས།
The power of fully engaging in remedial action	གཉེན་པོ་ཀུན་ཏུ་སྤྱོད་པའི་སྟོབས།
The power of reparation	སུན་འབྱིན་པའི་སྟོབས།
The power of reversal	སླར་ལྡོག་པའི་སྟོབས།

The four ways of gathering disciple	**བསྡུས་པའི་དངོས་པོ་བཞི།**
Giving	སྦྱིན་པ།
Speaking pleasantly	སྙན་པར་སྨྲ་བ།
Acting in accord with the teaching	དོན་མཐུན་པ།
Being helpful	དོན་སྤྱོད་པ།
The four bodies of a Buddha	**སྐུ་བཞི།**
The emanation body (nirmāṇakāya)	སྤྲུལ་པའི་སྐུ།
The enjoyment body (saṃbhogakāya)	ལོངས་སྤྱོད་རྫོགས་པའི་སྐུ།
The truth body (dharmakāya)	ཆོས་ཀྱི་སྐུ།
The essence body (svabhāvikakāya)	ངོ་བོ་ཉིད་ཀྱི་སྐུ།
The five aggregates	**ཕུང་པོ་ལྔ།**
Form	གཟུགས།
Feeling	ཚོར་བ།
Perception	འདུ་ཤེས།
Mental formations	འདུ་བྱེད།
Consciousness	རྣམ་ཤེས།
The five paths	**ལམ་ལྔ།**
The path of accumulation	ཚོགས་ལམ།
The path of junction	སྦྱོར་ལམ།
The path of seeing	མཐོང་ལམ།
The path of meditation	སྒོམ་ལམ།
The path of no more learning	མི་སློབ་པའི་ལམ།
The six realms	**རིགས་དྲུག**
Hell beings	དམྱལ་བ།
Hungry ghosts	ཡི་དྭགས།

Animals — དུད་འགྲོ།

Humans — མི།

Demi-gods — ལྷ་མིན།

Gods — ལྷ།

The six sense consciousness(es) — **རྣམ་ཤེས་ཚོགས་དྲུག**

Eye consciousness — མིག་གི་རྣམ་ཤེས།

Ear consciousness — རྣ་བའི་རྣམ་ཤེས།

Nose consciousness — སྣའི་རྣམ་ཤེས།

Tongue consciousness — ལྕེའི་རྣམ་ཤེས།

Body consciousness — ལུས་ཀྱི་རྣམ་ཤེས།

Mental consciousness — ཡིད་ཀྱི་རྣམ་ཤེས།

The six perfections — **ཕ་རོལ་ཏུ་ཕྱིན་པ་དྲུག**

Generosity — སྦྱིན་པ།

Moral discipline — ཚུལ་ཁྲིམས།

Patience — བཟོད་པ།

Diligence — བརྩོན་འགྲུས།

Absorption — བསམ་གཏན།

Wisdom — ཤེས་རབ།

The eight unfavorable states — **མི་ཁམས་བརྒྱད།**

Incarnation as a hell being — དམྱལ་བའི་ལུས་སུ་སྐྱེས་པ།

Incarnation as a hungry ghost — ཡི་དྭགས་སུ་སྐྱེས་པ།

Incarnation as an animal — དུད་འགྲོར་སྐྱེས་པ།

Incarnation as a barbarian — ཀླ་ཀློར་སྐྱེས་པ།

Incarnation as a god — ལྷར་སྐྱེས་པ།

Having wrong views — ལོག་ལྟར་གནས་པ།

Incarnation in a world where the Buddha's teachings do not exist	སངས་རྒྱས་ཀྱིས་སྟོང་པ།
Birth as a human without sensual or mental functioning	དབང་པོ་མ་ཚང་བ།
The eight worldly preoccupations	**འཇིག་རྟེན་ཆོས་བརྒྱད།**
Gain	རྙེད་པ།
Loss	མ་རྙེད་པ།
Fame	སྙན་པ།
Disgrace	མི་སྙན་པ།
Slander	སྨད་པ།
Praise	བསྟོད་པ།
Pleasure	བདེ་བ།
Pain	སྡུག་བསྔལ།
The eight types of *pratimoksha* ordination	**སོ་ཐར་རིགས་བརྒྱད།**
Monk	དགེ་སློང་།
Nun	དགེ་སློང་མ།
Novice monk	དགེ་ཚུལ།
Novice nun	དགེ་ཚུལ་མ།
Layman practitioner (holding lay vows)	དགེ་བསྙེན།
Laywoman practitioner (holding lay vows)	དགེ་བསྙེན་མ།
Postulant nun vows	དགེ་སློབ་མ།
Holder of single day vows	བསྙེན་གནས།

The ten opportunities	**དལ་བ་བཅུ།**
Birth as a human	མི་རུ་སྐྱེས་པ།
Birth in a land where Buddhism has spread	ཡུལ་དབུས་སུ་སྐྱེས་པ།
Born with sense faculties intact	དབང་པོ་ཚང་བ།
Possessing "uncorrupted karma"	ལས་མཐའ་མ་ལོག་པ།
Having trust in the Three Jewels	གནས་ལ་དད་པ།
Living in an age when a Buddha has come to the world	སངས་རྒྱས་འཇིག་རྟེན་དུ་བྱོན་པ།
Living at a time when the Buddha teaches	སངས་རྒྱས་ཀྱི་དམ་པའི་ཆོས་གསུངས་པ།
Living at a time when the Buddha's teachings survive	ཆོས་གསུང་པ་རྣམས་གནས་པ།
Living at a time when the teaching has many followers	ཆོས་གནས་པ་རྣམས་རྗེས་སུ་འཇུག་པ།
Living at a time when sponsors support Dharma practice	གཞན་གྱི་ཕྱིར་སྙིང་བརྩེ་བ་ཡོད་པ།
The ten virtuous actions	**དགེ་བ་བཅུ།**
Saving live	སྲོག་སྐྱོབ་པ།
Giving	སྦྱིན་པ།
Guarding moral conduct	ཚུལ་ཁྲིམས་སྲུང་བ།
Telling the truth	བདེན་པར་སྨྲ་བ།
Speaking gently	ངག་འཇམ་པོར་སྨྲ་བ།
Reconciling friends	ཁྲམ་མི་བྱེད་པ།
Speaking meaningfully	དོན་དང་ལྡན་པའི་གཏམ་སྨྲ་བ།
Contentment	ཆོག་ཤེས་པ།
Altruism	ཕན་སེམས་སྐྱེས་པ།
Abandoning wrong views	ལོག་ལྟ་སྤོང་བ།

The ten non-virtuous actions	**མི་དགེ་བ་བཅུ།**
Killing	སྲོག་གཅོད་པ།
Stealing	མ་བྱིན་ལེན་པ།
Sexual misconduct	འདོད་ལོག་སྤྱོད་པ།
Lying	རྫུན་སྨྲ་བ།
Harsh speech	ཚིག་རྩུབ་སྨྲ་བ།
Slander	ཕྲ་མ།
Meaningless chatter	ངག་འཁྱལ།
Covetousness	རྣབ་སེམས།
Harboring malice	གནོད་སེམས།
Wrong views	ལོག་ལྟ།

The twelve sources	**སྐྱེ་མཆེད་བཅུ་གཉིས།**
Form	གཟུགས།
Sound	སྒྲ།
Odor	དྲི།
Taste	རོ།
Tangible object	རེག་བྱ།
Phenomena	ཆོས།
The eye faculty	མིག་གི་དབང་པོ།
The ear faculty	རྣའི་དབང་པོ།
The nose faculty	སྣའི་དབང་པོ།
The tongue faculty	ལྕེའི་དབང་པོ།
The body faculty	ལུས་ཀྱི་དབང་པོ།
The mind faculty	ཡིད་ཀྱི་དབང་པོ།

The eighteen constituents [the twelve sources plus the six consciousnesses]	ཁམས་བཅོ་བརྒྱད།

The six god desire god realms	**འདོད་ཁམས་དྲུག**
Heaven of the Four Great Kings	རྒྱལ་བཞིའི་རིས།
Heaven of the Thirty Three	སུམ་ཅུ་རྩ་གསུམ་པ།
Free from Strife	འཐབ་བྲལ།
Blissful	དགའ་ལྡན།
Delighting in Creation	འཕྲུལ་དགའ།
Enjoyment of Emanations	གཞན་འཕྲུལ་དབང་བྱེད།
The seventeen form god realms	**གཟུགས་ཀྱི་ཁམས་བཅུ་བདུན།**
Brahma's Heaven	ཚངས་རིས།
Acolytes of Brahma	ཚངས་པ་མདུན་ན་འདོན།
Heaven of the Great Brahma	ཚངས་པ་ཆེན་པོ།
Limited Light	འོད་ཆུང་།
Boundless Light	ཚད་མེད་འོད།
Clear Light	འོད་གསལ།
Limited Virtue	དགེ་ཆུང་།
Boundless Virtue	ཚད་མེད་དགེ།
Extensive Virtue	དགེ་རྒྱས།
Cloudless	སྤྲིན་མེད།
Increasing Merit	བསོད་ནམས་སྐྱེས།
Great Maturity	འབྲས་བུ་ཆེ་བ།
None Greater	མི་ཆེ་བ།
Without Affliction	མི་གདུང་བ།
Glorious Appearance	གྱ་ནོམ་སྣང་བ།
Most Lovely	ཤིན་ཏུ་མཐོང་།
Highest Heaven	འོག་མིན།

The Four Formless Realms	**གཟུགས་མེད་ཁམས་བཞི།**
Sphere of Boundless Space	ནམ་མཁའ་མཐའ་ཡས་སྐྱེ་མཆེད།
Sphere of Boundless Consciousness	རྣམ་ཤེས་མཐའ་ཡས་སྐྱེ་མཆེད།
Sphere of Nothingness	ཅི་ཡང་མེད་པའི་སྐྱེ་མཆེད།
Sphere of neither Perception nor Non-Perception	འདུ་ཤེས་མེད་ འདུ་ཤེས་མེད་མིན་གྱི་སྐྱེ་མཆེད།

Endnotes

1. Zangpo. *Retreat Manual.* (1994): 82.
2. Information in this paragraph from Riggs (2001): 4-6, 249-262; Taranatha (1981): vii; and Zangpo (2003): 1-5.
3. Zangpo (2003) 3.
4. Yu mo ba mi bskyod rdo rje.
5. Khyung po rnal 'byor.
6. Kun spangs thugs rje brtson 'grus.
7. Dol po pa shes rab rgyal mtshan.
8. Historical information about Jomonang in the 17th century and Jonang institutions from Snellgrove and Richardson (1980): 196-99; Taranatha (1970): vii; Powers (1995): 146-47; Zangpo (2003): 1-5.
9. Kongtrul. Retreat. (1994): 28, 82.
10. Tsong-kha-pa (2000): 130.
11. Skt. *saṃsāra,* Tib. *'khor ba.* Cyclic existence means the cycle of birth and death that sentient beings experience. Cyclic existence is characterized by suffering, and is denoted in the sutras as the opposite of nirvana.
12. Skt. *vinaya,* Tib. *'dul wa* is one of the "three baskets" or collections of teachings that claim to be directly connected to Shakyamuni Buddha's original teachings. This collection contains descriptions of the various sorts of lay and monastic discipline, and outlines the formal rules for the spiritual community.
13. Skt. *karma,* Tib. *las* is one of the few words I have decided to leave untranslated in many instances in this text. The word can generally be translated as "action". However, it often carries the connotation of being a non-volitional link in the relationship between cause and effect and, in those cases, implies more of a tendency than an action.
14. Tsong-kha-pa (2000): 130.
15. Tsong-kha-pa (2000): 131.
16. Skt. *bodhicitta,* Tib. *byang chub kyi sems.*
17. Sanskrit for "Homage to the buddhas and bodhisattvas."
18. The three lineages refer to disciplines and practices of the Hinayana, Mahayana and Vajrayana traditions.

19. Buddhas, bodhisattvas, solitary-realizers and hearers are four types of individuals who have reached varying levels of attainment determined by their aspirations and characteristics (see Glossary of Technical Terms and Proper Names).
20. The "seven branch prayer" is a traditional genre of Buddhist prayer that includes seven parts: paying homage, making offerings, confessing negative actions, rejoicing in the merit of others, exhorting the Buddha to teach, supplicating the teacher not to pass away and dedicating the merit to the enlightenment of all sentient beings (See Glossary of Classifications).
21. The two sacred states are the "form body" and "truth body" of a Buddha. The former (Skt. *rupakaya*, Tib. *gzugs sku*) refers collectively to the emanation body and enjoyment body that a buddha attains for the benefit of others. The latter (Skt. *dharmakaya*, Tib. *chos sku*) refers to the truth body that a Buddha attains for his own benefit (See Glossary of Classifications).
22. Throughout the text, the instruction to "think this way again and again" frequently follows portions of the contemplations. Traditionally, contemplation and meditation sessions are lengthy (2-4 hours). The instruction to repeat the contemplation refers to a directive to repeat the contemplation a number of times per session. It is also a recommendation to reinforce the contemplation between sessions as a mental exercise.
23. Throughout the text "the contemplation on impermanence and death" and "the contemplation on impermanence" refer to the same contemplation.
24. Meditation on impermanence is the basis for understanding that everything, including the individual self, is impermanent, transitory and therefore lacks ultimate existence. Although this understanding is the goal of meditation on impermanence, it can lead to the misapprehension that everything is meaningless. This misunderstanding could potentially turn into a view tainted by nihilism or hedonism (hence "I may as well enjoy myself"), without regard for the workings of karma or the importance of striving to free oneself from cyclic existence.
25. The four contemplations mentioned here and elaborated on in the first part of *Essence* are the fundamental contemplations comprising the first part of the preliminary practices (Tib. *sngon 'gro*) embraced by all forms of Tibetan Buddhism.
26. For this and all subsequent references, see note 20.
27. From the *Sutra of the Sublime Dharma of Clear Recollection* (Skt. *Saddharmāsmṛty-upasthāna*, Tib. *'Phag pa dam pa'i chos dran pa nyer bar*

gbzhag pa). The eight unfavorable states refer to eight states of incarnation with circumstances unfavorable to the pursuit of spiritual development: incarnation as a hell being, incarnation as a hungry ghost, incarnation as an animal, incarnation as a barbarian, incarnation as a god, incarnation as a person with a cynical disposition, incarnation in a world where the Buddha's teachings do not exist and birth as a human without complete sensual or mental functioning. For an explanation of the cosmology of the six realms, see the Introduction; (see also Glossary of Classifications).

28. Trance (Skt. *samadhi,* Tib. *ting nge 'dzin*) is a meditative absorption in which the mind is in a state of tranquility endowed with bliss. While this state entails a withdrawal of the senses internally, it is not a hypnotic state but one where the meditator is developing concentration and control of the mind.

29. Skt. *asura,* Tib. *lha min.* Demi-gods, the beings in this realm, are jealous of the splendor and wealth of the gods and spend their lives battling for a place in the gods' divine abode.

30. From the *Sutra of the Sublime Dharma of Clear Recollection.* The ten endowments are ten conditions of incarnation that make the pursuit of spiritual development possible. They are birth as a human, birth in a land where Buddhism has spread, born with sense faculties intact, possessing "uncorrupted karma", having trust in the Three Jewels, living in an age when a Buddha has come to the world, living at a time when the Buddha teaches, living at a time when the Buddha's teachings survive, living at a time when the teaching has many followers and living at a time when sponsors support Dharma practice. Kongtrul. *Torch.* (1977): 32 (see Glossary of Classifications).

    The first five of these are called the "five inner endowments." The latter five are called the "five outer endowments". Kongtrul defines "uncorrupted karma" as being uninvolved with people who are non-Buddhists. Patrul Rinpoche defines it as having a lifestyle that conflicts with basic Buddhist precepts, such as acquiring a livelihood through hunting or prostitution (Kongtrul. *Torch.* (1977): 33; Patrul Rinpoche. (1998): 24.

31. The five acts of immediate consequence are matricide, patricide, killing an Arhat or guru, causing a schism in the spiritual community and intentionally wounding a Buddha. Kongtrul. *Torch.* (1977): 89 (see Glossary of Classifications).

32. Skt. *vinaya,* Tib. *'dul ba*: The "rules of discipline" is one of the "three baskets" making up the Buddhist Canon. This section of the canon presents the code of discipline for monastics, novices and lay

practitioners. The other two baskets are the *sutra* and *abhidharma* (see Glossary of Classifications).

33. The most common story cited to illustrate 'understanding the difficulty of obtaining a human rebirth by way of example' is the story of the turtle and the yoke:

    Suppose that this whole earth were an ocean, and a person threw in a yoke that had only one hole. The yoke would float back and forth in all the four directions. Underneath that ocean, there is a blind tortoise who lives for many thousands of years but who comes up above the surface once every hundred years. It would be very difficult for the tortoise's head to meet with the yoke's hole; still, it is possible. To be born in a precious human life is much more difficult *Gampopa.* (1998): 62.

34. Hearers (Skt. *srāvaka,* Tib. *snyan thos*) and solitary-realizers (Skt. *pratyekabuddha,* Tib. *rang rgyal*) achieve a temporary liberation from the suffering of cyclic existence by entering a state of meditative absorption: "They maintain unafflicted states of meditative concentration, but those states are based on the psychic imprint of ignorance. Since their meditative concentrations are unafflicted, they believe they have achieved nirvana and remain that way" (Gampopa. (1998): 52 (see Glossary of Technical Terms & Proper Names for definitions of each).

35. Skt. *Bodhisattva-caryāvatāra,* Tib. *byang chub sems dpa'i spyod pa la 'jug pa.*

36. Shantideva. *Guide to the Bodhisattva's Way of Life.*

37. Prajnavarman. *The Collection of Indicative Verses* (Skt. *Udana-varga,* Tib. *Ched du brjod pa'i tshoms kyi rnam gyi 'grel pa*).

38. At the time this text was composed in the 16th Century, it is likely that the ordinary lifespan did not usually exceed sixty years of age, as the author indicates. The intention of this section is not to imply that older people cannot practice religion but to encourage the aspirant not to procrastinate since the challenges of practicing religion become greater with age.

39. According to Buddhist cosmology, the universe is created and destroyed many times over. At the end of each eon, the universe is incinerated by seven suns over the course of seven days. Patrul Rinpoche. (1998): 40.

40. Nagarjuna. *The Friendly Letter* (Skt. *Suhṛl-lekha,* Tib. *bShes pa'i spring yik*).

41. Here, freedom of mind is synonymous with the realization of buddhahood. The attainment of buddhahood ensures freedom over one's mental state in this life and freedom to choose the place and type of one's rebirth.

42. Maticitra. *Letter to King Kaniṣka* (Skt. *Mahā-rāja-kaniṣka-lekha,* Tib. *rGyalpo chenpo kanika la springs pa'i spring yik*).
43. *The Precious Garland* (Skt. *Ratnāvalī,* Tib. *rGyalpo la gram bya ba rinpoche'i phreng ba*).
44. *Guide to the Bodhisattva's Way of Life.*
45. Matricita. *Letter to King Kaniṣka.*
46. Vasubandu. *The Treasury of Phenomenolgy* (Skt. *Abhidharma-kośa,* Tib. *Chos mgnon pa'i mdzod kyi tshig le'ur byas pa*).
47. "Karmic demons" are the wardens of hell that are ultimately mental projections appearing due to the negative karma of the beings born into this realm.
48. Tib. *bardo,* Skt. *antarabhava.* The intermediate state refers to the state between death and rebirth.
49. The beings in the hell realms have "mental bodies" and do not exist in physical form. Therefore, after they have lost consciousness or been mutilated, they wake up with the sense that their bodies are complete and whole again.
50. The four kinds of birth present in the six realms are birth from a womb, from an egg, from heat and moisture and miraculous birth (Gampopa. (1998): 439 (see Glossary of Classifications).
51. See footnote 45.
52. Vasubandu. *Treasury of Phenomenology.*
53. Candragomin. Skt. *Śiṣya-lekha,* Tib. *slob ma la spring pa'I spring yig.*
54. The nine disgusting things are bluish corpses, decaying corpses, worm-eaten corpses, swollen corpses, bloody corpses, corpses being devoured by predators, scattered body parts, burning corpses and dry bones. Dhammapada. (1985): 278.
55. The beings in the ephemeral hells have, depending upon the nature of their karmic projections, a wide variety of modes of existence. For example, some beings may mentally project themselves onto inanimate objects. Patrul Rinpoche explains: "Beings may be crushed between rocks or trapped inside a stone, frozen in ice, cooked in boiling water, or burnt in fires. Some feel that, when someone is cutting a tree, they are the tree having their limbs chopped off. Some suffer through identifying their bodies with objects that are constantly put to use, such as mortars, brooms, pans, doors, pillars, hobs and ropes". Patrul Rinpoche. (1998): 69.
56. A translation of this story may be found in Gampopa. (1998): 357-361.
57. Skt. *Sad-dharmāsmṛty-upasthāna,* Tib. *'Phag pa dam pa'i chos dren pa nye bar gzhag pa.*
58. Poison that issues spontaneously from their breath or bodies.

59. According to Buddhist belief, Brahma is chief of the first level of the form realm. Indra is sovereign of the Heaven of the Thirty-Three (Gampopa. (1998): Glossary). Both of them are very important gods in pre-Buddhist India. They are carried over into Buddhism although they are demoted in status. A universal monarch (Skt. *chakravartin,* Tib. 'khor los sgyur ba'i rgyal pa) "connotes worldly supremacy, the secular equivalent of the Buddha's spiritual supremacy" (Kongtrul. *Torch* (1977): 113. For an interesting discussion of the origin of the concept of the universal monarch, see Kongtrul. *Myriad.* (1995): 134-138.
60. To explain environmental results another way, the karmic propensities carried into a given environment by beings who live together in the same locale determine the nature of that environment. The environmental results used as examples in this passage concur with an agrarian society. In a modern context, the results might be reflected in a number of other ways, such as computer viruses and car problems for instance.
61. "The time of ripening is uncertain" means that the ripening of an action may be delayed for several lifetimes.
62. Taranatha does not go on to explain the ten virtuous actions explicitly as he is emphasizing the attitude of abandonment in this contemplation. The ten virtuous actions are to save life, to give generously, to preserve moral conduct, to speak the truth, to reconcile friends divided by slander, to speak gently, to speak meaningfully, to rejoice in the good fortune of others, to have a loving mind towards others and to have faith in the Buddha's teachings. Gyamtso. *Shes rab.* (1992): 40 (see Glossary of Classifications).
63. In other words, saving life leads to having a long life oneself; giving leads to being wealthy and so forth.
64. The four powers are four elements that must be present for an act of confession to be effective and complete. The procedure for confession is often taught in tandem with meditation on the deity Vajrasattva (see Glossary of Classifications).
65. The literal translation of this phrase seems to be "befriending men", but it can be translated as it is here. Taranatha was writing for ordained monks, who would be encouraged to befriend people of the same sex in order to maintain the purity of their ordination vows.
66. The three realms are the desire, form and formless realms (see Glossary of Classifications).
67. The eighth suffering is the suffering of the five aggregates, discussed in the 30th Contemplation.
68. According to Buddhist cosmology, there are six desire god realms, seventeen form god realms and four formless god realms. The two

mentioned here are among the lowest of the desire god realms (see Glossary of Classifications).

69. Nagarjuna. *The Friendly Letter.*
70. The eyes of the god are called "pleasure eyes" here because they are accustomed to seeing pleasant forms only.
71. Tib. *'phags pa,* Skt. *ārya.* Noble beings are those who have reached the first bodhisattva level.
72. The suffering of composite existence is one of the three types of suffering (see below) and is the subtlest of the three types. It refers to the suffering inherent within conditioned existence, the dissatisfaction that exists in the absence of transcendent wisdom (see Glossary of Classifications).
73. Skt. *skanda,* Tib. *phung po.* The mind and body of every sentient being (the living organism) is composed of five aggregates: form, feeling, perception, mental formations and consciousness (see Glossary of Classifications).
74. Nagarjuna. *The Friendly Letter.*
75. Literally, this line reads "Those who have been my mothers are equal to the number of juniper berries." The line makes reference to a Kadampa teaching that compares the number of one's mothers to the number of pellets of soil in the earth if those pellets were the size of juniper berries. See *Mind Training Like the Sun,* Library of Tibetan Works & Archives. (2002): 38.
76. Tib. *gnas lugs.* The "natural state" is ultimate truth and its expression as the essence or nature of mind.
77. The expanse (Skt. *dhātu,* Tib. *dbying*) refers to the true nature of all phenomena reflected, in this case, in the true nature of mind.
78. Skt. *shamatha,* Tib. *zhi gnas.*
79. "Knowing things as they are" refers to a buddha's realization of the ultimate essence of all phenomena. "Knowing things in their multiplicity" means the omniscient quality of a buddha's mind that is aware of every specific phenomena and occurrence.
80. gTum ston blo gros grags (1106-1166), student of Kadampa master Sharawa (1070-1141).
81. gTsang pa rdo rje mi bskyod (11th Century), student of Kadampa master Bya yul ba gzhon nu 'od (1075-1138).
82. Mus sman pa bdud rtsi char chen (11th Century).
83. Tib. *Theg pa chen po blo sbyong gi rim pa.*
84. Tib. *Bya yul wa* (1075-1138), also known as *gZhon nu 'od,* authored an important early Kadampa *lamrim* text.
85. Tib. *sNar thang pa,* also known as *'Jam bdyang rin chen,* was a 14th Century Kadampa master.
86. The three types of beings are those living on, below and above the earth.

87. Skt. *Jambudvīpa,* Tib. *'Dzam bug ling.* This is the continent to the south of Mount Meru considered in Buddhist cosmology to be our world.
88. Skt. *Videha,* Tib. *Lu 'phags po.*
89. Skt. *Godānīya,* Tib. *Ba lang spyod.*
90. Skt. *Kuru,* Tib. *sGra mi snyan.*
91. Skt. *yakṣa,* Tib. *gnod sbyin.*
92. See the Glossary of Classifications for an enumeration of the god realms.
93. Skt. *dhyāna,* Tib. *bsam gtan.*
94. The reference to "original sources" is probably a general reference to sutra sources that discuss cosmology and Vasubhandu's *Treasury of Phenomenology,* a text that Taranatha draws on frequently in this section.
95. "Brahma realms" refers to a set of the three heavens of the first stage of absorption.
96. Tib. *stong gsum.*
97. Tormas are cakes (usually made of barley flour) offered to please and propitiate deities and spirits.
98. The three spheres are subject, object and action. The seal of not conceiving of the three spheres means to cease to apprehend in a dualistic manner.
99. The "so forth" here refers to the rest of the seven branches (explained in Note 20).
100. The Ceremony of the Vow of Awakening Mind is explained later in the Appendix of this text.
101. Tib. *byang chub sems dpa'.* A bodhisattva (literally "a heroic being of enlightenment") refers generally to anyone who has taken the Mahayana commitments of awakening mind but more specifically to a person who strives in the six perfections (explained below) and (see Glossary of Classifications).
102. The six perfections plus the perfections of skillful means, aspiration, strength and wisdom (see Glossary of Classifications).
103. The idea here is that people that do not engage in meritorious actions themselves can only hope to be helped by the aspiration prayers and kindness of others.
104. Because a bodhisattva must perfect patience as a cause for attaining buddhahood, harm is an indirect cause of enlightenment.
105. The "signs of heat" refer to signs accompanying successful meditation practice.
106. Skt. *dhyāna* Tib. *bsam gtan.* This word refers to meditative absorption, a state of one-pointed concentration endowed with the attributes of clarity, bliss and relaxation (see Glossary of Technical Terms and Proper Names under absorption).

107. Refer to Note 28.
108. The perfection of absorption is accomplished through the practice of tranquility meditation (Skt. *shamatha*, Tib. *zhi gnas*) and the practice of wisdom is accomplished through the practice of insight meditation (Skt. *vipassana*, Tib. *hlag mthong*). In this section, Taranatha does not explain the methods of tranquility meditation, apparently leaving that to the instructor. A presentation of methods of tranquility meditation may be found in *Mahamudra: The Quintessence of Mind and Meditation* by Takpo Tashi Namgyal and in a number of other sources.
109. According to Rigzin (1986): 150, the last way is "consistency between words and actions".
110. This position, called the seven point or Vairocana position, is one with each foot resting on the opposite thigh.
111. Here the word "essence" indicates an inherent nature of "personhood" that transcends the any individual case of a single person. That hypothetical essence is given the name "self of person."
112. The reasoning here is that the aggregates are always subject to deterioration.
113. The reasoning here is that the self is the one that experiences phenomena. Therefore, if one of the aggregates such as (visual) perception were not a part of the self, then something else (such as the form of the body) would have to experience the object. For a detailed analysis of selflessness, see *Meditation on Emptiness* by Jeffery Hopkins.
114. Skt. *skanda, dhātu, āyatana*, Tib. *phung po, khams, skye mched.* The 5 aggregates, 18 constituents and 12 sources (see Glossary of Classifications) make up the body-mind continuum of each sentient being and determine the nature of individual and collective experience.
115. Skt. *samtana*, Tib. *rgyud.* The term "continuum" implies both the mental and physical components of a sentient being.
116. At this point, the logic is working with the idea that something that is "established as a valid entity" cannot be divided into parts—that it is an absolute unit.
117. These are standard names for these particles and have nothing to do with the animals and elements after which they are named. It is rather like our names of elements such as "iron molecule" and "copper molecule".
118. The reasoning is that it would not be three dimensional.
119. The four others are consciousness, feeling, perception and mental formations (see Glossary of Classifications).
120. The eight consciousnesses are the eye, ear, nose, tongue, body, mental, emotional and foundational consciousness.

121. In this analogy, the aggregates, constituents and sources [that define "phenomena"] are likened to the mountain. The mind is likened to the lake. The reflection of the mountain [of phenomena] in the water [of mind] is like our perception of appearances. The analogy of the reflection of a mountain [or moon] in water is often used to indicate the illusory nature of appearances.
122. In the Tibetan it says "*Chegemo*" and "*Gagemo*", two generic names.
123. The argument here is that "the son of a barren woman" (like emptiness) is validated by discussing its lack of existence. The idea is absurd, so further proofs posited on the basis of this idea are invalid.
124. In the case of this meditation, the object of focus is non-conceptuality.
125. From here forward, Taranatha is describing the nine stages of resting the mind (See Glossary of Classifications).
126. Skt. *Bhāvanā-krama,* Tib. *sGom pa'i rim pa.*
127. Tib. *Be'u bum.*
128. Potowa was a renowned Kadampa teacher and disciple of dGeshes 'Brom ston pa.
129. In other words, suffering cannot be non-existent and truly existent at the same time.
130. Shantideva. *Compendium of Trainings.* Skt. *Śikṣā-samuccaya,* Tib. *bSlab pa kun las btus pa.*
131. Potowa. *Be'u bum.*
132. The original treaties are the works in the Mahayana Buddhist canon.
133. The five paths that are discussed here are the path of accumulation, the path of junction, the path of seeing, the path of meditation and the path of no more learning (see Glossary of Classifications). Each path has three levels: lesser, middle and greater.
134. Tathāgata is an epithet for a fully enlightened Buddha.
135. Skt. *svabhāvikakāya,* Tib. *ngo bo nyid sku* (see Glossary of Classifications).
136. Skt. *saṃbhogakāyà,* Tib. *long sku.*
137. Skt. *nirmāṇakāya,* Tib. *sprul sku.*
138. One of the titles Taranatha gives to *Essence of Ambrosia.*
139. A "support" is a sacred representation of the Buddha's body, speech and/or mind typically in the form of a thanka, painting or statue (representing enlightened body); a sacred text (representing enlightened speech); and a stupa (representing enlightened mind).
140. A mandala is a symbolic representation of the universe.
141. Tib. bzang po'i spyod pa'i smon lam, the Aspiration Prayer for Excellent Conduct, from which the seven-branch prayer is taken, is a long prayer often recited at the beginning of ceremonies and rituals to allow participants to purify negative actions and accumulate merit (see Note 20 for the seven-branch prayer and see Glossary of Classifications).

142. Skt. *Gaṇḍa-vyūha-sūtra,* Tib. *sDong po bkod pa'i mdo.*
143. For the list, see Glossary of Classifications.
144. Tib. *Byang chub sems dp'i sde snod.*
145. Skt. *Ratna-kūṭa,* Tib. *dKon brtsegs.*
146. Asanga. Tib. *byang chub sems 'pa'i sa.*
147. Candragomin. Skt. *Śiṣya-lekha,* Tib. *slob ma la spring pa'i spring yig.*
148. Skt. *Ratna-megha-sūtra,* Tib. *'Phags pa rin po che'i phung po shes bya ba theg pa chen po'i mdo.*
149. Skt. *Akasagarbha-sūtra,* Tib. *Nam mkha'i snying po'i mdo.*
150. In the case of taking the vow, the ideal supports are the spiritual master representing the Buddha, sacred texts representing the Dharma and members of the spiritual community representing the Sangha. Or, alternately, the supports can be a statue representing enlightened body, texts representing enlightened speech and a stupa representing enlightened mind.
151. Tib. gSer gling pa chos kyi grags pa (10th Century) was one of Atisha's teachers.
152. Tib. 'Brom ston rgyal ba'i 'byung gnas (1004-1064) was one of Atisha's main disciples.
153. Sha ra ba yon tan grags (1070-1141), Potowa's disciple, was the author of two important Kadampa *lamrim* texts.
154. gTum ston blo gros grags (1106-1166) was a student of Sharawa.
155. gDo ston pa (12th Century) was a student of Tumton Lodro.
156. Gro mo che ba bdud rtsi grags (12th Century), student of Dotonpa, was the author of *Lam mchog.*
157. Sangs rgyas sgom pa sengge skyabs (1179-1250) was the student of Palden Dro.
158. mChims nam mkha' grags pa (1210-1267?), student of Kyoton Senge, wrote texts on the *lamrim* and logic.
159. sMon lam tshul khrims (1219-1299) was a student of Chimchen Namka.
160. Ze'u grags pa brtson 'grus (1253-1316), student of Monlam Tsultrim, was the abbot of Narthang for 12 years.
161. mChims blo bzang grags pa (1299-1375), student of Zeu Drakpa, was the author of a commentary on Vasubandhu's *Treasury of Phenomenology,* and was abbot of Narthang for 39 years.
162. Gro ston kun dga' rgyal mtshan (1338-1401), student of Lozang Chim, was the abbot of Narthang for 27 years and author of a commentary on Shantideva's *Compendium of Trainings.*
163. sPang ston grub pa shes rab (1357-1423), student of Droton Kungyalwa, was the author of a commentary on Shantideva's *Bodhisattva's Way of Life.*

164. mKhan chen bsod nams mchog grub (1399-1452), student of Sherab Pangton, was the author of two commentaries on the practice of mind training.
165. mKhan chen Bzod pa dpal grub (15th Century) was a student of Sonam Chokdrup.
166. 'Phags mchog grags pa bsod nams (15th Century) was a Sakya teacher of Kunga Chokdrup.
167. Kun dga' mchog grub (15th Century) was a Sakya teacher of Kunga Drolchok.
168. Jo nang rje btsun kun dga' grol mchog (1507-1565), prolific author of Jonang texts, was the holder of the Jonang, Shangpa and Kalachakra transmissions.
169. sPen lung pa mkhan chen lung rig rgya mtsho (16th Century) was Taranatha's root teacher.
170. Bya yul ba gzhon nu 'od (1075-1138), author of a Kadampa *lamrim*, was founder of Dakpo Lhogyu Jayul monastery.
171. gTsang pa rdo rje mi bskyod (11th Century) was a student of Jayulwa.
172. Mus sman pa bdud rtsi char chen (11th Century) was a student of Jayulwa.
173. The five Kadampa disciples of Jayulwa.
174. bSod nams mchog grub grags bzang (1399-1452).
175. Sron pa kun dga' rgyal ba (13th Century)was the originator of the Sron tradition of the Jonang lineage.
176. Yeshe Rinchen is the same as Lhachung (see below).
177. Lha chung ba ye shes rin chen (16th Century) was a student of Kunga Gyaltsen.
178. mKhas dbang byams pa lhun grub (16th Century) was one of Taranatha's teachers.
179. Chos kyi senge (1109-1169). *dBu ma bden gnyis kyi 'grel pa.*
180. Nam mkha' grags. *dBu ma'i man ngag gsal sgron.*
181. Gro mo che ba bdud rtsi grags (12th Century).
182. *Lam mchog.*
183. mChims nam mkha' grags pa (1210-1267?).
184. *gSung rgyun.*
185. Taranatha's nickname for himself (see Introduction on Taranatha's life for Tibetan).
186. Hopkins. *Meditation.* (1983): 175.

References

Banerjee, Anukul Chandra. *Aspects of Buddhist Culture from Tibetan Sources.* Calcutta: Firma Private Limited, 1984.

Dharma Publishing Staff, translator. *Dhammapada.* Berkeley: Dharma Publishing, 1985.

Gampopa. *The Jewel Ornament of Liberation.* Translated by Khenpo Konchog Gyaltsen Rinpoche, edited by Ani K. Trinlay Chodron. Ithaca: Snow Lion Publications, 1998.

Gyatso, Khenpo Tsultrim, *Shes rab snang ba* (no place, no date).

Hopkins, Jeffery. *Meditation on Emptiness.* Boston: Wisdom Publications, 1983.

Kapstein, Matthew. "The Shang-pa Bka'-brgyud: An Unknown Tradition of Tibetan Buddhism." In *Tibetan Studies in Honor of Hugh Richardson,* ed. Michael Aris and Aung San Suu Kyi, pp. 138-144. Warminster, England: Aris and Phillips Ltd., 1980.

Kongtrul, Jamgon. *The Torch of Certainty.* Translated by Judith Hanson. Boston: Shambala, 1977.

Kongtrul, Jamgon. *Myriad Worlds.* Translated and edited by the International Translation Committee of Kunkhyab Choling. Ithaca: Snow Lion Publications, 1995.

Patrul Rinpoche, *The Words of My Perfect Teacher.* Translated by the Padmakara Translation Group. Shambala: Boston, 1998.

Powers, John. *Introduction to Tibetan Buddhism.* Ithaca: Snow Lion Publications, 1995.

Riggs, Nicole. *Like An Illusion: Lives of the Shangpa Kagyu Masters.* Eugene, Oregon: Dharma Cloud Press, 2001.

Rigzin, Tsepak. *Tibetan English Dictionary of Buddhist Terminology.* Dharamsala: LTWA, 1986.

Sherburne, Richard. *The Complete Works of Atīśa.* New Delhi: Aditya Prakashan, 2000.

Smith, E. Gene. *Among Tibetan Texts: History and Literature of the Himalayan Plateau.* Boston: Wisdom Publications, 2001.

Snellgrove, David and Hugh Richardson. *A Cultural History of Tibet.* Boulder: Prajna Press, 1980.

Sterns, Cyrus. *The Buddha From Dolpo: A Study of the Life and Thought of the Tibetan Master Dolpopa Sherab Gyaltsen.* Edited by Matthew Kapstein. Albany: State University of New York Press, 1999.

Taranatha. *History of Buddhism in India.* Translated by Lama Chimpa and Alaka Chattopadhyaya, edited by Debiprasad Chattopadhyaya, Simla: Indian Institute of Advanced Study, 1970.

Tibetan Buddhist Resource Center Website, www.tbrc.org.

Taranatha, Jonang. *The Origin of Tara Tantra.* Translated by David Templeman. Dharamsala: Library of Tibetan Works and Archives, 1981.

Tsong-kha-pa. *The Great Treatise on the Stages of the Path to Enlightenment.* Translated by The Lamrim Chenmo Translation Committee, Ithaca: Snow Lion Publications, 2000.

Vasabandhu, *Abhidharmakośabhāṣyam.* Translated by Louis de La Valee Poussin. Translated into English by Leo M. Pruden. Berkeley: Asian Humanities Press, 1988.

Zangpo, Ngawang, translator. *Jamgon Kongtrul's Retreat Manual.* Ithaca: Snow Lion Publications, 1994.

Zangpo, Ngawang. *Taranatha.* Unpublished biography, 2003.

Zangmo, Tenpa. *Dharma Vocabulary.* Wappingers Falls, NY: Kagyu Thubten Choling (no date).